A Different Kind of War

A Different Kind of War

The UN Sanctions Regime in Iraq

Hans C. von Sponeck

Berghahn Books
New York • Oxford

Published in 2006 by

Berghahn Books
www.berghahnbooks.com

First published in Germany as *Ein anderer Krieg:*
Das Sanktionsregime der UNO im Irak
© 2005 Hamburger Edition

© 2006 Hans C. von Sponeck
Reprinted in 2007

Library of Congress Cataloging-in-Publication Data
Sponeck, H. C. von
  A different kind of war : the UN sanctions regime in Iraq / H.C. von Sponeck.
    p. cm.
  Includes bibliographical references and index.
  ISBN 978-1-84545-222-3 (hardback) -- ISBN 978-1-78238-752-7 (ebook)
  1. Economic sanctions--Iraq. 2. Sanctions (International law)--Case studies.
3. United Nations--Sanctions--Case studies. 4. Iraq--Politics and government--
1991-2003. 5. Iraq--Foreign relations--1991- I. Title.

JZ6373.S66 2006
341.5'8209567--dc22

                                           2006013936

British Library Cataloguing in Publication Data

A catalogue record for this book is available
from the British Library.

Printed on acid-free paper.

ISBN 978-1-84545-222-3 hardback
ISBN 978-1-78238-752-7 ebook

إلى شباب العراق
من أجل مستقبل أفضل لهم

To the youth of Iraq
for a better future

Contents

IRAN

TURKEY

SYRIA

IRAQ

SAUDI ARABIA

JORDAN

ISRAEL

LEBANON

KUWAIT

Zagrosgebirge

Lake Urmia

Mediterranean Sea

Persian Gulf

Schatt-el-Arab

Kermanshah

Korramshah
Abadan
Abu Flos
Basra
Abu al-Kassib
Umm Kasr

Kuwait

Kurdish controlled area

Amara
Nassirija
Al Hayy
Kut
As Samawah
As Suwayrah
Hilla
Safua
Nadschaf
Kerbala

Baghdad
Al-Dora
Baqubah
Al-Khalis
Falludscha
Khanaqin
Derbandikan
Tuz Khurmatu

Suleimanija
Halabdscha
Kalachualan
Dokan
Kirkuk
Erbil
Al-Awdscha
Tikrit
Baiji
Samarra

DIALA

Khaser Zap

Grosser Zap

TAMIM

SALAH AD-DIN

Tigris

Euphrat

Sacho
Amadija
Aqrah
Dohuk
Niniveh
Mossul
Kuban
Tall'Afar
Tall Uwaynat
Al Badi
Ash Sharqat

Hadithah

Ramadi

Nukhayb
Ar'Ar

Deir es Sor
Abu Kemal

Rutba

Al-Walid
Trebil

Syrische Wüste

Euphrat

Buhayrat al-Asad

Ataturk Baraji

Damascus

Amman
Jerusalem
Ramallah

Dead Sea

Beirut

0   50   100   150km

Figures, Maps and Tables

List of Figures

List of Maps

List of Tables

Acknowledgments

A conductor cannot perform a symphony without musicians. As an author, I could not have written this book without support. During the year of writing, help came from many and in ample measure.

Per Klevnäs, Nathaniel Hurd, Richard Garfield, Colin Rowat, Seth Kumi and Jonathan Stevenson helped in getting the statistics right and in designing tables and charts. Lutz Oette clarified humanitarian law and other legal issues. Naji Haraj translated from Arabic sources and patiently provided background information, as did Jasim Khalef, better known as Abu Laith. Paolo Palmero searched and designed appropriate maps. My wife Nelda ensured that I was doing justice to the English language. Tarik Mitri helped me in interpreting the broader picture in the Middle East. Matthias Schwoerer converted perceptions into the three political cartoons. Srinivasan Venkatasubramanian, my able office manager, first in Delhi and then in Baghdad, maintained my data base. Anne de Riedmatten and Lara Milosovic organised large volumes of documentation and Beverly Antilles transcribed the drafts and produced an impeccable final manuscript.

There were many others in Iraq, the wider Middle East, Europe, Africa and North America who generously shared their relevant experiences with me. I am grateful to all for the commitment and professionalism with which they assisted me.

Fourteen months of research and writing would not have been possible without the generous support I received from Professor Jan P. Reemtsma and the Hamburger Stiftung zur Förderung von Wissenschaft und Kultur for the entire book project. The Swiss Agency for Development and Cooperation's (DEZA) stipend allowed me to travel to the Middle East and other places.

Thanks to Dr Konrad Raiser, General Secretary of the World Council of Churches, and his successor, Dr Samuel Kobia, I was given 'refuge' at their headquarters in Geneva where I could do my writing in the most congenial setting possible. Luzia Wehrle made sure that this remained so throughout my stay at the WCC.

Denis Halliday, my predecessor in Baghdad, and I became staunch allies in our demands for accountability for all, losers and winners, for the injustices against the people of Iraq and for the misuse of the United Nations. His unrelenting outspokenness added to my determination to write this account.

I cannot end my words of gratitude without thanking my wife Nelda for her seemingly endless tolerance, patience and support and to our children Alexander, Mark and Anna for their persistent encouragement.

Hans C. von Sponeck
Spring 2005

Double punishment.
Courtesy of Matthias Schwoerer.

Foreword

At a moment when the international community is engaged in a necessary debate on how to update international structures, the book *A Different Kind of War* by Hans C. von Sponeck offers a significant contribution. The reflection proposed by Sponeck, from the point of view of his experience as a UN Humanitarian Coordinator to Iraq, points to the need for a profound restructuring of the United Nations and of the Security Council, so that they can effectively contribute to the objective of promoting peace and social justice.

I met Hans Sponeck during the Iraq Panels (that Sponeck graciously calls the 'Amorim Panels'), held in the United Nations from February to April 1999. After eight years of comprehensive sanctions, the Anglo-American bombings known as Operation 'Desert Fox' (16 to 18 December) again placed the Iraqi issue on the Security Council's agenda.

I vividly recall Sponeck's presentation to the Panel on the Humanitarian Situation in Iraq. In a little more than forty minutes, the former Humanitarian Coordinator summarised to Panel members the grim picture revealed today in all its detail in this informative and courageous book.

A Different Kind of War tells the story of a people placed by fate between two powerful forces: the dictator Saddam Hussein and the United States. The focus of Sponeck's analysis falls on the most fragile variable in the Iraqi equation: the civilian population and, most particularly, what one can call the lost generation of Iraq, a country known for its vigorous centuries'-old culture.

For twelve years under sanctions, Iraq went from an affluent society, equipped with modern infrastructure, as well as educational and health systems among the most developed in the Middle East, to a country made up of large numbers of poor and destitute citizens, condemned to live on less than one dollar a day. Children, youngsters, women and the elderly bore the heaviest burden.

Important as it may be, the debate on the extent to which the Iraqi Government complied with the rigid conditions imposed by the Security Council for the lifting of the sanctions imposed by Resolution 687, by which Iraq accepted the ceasefire in the first Gulf War, is beyond the scope of Sponeck's analysis. But the truth is that the process of disintegration of the fabric of Iraqi society became – for better of for worse – viscerally linked to the dismantling of the Iraqi programs of weapons of mass destruction.

While analysing the United Nation's Humanitarian program in Iraq, Sponeck calls our attention to another controversial topic: the capacity of the Organisation to fulfill its mandates without allowing basic human rights – to food, health and education, considered by some 'unwelcome collateral effects' – to be ignored. Sponeck demonstrates that this was the case in the implementation of the 'Oil-for-Food' programme: the mechanism conceived by the Security Council to alleviate the dramatic humanitarian situation in Iraq.

Routine delays, inept bureaucracy, budgetary constraints, and, above all, the determination of some permanent members of the Security Council not to allow Saddam Hussein's Iraq to recover all the attributes of its sovereignty, condemned – as indicated by Sponeck – the Iraqi population to a process of rapid impoverishment, perhaps unprecedented in history.

Sponeck's great achievement is to highlight both the high human costs of the comprehensive sanctions regime and the incapacity of the humanitarian programme to improve the situation of ordinary Iraqis, without any complacency towards Saddam Hussein, or, in his own words, 'without becoming an ally to a repressive regime'.

As a member of the Security Council, in the biennium 1998/1999 – almost the same period covered by *A Different Kind of War* – and having presided over the Iraq Panels, I cannot but agree with Sponeck's conclusion with regard to the limitations of status quo within the United Nations, to promote a truly global agenda. I salute Sponeck for his intellectual honesty and independence in concluding that the United Nations must be able to overcome the 'power of parochial interests'.

Celso N. Amorim
Minister of External Relations of Brazil
Brasilia, Spring 2005

Introduction

The years between two wars, 1991 to 2003, were not years of peace for the Iraqi people. A dictatorship at home and a divided UN Security Council abroad brought Iraqis fear, deprivation and suffering.

The Arab League, the Organisation of Islamic Countries and the European Union all failed to play a role in this conflict because of their own internal ineptitude and weakness. The international public, citizens in all parts of the world, displayed a sense of justice and took over the role governments should have played in the Iraq crisis in supporting peaceful solutions based on human rights and international law.

Much has been written on this period, often with great insight and value in contributing to the debate about the international structures needed to prevent a recurrence of a conflict of such a kind and origin. However, most reviews look at Iraq from the vantage point of disarmament and international security.

As an insider who became an outsider, I cannot accept the politically convenient notion that the desolate state of Iraq can be explained in simple black and white terms. It cannot.

My interaction with the Government of Iraq, with the UN Security Council, with the UN Secretary General, with an intricate system of UN agencies, programmes and units and with non-governmental organisations confirmed an unusual complexity of participation in the Iraq crisis. This complexity needs to be explained in order to fully understand the causes of the conditions in Iraq as they evolved from 1990 onwards.

More than three decades in the United Nations, including my time in Baghdad, made it almost mandatory that I should contribute to such an understanding. Many UN colleagues at senior levels and others no longer in the organisation were persistent in reminding me to do so.

From the beginning I knew that an analysis of the causes of the Iraq crisis would not be enough. In order to contribute to the pressing debate about the reform of the multilateral machinery created in 1945 to prevent conflicts, the canvas needed to be broader. The review had to deal with the intractable issue of the options that the Government of Iraq, the UN Security Council and the wider international community had in dealing with this crisis. The question which must be answered is: why were these options forfeited at the expense of the people of Iraq, the standing of the United Nations and the wider Middle East peace process.

The picture which emerged in the course of a year of reflecting, consulting and writing did not come as a surprise. All parties to this conflict, including the UN Secretariat, had options. The fate of a nation could have been different – more humane and consistent with internationally defined standards of life – had the protagonists opted for dialogue and honest intentions. The United Nations could have emerged as a winner by helping to solve a crisis. International law would have been confirmed as the universally acceptable basis for international relations. The world would have been less confused and a more secure place today.

This was not to be. Narrow national interests, rather than the needs of the international community for security, peace and development prevailed.

A dictator has been removed, economic sanctions have ended, weapons of mass destruction have not been found. The aftershock of this turbulent time, however, continues to be felt with far reaching consequences for the people of Iraq, for peace in the Middle East and for global political stability.

The investigation of the $64 billion UN Oil-for-Food Programme is part of this aftershock. It was a wise decision by UN Secretary General Kofi Annan to appoint an independent commission headed by Paul A. Volcker, the former chairman of the US Reserve Bank, to look into allegations of UN corruption but allocating $35 million of Iraqi funds to finance this investigation was a serious impropriety, which will not be forgotten by the Iraqi population.

The Volcker commission's 2005 findings point to weaknesses in the UN Secretariat's management of the humanitarian programme but not institutional misuse of entrusted resources, or corruption. Unfortunately, the role played by the UN Security Council in the conduct of the Oil-for-Food Programme was outside the remit of the commission. I consider this a serious omission because ultimate oversight of the Programme rested with the UN Security Council and not the UN Secretariat.

The failure of the UN to protect the people of Iraq cannot be explained by the commission's findings. Political manipulation and fundamental shortcomings within the UN Security Council, however, would have been proper subjects for the investigation.

Chapter 1

The Oil-for-Food Programme: An Adequate Humanitarian Exemption?

I arrived in Baghdad on 8 November 1998. It was an overland journey of some 900 km from Amman: UN sanctions regulations did not allow scheduled air links, and special flights were rare. As the convoy of UN vehicles that had travelled with me from the Jordanian/Iraqi border at Trebil entered the compound of the Canal Hotel in Baghdad, where United Nations offices were located, foreign and Iraqi Press were waiting. They wanted to hear the newcomer's perception of the political clouds which had started to gather since the Iraqi Government had suspended cooperation with UNSCOM[1] and UN arms inspectors had just been withdrawn from Iraq. The Press also wanted to get an impression of how I perceived my assignment as the UN Humanitarian Coordinator for Iraq and what I had to say about the deepening confrontation over arms inspection. I did not know much about the state of weapons inspections and the disarmament of Iraq: this was not part of my brief. I had no difficulty, however, nor any hesitation, in answering questions concerning my responsibilities. I made it clear that I felt I had a dual role to play: firstly, to be a good manager of the Oil-for-Food Programme, the humanitarian initiative agreed between the UN Security Council and the Government of Iraq to mitigate the impact of economic sanctions; secondly, to function as an interpreter, to the UN Secretary-General, the Security Council and the wider international community, of the human conditions in Iraq. Much later I learned that my understanding of this second function was not shared in Washington and London. James Rubin, spokesperson for the US Secretary of State, Madeleine Albright, at a Press briefing in the US State

---

1. UNSCOM = United Nations Special Commission. Responsible for disarmament in Iraq.

Department, made this clear when he said, 'This man in Baghdad is paid to work, not to speak'.[2] Was a UN Humanitarian Coordinator a tool of convenience or an accepted participant in the Iraq debate? This was a controversy early on and remained one throughout my Iraq assignment.

In late 1998 Iraq was in its ninth year of comprehensive economic sanctions and a stringent arms embargo.[3] Much to the disadvantage of the Iraqi population, the Oil-for-Food Programme that had been agreed upon between the Government of Iraq and the United Nations Security Council in April 1995 became operational only after further, detrimental delays in December 1996.

During the preceding years the Iraqi authorities and the United Nations had been entangled in arguments and disagreements over how economic sanctions were to be implemented and eventually terminated. Dependent upon the import of food,[4] medicines and industrial goods to maintain its sophisticated infrastructure and health system, Iraq was highly vulnerable. Frozen assets, a dilapidated oil industry and imports severely curtailed by sanctions had a quick and devastating impact on the economy, the social and physical infrastructure and the livelihood of the vast majority of the Iraqi population. Retaining this status quo for any length of time would lead to death and destitution on an unprecedented scale.

At the time of their Government's invasion of Kuwait in August 1990, followed by Gulf War II[5] in early 1991, the Iraqi population had already been significantly weakened from eight years of war with Iran (1980–88) and an increasingly disabling internal dictatorship. Governments, the United Nations Security Council and the UN Secretariat were all well aware of these realities.

In early 1991, an international coalition of armed forces led by the United States forced the Iraqi military to end its illegal occupation of Kuwait and eventually accept defeat. The Government of Iraq and the Iraqi population at that time assumed that the demands of UN Resolution 660 of 2 August 1990 had been met and, therefore, economic sanctions would end. Instead, UN Resolution 687 of 15 April 1991 confirmed the continuation of economic sanctions. This was justified by new UN demands for disarmament.

Iraq had lost a war and surrendered. Its people were exhausted and traumatised. Yet, their dictator remained alive, in office and in charge of a weapons of mass destruction programme. The size of this WMD programme was fairly well known since Western and Eastern governments and multinational companies had actively participated in its development.

2. James Rubin, Spokesman, US Department of State, Daily Press Briefing, 1999.
3. See UN SCR 661 (1990) and UN SCR 687 (1991).
4. In the late 1980s Iraq imported about 70 per cent of its food.
5. Gulf War I was the Iran-Iraq war (1980–88).

Such a constellation was politically convenient, at least for the United States, since it justified a continuing military presence in the Gulf with its geo-strategic, political and economic advantages.

The price for the Iraqi population was high. No country had ever been subjected to more comprehensive economic sanctions by the United Nations than Iraq. The years following the 1991 Gulf War were, therefore, catastrophic for Iraqis. Existing UN and other documentation provides extensive and credible evidence[6] that in the first half of the 1990s malnutrition and morbidity escalated rapidly. Communicable diseases in the 1980s not considered public health hazards, such as measles, polio, cholera, typhoid, marasmus and kwashiorkor, reappeared on epidemic scales.

Two United Nations missions visited Iraq during the first half of 1991 to assess the human conditions after the introduction of sanctions in 1990 and the war in 1991. By this time much of the physical infrastructure (electricity plants, water and sewerage facilities, bridges and railroads, etc.) had been destroyed. Undersecretary-General Marti Athisaari[7] and the Executive Delegate of UN Secretary-General Pérez de Cuéllar, Prince Sadruddin Aga Khan,[8] who led these missions, found immense suffering. Not surprisingly, they concluded that substantial financial resources had to become available quickly to avert a deepening of the existing human catastrophe in Iraq. Despite the evidence of a mounting tragedy and appeals by the United Nations and others for resources to end the worst manifestations of destitution, international generosity was poor. Five UN humanitarian appeals, during the years 1991 to 1996 calling for voluntary contributions totalling $1.2 billion, resulted in contributions of only $420 million, or 35 per cent of the funds needed.[9]

Even though organizations such as Caritas, Care, IPPNW,[10] The World Council of Churches, Amnesty International and, of course, the International Committee of the Red Cross had corroborated UN findings. They published their own accounts of the rise in malnutrition, the shortage of drugs, the increase in water-borne and other diseases. The

6. For a comprehensive coverage of the socio-economic conditions in Iraq during the period 1990–96 see : (i)*The United Nations and the Iraq Conflict, 1990–96*, Dept. of Public Information, Vol. IX, New York, 1996; (ii)*The Impact of UN Sanctions on Humanitarian Assistance Activities, Braunmühl and Kulessa, Gesellschaft für Communication Management*, Berlin, December 1995.
7. Mission to Iraq from 16–21 February 1991 – see UN/doc S/22366, 20 March 1991.
8. Mission to Iraq from 29 June to 13 July 1991 – see UN/doc. S/22799, 17 July 1991.
9. *The United Nations and the Iraq Conflict, 1990–96*, Dept. of Public Information, Vol. IX, New York, 1996, p. 59.
10. International Physicians for the Prevention of Nuclear War.

international public, however, and many governments had difficulties in distinguishing between the plight of an innocent population and the policies of a dictatorial regime. This affected their willingness to support emergency programmes for the civilian population in Iraq. The same cannot be said for those governments who made up the UN Security Council during these years, particularly its five permanent members. They were aware that Iraq had always been a food import country and, with the devastation of war, had become even more dependent upon such imports. The Security Council Resolution 666 of 13 September 1990 illustrates that there was no foresight in the Council for taking immediate measures to protect the Iraqi people. It simply requested the UN Iraq Sanctions Committee to 'determine whether there is an urgent humanitarian need to supply food stuffs to Iraq or Kuwait'.[11]

Had there been a genuine concern for the welfare of the Iraqi people, the warnings by Secretaries-General Pérez de Cuéllar and Boutros Boutros-Ghali about the deteriorating circumstances in Iraq would have been taken more seriously. The meagre response to the UN appeals for voluntary pledges could have been supplemented without difficulty. Additional government contributions of $820 million, or the small amount of about $200 million per year, would have made up the shortfall and guaranteed the financing of minimum requirements for survival during the 1992 to 1996 period.[12] In retrospect, and keeping in mind the evolution of the Iraq crisis in subsequent years, until Gulf War III of 2003, it can be argued that a combination of deliberate containment and a focus on disarmament overrode concerns for the human condition. This constituted the international Iraq policy of the United States and other governments during the first five years of sanctions.

Evidence of the seriousness of the human misery in Iraq became clear in the course of the 1990s.[13] Pressure mounted on the Government of Iraq and the UN Security Council to come to an agreement upon Iraq's humanitarian needs in order to avoid a total collapse of Iraqi society. The Government of Iraq proved to be a reluctant negotiating partner. For them sanctions had been introduced to secure the compliance of Iraq with the demands to withdraw 'immediately and unconditionally all its forces (from Kuwait)',[14] and to 'restore the authority of the legitimate Government of Kuwait.'[15] The de facto dismantling of the sovereignty of

---

11. See S/RES/666 (1990), 13 September 1990.
12. *The United Nations and the Iraq Conflict, 1990–96,* Dept. of Public Information, Vol. IX, New York, 1996, p. 59.
13. See also the report by the Harvard study team entitled 'The Effect of the Gulf Crisis on the Children of Iraq', *New England Journal of Medicine*, 1991.
14. UN Security Council Resolution 660 (1990), para. 2.
15. UN Security Council Resolution 661 (1990), para. 2.

the State of Iraq in subsequent UN resolutions[16] constituted, for the Iraqi authorities, a breach of the agreement they thought they had reached in 1990. Resolution 661 imposed sanctions on Iraq until it withdrew from Kuwait. The UN Security Council was not willing to discuss this Iraqi objection. In fact, the US and UK Governments took Iraq's rejection of Resolutions 706 and 712 as well as other attempts by the UN Security Council to establish a humanitarian programme in Iraq as a confirmation that the Government of Saddam Hussein was willing to sacrifice the Iraqi people in a game of political one-upmanship.

The reasons for Iraq's rejection of the UN's proposals were much more complex. First of all, there was no precedent for sanctions of the kind to which Iraq had been subjected. Secondly, the UN Security Council demanded that Iraq hand over responsibilities for its oil revenue to the UN. Oil production would be internationally supervised and subjected to strict export and import controls. Thirdly, compensation payments were to be made to parties claiming losses due to Iraq's invasion of Kuwait.

In addition, the agreement that a large team of UN workers would have a presence in Iraq generated deep fears about Iraq's independence. There was a sense of hurt pride and a feeling of humiliation to an ancient culture which had to submit to those whom Iraqis perceived as relative newcomers on the horizon of civilization.[17]

After years of frustrating negotiations and the concurrent worsening of Iraqi conditions of life,[18] Deputy Prime Minister Tariq Aziz and UN Secretary-General Boutros Boutros-Ghali in early 1996 finally agreed to work out practical arrangements for the implementation of what became known as the 'Oil-for-Food Programme', the humanitarian exemption for Iraq under sanctions. The legal framework for this programme had been laid down in UN Security Council Resolution 986 of 14 April 1995.[19] At the time of my arrival in Baghdad in November 1998, two years of this programme had been completed. The Government of Iraq and the United

16. See for example S/RES/706 (1991), 15 August 1991 and S/RES/712 (1991), 19 September 1991.
17. Pride and honour are national traits of fundamental importance in Iraqi culture. Whether perceived interference in Iraq's internal affairs through UN Resolutions or through US/UK occupation, Iraqis at all levels did not and do not hesitate to register their opposition.
18. D. Cortright and G.A. Lopez in *The Sanction Decade, Assessing UN Strategies in the 1990s*, Boulder, CO: Lynne Rienner Publishers, 2000, p. 37, make the important observation that 'continuing political animosity between Iraq and the West ... prevented the development of a bargaining dynamic and unnecessarily prolonged both the political crisis and the agony of the Iraqi people'.
19. S/RES/986 (1995) – Security Council Resolution concerning sales of Iraqi petroleum and petroleum products.

Nations had started the joint preparation of the fifth phase of six months of the Oil-for-Food Programme,[20] for the period November 1998 to May 1999.

The United Nations had never undertaken a larger, more intricate and more politicised humanitarian programme. The briefing I had received a few weeks earlier by colleagues at the UN Office of the Iraq Programme (OIP) in New York had been a useful and necessary introduction to administrative and personnel issues. Yet, despite my repeated requests, it did not include the much needed political briefing. At the time I was not sure whether this was due to incapacity or because the political aspects of UN/Iraq relations were considered a prerogative of New York and, therefore, not part of the humanitarian coordinator's brief. Subsequent visits to UN headquarters convinced me that as far as the Office of the Iraq Programme (OIP) was concerned, it was clearly both. There were numerous specific issues on which I needed a good grounding and, more importantly, a familiarisation with UN policy which I was to represent in Iraq. It was vital for me to understand the Iraqi approach in negotiating the phases of the Oil-for-Food Programme. I also sought to understand the relations between the Government in Baghdad and the Kurdish autonomous authorities in the North. Was the UN ready to use its good offices to facilitate a dialogue between the three Kurdish governorates and the central authority in Baghdad? What did the UN have to say about infrastructure rehabilitation involving the country as a whole? I also had hoped to receive a good briefing on the special political conditions prevailing in the marsh areas of southern Iraq which figured so prominently in the reports of the Human Rights Rapporteur for Iraq.[21] I needed to know if there was to be any relationship with the UN Special Rapporteur on Human Rights in Iraq, Max van der Stoel, the former Foreign Minister of the Netherlands. I was eager to be informed about senior government officials with whom I would have to deal on a regular basis. I assumed that both Iraqi and foreign intelligence would monitor our operations where we had offices in Iraq, particularly in Baghdad and in the Kurdish areas. I was therefore anxious to know what the UN's experience had been in this respect. UNOHCI[22] was located in the same

20. Each phase had a duration of six months.
21. See UN Economic and Social Council: Report on The Situation of Human Rights in Iraq, E/CN.4/1994/58, 25 February 1994, pp. 43–4 and A/47/367, 10 August 1992.
22. UNOHCI = United Nations Office of the Humanitarian Coordinator for Iraq. This office was located at the Canal Hotel, a former hotel training school at the outskirts of Baghdad together with other UN offices including UNSCOM = United Nations Special Commission dealing with Weapons Verification and Disarmament, the Office of the Special Envoy of the UN Secretary-General, the World Food Programme and the Liaison Office of UNIKOM, the United Nations Iraq-Kuwait observation mission. Other UN agencies, i.e., UNDP, UNICEF, WHO and UNESCO, had their offices in central Baghdad.

premises in Baghdad as the United Nations Special Commission (UNSCOM), the disarmament group. Was there a policy on interaction? To what extent did we, on the humanitarian side, cooperate with UNSCOM in areas such as administration, security and medical services?

I was aware that there were not many international non-governmental organisations with programmes in areas under the control of the Government in Baghdad. Did the UN encourage joint programmes with NGOs? What were their motives for being in Iraq? Could we co-finance their programmes?

I was disappointed, not to say shocked, that the Office of the Iraq Programme (OIP) in New York was entirely unable to equip me for the Iraq assignment with answers to any of these basic questions.[23]

Since I held the additional appointment as the UN Secretary-General's designated official for security of UN staff in Iraq, I also expected to receive detailed briefings on the security situation in Baghdad and elsewhere in the country.

In November 1998 about 450 international and some 1,700 Iraqi personnel were serving the United Nations in humanitarian programmes in Iraq. In addition there were about 200 UN staff involved in disarmament work. Apart from Baghdad, the United Nations had a sizeable presence in Erbil and Suleimaniyah, two of the three Kurdish governorates in northern Iraq.[24] While there were only small numbers of UN staff resident in other locations such as Mosul and Kirkuk, mainly to look after food storage facilities, there was extensive and daily road travel by UN humanitarian staff in this country of 437,000 km^2 and distances from the northern border with Turkey to the southern border with Kuwait of 1,200 km.

As in other countries where the United Nations is present, security management plans are meant to ensure that the United Nations is in a position at any time to respond to changing security circumstances in the interest of staff safety. It need not be emphasised that this was of special importance in the case of Iraq. At the time of my initial briefings the UN Security Office in New York was unable to even locate the Security

---

23. In the course of my stay in Baghdad, I discovered a financial account in New York in which $1 million was lying idle because no one had remembered that this money existed and could be used for special projects.
24. Iraq has a total of eighteen governorates or regions; fifteen of these were under the direct control of the Government in Baghdad. The three Kurdish governorates of Dohuk, Erbil and Suleimaniyah were considered locally autonomous and in accordance with UN Security Council Resolution 986 of 1995 administered by the United Nations 'on behalf of the Government of Iraq'. The term 'governorate' originally was used to refer to the administrative structure which prevailed during the Ottoman Empire. At that time Iraq consisted of only three governorates: Mosul, Baghdad and Basrah and Kuwait.

Management Plan for Iraq, let alone outline security issues in some detail. Eventually, a security officer found an outdated copy even though, as I discovered after my arrival in Iraq, the security section in the Baghdad office had prepared and earlier transmitted this vital document to UN headquarters.

The last day of my briefing in New York included a meeting with UN Secretary-General, Kofi Annan. It was he who, earlier in the year, had made all of us in the United Nations proud when in February 1998 he had courageously decided to travel to Baghdad despite signals of discouragement from the US Government, particularly the Secretary of State, Madeleine Albright. He had successfully diffused a major crisis which had arisen between the United States and Iraq as a result of a breakdown of cooperation between UNSCOM and the Government of Iraq.

When we met in his office on the 38th floor of the UN Secretariat on 30 October Kofi Annan's message to me was that the humanitarian situation in Iraq under sanctions was serious, and the tools at our disposal to redress the suffering of the people were inadequate. 'My expectation is that you will do your utmost to get the maximum out of the Oil-for-Food Programme for the benefit of the Iraqi people!' This was clear language. I was deeply inspired by the compassion and warmth which emanated from the UN Secretary-General. This meeting was a good ending to an otherwise disconcerting week at UN headquarters.

In Geneva, on my way to Iraq, I met with Denis Halliday, a colleague of thirty years who had resigned six weeks earlier from the post I was about to assume. After a few days together I had learned a lot about the politics of sanctions, the plight of a people and UN bureaucracy, and also about an honourable civil servant who had no longer been willing to be part of what he believed was 'a criminally flawed and genocidal UN Security Council Iraq policy'.

In Baghdad initial work priorities were fairly obvious. Apart from getting acquainted with UN colleagues, the Government of Iraq, the diplomatic community and NGO representatives, I had to familiarise myself with the humanitarian exemption. The Oil-for-Food Programme, covering 26 November 1998 to 24 May 1999, was in the final stages of preparation and involved the Government of Iraq, the Kurdish authorities and the UN offices in Baghdad. This programme had to be submitted by the Government of Iraq to New York for approval by the UN Secretary-General on 26 November 1998.

Distribution Plan v: An Example of Iraq's Humanitarian Exemption

On my desk I found the draft distribution plan for 'phase v', as it was called. It contained proposals worth $2.7 billion[25] for the survival of a population of some 22.5 million Iraqis[26] during the six months' period 26 November 1998 to 24 May 1999. The full budget would only be known at the end of phase v, when the UN Treasury in New York prepared the final accounts on the income from the Iraqi oil sold in the course of the phase. In other words, the humanitarian programme had no assurance of financial coverage during any given phase. Essential civilian supplies involving life-saving food commodities, medicines and equipment would only be processed at UN headquarters when the holder of the Iraq oil account, the Banque Nationale de Paris (BNP), confirmed that enough funds were available to cover a contract. The UN Secretariat and the UN Security Council were aware of what a shortfall in oil income would mean for the population of Iraq. A mechanism for the international community to make up for shortfalls through voluntary contributions, however, did not exist and was never contemplated.

Throughout the lifespan of the Oil-for-Food Programme, from 10 December 1996 to 21 November 2003,[27] the source of funding was entirely Iraqi. This is a fact which is frequently overlooked. The reference to 'humanitarian assistance' reinforces the false perception that external financial support was involved. The Iraqi source of funding was one of the reasons why I never felt comfortable with my designation as 'UN Humanitarian Coordinator'. Neither did the Iraqis, since they rightly felt that the United Nations was using 'their' resources. Some Iraqis additionally observed that not only was it their money we used, but had they control over this resource, they would have used it more efficiently.

During visits to the US State Department in Washington, I often heard: 'Yes, they would use this money to enhance their weapons of mass destruction programme'. In Baghdad, Washington and London the Iraq debate always seemed to result in black and white pictures. I soon realised that all participants in the Iraq drama were classified as either belonging to one or the other camp. It did not occur to these staunch

25. In comparison, the annual budget for 1998 of the UN in New York amounted to $2.4 billion.
26. Iraq had not had a published census since 1987. The population estimate was based on statistical projections emanating from data involving the 1997 census for which the government of Saddam Hussein never released the report and the number of food ration cards the UN World Food Programme had issued in the eighteen governorates.
27. In accordance with UN S/RES/1483 (2003) the Oil-for-Food Programme came to an end on 21 November 2003.

protagonists that one need not belong to either group, but could determine one's position on the basis of what was in the interest of the Iraqi people and legally correct.

The situation which emerged from phase to phase was an uncertainty of income and, therefore, one of hesitation on the part of the United Nations in the implementation of the humanitarian programme.

Figure 1.1 shows not only the serious inadequacy of the financial resources during the initial three phases of six months each, from 10 December 1996 to 29 May 1998, but also the systemic income volatility and erratic arrival of supplies facing the humanitarian programme throughout the thirteen phases until the beginning of Gulf War III in March 2003.

An analysis of Figure 1.1 provides an important insight into the operations of the Iraq sanctions regime in general and the Oil-for-Food Programme in particular. Without this, the extent of the politicisation of the Iraq Crisis, occurring at the expense of common Iraqis, will not be fully understood. It is significant that the uncertainty of funding and the inadequacy of actual available resources characterise not only the years of

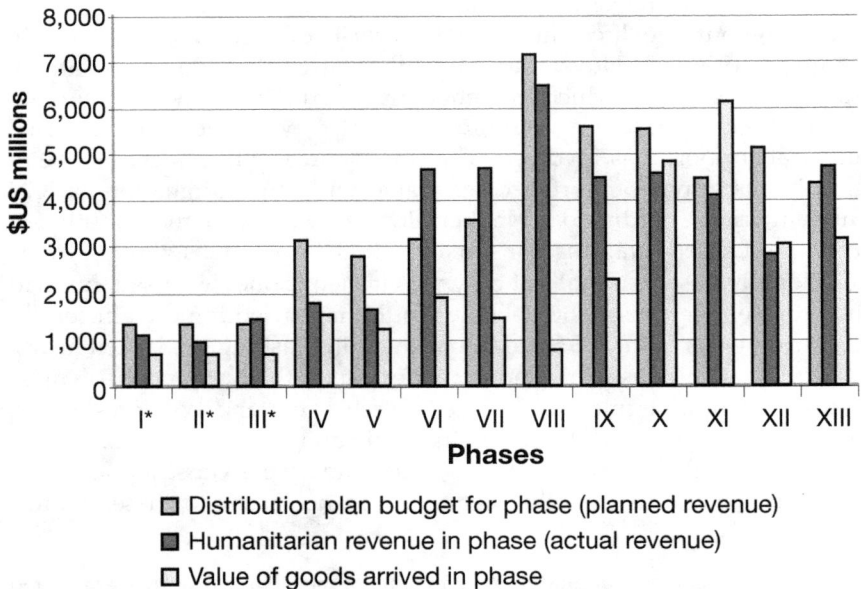

□ Distribution plan budget for phase (planned revenue)
■ Humanitarian revenue in phase (actual revenue)
□ Value of goods arrived in phase

Figure 1.1 Oil-for-Food Programme: Planned Budgets, Actual Revenues and Goods Arrived (Phases I to XIII), 1996–2003

Source: *Secretary-General's 180-day reports on the Oil-for-Food Programme, phases I–XIII.*
Notes: *Figures for the value of goods arrived in phases I–III are not available. The figure stated is the average over phases I–III, based on the cumulative value of goods arrived at the end of phase III.*

the Oil-for-Food Programme but also the years preceding it. There was no shortage of warnings of an evolving human catastrophe in the early years of sanctions as well as in the years leading up to the 2003 Gulf War. Calls for 'humanising' sanctions for Iraq by United Nations agencies, UN officials in Iraq, civic and religious organisations worldwide, Pope John Paul II, President Nelson Mandela and other eminent persons made no difference whatsoever in UN Security Council policy: they were ignored.

In fact, the design, funding and implementation of the Oil-for-Food Programme reflect a remarkable cold bloodedness on the part of the UN Security Council. Phases I to III received an allocation of $2 billion per phase of six months. These amounts do not readily reveal the severity of their inadequacy. Iraq under sanctions was prohibited, during these and subsequent phases, from free trading with its neighbours or anyone else. As shown in Figure 1.1, Iraq was only allowed to sell limited quantities of oil on the international market under UN supervision. Humanitarian supplies had to be imported under tight UN Security Council controls. No local products, including food, could be purchased under the Oil-for-Food Programme, even though the source of funding was Iraqi oil revenue.

The oil industry and private Iraqi enterprises were ravaged by war and neglect, yet not allowed to be rehabilitated beyond repairs and some replacements. Iraq's central bank had to surrender its functions to the Treasury of the United Nations. Oil income had to be deposited into the so-called Iraq 'Oil Account' at the Banque Nationale de Paris (BNP). Fees and interest rates for the Iraqi deposits in the BNP account were negotiated by the United Nations on behalf of Iraq. The Iraqi authorities had no access to foreign exchange and certainly not to Iraqi tax income since there were no tax payers in such a mothballed economy. Their overseas assets, including those of individual Iraqi citizens, were frozen. Iraq as a nation and Iraqis as individual citizens were dependent upon the UN Security Council for survival, particularly in the initial years of sanctions. These conditions encouraged the growth of an influential economic mafia linked to the Iraqi regime. Over time this prompted more and more attempts by the Government of Iraq to circumvent trade and oil export regulations. Illegal exports of oil via the Gulf,[28] Turkey and Jordan and, in the late 1990s also to Syria, not surprisingly began to mushroom.

The UN Security Council had agreed to $2 billion for each of the phases I to III. Figure 1.1 reveals the total inadequacy of this allocation:

- $2 billion was not the amount actually available to finance humanitarian supplies; it represented the gross oil revenue to be

28. After Operation Desert Fox of December 1998 this became more and more difficult as the US-led multinational maritime interception force carried out continuous and careful air and sea patrols of the Gulf shipping lanes.

apportioned to various accounts, only one of which involved the Oil-for-Food Programme.

- 30 percent of the $2 billion[29] was allocated to the UN Compensation Commission (UNCC) in Geneva to pay for claims made by individuals, commercial companies and governments for losses they allegedly had incurred as a result of Iraq's invasion into Kuwait in August 1990.[30]
- The amount available for the Oil-for-Food Programme was further reduced by 4 percent which the United Nations deducted to pay for the administration of the humanitarian programme (2.2 percent), the disarmament operations (0.8 percent) and a reserve fund for unexpected expenditures (1.0 percent).
- The actual (net) amount for helping the Iraqi population to survive was therefore only 66 percent or $1,32 billion of the allowable (gross) allocation of $2 billion for each of the three phases.

This means that during this period the Government of Iraq was permitted to purchase biannually food, medicines and other essential goods[31] worth $1.3 billion for a population, estimated at that time, of 22 million.

UN Resolution 986 of 14 April 1995, on which the humanitarian Oil-for-Food Programme is based, states in its opening paragraph that the UN Security Council is 'concerned by the serious nutritional and health situation of the Iraqi population and by the risk of a further deterioration in this situation'. The dollar value of this 'concern' amounts to $2.6 billion per year or $118 per year on a per capita basis. This means that for each Iraqi citizen 32 cents per day was available for food, medicine, agricultural inputs, electricity, water, sewerage, and education.

What must be emphasised is that the allocations the Security Council permitted per phase could only have been fully used through 100 percent delivery of the purchased humanitarian supplies. The figures included in Figure 1.1 show that neither during the initial three phases (1996 to 1998) nor during the subsequent ten phases (1998 to 2003), with the exception of a spike in 2001, did the value of the arrived goods come even close to the amounts the Government of Iraq and the UN had budgeted in the individual distribution plans.[32] This, therefore, confirms not only the

---

29. The UN Security Council on 15 August 1991 decided on this amount – see UN S/RES/705 (1991), para. 2.
30. In view of the deteriorating human conditions in Iraq, this amount of 30 percent was eventually reduced by the UN Security Council in 1999 to 25 percent. For more details on the UNCC see Chapter 2.
31. The sectors included in these initial distribution plans, apart from food and medical supplies, comprised electricity, water and sanitation, agriculture, irrigation and education; in the Kurdish areas it additionally comprised settlement rehabilitation and mine clearance.
32. This spike of arrivals in phase XI was entirely due to a backlog of ordered goods going back several phases.

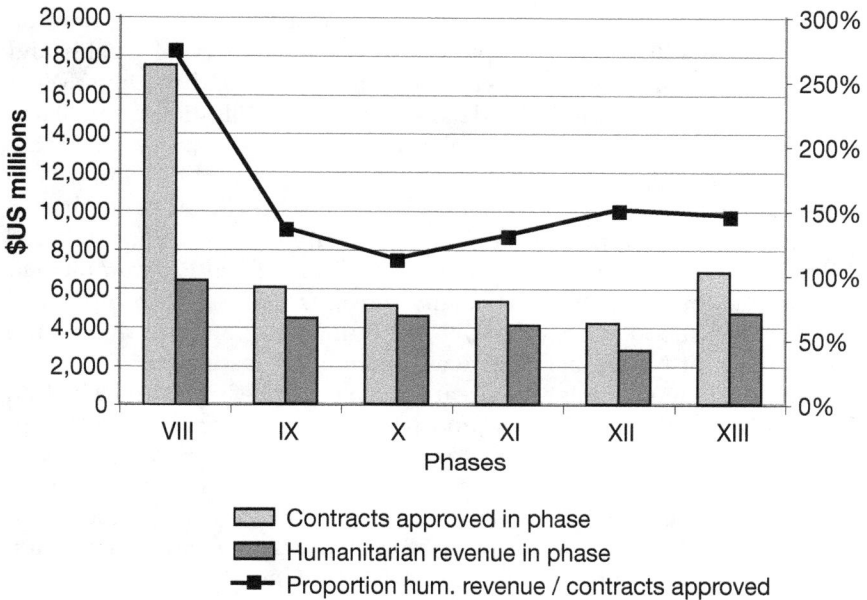

Figure 1.2   Contracts Approved and Humanitarian Revenue Per Phase

Source: *Secretary-General's 180-day reports on the Oil-for-Food Programme, phases VII-XIII.*
Notes: *No data are available on the value of contracts approved before phase VII.*

inadequacy of available resources, but also the fact that these pitifully small allocations could not even be fully utilised, mainly due to sanctions regulations. Such a situation should have been a warning light to the UN Security Council and led to an early increase in permissible funding and the easing of the bureaucratic controls to speed up arrivals of essential supplies in Iraq. This did not happen.

The US and UK governments insisted that the blame for the inability to utilise allocated funds lay entirely with the Government of Iraq. This is a serious misrepresentation of facts since there were no wilful delays in the ordering of humanitarian supplies on the part of the Iraqi Government.

Figure 1.2 shows that for the six final phases for which contract data are available, the value of approved contracts exceeded available revenue.[33] This does not mean that there were not delays because of the politicised nature of Iraq's trade relations. There were. At times delays also occurred

33. The value of approved plus proposed but not yet approved contracts significantly exceeded available revenue. It proves those wrong who accused the Iraqi authorities of procrastinating in the use of oil-for-food resources. See also Table A.10, page 290.

because of disagreements between an Iraqi ministry and a UN partner on the value of an item, for example between the Ministry of Health and UNICEF on the value of therapeutic milk for infants and mothers. What constituted the major cause for delays and under-utilisation of available resources, however, was the complicated procurement process and the permanent or temporary blocking of ordered supplies.[34] These are facts which cannot be dismissed by using references to the dictatorial regime of Saddam Hussein and the ruthlessness of his treatment of the Iraqi people.[35]

Briefings on the proposed phase v of the Oil-for-Food Programme had been set up for me with units in my office as well as with other UN agencies. The mood within the UN community in Baghdad during the second week of November 1998 was sombre. We feared that a military strike by the United States and Great Britain could be imminent. The Iraq Government suspended cooperation with UN inspectors on 31 October and the inspectors left the country. The US Government reacted with unusual sharpness to these developments. The words of Samuel Berger, the US national security adviser at that time left little room for interpretation: 'We are poised to take military action and we remain poised to take military action!'[36] The US had not forgotten previous similar crises between the UN arms inspectors and the Iraqi Government. The Clinton Government indeed seemed ready to strike. The UN Secretary-General and France, Russia, Malaysia (a temporary member of the UN Security Council) and others engaged intensively with the Iraqi and US Governments to avert military action. For some time these efforts paid off. On 14 November the Government of Iraq allowed UNSCOM to resume its arms monitoring and verification work. The crisis seemed over. As a result, tension eased among the UN humanitarian agencies in Iraq. We could concentrate once again on our mandate.

During the UN Secretary-General's historic visit to Baghdad in February 1998, he was able to convince the UN Security Council that permitted finance for the humanitarian exemption was no longer defendable and that the allowable resources for the Oil-for-Food Programme should be doubled, from $1.3 billion to $2.6 billion per phase. This increase, while a step in the right direction, would not be enough to reverse the deteriorating circumstances facing the Iraqi population. As I was told by UN colleagues, and quickly experienced myself, a shortage of finance, the bureaucratic obstacles to efficient delivery, as well as the deliberate withholding of humanitarian supplies by the UN Sanctions Committee, were ingredients of an international policy of disregard for

34. See outline of procurement structure on pages 80–2.
35. For a discussion of the delivery constraints the Oil-for-Food Programme faced see pages 83–6, including Fig. 5; for the specific issue of blocking of goods or putting on hold of humanitarian supplies see Fig. 7 on p. 132.
36. Press briefing, US White House, 14 November 1998.

the welfare of the Iraqi people. This was not the entire story, however. A simplistic purchase and supply mentality emphasising the ordering and distribution of goods and equipment during a six-month period had taken hold within the UN community and among the concerned Iraqi ministries. The latter were further demotivated from planning ahead by the constant and continuing unrealistic anticipation that economic sanctions would soon be lifted. During the preceding phases of the Oil-for-Food Programme, there had been no resources allocated for the training of teachers, technicians, managers and other categories of civil servants. There were no plans for institutional improvements of ministries and other government offices, let alone any effort to carry out national planning or to define national priorities.

International policy and national apathy had reduced Iraq to a nation compelled to take ad hoc day-to-day measures for basic survival.

My reading of the distribution plan for phase IV and the implementation reports of the United Nations confirmed this perception. The additional resources which the United Nations Security Council had permitted on 20 February 1998[37] beginning with phase IV did not alter the fact that the Oil-for-Food Programme was little more than a goods and equipment supply programme. There was no provision of funding for overheads, training and research. This did not change throughout the thirteen years of sanctions and in the course of time became a more and more serious constraint in the implementation of the Oil-for-Food Programme.

The distribution plan for this phase, as in earlier phases, contained an allocation for food as the single largest expenditure item. This would remain as such throughout the entire sanctions period. I was surprised by the absence of funding for housing, telecommunications and infrastructure repair. The oil industry had been significantly destroyed during the 1991 war and, therefore, funding for repair and maintenance of both the upstream and downstream oil industry was needed. This necessary funding was never allocated. The budget for phase IV reflected a serious lack of concern for Iraq's youth: the education budget allocation for this phase was a mere $100 million. It remained inadequate throughout the years of sanctions.

Finally, in accordance with UN Resolution 986 of 1995, the Oil-for-Food budget was divided into two segments. One was to cover the humanitarian needs for the population in the fifteen districts or governorates under the control of the government in Baghdad. The other was to do the same in the three locally autonomous districts or governorates in Iraqi Kurdistan. In Kurdistan the UN functioned as the implementing authority, in consultation with the local authorities in

---

37. See UN S/RES/1153 (1998).

Dohuk, Erbil and Suleimaniyah and the government in Baghdad. The budgets for these two areas did not correspond to the respective size of the population in central and southern Iraq and in the Kurdish areas. $1.96 billion had been allocated for the centre and south and $482 million for the three northern districts. This means that 80.3 percent of the funds were for 87 percent of the population, or 19.2 million persons, and 19.7 percent for 13.9 percent of the population, or 3.3 million persons living in Iraqi Kurdistan. These allocations were based on a political decision in the UN Security Council to calculate the budget of the humanitarian programme for the 13 percent of Iraqis living in Iraqi Kurdistan on the basis of the gross revenue of $2 billion. In contrast, the funds for the population under the control of Baghdad were based on the gross revenue of $2 billion minus the allocations for the UN Compensation Commission (UNCC), the allocation to Iraqi Kurdistan and UN overheads. This means that those living in the part of Iraq under the control of Baghdad had to shoulder the full burden of funding both UN overheads and compensation payments. The UN Security Council cannot escape the accusation that it thus victimised Iraqi citizens living in Central and Southern Iraq. They were made to pay for the wrongdoings of their government.

In the course of time this allocation formula raised more and more objections not only from the Government of Iraq, but also from others who felt this was an unfair apportioning of scarce resources. There were, however, also those who argued that this 'affirmative action' was fully justified because Iraqi Kurdistan had long been neglected by the central authorities in Baghdad. Moreover, the Kurdish areas, they stressed, had distinct requirements which other areas of Iraq did not have. Two such examples were the resettlement of internally displaced Kurds and the de-mining of large areas of northern Iraq, a legacy of the Iraq/Iran war.

Once this 'Kurdish' budget had been accepted by the Government in Baghdad and the UN Secretary-General, the Kurdish local authorities, in close cooperation with the United Nations, were responsible for the implementation of the six-month distribution plans. Procurement of humanitarian supplies for the sectors included in their budget was carried out directly between the Kurdish authorities and the United Nations agencies. For example, building materials were procured by the UN Centre for Human Settlements and the local (Kurdish) 'ministries'[38] for housing and resettlement; teaching aids and school books acquired by UNESCO and the local 'ministries' of education, etc. However, the purchase of food and medicines remained a central responsibility of the Government of Iraq in Baghdad.

---

38. The plural is used here because the Kurdish areas were divided into two political areas, one under the control of the Kurdish Democratic Party (KDP), the other under the Patriotic Union of Kurdistan (PUK).

From the point of view of equitable food security and medical protection for all Iraqis, whatever their religious or ethnic background, bulk purchasing made good sense. After all, it confirmed, at least in the context of the Oil-for-Food Programme, that the concept of 'territorial integrity' – again and again referred to in UN Security Council Resolutions[39] – had not lost its meaning. The anomaly, with negative implications for the budget under the control of Baghdad, was the fact that food and medicines destined for Iraqi Kurdistan had to be prepaid out of the Baghdad component of the Oil-for-Food Programme budget. Reimbursement often took an inordinate amount of time, thus depriving Central and Southern Iraq of timely access to much-needed resources. The UN Secretary-General repeatedly acknowledged this as an unfortunate constraint. In his report to the Security Council on 18 May 1999 he stated: 'The availability of funding [for Central and Southern Iraq] for phases III and IV continued to be adversely affected by the slow rate of reimbursement'.[40] At the end of phase IV, the budget for the fifteen governorates under the authority of Baghdad was awaiting reimbursement of $238 million advanced for the purchase of food and medicines for Iraqi Kurdistan. This constituted 15 percent of the Government's Oil-for-Food budget for the phase.[41] This was again at the expense of the Iraqis living in that area. The overall procurement flexibility for the Baghdad budget was obviously reduced. It took time for me to discover this. Efforts on my part to rectify this disadvantage, or at least to reduce the time between charging and crediting the account in Baghdad, failed.

The Secretary-General's report noted in terse and matter-of-fact language that progress in all parts of the country had been held up by funding constraints due to low oil prices as well as the all pervasive logistical constraints (warehousing, transport, communications) and the lamentable state of the oil industry. Nevertheless, in Central and Southern Iraq food distribution had been good. Some progress had been made in the distribution of medicines, water and sanitation materials and the delivery of agricultural inputs. Only slow improvements were noted in electricity generation. Poor progress in improving education remained.

In Iraqi Kurdistan, with the exception of the electricity supply, conditions were better in all sectors than they were in the areas under Baghdad's control. Progress was also reported in the northern areas in mine clearance and in the resettlement of displaced persons.

---

39. See Resolution 688 and ten other Iraq resolutions during the years 1991 to 1997.
40. See UN/S/1999/537, p. 24.
41. See UN/S/1998/1100, 19 November 1998, p. 18.

Having reviewed distribution plan IV prior to my arrival in Baghdad and the UN Secretary-General's assessment of this phase soon after my arrival, I had a sense of what was involved in the finalisation of the next phase.

The awareness of being part of an international effort to keep a nation under comprehensive economic sanctions alive and healthy weighed heavily upon me, both intellectually and emotionally. The UN Security Council, the UN Secretariat and the UN Humanitarian Programme in Iraq all were involved in a sanctions regime and, at the same time, had the responsibility to protect innocent lives. We were to ensure that at least the international community, if not the Government of Iraq, maintained a human rights based agenda and respected the dignity of the Iraqi population.

The days in November 1998 passed quickly. Professional and support staff in my office were preparing for final meetings with the Government of Iraq on the phase V distribution plan. There would be similar meetings with the World Health Organisation (WHO), the Food and Agricultural Organisation (FAO), the World Food Programme (WFP), UNDP, UNICEF and UNESCO, the agencies with resident offices in Baghdad.[42] Part of this process had been extensive consultations between the UN agencies and UNOHCI as well as between individual UN agencies and their ministerial counterparts in the Government of Iraq. The calorific value of the proposed food basket, targeted nutrition for vulnerable groups, priority needs in the electricity, water and sanitation sectors were major issues of concern to us. The special requirements of the oil industry were handled directly between the Government and the UN Secretariat in New York.

During those November days of 1998, UNOCHI was waiting for a signal from the Iraqi Foreign Ministry that the Government was ready to discuss the draft phase V distribution plan. It was the time for getting acquainted with my international and Iraqi colleagues and to learn about the structure of the Humanitarian Coordinator's Office. As one would expect of a UN office, there were colleagues from all parts of the world, with a majority from Africa and Asia. My deputies were initially Farid Zarif, an Afghan national, followed by Wurie Umaru from Sierra Leone. Zarif had been Permanent Representative to the UN in New York and, earlier, Adviser on Foreign Affairs to President Najibullah in Kabul,

---

42. UN Agencies which had closed their offices at the outbreak of Gulf War II in January 1991 and had no direct link to humanitarian programmes had subsequently not been invited back to Iraq. Over time, however, the Government of Iraq decided to re-establish relations with some of these, e.g., the International Telecommunications Union (ITU). In 2000 Iraq agreed that ITU could reopen its office in Baghdad. There was no contact with the Bretton Woods Institutions (World Bank and IMF) throughout the sanctions period.

Umaru his country's Ambassador to Germany. They were not the only former diplomats in my office. Two programme officers from Somalia and Yemen had served as Ambassadors in Kuwait and New York. Another from the Gambia had been, at one time, Foreign Minister in his Government. In my immediate office were colleagues from India, Malta, Australia, Kenya and Lebanon. My personal assistant, Srinivasan, had worked with me during earlier years in New Delhi where I had been the United Nations Resident Coordinator to India. There were a good number of staff on secondment from their UN parent organisations around the world, including the UN Secretariat in New York. The world truly came together at the Canal Hotel located in the Balladiyat district of Baghdad. This building housed what unquestionably had become at that time the most high profile UN humanitarian operation anywhere. Posts here for foreigners and Iraqis alike were much sought after, for some because of the special circumstances, for many because the remuneration was exceptionally high.[43]

Apart from the existence of standard units of a UN mission with responsibilities for finance, transport, personnel and general administration, the UNOCHI office also had a medical unit, a legal office, a resident auditor and an information section with a spokesman. A fairly large security office was under my mandate since I held a security brief on behalf of the UN system in Iraq for all UN staff with the exception of UN arms inspectors serving in the UN Special Commission (UNSCOM).

The key UNOHCI units concerned with the implementation of the Oil-for-Food Programme were two monitoring units. They had been established by the 'MOU', the Memorandum of Understanding the Government of Iraq and the United Nations had signed in May 1996. These units had the responsibility to confirm 'the equitable distribution of humanitarian supplies' to all groups of Iraqi society and 'to determine the adequacy of the available resources to meet Iraq's humanitarian needs'.[44] This was, indeed, a formidable responsibility. It seemed to suggest that such monitoring and reporting to the UN Security Council would lead to a continuous adjustment of the humanitarian programme in order to ensure that the needs of the Iraqi people were adequately met at all times. This was not to be the case, much to the detriment of the Iraqi people. To meet this responsibility, the UN Security Council, the Office of the Iraq

---

43. All international staff regardless of rank received $100 per day as a special mission allowance. Iraqi support staff would receive an average salary of $400–500 a month, an extraordinary amount in comparison to salaries in the Iraqi civil service where a primary school teacher would earn about $5 per month and a middle level functionary in a Ministry between $8 and $10.
44. See Memorandum of Understanding signed on 20 May 1996 in New York between Ambassador Abdul Amir Al-Anbari on behalf of Iraq and the UN Legal Counsel Under-Secretary General Hans Corell.

Programme had set up a 'Geographical' Observation Unit and a 'Multidisciplinary' Observation Unit.

The first of these was assigned to participate with UN agencies and programmes in observing the distribution of humanitarian supplies to end-user points (hospitals, clinics and pharmacies, schools, waterworks, sewerage plants, electricity facilities, warehouses for food, etc.). The other observation unit was charged with sectoral and technical observation responsibilities with emphasis on water, sanitation, electricity, medical supplies and equipment and agricultural inputs. Even though the Geographical Observation Unit was concerned with general observation of the distribution process and the Multidisciplinary Unit with the deployment of equipment and with technical issues related to the adequacy of the humanitarian supplies, there was a distinct overlap in functions. For this reason alone it was not at all surprising that tension existed between these two units.

The UN observation system in Iraq, however, was more complex than that. All of the UN agencies and programmes had their own sectoral observers and would join the UNOHCI observers on their daily verification visits. Such a three-tier observation structure proved to be a fertile ground for duplication, competition, and, ultimately, confrontation within UNOCHI and between UNOCHI and the other UN entities. Each was accusing the others of not being professional. All of this had less to do with personalities and more with the observation structure the UN had put in place.

In carrying out monitoring assignments all over Iraq these mixed UN teams would have to be accompanied by government minders. Some no doubt with intelligence responsibilities, they were junior functionaries whose job it was to assist during travels and observation visits with translations and to resolve any difficulties en route, at police checkpoints or in local government offices. Without their presence the Government would not permit monitoring. The shortage of such government staff in some ministries, for example the Ministry of Education and late arrivals at arranged points of departure in Baghdad, often caused delays and irritation. Iraqi counterparts did not have the convenience of assigned vehicles as UN staff had[45] and instead had to depend on unreliable public transport.

The overall coordination of the UN observation process rested with my office but, as I soon became aware with much concern, coordination within my own office left much to be desired. Concern eventually became anger and disbelief when I discovered that the Multidisciplinary

---

45. This is an example of the many inherent inequities between the two sides. UN staff had ready access to latest model vehicles which were paid for with Iraqi oil revenue, yet no vehicles were available to the Iraqi counterparts.

Observation Unit was reporting directly to the UN Office of the Iraq Programme in New York instead of to the Humanitarian Coordinator in Baghdad as the Geographical Observation Unit did. A year later this was confirmed to me in a written communication: 'The Chief of the Multidisciplinary Observation Unit (MDOU) will continue to report its analysis, conclusions and recommendations directly to the Executive Director (in New York) …'.[46]

Managerially this made no sense and spelled disaster. It constituted an untenable obstacle to carrying out daily monitoring responsibilities in an efficient manner. I wrote, telephoned and met on this issue with many in both Baghdad and New York. Requests for immediate changes to the Deputy Secretary-General overseeing the Iraq Programme, Louise Frechette, and my direct superior, the Executive Director of the Office of the Iraq Programme, Benon Sevan, fell on deaf ears. The latter was adamant that the existing structure was the right one and had to stay in place. He also cited a 'demand' from the UN Security Council that it wished to have the Multidisciplinary Observation Unit report to the UN Secretariat. This indicated to me that both OIP and the Security Council wanted to have a direct channel of communications between New York and Baghdad. Much later, in the winter of 1999, during a visit to UN Headquarters, I brought this serious structural anomaly to the attention of Secretary-General Kofi Annan. He looked at me in astonishment. 'This is difficult to believe', he said. He was truly surprised to see an organisation chart which showed that one of the two observation units in my office reported directly to New York.

Additionally, the entire UNOCHI administration in Baghdad, as I had discovered, to my horror, after a few weeks into my assignment, reported not to the UN Humanitarian Coordinator in Baghdad but directly to the Department of Peace Keeping Operations (DPKO) in New York. The Secretary-General was quick to reassure me that he shared my concern and would do something about what can only be described as a managerial nightmare. This reality, unfortunately, did not change during my tenure in Baghdad. It remained a never-ending source of conflict and frustration. It siphoned off much energy which should have been available for the implementation of the humanitarian programme.

Because of the eight-hour time difference between Baghdad and New York, the work day at UN Headquarters started more or less when the work day in Baghdad came to an end. This meant awkward working hours, especially for the senior staff in Baghdad.

Our long days were charged with a mixture of fear of the unknown and a determination to make the best out of a demanding work environment. Intensive debates would take place spontaneously about the latest

46. Letter from Chef de Cabinet, Iqbal Riza dated 23 November 1999 to author.

theories on the whereabouts of an elusive President Saddam Hussein or speculation about the next steps in the 'great game' between Washington, London and Baghdad. Other topics which occupied UN minds ranged from the sudden arrest of a local employee[47] to traffic accidents and the misconduct of UN staff. There were whispered stories of anti-government unrest in areas with Shi'ite majorities, such as in Madinat Saddam, a desperately poor part of Baghdad, or in Najaf, Karbala and tribal communities in the Shatt-el-Arab areas of Southern Iraq where the Tigris and Euphrates rivers join.

Regular US/UK air strikes in the two no-fly zones north of the 36th and south of the 33rd parallels added[48] to the unease of UN staff.

I was fortunate to have dedicated telephone connections to New York and Geneva in my office as well as in my flat in the Djadriya district of Baghdad. Thus, there was no danger that leaving the office would mean missing incoming calls from senior colleagues in New York or from our offices in Erbil and Suleimaniyah in Iraqi Kurdistan. Moreover, all UN vehicles in Iraq were equipped with mobile phones, chiefly to maintain a local security network but also to respond to calls from UN offices, the Government,[49] the diplomatic community in Baghdad and the media. We could not escape the twenty-four-hour connectivity!

The twenty-minute ride between the office and my flat was depressing. There was little that could possibly remind one of Haroon al Rashid's Baghdad of the eighth century AD. The enticing jewel of the Middle East, the Baghdad of Sheharazade, had long disappeared. Baghdad had become a conglomerate of dilapidated buildings, a city of open sewerage and broken water mains, with pavements clogged with mounds of uncollected rubbish and rubble from unfinished roadworks. Tree stumps lined the roads where once flamboyants, acacia and palms had been. I am told that they were plentiful in earlier years and carefully maintained by a well endowered Amanat al-Asima, the municipality of Baghdad. Along the route we would pass military buildings and an abandoned airport with remnants of the erstwhile Iraqi air force. These were all testimony of a city under siege. Baghdad was a city whose soul and mind were

---

47. Local staff with UN contracts enjoy worldwide immunity from arrest until the UN Secretary-General decides to waive this immunity. The Government of Iraq, as many other governments with whom I had to deal, often did not honour the UN Convention on Privileges and Immunities of UN Staff and would arrest UN local staff, e.g., for minor traffic offences.
48. For more detailed review of these no-fly zones see chapter 3.
49. The Government of Iraq had a work day not dissimilar to other parts of the Middle East. The official day began around 10 A.M; between 2 and 7 P.M. it would be difficult to find staff in their offices; after 7 P.M. and into the late evenings was an active time in government offices. The UN and diplomatic community were expected to be available during these hours for meetings, often at a moment's notice.

disturbed, a city with people who had hardship written on their faces, and looked as run down as the buildings in which they lived.

The picture of Baghdad in 1998 would not be accurately described without reference to the 'islands of glitter', the palaces of Saddam Hussein and the beautiful mosques. Some of these had been built recently and in their magnificent architectural designs were witnesses that Iraqi craftsmanship was still very much alive. And then there was, of course, during every moment of the drive the omnipresence of the Iraqi leader in the form of statues, observing the misery facing his people. Not a week passed without evidence of a new portrayal of 'the President of all Battles' along the road between the Canal Hotel office and the Carthage Hotel in Djedriya, the district in which I stayed. He looked at you as a general, a sportsman, a teacher, a father surrounded by children, or dressed as a Kurd, a tribal leader, a statesman – the one missing picture was that of Saddam Hussein as the dictator.

At night, darkness added a veil of mysteriousness to this picture of misery and contradiction. The horrific electricity shortages would make the trip to my flat a journey between areas of total darkness or dimly lit blocks of houses attesting to low voltage and those of the bright lights of government offices, palaces and the few homes of those who owned generators. Given the atrocious conditions of many of Baghdad's roads, I was fortunate in having Basim Khalaf, or Abu Laith as he was affectionately known by his colleagues, as my driver. Driving in Baghdad was hazardous at any time, and, by any standards, particularly at night. He knew his city superbly well and even though he often spoke of the better days Baghdad had seen, he had an imaginary road map of potholes in his mind which never seemed to fail him in navigating us safely around town. Not everyone was as fortunate, as the innumerable cars with broken axles testified.

The Iraqi Government required all UN staff on humanitarian or disarmament assignments[50] to stay in eighteen specified hotels. The Muchabarat, Iraq's intelligence agencies, wanted to keep track of us but particularly those working with the UN Special Commission (UNSCOM). The Government also refused private residences for staff in these two categories and disallowed families to join these UN staff members. The authorities wanted to make the point that staff in these categories were indeed involved in 'temporary' assignments as was specified in UN resolutions.[51]

---

50. This comprised 95 percent of the 200 to 250 UN staff living in Baghdad at any one time.
51. E.g., in UN SC Resolution 986 of 14 April 1995 which refers in the third paragraph to the humanitarian programme as 'a temporary measure to cover the humanitarian needs of the Iraqi people'.

The Carthage Hotel, my 'home' for seventeen months, was one of the smaller 'UN hotels' on the left bank of the Tigris. Those living in the approximately twenty studio apartments in this hotel were men and women either working for humanitarian programmes or involved in the multifarious disarmament activities of the UN Special Commission.

I do not know how my colleagues felt when they returned to the Carthage Hotel in the evening. Despite the differences in cultural backgrounds, professional training and rank, experience in international affairs and attitude to the human catastrophe, there were aspects of life common to all. For example, stress: no one was spared it, and we shared an awareness that we were participants in a huge, dramatic and unique experience of international relations. This reality made it important, at least for me, to create the space to 'digest' the day and reflect on what was likely to lie ahead.

Press clippings, status reports, communications from the Iraqi Government and the UN in New York – full briefcases accompanied me whenever I entered the 'private' world of my apartment. They neither distracted nor discouraged me from taking time out to reflect on broader issues, on the reasons for being in Iraq or on the approach that the UN had chosen. Evenings were long and the demands of the moment could wait. I was intensely occupied during these evenings of the initial weeks in Baghdad as I attempted to understand:

- the motives and dynamics of the fifteen-member UN Security Council dealing with an Iraq humanitarian programme that so obviously was severely lacking, financially and substantively;
- how the UN community in Baghdad could organise itself to increase pressure on all parties, the Government of Iraq, the UN Security Council and the UN Secretariat to improve the Oil-for-Food Programme for the benefit of the civilian population;
- the reasons for the existence of a large but fragmented UN presence in Iraq and whether anything could be done to change it.

Every day I saw more evidence of the inadequacy of resources and the corresponding poor human conditions. I also noticed a disturbing 'routine mentality' in many UN offices.

The explanation for the UN Security Council's position could not be that member governments were unaware of conditions in Iraq. It was in the hands of the UN Security Council to do something about the Oil-for-Food Programme. The Council could increase oil revenue, remove sectoral limitations and allow a freer flow of goods. Why did this not happen? In these early days of my stay in Baghdad it was difficult for me to believe what my colleague Denis Halliday had told me in Geneva: that the motive of some governments was punitive and destabilising, putting deliberate limitations on the humanitarian programme and thereby knowingly maintaining conditions of misery in the hope that this would lead Saddam Hussein and his government to change their ways.

Should more efforts have been made on the part of the UN system in Baghdad to expand the existing reporting requirements to assess and report in greater detail on the implications of existing UN policies? To what extent was the UN becoming a culpable party? Assuming that no additional resources would become available, what were the alternatives the UN had to extend more benefits to the people of Iraq? We had to be creative and convince the Government in Baghdad and the UN in New York that improvements of living conditions in Iraq were absolutely necessary. Lifting the present restriction of purchasing food locally would be one. It would save a lot of money. Refurbishing local medium- and small-scale industries in order to produce within Iraq items needed by the Oil-for-Food Programme would be another. Such measures would reduce cost and generate employment. There was no acceptable reason why, for example, school furniture, general medicines and some spare parts could not be made in Iraq. However, rehabilitating the economy was strongly opposed by the US and UK Governments in the UN Security Council with the argument that many products, e.g., in the pharmaceutical industry,[52] were of dual use and could be diverted to the military for the production of weapons of mass destruction. Additional resources could have become available through a reduction of the exorbitant 30 percent of oil revenue that was diverted to the UN Compensation Commission (UNCC) in Geneva. Also draining resources was the use of Iraqi oil revenue for the payment of UN overheads. Four percent was deducted by the UN for the cost of running humanitarian programmes, disarmament administration and a special reserve at the time we were finalising phase v of the Oil-for-Food Programme in late 1998.[53]

The question I asked myself again and again in these early days in Baghdad was why should limited Iraqi resources that were badly needed to keep a nation alive and, in particular, to reduce malnutrition and child mortality, be used for the payment of UN staff salaries? One of my first special initiatives in early 1999 was to telephone the Swedish Foreign

52. In 1998, the Samara Drug Industry (SDI) was practically defunct. Partial rehabilitation to produce some general prescription drugs would have been possible. The UN could have without difficulty monitored production and distribution.
53. Until 21 March 2003, 64.2 billion had become available to the UN from the export of Iraqi oil. Taking into account slight changes in the calculations of overhead deductions over the 1996–2003 period, amounts around $2 billion were available to finance the administration of UN humanitarian and non-humanitarian programmes. These funds could have made some difference in the living conditions of Iraqis.

Secretary, Jan Eliasson, in Stockholm. I knew him well from the time when he had been Undersecretary-General for humanitarian affairs in New York and I felt that I could talk to him freely. I asked him whether he saw a possibility that Sweden could provide about $1.4 million to finance the cost of maintaining three hundred UN humanitarian staff in Iraq during phase v operations. He was receptive to the idea and promised to discuss the suggestion with his government. This sounded encouraging and I was looking forward to good news. To my great disappointment and anger, I heard later that the Swedish Permanent Representative to the UN in New York had been told by an unnamed senior official in the UN Secretariat that this would not be a good idea. This ended what I thought had been an imaginative alternative for additional funding of humanitarian activities. It certainly would have enhanced UN credibility in Iraq. Many Iraqis, not only those in government, criticised the UN's use of Iraqi money for high salaries while they were starving. I felt that this was a legitimate issue and that the 'senior official in New York' whoever he was – I, of course, had a hunch – was out of order.

My concern for more benefits within the various sectors included in the Oil-for-Food Programme was based on the initial impression that a programme year after year entirely focused on the purchase and distribution of goods, spare parts and equipment, could not be in the best interest of the Iraqi people. Training, institution building, inter-sectoral planning, curriculum development and other elements which the United Nations in its humanitarian and development programmes elsewhere advocated should have their place in Iraq as well. Were they deliberately excluded even though training and institution building, for example, would cost relatively little? Why were there no provisions to assist in inter-ministerial planning? Why were no efforts made to engage in curriculum development at the various levels of education? I had no answer to these questions, only an awareness that the Oil-for-Food Programme did not pay much attention to these areas. I was determined to find answers. The Iraq Programme's Director in New York, Benon Sevan, was not even willing to discuss these issues which could no longer be ignored because of the 'temporary' nature of sanctions, not after nine years! 'This is an emergency not a development programme' was all he had to say.

The Government of Iraq, in the initial three-draft distribution plans (1996–8) had included justified funding requests for the transport and telecommunication sectors. The UN Security Council simply rejected them. Living in Baghdad, it was not difficult to realise why these sectors were badly in need of improvement. To call New York or Geneva on dedicated UN telephone lines[54] and have instant connections made one

54. These special lines for UN offices in Baghdad had New York telephone numbers. Dialling 1-212-963-3010 from anywhere around the world would connect automatically to the Baghdad's UN telephone exchange.

forget that it was a different situation for Iraqis. On the other hand, to make a local call was an exercise in self control. It was not at all unusual to have to dial five, six or more times to get a connection. To get through did not guarantee that one would be able to understand the person at the other end. The telephone system was in a truly chaotic state.

As far as transport was concerned, the needs were also all too obvious. There was a severe shortage of public road transport, as one could see daily from the long lines of Baghdadis patiently waiting for their turn. The Iraqi railways were practically defunct, with only a few trains operating between Baghdad, Mosul and Basra. Train travel was not safe, given the conditions of the tracks, victims of the 1991 Gulf War and years of forced neglect. These proved to be considerable inconveniences for the average Iraqi but they were not life-threatening. It was different for the state of the transport fleet required to carry food and medicines to warehouses, hospitals, clinics and food distribution points throughout Iraq. During my briefings the representatives of the World Health Organisation, the World Food Programme and UNICEF had repeatedly expressed their concern for the poor state of transport, particularly refrigerated vehicles. The recurrent breakdowns and the overall shortage of transport posed a serious threat to the welfare of the Iraqi people. There were, of course, funding limitations but it was more than that. It was an unwillingness by the UN Security Council or, more accurately, the US and UK representatives on the Council, to approve contracts for these sectors for fear that improved telecommunications and transport[55] would benefit the Iraqi military. In Distribution Plan v the Government of Iraq, yet again, had included both of these sectors. I would attempt to support this request with all the good arguments the UN in Baghdad had at its disposal.

Why did the Security Council exclude such sectors as transport and telecommunications and even housing when the civilian population badly needed them? Why was there a severe shortage of funding despite the repeated reassurances by the Security Council that the needs of the Iraqi people had to be met? Why was a UN observation mechanism hampered by fragmentation and multiple lines of authority?

The privacy of my flat was the right place for me to grapple with these issues. No one disturbed me here, not even the tropical fish which my predecessor, Denis Halliday, had left behind, nor the perroquet which Amer Abdullah, the caretaker of my flat, had added without a warning:

---

55. As an example, in the course of my stay in Baghdad, US representatives on the Security Council Iraq Sanction Committee blocked for many months the release of 800 badly needed ambulances. They were only released when the UN could confirm that the communication equipment, a standard life-protecting item in ambulances, had been removed.

he simply went one day to the Zukk al Gazil, the animal market in central Baghdad, and bought it. The Zukk had a wide array of fish, fowl and other animals. Depressed-looking and poorly clad owners were at the market, eager to pass on to others the food bill for the pets they could no longer afford. Amer installed this small orange bird in my living room because 'I feel sorry for you. You are alone here'. I accepted the bird as 'the lonely tenant whose family was far away in Geneva'. 'Mortin', as Amer Abdullah decided to call the new co-tenant of my flat, was quite discriminating in his dietary habits, preferring local seeds to the Swiss varieties I would bring back for him. He also clearly rejected Telemann, Boccherini and Vivaldi and preferred the Spice Girls, Boyzone and father and son Iglesias, the music my daughter insisted I should take with me to Baghdad. The moment I played baroque music, Mortin would move to a corner of his cage and sulk, keeping quiet, yet displayed Pavaroti-like temperament and vocal ability when he heard the music my daughter had added to my 'Baghdad collection'.

Similarly concerned for my welfare was Abu Laith, my colleague and driver, and his family. This Kurdish-Arab family ensured that my diet would not be monotonous. Abu Laith regularly brought me Iraqi culinary delights prepared by his wife. There was an abundance of Iraqi kindness around me.

Whenever I left the tranquillity of my flat I re-entered another world, a grim world in which people struggled to survive. Abu Laith and I would usually join a cavalcade of white, recent model UN vehicles, which were purchased with Iraqi oil money, taking staff from their hotels in Djedriye and other parts of the city to the UN offices at Canal Hotel. I could not help but perceive us, the UN staff, as rolling islands of affluence. Iraqi cars were mostly of old vintage, with the exception of occasional shiny limousines of high government officials which would speed past us, their curtains drawn to protect the identity of their passengers. Then there were a few recent model cars of diplomats[56] and well-to-do local businessmen.

During the first two weeks in November 1998 I often spent time in those government ministries which participated in the Oil-for-Food Programme. The key ministries for the Office of the United Nations Humanitarian Coordinator were the Ministry of Foreign Affairs, our focal point, and the Ministries of Health and Trade. The Minister of Trade, Mohamed Medi Saleh, was in charge of procuring food. His Ministry,

---

56. In 1998 there were some thirty-five embassies in Baghdad representing countries in Africa, Asia, Europe and Latin America. The United States maintained an interest section which was located in the old US Embassy but formed part of the Polish Embassy. The largest representations were those of Russia, France, China and Iran.

therefore, was the biggest user of Oil-for-Food revenue.[57] While my colleagues from UNICEF, WFP, FAO, WHO, and UNESCO[58] were busy discussing proposed humanitarian supplies with technical staff in their respective ministries, I would meet, at the Ministry of Foreign Affairs, or 'MOFA' as it was called locally, with the Under Secretary of Health, Dr Shauki Murqus, the Director-General of the Ministry of Trade, Dr Fakri Rashan, and the Director of the International Organisation Department of MOFA, Ambassador Adnan Malik.[59]

Negotiating the Humanitarian Exemption

New for me at the time of negotiating phase v in November 1998, but a standard feature of negotiations on the Iraqi side, was the Foreign Ministry representative's warning at these meetings that the Government of Iraq was running out of patience with sanctions: 'I cannot guarantee we will submit this distribution plan to the UN'. He knew, however, that I was aware that a political decision at the highest level, meaning by President Saddam Hussein himself, had already been taken to forward this document to the United Nations, thereby accepting another six months of sanctions.

The four of us always met in Ambassador Malik's small office on the fourth floor of the Foreign Ministry. As with so many other government offices I had seen in Baghdad, it had the standard rundown furniture, faded curtains and the ubiquitous photo of an eternally youthful-looking President Saddam Hussein, taken by Babylon, a well known Baghdad photo house specialising in official photographs ever since President Abdul Salam Aref in the 1960s.

Ambassador Malik would always criticise the long delays in the arrival of '986 commodities'[60] and invariably referred to the increasing number of humanitarian supplies put on hold by the US and UK representatives

---

57. In phases i–iii, the food element came to 80 percent of the total budget; for phases iv to vi the food element was 30 percent, 45 percent and 31 percent respectively. The lower average is explained by the increase of overall funding due to higher oil revenue ceilings and better oil market prices allowing more funds to go to other sectors.
58. UNCHS, the United Nations Centre for Human Settlements, was also represented in Baghdad but its programmes were confined to Iraqi Kurdistan. UNCHS, therefore, did not participate in preparatory meetings with the Iraq Government.
59. In the course of 1999 Ambassador Adnan Malik was assigned as Iraqi Ambassador to Malaysia and replaced in Baghdad by Ambassador Osama Badruddin. He had recently returned to Baghdad from Islamabad.
60. Reference to UNSCR 986 of 14 April 1995 establishing the Oil-for-Food Programme.

on the Iraq Sanctions Committee in New York. At the time the Government of Iraq and the United Nations were finalising phase v, these holds amounted to about $200 million – a very small amount compared with the value of holds in subsequent phases.[61]

I expected additional criticism of the budget for Iraqi Kurdistan since it was prepared between the UN and the local authorities in Iraqi Kurdistan without any direct involvement by the authorities in Baghdad. Such criticism neither came during phase v negotiations nor in the talks during subsequent phases. The only remark Ambassador Malik made regarding the budget for Iraqi Kurdistan related to what he thought were the 'outrageous' costs for the UN de-mining operations in the northern areas. I would hear similar complaints from Kurdish officials during my visit to Iraqi Kurdistan.

The bearer in Ambassador Malik's office, Raad, a Baghdadi midget, seemed to know when this mandatory tirade of opposition to the Oil-for-Food Programme was over. He would then enter to serve us *stikan*, the tea in small glasses, appreciated all over the Middle East, Turkey and Muslim South Asia. This eased what could have been a much more charged atmosphere. Instead it became more light hearted and congenial – a good beginning, I thought, for jointly reviewing a $2.7 billion phase v distribution plan covering the period 26 November 1998 to 24 May 1999.

Ambassador Malik, Dr Murqus, Dr Rashan and I were literally huddled together around a low table as if in a conspiracy on behalf of the Iraq people. Had the US State Department or British Foreign Office been privy to such meetings they would have been surprised. The budget review and the many preceding joint working group meetings between UN staff and Iraqi ministerial officials attempted to make the best out of a totally inadequately funded and seriously restricted programme. US and UK officials would have been astonished by the deep sense of purpose that characterised these meetings, on both the UN and the Iraqi sides.

The WFP representative, Holbrooke Arthur, my Ghanaian colleague[62] and his team, were working with their counterparts in the Ministry of Trade to put together a food basket of 2,200 kilo calories per person per day for a population of about 23 million. Their task was to prepare for the timely import of some 2.64 million tons of food for the six months period. Dr Habib Rejeb, the Tunisian WHO representative, and his team were discussing with the Ministry of Health, particularly with Kimadia, the Iraqi state company for importation of drugs and medical supplies, an intricate programme for the procurement of medicines and health equipment. Dr Amir Khalil, my Sudanese colleague, representing the UN

61. See Fig. 7 on page 132.
62. He was replaced in early 1999 by Jutta Burckardt, a German civil servant on loan from the Ministry of Economic Cooperation in Bonn.

Food and Agricultural Organisation, and his colleagues, were negotiating with the Ministries of Agriculture and Irrigation. Time-bound seasonal inputs (fertilizer, seeds, pesticides, etc.) to meet some of the needs of about 260,000 Iraqi farmers were required. Dr Philippe Heffink, the UNICEF representative[63] and colleague from Belgium, and his team were reviewing with the Ministry of Education the use of the meagre $100 million available for the education sector. They also discussed mother and child and nutrition issues with the Ministry of Health. The Ministry of Interior, UNICEF's focus, was on safe water and sanitation programmes. UNESCO, responsible for education programmes beyond the primary level, was represented in Iraq by Claudine Courtel, a Canadian.[64] She and her small team were in contact with the Ministry of Higher Education to identify educational needs, mainly school books, teaching aids and school furniture that could be met from the slim resources available to that sector. The electricity, resettlement and de-mining sectors, the latter two limited to Iraqi Kurdistan, had been reviewed in Erbil and Suleimaniyah. Their budget requirements were defined by UNDP for electricity, by UNOPS for de-mining and by UNCHS[65] for resettlement. These budgets needed to be vetted by the Government of Iraq and by my office. Meetings at the Foreign Ministry served, *inter alia*, this purpose.

Derogatory statements from Washington and London such as 'the regime is getting drunk while it claims that its people don't have enough to eat. So we are a little tired of hearing that sanctions are responsible for the problems of the people of Iraq',[66] made all of us in the UN in Baghdad upset. They simplistically dismissed that sanctions had a great deal to do with the plight of Iraqis. Apart from this, there was also a genuine sense of responsibility with which the Iraqi ministry officials and their UN counterparts dealt with a complicated physical and mental survival programme. The dictatorship aside, Iraqi civil servants and even the portfolio ministers involved in the programme, such as the Ministers of Education, Higher Education, Health, Social Welfare, Agriculture, Irrigation, and Trade, as strange as it may sound, had concern for their people. They did not use, certainly not during my time in Baghdad, the Oil-for-Food Programme as a bargaining tool. Trade involving Oil-for-Food Programme commodities at the same time was politicised, as has been pointed out. Minister of Trade, Dr Saleh, openly admitted that countries which supported Iraq politically and were critical of economic

63. He was replaced in 1999 by Dr Anupama Rao Singh from India.
64. Courtel was headquartered in Iraqi Kurdistan since UNESCO headquarters in Paris believed that the focus of its involvement would lie in Northern Iraq.
65. UNDP = UN Development Programme, UNOPS = UN Office for Project Services and UNCHS = UN Centre for Human Settlements.
66. US State Department, Daily Press Briefing by James P. Rubin, Assistant Secretary of State, Bureau of Public Affairs, 25 February 2000.

sanctions would be the preferred trading partners. Others would only get contracts for goods which Iraq needed and could not purchase elsewhere. This applied, for example, to oil industry spare parts and equipment. Many of these had to be procured in the United States since Iraq's oil industry, in days of better relations with the US, had developed its upstream and downstream oil facilities with US technology. Iraqi and UN statistics concerning procurement readily confirmed the link between source and political relations. Russia, France, China, Pakistan, India, Vietnam, even Yemen and, of course, Jordan and later Egypt and Syria had 'most favoured nation' status.

Reviews of draft distribution plans usually stretched over many days and often late into the night. These plans were based upon a consensus of the sectoral ministries and their counterparts from Baghdad-based UN agencies. The representatives of the Ministries of Foreign Affairs, Health and Trade, and myself, were to ensure that the proposed sectoral budgets reflected the best possible distribution of the limited funds available.

Neither UN Resolution 986 of 1995 nor the accompanying Memorandum of Understanding, signed between the UN and the Government of Iraq in 1996, specifically identified food and health supply as priorities. It was obvious to the Iraqi and UN sides that the distribution plans had to ensure that the monthly food basket, upon which the vast majority of Iraqis depended, came as close to the caloric value which Government and the UN had jointly calculated. The UN Secretary-General would, in any case, not have approved a distribution plan unless he was satisfied that food and medicines had been given priority attention. This explains why in phases I to III (1996–8) an average of 80 percent of the $1.3 billion available for the humanitarian programme, per phase, was allocated to these two sectors. As oil income increased in subsequent phases, funds allocated to these two sectors increased. Their priority was never questioned. This was in order. However, unfortunately, nothing was done to rectify the inadequacy of allocations to other sectors.

For phase V,[67] the first phase in which I was involved, $1.1 billion or 41 percent of the total budget of $2.7 billion was proposed by Government for food and $240 million or 8.9 percent for health supplies.[68]

I regret that at the time we did not disaggregate sectoral allocations to a per capita level in order to show in some detail the irresponsibly low levels of funding authorised by the UN Security Council. To give one example, each Iraqi received a food allocation worth $49 for the six-month period or 27 cents per day![69]

---

67. The UN Secretary-General approved Distribution Plan V (November 1998 to May 1999) as submitted by the Government of Iraq on 26 November 1998.
68. See Table A.7, p. 287.
69. See Table A.12, p. 297.

In retrospect, it is surprising that while the Government of Iraq was continually complaining of the shortage of resources, in all sectors, it did not present its case more strongly.

The Food Sector

The Distribution Plan for phase v identifies 55,864 'food ration agents' in Iraq. The Government of Iraq had already introduced a food rationing system in September 1990, in response to the UN embargo. These agents were authorised by the Government of Iraq to hand out to 'every Iraqi citizen, Arab and foreigner'[70] the monthly food ration in return for coupons which were included with the individual ration cards. The food basket included wheat flour, rice, sugar, tea, cooking oil, milk powder, dried whole milk cheese, fortified weaning cereals, pulses and iodised salt. Soaps and detergents were also distributed. These ration cards had to be renewed annually and were valid only in the location of permanent residence. Change of residence would require a new ration card to be issued by the registration centre in the community to which an individual or family had moved. Apart from facilitating the distribution of food, this system was a convenient way for Iraqi intelligence services to keep track of the location and movement of Iraqi citizens as well as others.

The Kurdish Budget

All thirteen distribution plans covering the lifespan of the Oil-for-Food Programme from 10 December 1996 to 21 November 2003 contain separate budgets for Iraqi Kurdistan.[71]

Details of the budgets for Iraqi Kurdistan were worked out by the United Nations agencies operating in northern Iraq in cooperation and the two Kurdish local authorities, the Kurdish Democratic Party (KDP) in Erbil and Dohuk and the Patriotic Union of Kurdistan (PUK) in Suleimaniyah. Budgets for Iraqi Kurdistan excluded food and medicines since these were procured centrally by the Government of Iraq. Budget negotiations, as UNOCHI carried them out with the two Kurdish factions and eventually with the Central Government in Baghdad, involved the

---

70. This provision was contained in all thirteen distribution plans the Government submitted to the UN during the 1996–2003 Oil-for-Food Programme period.
71. See Table A.7, p. 287.

sectors of water and sanitation, agriculture, and primary and higher education. Budgets for resettlement programmes and de-mining, two sectors unique to Iraqi Kurdistan, were negotiated separately between the UN and the Kurdish authorities.

Settlement Rehabilitation in Iraqi Kurdistan

The Government of Iraq did not question the Kurdish budget proposals for the four sectors. They showed more interest in the sectors' 'settlement rehabilitation' and 'mine-related activities', since these were specific to the Kurdish areas. Settlement rehabilitation consisted primarily of housing programmes for the so-called 'IDPs' or internally displaced persons, who, because of the conflict between the KDP and PUK factions, had left their homes to settle in other parts of the Kurdish north. While no count was ever made, the UN Centre for Human Settlements (UNCHS), the main UN entity responsible for assisting the IDPs, estimated that 100,000 lived in areas under the control of the KDP. The PUK had admitted 150,000 into their areas. For Distribution Plan v, UN and Kurdish authorities had suggested an amount of $40 million for the rehabilitation of resettled villages, infrastructure and services rehabilitation in townships and urban areas, and basic assistance to resettled families. This programme also included support to IDPs who had come across the Arab/Kurdish line of control, out of areas controlled by Baghdad, particularly in Kirkuk and Mosul and rural communities surrounding these two cities. Using ration cards cancelled by the Central Government as information the UN assumed that the number of such IDPs was relatively small during the period 1998 to 2000, when I served in Iraq. They probably numbered not more than a few thousand. They, however, constituted a high profile group which the Central Government played down as insignificant arguing that it was not bigger than the group of Arab Iraqis who had crossed the line of control in the opposite direction. This was factually incorrect since not many Arabs had opted to stay in the Kurdish areas after Iraq's 1991 Gulf War defeat.

The Kurdish side, on the other hand, regularly issued strong statements of condemnation about the 'Arabisation' of the Kirkuk and Mosul areas in order to remind Baghdad and capitals around the world that they considered these 'expulsions' clear evidence of the severe human rights violations committed by Saddam Hussein's Government against the Kurdish minority. It was also a reminder that both KDP and PUK considered oil rich Kirkuk and Mosul traditional Kurdish territory.

The plight of these unfortunate Kurdish groups was obvious to anyone travelling in the Khanaqin area of Iraqi Kurdistan. They were housed in tents which only poorly protected them against harsh weather conditions, particularly in the winter. Inadequate medical services, poor schooling facilities for their children, little hope of employment, and total dependency on food assistance from the UN reflected their predicament. Long waiting periods before their relocation to more permanent quarters in the Kurdish north intensified their hardship.

The settlement rehabilitation component of the Oil-for-Food Programme was meant to help them and their somewhat more fortunate fellow IDPs who had merely crossed from one part of Iraqi Kurdistan to another. No doubt, the Iraqi Government must take responsibility for a large portion of this human drama. The bickering between the various Kurdish political factions, however, added significantly to the displacement and suffering.

The US State Department's September 1999 publication entitled *Saddam Hussein's Iraq*[72] chose to ignore this 'internal Kurdish factor' and blamed the Government of Iraq entirely for the IDP tragedy. To make its point, the US State Department cited, *inter alia*, as facts the 'destruction by Iraqi forces of civilian homes in the citadel of Kirkuk'. Two photos in this publication show the citadel of Kirkuk before and after the destruction of houses. During a stay in Kirkuk in the spring of 1999 I visited the citadel. Houses had indeed been demolished. This had been done, as I learnt, under the supervision of the Department of Archaeology to excavate and restore historic sites, including mosques and Arab houses.[73] The Director of Archaeology, who had heard of my arrival, came to the citadel to show me these sites and the ongoing restoration works. He confirmed that homeowners had been evicted and their houses had been demolished, yet 'we offered them alternative properties in the vicinity of the citadel'. Later, just outside the citadel, I engaged a Kirkuki in a conversation. He turned out to be a Turkoman who reconfirmed that those who had been asked to leave the citadel area had been offered new houses. Back in Baghdad I heard the same story.

De-mining in Iraqi Kurdistan

The Kurdish de-mining programme represented a more contentious issue in discussions with the Iraqi Government. For phase v the Kurdish authorities and the UN Office for Project Services (UNOPS), as the

72. *Saddam Hussein's Iraq*, prepared by the US Department of State, 13 September 1999.
73. Journalist Neil MacFarouhar wrote in the New York Times of 28 September 2003: 'In the ancient citadel, Mr. Hussein's Government paid the mostly Turkomen and Kurdish population to move out and in 1998 bulldozed all but a few historical mosques and exquisite Arab houses.'

implementing agency, had proposed a budget of $9 million. This was a relatively small amount considering that a mined area of thousands of square kilometres was involved. In fact, an estimated 20 percent of the arable land in Iraqi Kurdistan could not be cultivated because of landmines. The Government of Iraq did not like the existence of this programme for a variety of reasons. First of all, it involved international personnel with a military background. The Iraqis feared that this would encourage intelligence activities. The Government, for example, was convinced that the British Mine Action Group (MAG) operating in Iraqi Kurdistan long before the UN's involvement was a front for British intelligence. MAG was, however, appreciated by the Kurds for its competence.

Considering this conviction and the Government's experience with UNSCOM, the UN disarmament group, which had been misused repeatedly by bilateral intelligence, this reservation was understandable. Our efforts to reassure Iraqi officials that we would carefully monitor this programme and that any misuse would result in disciplinary action and dismissals of those involved did not have the desired effect on Ambassador Malik of the Foreign Ministry and other officials.

The Iraqi authorities were also concerned that the de-mining programme would ignore the Government's demand to desist from all mine-related activities in the 5km buffer zone along the Iraq/Iran border of Iraqi Kurdistan. In fact, the Government in Baghdad tried to boycott this programme in a variety of ways. Our repeated requests for special maps of the areas possessed by the Iraqi army were always refused. Clearance of ordered de-mining equipment was delayed for long periods of time. The Government also questioned the number of personnel UNOPS wanted to deploy in this programme.[74] A particularly contentious issue concerned the de-mining dogs which the UN had brought from South Africa. I had to repeatedly face the accusation that the UN was more humane with its dogs than with the Iraqi people: 'For each dog you are spending $160 of our money for food, yet, the value of the monthly food basket for our people is a fraction of this.'[75] This became a standard accusation. It was futile to deny this fact. I could well appreciate the Iraqi anger.

However, eliminating this important activity would have been irresponsible. During the course of phase V and subsequent phases I often questioned the Ministries of Foreign Affairs and Defence's objections to expanding de-mining activities into areas under Iraqi Government control. A polite 'we will look into it' was the standard reply. However, each year the desert areas of Southern Iraq reminded me of the presence

74. UNOPS asked for two hundred new visas in 1999 alone.
75. The monthly food baskets had a value of between $20 and $25.

of lethal, unexploded ordnance. During the rainy season, in particular, mushroom pickers, many of them children, looking for the valuable black and white truffles became victims of mines. The German Maltese medical team stationed in Um Qasr, near the Iraqi/Kuwaiti border, were regularly called upon to perform emergency operations on mine victims. This team, with its superior medical facilities was part of the UNIKOM contingent. Iraqi health units in the area would bring particularly serious mine accident cases to this UN desert outpost. The Iraqis did so reluctantly since it hurt their pride to admit to outsiders the inadequacy of their professional and material resources.

The central Government should also have considered a much needed resettlement programme for citizens displaced to Central and Southern Iraq. This would have included mainly Kurds and Turkomen who had been forced by the Government to resettle, as well as tribes belonging to the Madan. These Marsh Arabs had lost their centuries old livelihood as semi-nomadic fishermen and herdsmen. Saddam Hussein's Government had decided to dry large parts of these swamp areas to reclaim land for modern agriculture and because of security concerns. The marshes straddled the Iraq-Iran border. A resettlement plan to be included in the Oil-for-Food Programme was never seriously considered by the Government due to lack of resources, more likely lack of interest or embarrassment in having to admit that resettlement was the result of forced migration.

During a visit to communities around Kut in southern Iraq in mid-1999, I experienced what life was like for some of these relocated communities. The Government had simply constructed blocks of houses in the middle of nowhere, in barren and desolate areas. There were no schools, no markets, not a single bush or tree, only houses surrounded by sand and subjected to scorching heat. Simple toilet facilities had been completed with assistance from the Middle East Council of Churches. Yet there was no running water. The open fields served as the humiliating community toilet.

In retrospect, it is difficult to understand why the UNOCHI and UN agencies did not press more strenuously for the implementation of the UN/GOI Memorandum of Understanding[76] which specifically called for 'equitable' coverage of the Oil-for-Food Programme to eliminate such pockets of particularly severe poverty. It was not that we were oblivious to the situation or had become immune to the suffering around us. The magnitude of daily pressures from Government, the UN Security Council and the UN Secretariat gave us little opportunity to pause and tackle such special problems of inequity.

76. Memorandum of Understanding (MOU) of May 1996, Section VII, Para. 35(a)

Agriculture and Irrigation

The food sector was relatively straightforward in terms of the content of the food basket and its caloric value. There were nevertheless a number of fundamental issues in this sector relating to the quality and the sources of procurement of food.

Iraq had always been a food deficit country. In 1990, the UN estimates, Iraq had 'to import between 60 and 70 percent of the food it consumed'. Between 1974 and 1990, the quantity of wheat imported by Iraq increased fivefold.[77] Such dependency on food supply sources abroad became, under sanctions, a significant cause of vulnerability. Financial resources were inadequate and purchases were politicised by both Iraq and potential countries of supply. The food basket, in its content, was unbalanced. Its caloric value, while over time quantitatively improving, at no time was qualitatively of an acceptable standard since it lacked animal protein, fresh fruits and vegetables. Iraqi agriculture assumed an important role as a supplementary source of essential foods such as meat, vegetables, fruit and also rice and wheat for both urban and rural dwellers. However, the average Iraqi could not afford these 'luxuries'.

While food was never put on hold by the UN Security Council, agricultural machinery, seasonal inputs, especially pesticides, irrigation equipment and spare parts, were heavily subjected to temporary or permanent holds.[78] As in other sectors, these holds refer almost exclusively to procurement for the fifteen governorates under the control of the authorities in Baghdad. Delayed approvals by the UN Security Council of the rehabilitation of the grape- and tomato-based industries in Iraqi Kurdistan, rather than formal holds, explain damage done to the local Kurdish economy. Food processing had to coincide with the harvesting period. Seasonal labour and the purchase of grapes, tomatoes and other fruits would otherwise be negatively affected. In addition, tomato paste and fruit juices would have to be imported from neighbouring countries at much higher costs. The Sanctions Committee in New York ignored these warnings of the FAO representative in Baghdad.

It must be stressed that the agriculture sector, a key element in the humanitarian programme, faced a range of manmade and natural constraints. Holds, protracted delays, due to the complex procurement

---

77. See Assessment of the Implementation of phases I–IV of the Humanitarian Programme (SCR 986), Section Four: Augmenting Agricultural Production, p. 1.
78. Out of a total of agricultural contracts submitted to the Sanctions Committee for phases IV, V and IV valued at $452 million, 8.1 percent or $36 million were on hold in October 1999 – see internal UN report on Applications on Hold, 9 November 1999, pp. 26–37.

process, the sector's seasonal nature, the UN restrictions of aerial spraying for crop protection on the farms located in the two no-fly zones and the emerging three-year drought constituted the main factors that explain why domestic agriculture could not play a supplementary role to ameliorate the nutritional conditions in Iraq under sanctions.

The FAO representative in Baghdad, Dr Amir Khalil, did everything he could to accelerate the agricultural procurement programme He tried to convince the UN Sanctions Committee in New York that pumps, generators, pesticides, sprinkler systems, sprayers and agro-chemicals would be used for Iraq's agriculture and not for the manufacture of biological and chemical substances for a weapons of mass destruction programme. My Sudanese FAO colleague and his organisation had intermittent success in obtaining the release of blocked agricultural items. Overall, however, the agricultural sector was in chaos. The fleet of tractors was mostly broken down. Seasonal inputs such as seeds, fertilisers and pesticides were not available in the required quantities or arrived at the wrong time of the cycle due to the procurement system, or, more likely, because the UN Security Council had blocked consignments. Agricultural implements such as seeders and hoes were lacking. Irrigation canals were clogged. A severe drought, started in 1998/99, would further aggravate the dilapidated state of Iraq's agriculture for three consecutive agricultural seasons.

At the time of phase v operations in 1998/99, the FAO representative and I would jointly visit the Ministers for Agriculture and Irrigation Abdul Ilah Hamid and Mahmoud Dhiyab Al Ahmed in their offices on Al Andalus Square and Palestine Street to reassure them of our commitment to present the case for Iraq's agriculture to the UN Security Council. They appreciated the support. The UN and FAO's record of ultimately succeeding in having blocked items released, unfortunately, was mixed.

In normal years, Iraq's rivers, particularly the Tigris and tributaries such as the Little and Greater Zap, were expected to provide irrigation water to Iraq's wheat basket in the Northern Provinces. Yet in 1999/2000 the two major dams, the Dokan and Derbandikhan Reservoirs, had the lowest water tables since they had been constructed in 1959 and 1962 respectively.

Both the Government of Iraq and the United Nations were fully aware that the import of generators, pumps, pesticides and earth-moving and drainage equipment had in previous phases faced difficulties in the UN Sanctions Committee. Such items were routinely put on hold. We had agreed, however, during phase v negotiations with the Iraqi authorities in Baghdad, that such items were most significant for improved food security, especially under drought conditions. The proposed DPV budget for agriculture of $180 million for the country as a whole, including $34 million for Iraqi Kurdistan, therefore contained a large irrigation component to cover an area of between 50,000 and 100,000 hectares in the fifteen governorates of Central and Southern Iraq.[79]

Functioning irrigation systems using local ground water were vital for protecting at least some of the cereal crops Iraqi farmers in Ninevah, Tamim and Salahaldeer governorates had dared to plant. This would not be possible unless the UN Security Council cooperated. This unfortunately rarely happened.

During one of my travels in Northern Iraq in early 1999, I witnessed the hopeless situation facing farmers in Ninevah and other cereal producing governorates. This is an area which, after rainy seasons and without sanctions, would produce most of Iraq's wheat and rice. I passed large mobile irrigation systems which were standing idle in vast expanses of dry soil. Carpets of green should have reassured farmers, at this time of the year, that they would soon have a crop.[80] All of this was not surprising. Some \$10 million worth of water pumps and electric motors were on hold during the 1998/99 season. However, even those farmers in the area who owned pumps and electrical motors had no guarantee that irrigation waters would be available because of the frequent electricity outages. Diesel generators were not easy to come by. While the civil servants back in Baghdad were indignant, the farmers whom I met seemed to be resigned to their fate.

The FAO's overall sombre conclusion for the agricultural year 1998/99 was that due to drought and sanctions the harvest prospects looked grim. The placing on hold of contracts in the irrigation sub-sector alone would lead to a reduction of wheat yields by 20,625 tons or a significant portion of a normal summer yield.[81] More generally, FAO maintained that 'the effect of holds was 50 percent of the potential per hectare production of cereals and up to 75 percent loss in orchards'.[82]

The questions that arise in connection with the food and agricultural sectors are once again similar in nature to those in other sectors:

- Why did the UN Security Council not permit procurement of locally produced food? Rice, wheat, pulses – all were imported from countries like Australia, Vietnam and Turkey, even though some quantities could have been purchased locally at significantly lower costs. This, in turn, would have freed funds for medicines, water supply and sanitation, education supplies and other humanitarian needs. The UN team in Baghdad would have been in a position to monitor the financial

79. See Procurement and Distribution for the Agricultural Sector.
80. See UN Internal Report on The Impact of Holds on Agriculture, dated 9 November 1999, pp. 27–9.
81. Ibid., p. 28.
82. Ibid., p. 26.

transactions to prevent Government from becoming an 'earner', if this was the Security Council's concern.

- Why could the nutritional value of the food basket not have been enhanced with fresh vegetables and meat? This would have brought down unacceptably high malnutrition and mortality rates.
- Why was no food policy strategy developed for Iraq and the Kurdish governorates? This could have provided rural employment and discouraged rural – urban migration, particularly in the Kurdish North. It would also have promoted economic linkages within the country as a whole and thereby given political meaning to the ubiquitous references in UN Security Council resolutions to 'territorial integrity'.

There were other questions for which the Security Council also did not have good answers:

- Why would an under-funded sector linked to the food security of the civilian population be subjected to such stringent import restrictions?
- Why would submersible pumps, generating equipment and seasonal inputs such as pesticides be blocked when the UN in Iraq had the capacity to monitor their deployment?
- Why did the UN Security Council not heed the advice of the FAO representative to facilitate special preparatory measures to forestall the worst effects of the emerging drought?

Defining the content of the health sector proved to be a much more complicated, as well as sensitive, undertaking.

Health

Medicines and other health supplies, such as food, were procured for the entire country in accordance with the agreement between the UN and Government of Iraq. Joint preparations between the World Health Organisation (WHO), UNICEF, Government and the Kurdish local authorities for the health sector in phase v (November 1998 to May 1999)[83] revealed the range of problems confronting the Government and the UN Secretariat. These problems had life-threatening implications for the Iraqi population. The health budget proposed for phase v amounted to $240 million.[84] This came to $10.70 for six months per person for an estimated

83. Individual sectors of the Oil-for-Food Programme are discussed in the context of phase v in the order in which they are listed in the Iraq Government Distribution Plan.
84. See Distribution Plan v (26 November 1998 to 24 May 1999), p. 5.

population of 22.5 million.[85] The inadequacy of such an amount is obvious, especially when one remembers that the medical infrastructure had been hard hit by the 1991 war, by years of neglect and by the severe restrictions the UN Security Council had put on the import of medical supplies. These restrictions involved laboratory and diagnostic equipment, chemicals, and vaccines. Apart from a shortage of funds, there were many other serious impediments facing the health sector, such as limited warehousing and, particularly, cold storage for medicines and health materials. Transport, refrigerated trucks in particular, was often not available. Modern management tools, especially computers, were in short supply – much needed items for which the UN Security Council refused clearance. The representatives of the US and the UK were exclusively responsible for the uncompromising posture of the UN Sanctions Committee. In addition, health officials and the medical faculties in Iraq's universities lacked knowledge of up-to-date treatment methods because the import of scientific and professional publications was also prohibited. The total picture which emerged was one of truly disastrous conditions for curative medicine. At the time when phase v was finalised, I had opportunities to acquire first-hand impressions of these avoidable realities.

In Karbala, a major town of Shi'ite pilgrimage[86] located 80 km south of Baghdad, I went to see two general hospitals, the Al Husseini Hospital and the Al Hindiya Hospital. Both were deplorable sights – dilapidated buildings, non-functioning elevators, broken down x-ray machines. These were long-standing problems according to hospital staff. Both hospitals had only intermittent water and electricity supplies. The incinerators were out of order. Infectious waste had to be burnt manually. At the Al Husseini Hospital I was told that after 10 o'clock in the morning, the dispensary had usually run out of medicines for outpatients. The doctor showing me around pointed out that the ratio of those who were fortunate enough to get medicines as against those who did not was one to fifty. Inside both hospitals it was a common sight to see patients, families, nurses, doctors and others fighting their way through waiting crowds. If they all had anything in common it was their decrepit appearance and their misery. Hospital staff, patients and visitors alike looked tired and tense. Aware of the excessively high mortality rates in all parts of Iraq, for both young and old, and the fact that even minimal medical treatment was difficult to obtain, I became acutely aware that for many patients these two hospitals would become their last residence. In the following months I would visit many more hospitals and rural health

85. See Fig. 1.5, p. 95. It should be noted that while $10.70 had been budgeted, only $5.80 worth of medical supplies actually arrived.
86. The burial ground for Imam Hussein, son of Imam Ali and his wife Fatima; Ali was the fourth Caliph and son-in-law of prophet Mohammed.

clinics in all parts of Iraq. The picture was always the same: crowded conditions, fearful faces, malnourished children and harassed looking medical staff. These hospitals reminded one more of disorderly and unkempt train stations than places of treatment.

During one of my subsequent visits to the US State Department in Washington, I tried to engage officials in a discussion on the sorry state of medical care in Iraq. I referred to the appalling conditions in Iraqi hospitals. As an example I singled out the Saddam Paediatric Hospital in Baghdad. Francis Ricciardone, the official whom the US Government had appointed as 'Special Coordinator for the Transition of Iraq' had asked a group of State Department officials to join him in meeting with me. My description obviously did not impress them. Their picture of Iraq was cast in iron, a UN official would not be able to replace it. One official merely said: 'Oh, you have visited Saddam Hussein's propaganda hospital'.[87]

In Baghdad, at least, there was full agreement among UNICEF, WHO and UNOHCI that in view of these conditions the proposed allocation of $240 million for phase v did not remotely meet health service needs. Additionally, the Minister of Health rightly stressed in our meetings that 'the public health sector could not be improved by the provision of medicines and medical appliances only. The infrastructure of hospitals, medical centres and warehouses was in need of basic rehabilitation through the provision of spare parts and replacement equipment.'[88]

During negotiations between the UN and the Government of Iraq, the dilemma of the shortage of funds was an ever-recurring subject for the entire humanitarian programme. On one occasion, the Minister of Trade, Mohammed Medi Saleh, metaphorically made the point that 'the cloth which we can buy with such severely limited funds we have under sanctions, can simply not cover the Iraqi body!' I could only agree with him.

Without safe water, sanitation and electricity, diseases such as cholera, malaria, leishmaniasis, intestinal parasitic infections, and hepatitis would remain serious threats to public health. Diarrhoea and acute respiratory infections, UNICEF kept reminding the Government and the UN Security Council, constituted major and avoidable causes of child mortality in Iraq.[89] The rehabilitation of water and electricity supplies and sanitation facilities to pre-1990 conditions and a more adequate supply of medicines would have prevented much illness and reduced mortality levels.

In the course of the 1991 Gulf War water, sanitation and electricity infrastructure were severely damaged in all parts of central and southern

87. Visit to US State Department, 9 December 2000.
88. Government of Iraq, DPV (November 1998 – May 1999), para. 34.
89. UNICEF/IRAQ – 2002, p. 20; UNICEF maintains that in the late 1990s, 70 percent of child mortality related to diarrhoea (more prevalent in summer) and acute respiratory infections (more prevalent in the winter).

Iraq.[90] Under sanctions, the once state of the art distribution networks were kept barely functional. Full rehabilitation or modernisation of waterworks, sanitation facilities and electricity units were not permissible under sanctions and, in any case, adequate resources to do so would not have been available. The high incidence of waterborne diseases constitutes the best evidence of this reality.

Water and Sanitation

The $150 million which the Government of Iraq requested for the water and sanitation sector during phase v would not at all suffice to alter these precarious conditions. Unsafe water supply and poor sewerage treatment would prevail as was predicted by WHO, UNICEF and UNOCHI. An additional concern which the United Nations shared with the Government of Iraq was the decreasing volume of available water per person. In 1990 Iraqis consumed, on average, 330 litres per person per day in Baghdad, 270 litres in other urban centres and 180 litres in served rural areas.[91] At the time of preparing phase v the Government and UNICEF indicated that the per capita share of water had gone down by 63 percent.[92]

This was also the time when the rainy season should have started, yet there was no sign of rain. In fact, a severe drought was in the making for Iraq and surrounding countries. This would, of course, further compound the difficulties Iraqis were facing with their water and sanitation facilities.

Apart from a few better off residential areas in Baghdad such as Al Mansur, Al Waziriya, Al Harthiya, the Baghdad of 1998/99 was covered with broken water mains which spilled the neighbourhood's precious water into the streets. This, together with clogged sewers and open sewerage, which was sometimes several feet deep along the roadsides, constituted typical and serious public health hazards.

Around the Al Carthage Hotel where I stayed, one was never far from high heaps of organic waste. Uncollected household rubbish added to the all pervasive stench characteristic of many parts of Baghdad This was especially noticeable in the summer when temperatures were consistently

90. There is a perception among some Iraq specialists that the US military deliberately targeted these civilian installations. Declassified US Department of Defence documents, e.g. a document of the US Defence Intelligence Agency with the titled 'Iraq Qater Treatment Vulnerabilities' (1991), are cited as evidence.
91. UN/OIP – Two-Year Assessment of phases IV and V, section three: Repairing Water and Sewerage Treatment Facilities, 28 April 1999.
92. This resulted in 218 litres consumed per day in Baghdad. 138 litres or 51 percent in other urban areas and 91 litres or 50 percent in served rural areas. DPV, para. 40.

above 35°C. This was not surprising. In 1990 there had been 800 refuse collection vehicles countrywide.[93] At the time of phase V, in early 1999, only 80 vehicles remained. At one of the final meetings on the distribution plan for phase V between the Government and the UN system, the Deputy Mayor of Baghdad, Adnan Jabour, came in great excitement to ask me whether I wanted to see the three yellow refuse collection trucks that had finally arrived in Baghdad from Sweden.

The refuse collection situation in other Iraqi cities was not any better. In fact, Basrah, the 'Pearl of the Middle East', as it was called during the days of the Ottoman Empire, when the city was part of 'the governorate of Basrah and Kuwait', was much worse. During the Ottoman administration, wide water channels had been constructed in the city. In the 1990s these had become large, stagnant cesspools and, of course, serious sources of contamination and infection. Far from the epicentre of Saddam Hussein's power and in Shiah territory this was not surprising, according to some of my Iraqi friends.

When visiting water plants, sewerage facilities, water pumping stations, or water distribution points in large urban areas such as Mosul, Kirkuk, Basra and Baghdad or in the smaller towns of Kut, Asmara, Nasiriya or Samara, one could readily witness the precarious conditions of the water and sewerage facilities: idle pumping units because of burnt-out motors, leaking water mains due to a lack of piping materials, insufficient amounts of alum sulphate, bleaching powder, chemical dosers and clorinaters, etc. Pumps, cesspit jetting units and generators were other items in great shortage.[94] The water and sanitation sector was among those most affected by the shortage of funds, a lack of professional staff and, as in the health sector, by the deliberate blocking of contracts by the US and UK representatives in the UN Security Council Sanctions Committee.[95]

An impact assessment of holds on water and sanitation contracts during phases IV, V and VI shows that $68.3 million or 32 percent of all contracts for water and sanitation facilities had been put on hold by US

93. UN/OIP – Two-Year Assessment of phase IV, and V, section three: Repairing Water and Sewerage Treatment Facilities, 28 April 1999.
94. UNICEF described for 1998 the following picture of the functioning of water boosting and sewage pumping stations in the fifteen governorates under Baghdad's control: (i) water boosting stations: moderate (poor efficiency: 37.5 percent; good/very good efficiency: 62.5 percent; (ii) sewage pumping stations: moderate/very poor efficiency: 60 percent; good/very good efficiency: 40 percent. UNICEF further points out that low efficiency rates (less than 50 percent) were due to continuous electricity outages! This information is contained in: UNICEF Statistical Outline prepared for UNOCHI on Water and Sewage Treatment, November 1998, p. 3.
95. Almost 100 percent of all items put on hold by the Sanctions Committee of the UN Security Council during the Oil-for-Food Programme period (1996–2003) was due to the US and UK Governments.

and UK representatives on the UN Security Council Sanctions Committee. This UN Baghdad report[96] stated that despite the high amount of holds in the water and sanitation sector, the impact on efficiency seemed 'minimal'. In retrospect, I have considerable misgivings that I had agreed to forward such an assessment to New York. This conclusion, while technically correct, was extraordinarily misleading. It would have been important to point out that in all phases included in the review, the severely inadequate financial allocations to the water and sanitation sector remained life-threatening for a large part of the Iraqi population. The blocking of supplies by the UN Security Council further aggravated an already serious situation. Non-UN institutions such as the International Federation of Red Cross and Red Crescent Societies and Care were much more forthright and to the point in describing the poor state of water and sanitation installations. The International Federation indicated: 'Major problems continue to exist in [the] water and sanitation and power industry. They are linked together in Iraq's flat landscape, where pumping is essential and more water treatment desperately required. For many millions, contaminated water from broken mains or a local river is the only option.'[97] A Care report points out: 'The majority of the urban population [is] not served by sewage disposal systems. During the past years [sewerage treatment plants in ten governorates in which Care assisted water and sanitation projects] have either been acting as lifting stations or have been completely out of action because of the lack of spare parts or replacement equipment.'[98] These conclusions corroborated the claim of Ambassador Adnan Malik of the Iraqi Foreign Ministry and his colleagues from the Ministries of Health and the Interior[99] that none of the sewerage treatment plants in Central and Southern Iraq were functioning properly. UNICEF estimates that in the late 1990s, '500,000 tons of raw sewerage were dumped directly into fresh water bodies every day'.[100]

The UN in Baghdad should have highlighted these fundamental water and sanitation problems much more intensively than we actually did. All of us in Baghdad had first-hand experience of conditions in this sector. WHO and UNICEF colleagues spent significant amounts of time convincing those on the UN Sanctions Committee in New York that the

---

96. Internal UN System/Iraq Report on Applications on Hold, Baghdad, 9 November 1999.
97. Letter of 6 March 1999 from the International Federation in Baghdad to the UN in Baghdad.
98. Care International, Iraq Project Report, January–March 2002, p. 3.
99. Water supply for human consumption was part of the Ministry of Interior's portfolio; since the fall of the Iraqi regime an independent Ministry of Water has been created.
100. The Situation of Children in Iraq, February 2002, p. 23.

chemicals, spare parts and equipment in this sector should be released for the sake of an endangered population and that UN observers could account for proper deployment of these supplies.

At times intervention with the UN Sanctions Committee would lead to the release of a blocked item. Often it would not. In the spring of 1999, an Italian NGO – Ponte Per Baghdad, one of the few private organisations active in Central and Southern Iraq, asked me to intervene with New York to release a small quantity of alum sulphate for a village water supply project in the Shatt al Arab area of Southern Iraq. Contacts with the UN Office of the Iraq Programme, the Sanctions Committee, Italy's Permanent Representative to the UN in New York, Ambassador Francesco Fulci, did not lead to the release. A community of a few thousand people was therefore prevented from receiving a safer water supply system. Alum sulphate was considered a dual-use item by the UN Security Council since it could be diverted to the Iraqi military for use in proscribed weapons programmes. The fact that a small quantity was involved, and that verification of use by NGO staff or by the UN would not have been difficult, made no difference.

Many towns and smaller communities either had no water treatment chemicals or regularly ran out of them. Not surprisingly, a UNICEF study carried out in Iraq in May 2000 showed that 'close to half of children under five suffered from diarrhoea within two weeks of that month'.[101] Anxious to understand this element of Iraqi deprivation better, I decided to spend some days in Safua, a community close to the town of Hilla, southeast of Kerbala. Safua had never been an affluent community. It did, however, at one time have running water in most homes. Sanctions changed that, forcing villagers to collect their water from an almost stagnant tributary of the Euphrates. The local school, too, had piped water before 1990. During my visit, the primary school with 250 students and 12 teachers, depended upon the weekly visits of an old water tanker. For 35 cents (!) the headmaster would purchase 800 litres of polluted water, if he had the money. I was told he often did not have it. Consequently, each student had about 3 litres water per week for drinking and washing. The students' parents remembered better days in the 1980s and spoke of school uniforms, school feeding, school transport, functioning toilet facilities and, of course, running water in the school. These were the years when the World Bank and the IMF considered Iraq a country in transition with an annual per capita income of about $2,400.

101. Ibid., p. 21.

Electricity Supply

In 1989, the year before Iraq's invasion of Kuwait, the country had an electricity grid connecting all eighteen governorates with an installed capacity of 9,295 megawatts.[102] The power plants, and the grid as a whole, suffered extensive damage during the Gulf War. Out of a total of 120 generating units in the twenty-four power plants, not more than fifty were operational at the end of the war in early 1991 and were capable of supplying only 2,325 megawatts. This represented a 75 percent loss of Iraq's pre-war generating capacity. Ten years later, in 1999, when phase v of the Oil-for-Food Programme was ongoing and some electrical equipment and spare parts had arrived, the generating capacity had still only risen to around 4,364 megawatts.[103] The two hydroelectric dams, Dokan and Derbandikhan, located in Suleimaniyah, the Kurdish governorate administered by the Patriotic Union of Kurdistan (PUK), were disabled as a result of the Iraq/Iran war (1980–8). Low water-tables due to the lack of inflowing water from melting snow in the mountains, in any case, hampered electricity generation.

The deliberate destruction of the pylons on the Kurdish side of the line of control constituted a further factor. With the exception of a single transmission line between Mosul and Dohuk all electricity links between the areas under the control of Saddam Hussein's Government and Iraqi Kurdistan had been disconnected. A national grid no longer existed. In accordance with the UN/Government of Iraq Memorandum of Understanding (MOU) of 1995, the three Kurdish governorates were free to plan their own electricity supply programme in consultation with the UNDP.[104] This UN organisation was solely responsible on the international side for the implementation of electricity programmes in Iraqi Kurdistan. While the UN Security Council Resolution 986 of April 1995 confirmed in its penultimate paragraph 18 that 'nothing in this resolution should be construed as infringing on the sovereignty or territorial integrity of Iraq', the MOU did not include such a reference. This may seem unimportant, yet ultimately had political consequences. The absence in the MOU of such a reference gave the Kurdish authorities and the 'United Nations Interagency Humanitarian Programme', as the programme for Iraqi Kurdistan was called, a free hand in implementing programmes which did not necessarily conform to the spirit of 'sovereignty' and 'territorial integrity'. In fact, over time this free hand intensified the determination of the local authorities in Dohuk, Erbil and Suleimaniyah to distance themselves more and more

102. See UN/OIP/Background Brief – Electricity, para. 2, 17 December 2003.
103. UN/OIP/Internal Report: Assessment of the Implementation of phases I–IV of the Humanitarian Programme (SCR 986), section 5, p. 1.
104. UNDP = the United Nations Development Programme.

from the central authorities in practically all sectors. The electricity sector constituted early and tangible evidence of a Kurdish plan to create institutions and facilities which would be independent from Baghdad. The UN did little to intervene.[105]

Distribution Plan v proposed a budget for the national electricity sector of $409 million of which $116 million were to be allocated for Iraqi Kurdistan. The electricity component thus comprised, with 28.4 percent, the second largest slice of funding in any single sector for the Kurdish areas. The largest amount of funding went to the food sector which utilised $166 million or 34.4 percent.

In Distribution Plan v negotiations, the Government of Iraq team, particularly the representatives of the electricity commission, agreed to such an allocation for the Kurdish areas to allow the rehabilitation of the two dams of Dokan and Derbandikhan. These were in the areas under Kurdish control and could supply power to these areas, while also providing valuable irrigation water to At ta'mim governorate and other areas under Baghdad's control. Funding would also be available for 'the urgent rehabilitation of the rundown transmission and distribution network'[106] in the Kurdish areas. Had an evaluation of the implementation of distribution plans for Iraqi Kurdistan ever been undertaken, Baghdad would have had reason to object since it would have shown that the UN and the three Kurdish governorates were, in fact, implementing an electricity programme with a dual strategy. On the one hand they pursued the repair of the two dams which would boost both power generation in their own territory and the supply of irrigation water which was of interest to Baghdad. The irrigation water could become a bargaining tool for the Kurdish side to obtain concessions from Baghdad. The Kurdish local authorities were also willing to invest in the repair and enlargement of transmission lines across the line of control between Dohuk and Mosul, and to pay for a portion of the costs. Yet, on the other hand, the Kurdish local authorities had no faith in obtaining their share of electricity from a rehabilitated national grid under Baghdad's control. Therefore, their first priority was to establish an independent parallel supply network over which they had exclusive control.

The UN Security Council Sanctions Committee no doubt was aware of these intentions. The type of equipment the Kurdish authorities wanted to procure with the help of UNDP, namely new transmission and distribution networks, made this quite obvious. The Security Council did

---

105. When the Kurdish authorities intended to introduce their own car licence plates for vehicles of the Kurdish local authorities supplied under the Oil-for-Food Programme, we did intervene and prevented this further sign of local independence.
106. DPV, part 4: Plan of Supplies and Equipment for (the) Electricity Sector.

not ask any questions. Paragraph 18 of UN Resolution 986 about 'territorial integrity' and 'sovereignty' was forgotten. The position taken by the US/UK representatives in the Sanctions Committee on procurement for the electricity sector, in fact, suggested that they fully supported the Kurdish approach. While they would painstakingly scrutinise Iraq Government orders for electricity spare parts and replacement equipment and would, phase by phase, block significant numbers of purchase requests for areas under Baghdad's jurisdiction, the Sanctions Committee approved, with rare exceptions, all orders for Iraqi Kurdistan. Relevant statistics speak for themselves: in October 1999 a review of the applications in the electricity sector for phases IV, V and VI discloses that $250.6 million worth of contracts in the electricity sector were blocked. These included water treatment pumps, replacement of aging boiler tubes, transmission lines, control and instrument systems, safety equipment, spare parts, etc. For Iraqi Kurdistan, on the other hand, not a single contract was put on hold. The only item the Sanctions Committee did hold back involved a theodolite worth $6,072 because of an invoice discrepancy. The differential handling of electricity contracts for areas under Baghdad and Kurdish control was a political act with serious implications for Iraqis living in central and southern parts of the country. It also provided an insight into the counter-productive micro-management approach of the Sanctions Committee and its profound lack of confidence in the monitoring competence of the UN team in Iraq! At the time of negotiating phase V, I was neither aware of these plans in Iraqi Kurdistan nor of the tacit support they had received in the Sanctions Committee of the UN Security Council. My first visit, in late 1998, and subsequent visits to Iraqi Kurdistan changed my perception. I began to realise how sensitive the implementation of the electricity programme was.

A vivid reminder of the Kurdish determination to become self-reliant was the hundreds of destroyed pylons along the road to Suleimaniyah, many with pieces of transmission lines still attached. As soon as one had crossed the line of control dividing Baghdad-held areas from territory under Kurdish control one could not help but notice these fallen witnesses of a more unified past. PKK sabotage, I was told, had destroyed these transmission lines and cut the supply links controlled by Baghdad. Much of whatever could be salvaged found itself smuggled across the border into Iran.

Both local ministers for humanitarian affairs, Dr Qazzaz in Erbil and Mr Sade Pire in Suleimaniyah, conveyed to me the policy of the KDP and PUK authorities for greater self reliance of the Kurdish areas in the electricity sector. In engaging the two local Kurdish administrations in discussions on the content of the Oil-for-Food Programme for Iraqi Kurdistan, I would stress the economic and, ultimately, political implications of an independent electricity network. In return, I would hear about their lack of confidence in Baghdad's reliability of electricity sharing and Kurdish determination to protect themselves accordingly. Dr Qazzaz would point out that the electricity authorities in Mosul never honoured their agreement with the Dohuk local authorities for fair and predictable power sharing. When the UN checked, it was found that, in view of the poor state of the power plant in Mosul, the supply situation for the population south of the line of control was as dismal as on the Kurdish side. Residents of Mosul did not receive more electricity than their compatriots in the Dohuk communities of Iraqi Kurdistan, i.e., on average two hours of supply per day at the time phase v was under implementation.

These were good opportunities for confidence-building measures between the Kurdish authorities and Baghdad. Moreover, as a UN official I felt an obligation to play a role in the interest of the Iraqi communities on both sides of the dividing line. After all, the different communities were encouraged by UN resolutions to maintain the country's territorial integrity. To jointly review options for an integrated electricity supply and development programme became for me an important issue. Other cross-line priority concerns were water, especially irrigation water supply, agriculture and transhumance issues, de-mining and medical services. My UN colleagues in Baghdad as well as in Erbil and Suleimanyah, enthusiastically supported this plan of trying to bring the two sides closer together.

The limited resources available under the various phases of the Oil-for-Food Programme and the mounting demands for investments in the electricity sector[107] made it quite urgent to meet as a tripartite group, i.e., Government, Kurdish authorities and the UN. After a series of separate consultations involving the Ministries of Foreign Affairs, Defence, Interior and the Electricity Commission in Baghdad and the two offices of humanitarian affairs as well as the local Prime Ministers of Erbil and Suleimanyah, agreement had been reached to begin in Baghdad with joint reviews of the electricity and the de-mining sectors. This was an important first step with the UN playing its rightful role as honest broker. At least I thought so. For the electricity review UNDP, as the lead UN agency for the sector, in consultation with Baghdad and the Kurdish authorities, had prepared a careful agenda for a series of meetings. The first meeting took place sometime in late spring 1999.

The agenda was straightforward. It confirmed what had already been negotiated in November 1998 between the UN and the Government of

---

107. The total value of proposed contracts for Iraqi Kurdistan alone amounted to about $900 million in 1999/2000. UNDP, as the procurement agency in this sector, therefore at the time managed in Iraqi Kurdistan a budget which was larger than its regular programme of technical assistance worldwide!

Iraq for DPV, the rehabilitation of integrated transmission and distribution networks in northern Iraq on both sides of the line of control, investment in new generation facilities and the repairs to the Dokan and Derbandikhan dams. I remember well this first meeting held in the conference room of the Electricity Commission in Baghdad chaired by Dr Jafar Al Jafar.[108] There was an air of uneasiness between the Kurdish group and those representing the Government of Iraq. There was also excitement since this was not a routine meeting or one that had recent precedents. There were regular contacts on many issues between the KDP and PUK factions and the central Government in Baghdad. This tripartite meeting, however, involving the future of investments in the electricity sector of the Oil-for-Food Programme, had a distinct degree of formality and transparency not normally associated with the direct and discreet meetings of emissaries from Iraqi Kurdistan and Iraqi officials. The ubiquous tea and words of welcome somewhat eased the tension. There were even some smiles appearing on the faces of those who not long ago had passed through such a cruel period of confrontation. No Kurd could forget 1988 when Iraqi forces mounted an attack across much of Iraqi Kurdistan in an Iran-Iraq war-related operation known as the 'Anfal campaign'. It was then that Saddam Hussein and his commander Ali Al Majid, the ruthless general and cousin from Tikrit, is said to have deployed gas against Kurdish villages.[109]

The outcome of this first round of talks in Baghdad between local authorities in Kurdistan and Central Government was agreement that the reconnection of a network destroyed by conflict within Iraq and war between Iraq and Iran was possible. For the Iraq Government reconnection was mainly a technical and financial issue, but for the Kurdish side it was mainly a political issue.

To bridge this gap would be a challenge for the UN in Iraq. After having had two similar joint meetings in Baghdad on de-mining that had preceded the talks on electricity, UN colleagues and I felt that an important process had been set in motion. I reported this to the UN Office of the Iraq Programme in New York with the enthusiasm I thought the initiative deserved, hoping to get advice on how to carry on in these as well as other areas. For agriculture, in particular, the FAO representative Dr Amir Khalil and I wanted policy guidance. An emerging outbreak of foot-and-mouth disease affecting the entire livestock of the country required urgent cooperation between the Government and the local Kurdish authorities and the UN/FAO.

108. Dr Jafar Al Jafar was a senior adviser to the Government of Iraq in the rank of a minister and had been in charge of Iraq's nuclear programme for many years.
109. See pp. 282–3.

We were dumbfounded in Baghdad when we received the response from the Executive Director of the OIP, Benon Sevan. In a memorandum, copied to the UN Deputy Secretary-General, Louise Frechette, and UN Under-Secretary-General for Political Affairs Kieran Prendergast and others, he pointed out that I should refrain from getting involved in local politics. 'Your predecessor has burned his fingers, don't you burn yours'. I was deeply troubled by such short-sightedness of a UN official. Keeping in mind existing UN Security Council resolutions, all stressing territorial integrity and the UN's responsibility to make the best of its constrained humanitarian resources, I thought what the UN system in Iraq had initiated was totally consistent with the UN's role in conflict resolution and peace-building through dialogue. In addition, it would encourage economically sound and managerially efficient programmes. UN/OIP remained adamant in its opposition. The Department of Political Affairs and the Office of the Deputy Secretary-General kept silent. A constructive and important initiative had been prevented.

The electricity situation was catastrophic for the country as a whole. Power cuts in Central and Southern Iraq during November 1998 to May 1999 involved an average of ten to twelve hours. Across Iraqi Kurdistan it was worse. To conserve electricity, the local authorities there had initially issued a directive that each household could use 2 amps of electricity, enough for three bulbs and one TV. This later became 4 amps, enabling the addition of one refrigerator. Only the ingenuity of Iraqi engineers and technicians explains how the electricity system did not collapse altogether.

Apart from the significant numbers of items blocked by the UN Security Council, there was the sanctions bureaucracy's problem of long lead-times for the arrival of electrical supplies. Additional constraints were missing parts, a lack of manpower, conditions of drought,[110] and seriously under-funded rehabilitation programmes. These affected all aspects of existence from household life to work in hospitals, offices, schools, at petrol pumps, flourmills, irrigation and drainage facilities, and the few industries that were still operating in Iraq.

A visit to the Al Taji electricity plant some 25 km from Baghdad, a main supplier of power for Iraq's capital, demonstrated to me the enormous fragility of the network.

The Taji plant was a major source of electricity. It functioned with the help of cannibalised parts[111] from obsolete equipment and road-side manufactured parts. Staff were working without protective clothing or

---

110. Iraq was affected by severe drought conditions during 1998–2001.
111. As a result of sanctions, many small roadside workshops had sprung up where artisans were manually manufacturing spare parts with minimal standardisation and quality control supplying civilian and even military sectors.

hard hats. They were subjected to extreme noise levels because there were no more silencers or insulation.[112] In 1999, Al Taji had an installed capacity of 100 mw. During the 1991 Gulf War it was partially destroyed and then rebuilt. During my visit it actually produced 75 mw.

To a layman, Al Taji looked like a heap of worn out pieces of metal, a patchwork that miraculously was producing electricity. The budget foreseen in phase v would be able to do little to redress these country-wide conditions in the electricity sector. The people of Iraq had no choice but to continue to endure extreme and life threatening inadequacies similar to the ones which prevailed in the water, sanitation and health sectors.

In Baghdad, the world of the UN staff did not face these difficulties, at least not in the offices from which we administered the Oil-for-Food Programme. Equipped with powerful generators, as well as standby equipment, there was a guarantee of uninterrupted power supply for lights, cooling in the summer, heating in the winter and for running the latest model computers. All expenses were paid for out of Iraq oil revenue. None of this was available for ordinary Iraqis, not even for Iraqi civil servants. For the six months of phase v the amount for UN overheads to administer the humanitarian programme would be $60.4 million, corresponding to 2.2 percent of the anticipated oil revenue. The UN had no resource constraints. This had been decided by the UN Security Council. Iraq was not consulted. The deductions from Iraq's oil income were not negotiable.

The UN's privileged position became blatantly obvious during the many electricity outages in the evenings when suddenly entire neighbourhoods around the UN Canal Hotel offices became clusters of darkness. The UN premises retained their brightness as did the nearby offices of Al Am Al Amn, Iraq's feared internal security agency, the palaces of President Saddam Hussein, homes of members of the leadership and embassies. This was indeed a disturbing alliance of the privileged which contrasted sharply with the conditions of the vast majority of Iraqis who had an equal right to light but only intermittently obtained it. During one of those evenings in the winter of 1998–9, when different areas of Baghdad alternated between light and darkness, I witnessed of the extent to which power cuts, most of them unscheduled, affected people's lives. A young Iraqi artist from Basra had invited guests to view his first exhibition of drawings in a rented room in central Baghdad.

112. A Caritas Europa delegation visiting Iraq in January 2001 strongly criticised the lack of safety equipment in the electricity and water/sanitation sectors. This was an issue which UNOCHI never raised, neither with the UN Sanctions Committee nor the Government of Iraq.

Due to a power cut in the neighbourhood, it took Abu Laith and I a long time to finally locate the building. In the ground-floor exhibition room I could hear but not see the other guests. They were waiting in the dark for electricity to return. About an hour later, ingenuity unexpectedly ended the artist's tribulations and the guests' impatience to view his works: Abu Laith convinced two other drivers to park their vehicles in parallel with his, directly in front of the exhibition room, with their headlights switched on. The guests could view the paintings. Sadness emanated from these works of art, for they all depicted human suffering, death and natural calamities. The artist could not afford canvas, brush and paints, nor even coloured pencils. Instead, he used what looked like recycled paper and ballpoint pens. His worn-out clothes and the humbleness with which he talked about life to explain the motif of his work did not detract from his dignity. On the contrary, it gave him an aura of refinement and an impressive artistic authority. He was, no doubt, a promising representative of a dynamic and well established community of painters and sculptors which enriched Baghdadi cultural life despite the immensely difficult circumstances of dictatorship and sanctions.[113]

Key sectors for the well-being of the Iraqi people such as health, water and sanitation and agricultural production all depended upon the supply of electricity. My UN colleagues in Baghdad and I failed to understand why the UN Security Council, aware of the extremely poor condition of the electricity sector, had not made special efforts to address this issue. Why had the Security Council not objected more vigorously to the fact that the US and UK representatives were aggravating the precarious condition of the Iraqi people by choosing the electricity sector as a major target for holds? Because generators were also useful to Iraqi armed forces? The UN in Iraq had no problem monitoring the deployment of electricity supplies. Why was it not given more authority to do so? Electronic tagging to keep track of items would have been an option in the electricity and other sectors. This would have been the positive alternative to the UN Sanctions Committee's act of putting such important items on hold.

Permanent members of the UN Security Council, Russia, China and France, having followed developments in Iraq since sanctions were introduced in 1990, were as aware as was the US and the UK, of the dire and unavoidable consequences of the situation in the electricity and other sectors. As supporters of Resolution 986 of April 1995 they had an obligation to remain sensitive to 'the risk of a further deterioration in this situation',[114] as they themselves had cautioned against at that time. The

---

113. For the modest amount of $15 one could obtain one of his drawings. Yet, for most Baghdadis whose earnings, if they were fortunate to be employed with an income between $5 to $12 a month, such a price was out of their reach.
114. See UN S/RES/986, 14 April 1995, para. 2.

risk had not been averted but, in fact, had grown as the situation on the ground amply demonstrated.

The Education Situation

Leaving the Carthage Hotel in the morning and returning at different hours in the evening, I was certain to meet Tariq, the eight-year-old beggar boy in residence. Barefoot, with a torn shirt and pants of an indescribable colour, he would make sure that he was standing close enough to me to receive something, anything – some sweets, a few Iraqi dinars or just a friendly word. He would, however, also stand far enough away to escape in case a bystander, remembering that begging was not part of the Iraqi tradition, should try to beat him or chase him away. Tariq was one of many children of primary school age who were not in school.[115] Neither a 'drop-in' nor a 'drop-out', he simply had never gone to school. His family, an unemployed and disabled father and a mother of five, needed him to be on the street. As a young beggar, standing in front of three UN hotels, he could average a thousand dinars or about 50 cents a day. This amount was three times more than a primary school teacher would earn per day. A headmistress in the Rassafa directorate of Baghdad would earn 15,000 dinars or about 15 dollars per month.[116] Little Tariq had no idea that he, too, had a 'right' to education and to the 'full development of his personality' as stipulated in article 26 of the Universal Declaration of Human Rights.[117] And yet his quick and astute dark brown eyes seemed to continually ask 'what have I done wrong, why can I not be at home with my family, eat warm meals, play with friends and go to school?' His reality was different. He rarely went home and usually ate what he was given on the street. He was a lonely child among adults. His 'bed' was a concrete space between the entrance to the Carthage Hotel and the wall of an adjacent restaurant that had been closed for years. His school was the street. To me, Tariq became the symbol of the most brutal manifestations of a dictatorship that was squandering resources on palaces and luxurious office buildings and a UN Security Council which showed no initiative to protect the most vulnerable and most innocent: the Iraqi youth who were eager to prepare for life. The more I saw of Tariq the more I wanted to help him leave the street and enter school. I asked him whether this was a good idea. He nodded shyly: 'Alayka an tasal

115. 23.7 percent of Iraq's primary school age children in 1998/99 according to UNICEF were not in school – see: *The Situation of Children in Iraq*, UNICEF, February 2002, p. 39.
116. Ibid.
117. The Universal Declaration of Human Rights was adopted by the UN General Assembly on 10 December 1948.

ummi!' – 'You must ask my mother'. I decided to despatch Amir Abdullah, the caretaker of my flat or the 'fishman' as I preferred to call him, since he also looked after the fishtank in my apartment, to Tariq's mother as the 'negotiator'. I had no idea where the family lived in Baghdad. A few days later, in early 1999, as I was preparing to go to my office I heard that Tariq's mother was waiting in front of the hotel to talk to me. A moment later I stood in front of a typical Iraqi matriarch: heavy-set, dressed in the traditional black abayya, stern looking. I quickly learned that this 'open-door' meeting on the street in Baghdad would not be any less formidable than the 'closed-door' meetings I had encountered in the UN Security Council in New York. The mother was uncompromising in her demands: 400,000 dinars per month, payable in two instalments per year. My counter-proposal: 40,000 dinars per month and the costs for Tariq's schooling. Her gestures signalled clear disagreement. She walked away, saying she would think about the offer. I knew what she meant. To encourage her to change her mind, I decided to have little Tariq taken to a local hamam, the traditional public bath in Turkey and the Middle East, then to a hair cutter, followed by a visit to a store where he was fitted with a new set of clothes. When I saw Tariq again, I could hardly recognise him: well groomed, neatly dressed, with a smile of anticipation. He seemed ready to go to school. Abu Laith and I would find the school. Amir Abdulah would continue the negotiations with the mother. A few days passed without seeing Tariq. What happened next I simply could never have imagined. Tariq eventually returned, as dirty as he had been before, wearing the same torn and worn clothes. His mother had taken the new clothes away and ordered Tariq to continue to beg. At that moment, I began to realise how little I understood the psychology of poverty in Iraq.

Tariq was only one of an ever-increasing number of boys and girls who had to earn a living for themselves and their families on the streets of Baghdad, Kut, Samarra, Ramadi, Kirkuk or anywhere else in Iraq. Abu Leith and I, in our daily commutes between the Carthage Hotel and my office, were witness to the arrival of more and more boys and also some girls at street corners trying to sell anything they could get hold of: chewing-gum, pencils, incense, candles or a range of newspapers with names such as Al Thawra, the paper of the Ba'ath Party, Al Jumhuriya, a broader government voice, and Al Iraq, the main Kurdish/Arab paper. The newspapers contained identical messages about the ultimate 'mother of victories' and the ever benevolent father of the nation, Saddam Hussein, whose age seemed never to change in the photos. Most of these little street 'entrepreneurs' did have families to whom they could return in the evenings with their profits. There were other less fortunate children, those who were abandoned. This was a phenomenon unheard of in pre-1990 Iraq. Whenever the Government became aware of these children, they would be taken to the Al Rahma Centre, literally the 'Centre of Compassion' near Baghdad's Al Wathig Square. In Iraq's history this was its first home for abandoned children. A visitor to Al Rahma could feel that it was indeed an oasis of compassion and warmth for these children whose parents, because of poverty or despair, had to give up what normally would have been their most valuable possession. Here at Al Rahma the children had their beds and their meals and teachers who cared for their welfare. They would learn educational fundamentals and trades such as tailoring or carpentry. Among the unfortunate without parents these few, at least, were the lucky ones.

In the initial three phases of the Oil-for-Food Programme, when only $113 per person per year had been allocated by the UN Security Council for all the sectors, the amount for education was $27 million for a school population of 4.8 million, or $5.60 per pupil for a six-month period. For phase v the Government proposed an education budget of $100 million for the entire country, including $25 million for Iraqi Kurdistan.[118] This was an improvement since it amounted to $10.4 per student. The UN Security Council's alleged concern for the well-being of the civilian population could easily have been translated into an 'incubator' programme for children that could have assisted in protecting their physical and mental well-being[119] and in providing basic standards of education.

There was no political and certainly no moral justification for including children in the implementation of comprehensive and economic sanctions. Pointing accusatory fingers at irresponsible spending by the Iraqi regime detracted from the UN Security Council's own responsibilities. This certainly did not help Tariq or the other children whose parents could not afford to send them to school.[120] Those in primary school were taught by teachers who had not enjoyed any refresher training for years. Their concern was necessarily with financial survival rather than with teaching. They tried to earn additional income either by giving private lessons or having other jobs.

According to UNICEF and UNESCO, many schools were in such poor physical condition that they did not provide a 'safe learning and teaching environment'.[121] School books were rare, outdated and in extremely poor shape. Only in early 2000 was school furniture provided to an increasing

---

118. See DPV of the Government of Iraq, part 6: Plan of Purchase of Materials and Requirements for (the) Education Sector.
119. School feeding programmes could also have been introduced and financed from special international contributions!
120. Out of the 23.7 percent of children not in school in 1998/99, girls comprised 31.2 percent or twice as many as the boys, for whom the figure was 17.5 percent! See *The Children of Iraq*, UNICEF, February 2002, p. 39.
121. Ibid., p. 41.

number of schools. Teaching aids such as overhead projectors and computers were rarely available. If they were, most of the time they could not be used because of power cuts. Toilet facilities, more often than not, were neither available to students nor to faculty. Had I not repeatedly seen schools in such conditions, I would have taken these descriptions as propaganda or, at best, wild exaggerations. In fact, compared to what I saw in schools in Saddam City (now Sadr City), in Dialla, in Basrah or Mosul, conditions in other parts of Iraq were worse. Most classrooms lacked blackboards; those which existed were in such poor shape that they could hardly be used. Chalk was not readily available unless parents gave it to their children for the teachers' use. During the 1998/99 school year, primary school children were fortunate when they had benches on which to sit: most children were forced to spend the school day sitting on the floor which was often moist or musty; lucky ones had stones on which to sit.

An example was the Safua School in Diyala, a primary school in the morning and a secondary school in the afternoon. One of the principals showed me classrooms where four students sat on benches meant for two. There were blackboards but no chalk. All classrooms, without exception, had no glass in their windows. Frequent dust storms had an easy time making their contribution to the students' discomfort. Here, as in so many other places, the ubiquous portraits of a well-dressed and smiling Saddam Hussein adorned the walls and the few available textbooks. The texts themselves were generously augmented with epitaphs of praise for the great leader, the co-contributor to the misery of Iraqi education under sanctions.

The primary school 'library' of the Safua School which was attended by 250 children[122] contained about fifty books. These were over ten years old and worn out from frequent use. They had lost their bindings and become a collection of loose leaf pages. When I saw this 'heap' of printed material I thought of the old proverb well known in the Middle East: 'books are written in Egypt, printed in Lebanon and read in Iraq'. This proverb certainly had lost its meaning as far as the Iraq of 1999/2000 was concerned. UNICEF and Care were the two international organisations which fought a courageous battle against these atrocious conditions. Their dedication, with little resources available, made a difference for a few thousand children whose teachers did have chalk and decent blackboards and even books, and where the children could find functioning bathrooms.

122. In the 1990s, more and more girls became victims of politics. The Safua School in Diyala is a good example. In 1998 there were fifty primary school age girls in the school; in 1999 girls numbered twenty and in 2000, during my visit, eight girls were left!

For the overwhelming majority of Iraqi primary school children their first learning experience was anything but this. Class 'holes' would be a more apt description of the places where they spent their school days. It was a world of stench from the poor sanitary conditions, overcrowded classrooms, broken furniture and usually long walks from home to school and back. There was a lack of just about anything that primary school children in Europe and Iraqi children before 1990 would have taken for granted: not infrequently they had no pencils, no paper, no erasers, no textbooks, no schoolbags. University students fared no better. Scientific equipment, computers, journals – all of these were lacking at Iraqi institutions of higher learning. At the law faculty of the University of Baghdad, 1989 was the last year for which British law journals, or for that matter, any journals were available. Apart from financial limitations, I was told by my host, Dr Nizar al-Anbaki, the Dean of the Law Faculty, even professors who had obtained their degrees in the UK or the US could no longer subscribe to journals of their alma maters. This confirmed what I had been told, namely that US and British postal regulations prohibited the sending of educational materials to Iraq. This, amazingly, included sheet music! Several visits to the campus of Al Mustansiriyah University[123] gave me a good insight into the desperate conditions there. Thirty thousand students, half of them females, wanted to obtain a higher education. Dr Riyadh al Dabagh, President of the University at the time, painted a dismal picture: there were no funds for maintenance and equipment; computers were a rarity since most were on hold by the UN Sanctions Committee; full professors would earn no more than 80–90,000 dinars or about $35–45, and as a result, many faculty members had left for employment in Libya, Yemen and elsewhere in the Arab world. A disproportionate number of students suffered from emotional disorders, mainly because of the dim prospects of finding employment after graduation: an architect student said to me, 'I find my studies exciting but what am I going to do after I graduate?' Another one, standing in a group of fellow students with whom I had engaged in an unplanned open-air discussion, summed up the feelings of her fellow students when she softly pointed out, with tears in her eyes: 'All we want is to study in peace with teachers who have up-to-date knowledge.' These students knew from their parents that in the 1980s and before, their university, together with others in Baghdad, Mosul and Basrah, had been among the best in the Middle East and attracted thousands of foreign students. All Iraqi and foreign students alike had been on scholarships. Iraqi students were, furthermore, encouraged by Government to accept generous grants to study abroad.

123. Al Mustansiriyah University is Baghdad's oldest university and one of the oldest universities in the Middle East. It was founded in 1204 by Khalif Al Mustansir.

Schools and universities were truly pitiful sights that made a mockery of the 1989 Convention on the Rights of the Child, which demands 'special protection' for children:[124] 'Children should be able to develop physically, mentally, morally, spiritually and socially in a healthy and normal manner and in conditions of freedom and dignity.'

No 'special protection' was given by either the Government of Iraq or the UN Security Council. While the Government of Iraq, under sanctions, retained a few 'islands of relative educational excellence', e.g., Baghdad College, the high school for children of mostly Ba'ath Party members, it could have done much more for the education sector as a whole, but so could the UN Security Council. Instead, the education budget for all thirteen phases of the Oil-for-Food Programme remained woefully inadequate.

What did it mean when 109 countries ratified the Convention on the Rights of the Child in 1990 after years of conferences and deliberations and concluded that 'There are children living in exceptionally difficult conditions and that such children need special consideration'?[125] Where could this have been more relevant than in Iraq? The issue of special support for education was not even discussed in the UN Security Council as an option. On the contrary, many educational materials meant to be purchased with inadequate Oil-for-Food Programme budgets were blocked by the UN Sanctions Committee, thus further disabling the education sector. The UNESCO representative in Baghdad gave me a document which showed that for phase IV (1998) the UN Sanctions Committee blocked educational materials, computers and teaching-support facilities for schools administered by the Ministry of Education in Baghdad amounting to $4.9 million or 26.1 percent of all supplies ordered; the corresponding figures of items blocked for the Ministry of Higher Education were $12.9 million or 73 percent of all orders![126] Fortunately no items for education programmes were on hold by the UN Sanctions Committee for Iraqi Kurdistan. When I discussed the state of the education sector in the spring of 1999 with a school administrator in Mosul he reacted angrily by saying: 'They have destroyed our economy, now they want to destroy our minds as well.' In the spring of 1999 I wrote to Deputy Secretary-General Louise Frechette, who was the ranking official overseeing the Iraq situation at UN headquarters, to alert her to the sorry state of education in Iraq. I pointed out to her that malnutrition was one additional factor which had to be identified as part of the negative learning circumstances of Iraqi children. My WHO, UNICEF and WFP colleagues in Baghdad were in agreement that chronic malnutrition

124. Declaration of the Right of the Child adopted by the General Assembly in resolution 1386 of 20 November 1959, principle 2.
125. UN Convention on the Rights of the Child, Preamble, 2 September 1989.
126. See Internal Report on Applications on Hold, dated 9 November 1999, pp. 40–1.

was still affecting every fourth child under five. The concern I wanted to convey to UN headquarters was that this would have a 'serious effect on the learning abilities in middle childhood' and eventually would make 'Iraqi youth ... increasingly ill-prepared to assume responsibilities in nation-building'.[127] I did not receive the benefit of a response.

Iraq still has a pool of well trained professionals. In a few years time, once this educated group is no longer active the permanent damage that sanctions have done to Iraqi society, particularly its youth, will be revealed.[128]

The UN Convention on the Rights of the Child also refers to 'freedom and dignity' for children and youth. These meant little to either the Iraqi regime or the UN Security Council. Ignoring this important convention went beyond the refusal by Government and Security Council to provide financial protection for education. Even primary students were forced to perform weekly salutes and recite poetry in the school courtyards in honour of the paramount leader. High school students were bribed by being given an additional five points in their exam scores if they joined the Ba'ath Party. This would be enough to ensure their admission to the country's better universities. Disarmament experts of UNSCOM would occasionally fly their white UN helicopters into university campuses to pay surprise visits. The inspectors would freeze the movements of faculty and students and interrogate students about what their professors, at that moment, had been teaching, in order to determine whether the lectures had any connection to weapons of mass destruction. Youth was not treated with dignity, either by Government or by the Security Council.

Given the pitiful state of education at all levels and the high number of children like Tariq not going to school at all or prematurely dropping out, it cannot be a surprise that the literacy gains of the 1970s and 1980s were quickly lost in the 1990s. UNESCO points out that Iraq received international recognition for the success of its literacy campaigns. In just ten years these campaigns had raised literacy from 52 percent in 1977 to 80 percent in 1987. This was not a mean achievement: Iraq's literacy level had become comparable to those of Hong Kong, Singapore and Panama.[129]

In 1995 Iraq's literacy rate had deteriorated to an estimated 58 percent.[130] In November 1998, UNESCO and UNICEF concluded that no more than 50 percent of Iraq's adult population were literate. This put

---

127. Internal Note to Deputy Secretary-General Louise Frechette, dated 12 May 1999.
128. Prior to 1990, Iraq had the most advanced educational system in the Middle East.
129. See 1990 UNDP Human Development Report, Oxford University Press, p. 131.
130. See internal submission from the author to the Chairman of the UN Security Council Panel on Humanitarian Issues dated 24 March 1999, p. 31.

Iraq at a literacy level below countries such as Malawi and Papua New Guinea.[131] UNICEF also alerted us to the fact that female literacy rates had fallen even faster, and in 1995 stood at 45 percent:[132] over half of Iraq's women could not read or write. It is difficult to imagine that this was the same country which only a decade earlier had the most modern education system in the Arab Middle East, a system in which females could participate without discrimination. While Iraq's youth of the 1990s had either poor or no opportunity to learn, their elders had little or no opportunity to apply what they had learnt in their days of formal education. Unemployment rates kept rising throughout the years of sanctions. No reliable recent unemployment figures were available during the time of my stay in Baghdad. In 1999 a rough estimate of 60 to 75 percent was used by the international community.

No wonder that educated, often highly trained professionals were willing to accept any employment, whether they had the training for it or not; many of them agreed to do even menial work. A report to the UN Security Council illustrated what I referred to in Baghdad as a process of 'deprofessionalisation'. A survey among professionally trained Iraqis employed by the UN system or NGOs in Baghdad involving 1,157 persons showed that 725 or 63.7 percent of those trained in natural sciences, engineering, medicine, architecture, etc., were actually working as drivers, clerks, secretaries, messengers and handymen.[133] One of the security guards at my office who would lift security bars to let our vehicles pass had been an Iraqi Airways pilot. There were few, young or old, who were not affected by either the state of the education system or the state of the economy, or both.

The education budget of $100 million, which the Government of Iraq and the UN system had negotiated for phase v, would not be able to prevent further deterioration. I nevertheless tried to impress on officials in the Ministries for Education and Higher Education that they should make their case for more funding in the Iraqi Cabinet and, if possible, directly with President Saddam Hussein. Of all the ministers I had met in the early days of my assignment, Dr Fahad Al Shagra, Minister of Education, had more portraits of Saddam Hussein in his office than did any of his colleagues. I counted twenty-six(!) pictures of all sizes, ensuring that the Minister, wherever he was in his large office, would never for a

---

131. See 1990 UNDP Human Development Report, Oxford University Press, pp. 196–7.
132. *The Children of Iraq*, UNICEF, February 2002, p. 39.
133. The Care Country Representative for Iraq, Margaret Hassan, wrote to the author on 17 March 1999: 'During the course of our work, we came across large numbers of people who are highly trained and working as taxi drivers or selling in shops. To highlight just one case, not long ago I was served ice cream by a qualified medical doctor.'

moment forget who was his President. Maybe he indeed had a more personal connection to the President and could discuss these funding constraints in education with him: he certainly was sympathetic to my proposal. Not until phase VI, however, was the pressure successful: the education budget was raised, in May 1999, from $100 million to $127 million. This was a sizeable increase but certainly did not suffice to change in any way the catastrophic learning environment in primary and secondary schools and universities in Iraq.

At the time when the UN Secretary-General approved the distribution plan V, on 11 December 1998, with a budget of $2.7 billion for the period 26 November 1998 to 24 May 1999, no one in New York or Baghdad had any inkling of the difficulties that were lying ahead in the immediate future for the United Nations, for Iraq as a nation and, most of all, for the Iraqi people. The plan which Kofi Annan had accepted was, unfortunately, yet another plan of inadequacy.

It was another plan which would provide further cover of legitimacy to the UN Security Council's economic sanctions policy on Iraq. The threshold between a negative but tolerable impact on the daily lives of a population and an increasing disregard for human rights by the Security Council had long been crossed.

As was customary, distribution plans were always subjected to one final formal meeting in the Foreign Ministry in Baghdad before Government would transmit this plan to the UN Secretary-General through, at the time, Ambassador Nizar Hamdoun, Iraq's Permanent Representative at the United Nations in New York. On this occasion, all participating UN agencies and government ministries came together in the conference room on the fifth floor of the Ministry of Foreign Affairs. This included the Iraqi Ministries of Foreign Affairs, Health, Trade, Agriculture, Irrigation, Interior, Education, Oil, the Electricity Commission and the Municipality of Baghdad. The United Nations was represented by UNOHCI, the WFP, the WHO, UNESCO, UNICEF, the UN Centre for Housing, the UNDP, the UNOPS and the FAO.

The phase V meeting, co-chaired by the Under Secretary of Health, Dr Shauki Murqus, and myself, took place in late November 1998. Ministerial representatives and Heads of UN agencies had an opportunity to make their concluding statements. For the Iraqi side this was an important occasion to yet again praise President Saddam Hussein's magnanimity to have 'accepted' another phase of the Oil-for-Food Programme and to state their determination not to have the sanctions programme continue beyond the phase which was about to start. This was verbalised in sharp, almost hostile language, by Ambassador Adnan Malik, the Director-General responsible for the Oil-for-Food Programme in the Ministry of Foreign Affairs. Once these statements had been made and tea was served, as always, the atmosphere became more congenial.

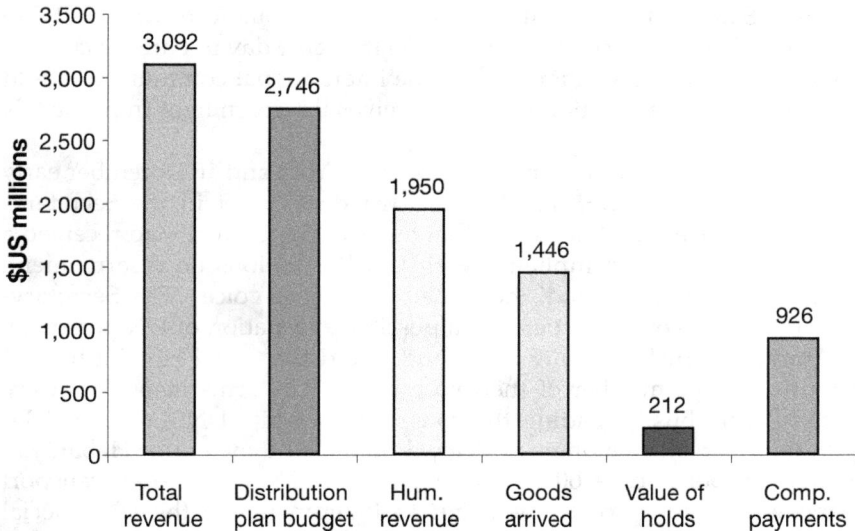

Figure 1.3 Data on Oil-for-Food Programme for Phase v

Source: *Secretary-General's 180-day reports on the Oil-for-Food Programme, phases V–VI.*
Notes: *Holds data for phase V refers to contracts from phases IV and V only and might therefore understate the total number of holds. Data have been pro-rated for a 180-day period. The reporting period for phase V stretches from 31 October 1998 to 31 March 1999, a period of 151 days. The distribution plan is for the whole 180 days of phase V, from 26 November 1998 to 27 May 1999. In order to render data comparable, the figures for revenue, goods arrived, and compensation payments have been scaled up by a factor 180/151, i.e., pro-rated for a 180-day period.*

Battles had been fought over issues such as the content of the food basket, the specification of equipment, the choice of drugs and their treatment methods, alternatives for water and sewerage plant repairs, cost-effective agricultural pest control, the choice of educational materials, etc. There was relief when negotiations were over and the more important stage of securing actual supplies for a suffering population could begin. What we, Iraqi and non-Iraqi, did not fully realise at the time was that our involvement in necessary detail for this survival programme had made us less sensitive to the stark injustice of the approach itself.

It should be remembered that the overall political climate in which phase V was prepared in 1998 was tense and confrontational. On 31 October Iraq had suspended cooperation with UN weapons inspectors. On 14 November Government had reversed its decision and agreed to their return. All along, however, signs were increasing that the United States Government was looking for a justification to 'use effective force if necessary,' 'to deter Saddam's aggression', as US National Security

Adviser Samuel Berger put it in a speech at Stanford University in California in early December 1998.[134] On the same day in Paris, Secretary-General Kofi Annan cautioned that 'the international community should refrain from military action unless it receives the green light from the UN Security Council.'[135]

On 15 December around midnight in New York and 16 December early morning in Baghdad,[136] Iqbal Riza, Chef de Cabinet in the Secretary-General's Office called me to say that the Security Council had received a report on Iraqi non-compliance with UN Resolutions on disarmament. 'Things do not look good', he added in a terse voice: 'The Secretary-General wants you to prepare for a possible evacuation of UN personnel to Amman'. I rushed to my office and found the Canal Hotel a hive of activity. A large number of the two hundred UN arms inspectors were already there busily loading the conspicuous white UNSCOM vehicles with their personal belongings. A few hours later they left for Habaniyah military airport, some 60 km from Baghdad. There a C-130 transport plane was waiting to fly them out to Bahrain where the UN Special Commission had a large field office. In the course of the day, I learnt that on 15 December Ambassador Richard Butler, UNSCOM Chairman, had submitted his report to the UN Security Council together with a letter addressed to Ambassador Buallay of Bahrain, President of the UN Security Council for the month of December. The letter concluded that Iraq had not been in full compliance with UN resolutions. The implications of such a conclusion were clear.

On 16 December 1998, US President Clinton, as his country's military Commander in Chief, authorised what became known as 'Operation Desert Fox'. During 16–19 December 1998 Baghdad, Basra and other strategic centres in Iraq were subjected to four nights of intensive and targeted bombardment of military and intelligence installations. This included residential facilities of the Republican and Special Republican Guards, who were the backbone for the protection of Saddam Hussein and his regime.[137]

After UNSCOM personnel had been evacuated on 16 December 1998, the UN Secretary-General decided, on the same day, to carry out a partial evacuation of the international humanitarian staff in Iraq. As the official responsible for security, I had declared the UN offices at the Canal Hotel as a safe-haven area, a point of concentration for all staff and the point of departure of most UN staff to Amman.

134. US newswire transcript of 8 December 1998 and article by Barton Gellman, *The Washington Post*, 9 December 1998.
135. Reported on 8 December 1998 by Agence France Presse (AFP).
136. The time difference between the US and Iraq is eight hours.
137. See also pp. 218–33.

UN Secretary-General Kofi Annan was wise to let the evacuated humanitarian staff quickly return to their duty stations in Baghdad, Erbil and Suleimaniyah. The six Iraqi buses which had taken some 250 staff to Amman only three days before returned to Baghdad on 20 December, a day after the US/UK air attacks had stopped. This was good for the morale of all the international staff whom I had asked to stay with me in Baghdad during the bombing, as well as for those who had been evacuated to Jordan. Many had been evacuated against their personal will, since they had wanted to remain. Iraqi UN staff were reassured as they had feared that the UN would pull out altogether, leaving them without jobs. The decision was also politically important. NGOs, the International Committee of the Red Cross and the Federation of the Red Cross and Red Crescent Societies had kept their staff in Baghdad. The UN did not want to give the Government, the Arab League and others the impression that the UN Secretariat was taking its humanitarian role in Iraq lightly. Nevertheless, the four nights of bombing did have a ripple effect with many negative consequences for the implementation of the Oil-for-Food Programme. The most immediate problem had been created by Lloyds Register, the UK agency which the UN had appointed in 1997 to inspect humanitarian supplies as they arrived at Iraq's borders. Lloyds had withdrawn its staff at the outset of the air strikes without consultation with the United Nations. The four UN authorised entry-points at Trebil (border with Jordan), Al-Walid (border with Syria), Zakho (border with Turkey), and Umm Qasr, the Iraqi Gulf port near Basra, had been abandoned. Without the presence of Lloyds personnel, goods could not be authenticated and, therefore, not brought into Iraq. As a UK-registered company, Lloyds management had taken this unilateral decision out of fear for Iraqi retribution. The Iraqi Government was quick in condemning Lloyds, and the UN Legal Office in New York rightly considered Lloyds in a breach of contract. In order to minimise the period of interruption in the flow of humanitarian supplies, the United Nations without losing time appointed a new clearing agent, Cotecna, a Geneva-based company. The handover from Lloyds to Cotecna was anything but an example of congeniality. After all, one company was dismayed to lose a lucrative contract, another company was eager to take over. It took a good part of January 1999 before Cotecna could start with the clearance of goods. In the meantime, the lines of trucks awaiting clearance at the three land-entry points got longer and longer every day. Several ships bringing wheat and rice waited in the open seas of the Gulf to avoid exorbitant demurrage charges.

In addition, the air strikes had left, in the minds of all parties concerned, a good deal of uncertainty about the future of the Oil-for-Food Programme. Exporters were hesitant to ship goods. Insurance companies wondered whether the risks were becoming too high to offer insurance.

Oil dealers took a wait-and-see approach to new oil contracts. The UN community and the Government of Iraq needed to catch their breaths and return to implementing the humanitarian programme in a routine way. A slowdown of shipment, contract processing and distribution of humanitarian supplies was a natural response to the December air strikes. Again, the price was paid by a people who were waiting for food, medicine, more electricity, cleaner water and improved sanitation.

It was only during these days of 'recuperation' that I realised that I had in my office a staff member whose sole job it was to troubleshoot contracts involving commodities which were held up either in the Government of Iraq or at border entry points. The daily routine of this staff member, a retired colonel of the Australian army, was to maintain contact between the Iraqi Ministry of Foreign Affairs, the office of the Lloyds/Cotecna clearing agent at the Canal Hotel and the UN Office of the Iraq Programme in New York. It was an immense struggle, not so much to find the cause of delays, but to convince those responsible for holding up the humanitarian supplies to do something about it. Contract processing for some became one of the hidden weapons in sanctions management. The retired Australian colonel was only a tiny element of a costly UN processing machinery mainly located at UN headquarters in New York. It had been set up in response to the UN Security Council's surveillance demands. Loyal to the dynamics of bureaucracies, this unit of the UN Office of the Iraq Programme was involved in continuous regulatory fine-tuning in order to justify its own existence, but primarily to satisfy the ever-present demands of the US/UK missions to the UN[138] for total control. To any outsider it may appear impossible that a humanitarian programme meant to protect innocent people from the worst effects of sanctions could possibly be subjected to such intense scrutiny.

To illustrate how cumbersome the procurement process was, Table 1.1 gives an example from phase V of the Oil-for-Food Programme: a manufacturer in Barcelona ready to ship equipment to Iraq for Baghdad's water authority, which included chlorinators, compressors, pipes and fittings, would face a true obstacle course of extraordinary dimensions and uncertainties.

This example reflects a process which the Government of Iraq and anyone who wanted to enter into a business relationship with Iraq had to accept. The twenty-three individual steps shown represent the 'routine'.

138. These two countries maintained large 'Iraq sections' within their missions to the UN and, of course, in various government departments in their capitals. These included technical specialists who would second-guess UN specialists in determining whether a humanitarian item could be of dual use. US/UK mission staff were regularly on a collision course with staff in the UN Secretariat, with the latter usually at the losing end.

Table 1.1   The Procurement of Humanitarian Supplies – an Example: Water Equipment from Barcelona to Baghdad, an Outline of 23 Major Steps[139]

Step 1:   The Government of Iraq seeks a contract with a Spanish manufacturer of water equipment.

Step 2:   The Barcelona-based company accepts the contract proposal.

Step 3:   The company forwards the contract to the Spanish Ministry of Foreign Affairs and the Spanish Ministry of Defence.*

Step 4:   The Spanish Government agrees with this business deal and forwards the contract to the UN Mission of Spain in New York.

Step 5:   The UN Mission of Spain forwards the contract to the UN Office of the Iraq Programme (OIP).

Step 6:   The UN/OIP checks the humanitarian nature of the contract, assigns a commodity number and advises the Spanish Mission to the UN that the contract is under review.

Step 7:   The UN/OIP submits the contract to the UN Sanctions Committee for approval.

Step 8:   The UN Sanctions Committee pronounces that the equipment is not of dual use and informs OIP of its agreement to the procurement.**

Step 9:   UN/OIP informs the Spanish Mission to the UN of the UN Sanctions Committee's approval after the Chairman of the Committee has signed the approval letter.

Step 10: UN/OIP requests the UN Treasury to confirm that there is financial coverage to purchase the water equipment.***

Step 11: UN Treasury confirms available funding to the UN/OIP and concurrently requests the Banque Nationale de Paris (BNP) to reserve the funds for this contract.****

Step 12: BNP opens a Letter of Credit once the Central Bank of Iraq has conveyed its agreement to the BNP.

Step 13: In parallel, the Mission of Spain in New York informs the manufacturer in Barcelona of the UN Sanctions Committee's approval.

Step 14: The manufacturer in Barcelona requests the Spanish Trade Ministry to issue an export licence for the water equipment.

Step 15: The Spanish manufacturer forwards the documentation to the BNP in Paris once the export licence has been granted by the Spanish authorities.

Step 16: BNP confirms to the UN Treasury that the documentation is in order.

Step 17: The UN Treasury recommends to BNP payment once the water equipment has arrived at the Iraqi border. BNP informs the manufacturer.

Step 18: The Spanish manufacturer selects a shipping agent and forwards the consignment to Iraq.

continued

Table 1.1 *continued*

Step 19: BNP pays the supplier once Cotecna, the clearing agent, has authenticated the consignment and agreed to its transport into Iraq.

Step 20: UN Treasury informs OIP when BNP has made the payment to the Spanish manufacturer.

Step 21: The trucks carrying the equipment proceed to Baghdad and unload the consignment at a central warehouse.

Step 22: The Government of Iraq carries out quality control tests, confirms that the consignment meets Iraqi standards and releases the equipment for pickup by the Baghdad water and sanitation authority.

Step 23: Installation at the site of need will depend on available transport and funds for the cost of installation.[140]

---

* Many export countries insisted on clearance by their Ministries of Defence to confirm that no military equipment was involved.

** If an item was found to be of dual use, UNSCOM/UNMOVIC and individual permanent missions to the UN would review a contract further to determine whether it should be put on permanent hold or whether technical clarification be sought.

*** There was frequently a need to prioritise contracts because of insufficient funds. Prioritisation always meant that contracts for food and medicines ranked first, education contracts usually were last on the list.

**** The Banque Nationale de Paris (BNP) during phase v was the exclusive holder of Iraqi oil revenue deposits. In the course of 1999 pressure from governments and large banks, e.g., Deutsche Bank increased to receive part deposits of the multibillion Iraqi oil income. As a result there was some account diversification. The BNP, however, remained the major account holder.

Apart from the procurement of three to four hundred thousand tons of food every month, which worked reasonably well, the procurement of humanitarian supplies constituted a nightmare, certainly not only, but also, because of the complexity of this process.[141] It should not come as a surprise, therefore, that it would often take a year, sometimes longer, for humanitarian supplies to reach Iraq from the time a contract was negotiated. There were other serious 'road blocks' that explain the poor

139. These were standard steps with some variations depending on the country of origin. Often additional steps were involved due to clarifications sought by one of the parties or an item that was initially blocked by the UN Sanctions Committee.
140. On 14 May 2002 the UN Security Council adopted Resolution 1409 as part of a 'smart sanctions' policy reducing these steps to seventeen.
141. Should a contract be held back by the UN Sanctions Committee, either because it involved a possible dual purpose item or because funding was lacking, various procurement steps had to be repeated, further delaying arrival in Iraq. At times a contract had also to be renegotiated because delays had resulted in significant price changes.

implementation record of the Oil-for-Food Programme,[142] one of which was the issue of quality control for imported items. UN Executive Director Benon Sevan and I had tried to convince the UN Sanctions Committee that all contracts for humanitarian supplies should include a 'commercial clause' to protect Iraqi importers and, ultimately, the Iraqi people from exploitation. Such a clause, a provision in any normal international business contract, would provide for withholding between 5 and 10 percent of the cost of an order until the goods had arrived in Iraq and were found to meet quality control standards. Neither Sevan nor I anticipated that this would be found objectionable by the UN Sanctions Committee. In mid-1999 we therefore proceeded, with the Ministry of Trade in Baghdad, to revise contracts to include such a provision. Accordingly contracts in the new format were negotiated by the Iraqi Government with the overseas suppliers. Satisfaction over this improvement did not last very long: the moment the Office of the Iraq Programme in New York sought clearance for contracts with this format, they were turned down by the UN Sanctions Committee. US and UK committee members demanded that the commercial clause be dropped: it would encourage, they argued, over-invoicing and provide cash into the hands of the Iraqi authorities which they would use for their weapons programmes. This made no sense whatsoever, since over-invoicing could not be prevented by dropping this clause. Rational arguments were unsuccessful. This was the end of the discussion. The contracts involved were returned and had to be rewritten with the delays and costs this entailed, Iraq was forced to remain vulnerable in its international trade relations, and shady international businesses could continue to exploit Iraq.

The statistics on humanitarian inputs failing to meet established quality standards are evidence that our concern was indeed justified: the monthly stock report for September 1999, for example, shows that $10.9 million or 2.1 percent of all items in stock at that time had failed quality controls.[143] Quality control problems were not limited to consignments from unknown or dubious suppliers. These stock reports, which were prepared by UN agencies for all sectors and included in the six-monthly distribution plans, showed that reputable and internationally known companies at times delivered defunct or sub-standard equipment and materials as well. During the time I served in Baghdad these included food, warehouse equipment, rice and wheat consignments, dental chairs, chemicals, spare

142. Blocked supplies by the Sanctions Committee, difficulties in finding a politically acceptable supplier, quality problems, lack of finance for training and installation of equipment were among the main causes of delays in the arrival of humanitarian supplies.
143. These stock reports were introduced by UNOCHI in August 1999 and published on a monthly basis.

parts for water plants, generators, school rehabilitation materials, medicines, etc. In other words, no sector was spared from this problem.

Cotecna, and previously Lloyds Register, regrettably were no more than 'clearing agents' for the Oil-for-Food Programme. Their staff would only check export documents and humanitarian supplies which had arrived at Iraq's land and sea borders and release goods once they had authenticated the consignment. These commercial firms were not expected to carry out quality control checks: they simply performed quantity-control functions on behalf of the UN Security Council, not quality controls on behalf of the people of Iraq.

Dr Amir Khalil, the FAO Representative, Jutta Burckardt, the World Food Programme Director, myself and others argued that this was a costly and simplistic exercise at Iraqi borders that could have been combined with quality controls: Iraqi institutions responsible for standards and quality control in the food, medical and other sectors could have been utilised. The dialogue with UN Headquarters concerning this issue proved futile. The struggle for fair trading practices and quality assurances for the Oil-for-Food Programme was left entirely to the Iraqis.

Keeping in mind the many steps that were involved in the procurement process, the delay in obtaining the humanitarian supplies at the required standard would often have serious consequences for the welfare of the Iraqi population. The fact that Government, in the absence of a commercial clause, had already paid in full for consignments that turned out to be defunct did not facilitate litigation. To agree on refunds or goods replacement was cumbersome and more often than not unsuccessful.

There existed the related problem of holds of complementary items, i.e., those humanitarian supplies which were required along with other items already in Iraq. Syringes without vaccines, irrigation equipment without pumps, teaching aids without electricity connections, warehouses for medicines without air conditioners, laboratory reagents without diagnostic facilities, or school furniture without trucks to transport them to their location, are examples of the problem of lacking complementary items. Failed quality controls, in many cases, aggravated the complementary item issue since items that were found to be below standard would have to be reordered and, in the meantime, held up the rehabilitation of a water plant or the distribution of medicines to rural areas or prevented a harvest in those areas where irrigation equipment was needed. The UN Sanctions Committee never reacted to UNOCHI's monthly stock reports and the supply and installation problems which they identified. The US/UK members of the UN Sanctions Committee did not manage, if they ever attempted, to convince their Foreign Offices in Washington and London to end their allegations that the Iraqi Government was purposely withholding humanitarian supplies from the civilian population.

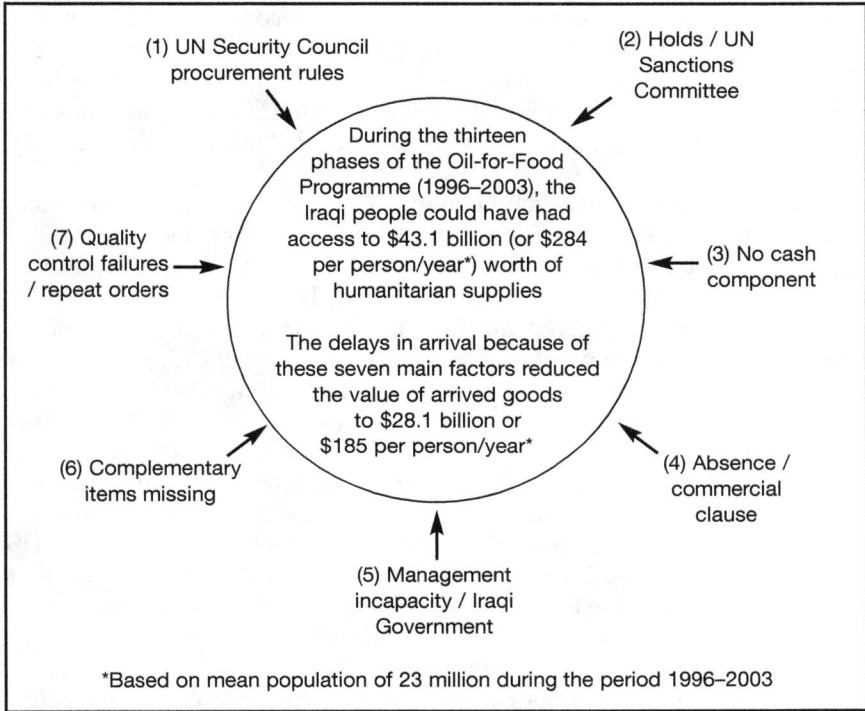

Figure 1.4 Humanitarian Supplies for Iraq: Causes of Delayed Distribution

In fact, UN stock report after stock report showed precisely the opposite picture. The distribution of humanitarian supplies was working well. The UN stock reports identified the reasons for the occasional distribution difficulties. These had nothing to do with 'refusal to distribute': they had much to do with the policy of the US/UK Governments and connivance by the UN Security Council. This policy resulted in lack of transport, non-release of cash for installation and training, putting on hold items without which repair or operation of equipment was not possible, objection to the inclusion of commercial clauses in contracts, and the excessively control-oriented procurement process.

During the thirteen phases of the Oil-for-Food Programme (1996–2003), the Iraqi people could have had access to $43.1 billion or $284 per person/year.[144] Delays in arrival of humanitarian supplies due to the indicated factors reduced this amount to $28.1 billion or $185 per

144. By coincidence, the total of the budgets the Government of Iraq submitted for the thirteen phases also amounted to $43 billion.

person/year. Had the earned oil revenue[145] become available in full during this period, instead of having been partially apportioned to the UN Compensation Commission (30 percent)[146] and UN overheads (3 percent), the per capita amount available for humanitarian supplies per year would have been $432 or more than twice the value of what actually reached Iraq.

It was within the jurisdiction of the UN Security Council to make changes at any time. The UN Secretariat in New York and all of us in Baghdad should have pressed much harder for such changes. The removal of any or all of these constraints would not have been problematic: it would not have endangered the UN disarmament programme, since a large team of UN monitors was available to verify the deployment of equipment and the use of cash. The Iraqi people, on the other hand, would have greatly benefited. US and UK representatives in the UN Sanctions Committee had repeatedly bemoaned and criticised the UN system in Baghdad which, in their opinion, had no concrete evidence that the distribution of humanitarian supplies was as efficient as our reports claimed. During a visit to New York in February 1999 I asked to see the US Acting Permanent Representative, A. Peter Burleigh, to reassure him that distribution of Oil-for-Food Programme goods 'worked'. He again brought up the issue of 'tangible evidence' to this effect. I could not give him specific statistics and only referred to the January reports of UNOCHI's monitoring units in Baghdad and to those of UN agencies. Ambassador Burleigh had a point. I realised that without such data the politicisation of distribution would continue. I thanked him for his suggestions and assured him that the UN system in Baghdad would revise its reporting to include detailed distribution statistics. It is ironic that the UN stock reports were introduced as the result of a US initiative but the US Government ignored them when they became available.

Back in Baghdad, I found full support for the idea of preparing monthly stock reports. It took, however, six months for agreement to be reached with the Government of Iraq and a reporting structure put in place. The first detailed stock report was issued in August 1999. Initially, the technical ministries in Baghdad had not been enthusiastic about cooperating. A turning point came after a meeting I had with Deputy Prime Minister Tariq Aziz in late March 1999. 'You must understand that our mid-level civil servants are suspicious when they are asked by outsiders to provide information. Too often the data they supplied were ultimately used against Iraq. When they believe in the honesty of a

---

145. Total oil revenue earned during the 1996–2003 period amounted to $64.7 billion.
146. In accordance with UN Security Council Resolution 1330 of 5 December 2000. This percentage was lowered to 25 percent from the year 2000 onwards.

request, they will be helpful. I will ask the Ministries to cooperate since I know that in this case the intentions are sincere.' Gradually, the ministerial response became more and more what we needed and increasingly the UN agencies too were prepared to take on this new task. WHO, faced with a stock of thousands of medical supply items, set up an entire unit staffed with four professionals and headed by an Egyptian colleague with solid experience in data collection. The stock reports went significantly beyond what US Ambassador Burleigh had requested. The first such report provided data for each sector, outlining what had been received in Iraq, what had been distributed and what had been kept in stock. Stocks were shown that were undergoing quality control tests or had failed such tests, and items that had arrived yet were awaiting complementary items. The report concluded that 88 percent of all humanitarian supplies which had arrived in Iraq had been distributed to end-user points, i.e., food to families, drugs to urban hospitals and rural health centres, educational materials to schools, equipment for water sanitation and electricity to the sites concerned, and so on.

I was extremely pleased that the UN system in Baghdad had been able to respond in such a comprehensive manner to justified US criticism. At this point I was still hopeful that good arguments and reliably collected information would make a difference in defining the parameters of the Oil-for-Food Programme. I was wrong again. In February 1999, the UN had been criticized because it 'lacked' data; when we had collected the data the UN was criticised because it lacked 'reliable' data. The US/UK criticism of UN data remained a standard aspect of the UN Secretariat's relationship with these two Governments. UNICEF's mortality surveys were attacked. WFP's and UNICEF's nutritional assessments were questioned. FAO's drought and foot-and-mouth disease alert was rejected. Data that did not fit the US/UK strategy of weakening Iraq under sanctions was ignored, questioned or rejected as Iraqi propaganda or inadequate UN data.

The US State Department wrote in September 1999: 'The Iraqi Government has refused to distribute to the people of Iraq billions of dollars worth of supplies delivered by the Oil-for-Food Programme.'[147] The State Department's spokesman added on one occasion the incredible accusation that I, as the UN Humanitarian Coordinator in Iraq, had helped the Iraqi Government to do so. The British Government's position was reflected in State Minister of Foreign Affairs Peter Hain's insistence that 'the Iraqi people continue to suffer because the regime is not spending the money made available by the UN on its people's needs'.[148]

---

147. See report by the US Department of State entitled 'Saddam Hussein's Iraq', Washington, September 1959, chart 3.
148. Peter Hain, MP, and Foreign Office Minister, *The Guardian*, London, 6 January 2001.

How completely false this assertion was can be seen in Figure 1.2. Iraq had always more contracts in the pipeline than resources to pay for them.[149] The US and UK Governments were simply not willing to admit that their position was wrong. The UN team in Baghdad was furious. The countrywide data was simply ignored in favour of politically convenient fabrications assembled thousands of miles away in Washington and London. The US Government argued, from a distance, that 'billions of dollars'[150] of humanitarian supplies were left undistributed without allowing the reader to know the basis for this conclusion while the UN in Iraq showed, transparently and in detail, that 88 percent of all supplies had been distributed.[151] Subsequent stock reports would identify an even better distribution picture and give good reasons for the existence of undistributed stocks.[152] For example, the fact that items had failed quality control tests and, therefore, had to be kept in stock. Goods were also in stock because they were awaiting complementary items either because these items were blocked in the UN Sanctions Committee or were late in arriving due to the Sanctions Committee's laborious procedures.

The US Government pointed out that 32 percent of all medicines were lying undistributed in Iraqi warehouses in 1999. This, in fact, was close to the figure of 30.7 percent of medicines in stock indicated by WHO in the UN stock report for August 1999. The overwhelming part of these stocks, WHO explained, were 'buffer stocks': the balance consisted of medicines that had failed quality-control tests or those undergoing quality controls at the time.[153] The stock situation for medicines, according to WHO, was totally acceptable. If anything, stocks should have been higher, since all countries are encouraged to keep what WHO calls 'just-in-time' stocks of their supplies ready and available to protect against outbreaks of epidemics. The Government of Iraq, however, insisted that such stock levels would not be possible given the inadequate funding available for the health sector. For the US State Department not to give the additional stock information shows a malicious intent. One can see the difficulties which the UN faced.

Why the United Nations and UN agencies like WHO did not protest over this deliberate and serious distortion of facts and provide a clarification to the Security Council, governments, and the media, once again shows how fearful and intimidated the UN system was of US retribution. Instead, it was left to the Government of Iraq to condemn

149. See Table A.10, p. 290.
150. US Department of State, op. cit.
151. UNOCHI Monthly Stock Report, August 1999, p. 6.
152. See, for example, UN Stock Reports for November 1999 and March 2000.
153. Ibid., note: Stocks comprised 87 percent of buffer stocks; 6.5 percent of stocks represented medicines and medical supplies that had failed quality control tests, 6.2 percent were undergoing quality controls at the time.

these false accusations – an act which neither governments nor the international community took seriously.

Soon after the December 1998 air-strikes were over, the Government started the rehabilitation of nearly all of the seventy buildings which had been either partially or extensively destroyed. Among them in Baghdad were the Ministry of Health building belonging to the Ministry of Defence and the Military Industrial Complex, residential quarters of the Republican and Special Republican Guards, and the massive building of the Am al Amn, the general security organisation near the UN offices at the Canal Hotel. Progress with the repair of the security building was extremely slow, as I saw driving past it every day during the following months. Appropriate building materials for this specially constructed building seemed to be lacking. It was, nevertheless, impressive to see the ingenuity with which labourers were at work to erase the outward signs of the damage inflicted on the Iraqi regime's structures. Just prior to the beginning of the air-strikes on 16 December, many of the government ministries had been totally emptied: furniture, filing cabinets, TV sets and office equipment were removed to other locations. On that day I happened to be at the Ministry of Foreign Affairs and in the Planning Ministry where Deputy Prime Minister Tariq Aziz's office was located, and could witness this exercise. It reminded one of a stage-set change in a comical drama. CNN had given the Government a helping hand with their 'avalanche' of advance warnings of possible US/UK military strikes.

Government, UN and those anxious to do business with Iraq tried to make up for lost time. There was, therefore, a flurry of meetings, communications and telephone calls with New York, UN agencies, exporters, Cotecna, our new clearing agent, Saybolt, the oil overseers, Iraqi ministries and Baghdad based embassies. The latter wanted to make full use of their presence to influence Government to intensify trade relations with the countries which the embassies represented. They also sought UN help in removing 'holds' from goods ready for export from their respective countries. For them trade with Iraq was much like a long-distance race. Some ambassadors and chargés d'affaires made it their regular habit to call or come to the United Nations at the Canal Hotel to get the latest statistics on the volume of contracts their manufacturers had received in comparison with other countries. This became a nuisance and, to the annoyance of some, made us decide to cease disclosing such information.

In early 1999, there were forty-three countries with embassies in Baghdad. Four were from Africa, ten from North Africa and the Middle East, fifteen from Asia, twelve from Europe and two from Latin America. Egypt, France, Italy and the United States maintained interests sections in the Embassies of India, Romania, Hungary and Poland respectively. Iraq was slowly moving out of its isolation.

UN contacts with the diplomatic community were close. For me there were daily contacts with the French, Chinese and Russian ambassadors representing permanent members of the UN Security Council, or the 'P3 Group' as they were called. All three ambassadors had much closer relations with Iraq's leadership, particularly with Deputy Prime Minister Tariq Aziz, than I had. They all were arabistes and had many years of experience with the Middle East. Their briefings helped me to better gauge the political pulse and put local events and rumours into some perspective. The stories, for example, about the intermittent and localised insurgencies in the Shi'ite South or the occasional confrontations of the intelligence agencies with Shi'ite groups in Saddam City are examples. I used these meetings with the P3 Group to prepare positions on a range of issues relevant to the welfare of Iraqis.

Most valuable were the discussions with Turkish Ambassador Selim Karaosmanoğlu. We reviewed the increasingly offensive nature of US/UK over-flights in the northern no-fly zone in violation of agreements that these two Governments had made with the Government of Turkey. He was extremely well informed on the developments in Iraqi Kurdistan and the situation of the Turkomen in Kirkuk, Telafar and other areas. His knowledge of northern no-fly zone developments was of importance to the UN and my preoccupation with the security of UN staff travelling on roads between Baghdad, Mosul and Kirkuk and the safety of trucks bringing humanitarian supplies to areas located in the northern no-fly zone. Most useful were the discussions with French Ambassador de la Mesuzière about Iraq resolution drafts, particularly Resolution 1284, which took almost the full year of 1999 to be finalised.[154] We both hoped that its final content would outline genuine and speedily implementable improvements for the Iraqi people. This was, of course, not to be the case as will be discussed later.

How to accelerate the flow of humanitarian supplies and increase the pressure on the US and the UK to end the harmful blocking of humanitarian supplies was a common and continuous concern for us all. For this purpose I would give the P3 ambassadors copies of our latest status reports and analyses. There was a flurry of senior Russian political figures coming to Baghdad during this period. They and other visitors from P3 countries would always get up-to-date information from us on the Oil-for-Food Programme. In turn I would be briefed about the evolving Russian, French and Chinese positions and sanctions policy in the UN Security Council. I made good use of this information in preparation for visits to New York.

Communications with Chinese Ambassador Zhang Weiqin were as cordial as with the others, but more complicated. A careful listener, he was

---

154. For a discussion of this resolution see p. 106, p. 120, p. 149.

anxious to hear how I saw political developments in Iraq and what constraints the Oil-for-Food Programme was facing. In responding he would – and this in an almost mechanical manner – not disclose more than the general and known positions of the Chinese Government on the 'injustices of sanctions' and the Chinese support of the humanitarian efforts. I never gained the impression that there was a deep personal involvement on his part. He simply carried out the 'business of government'. It was not I but the Ambassador of the then Yugoslavia, Enes Korabegovic, who on the occasion of a meeting in the house of the Russian Chargé d'affaires lost his patience with the Chinese Ambassador's reticence: 'All you are interested in is what happens to China and the Chinese', he shouted. There were also close and friendly contacts with the small but influential community of Arab ambassadors. I often met with them individually or as a group to discuss the Oil-for-Food Programme and the situation in the country. All of them, but particularly Riadh Al-Akbari, the Ambassador of Yemen, Hmood Al-Katarnh, the Ambassador of Jordan and the three ambassadors of the Mahgreb, Najib Belhaj Buliman of Tunisia, Lhassane Naciri of Morocco and Tayes Saadi of Algeria, who also was the Dean of the Diplomatic Corps, were exceedingly well informed on conditions in Iraq, well connected with Iraqi cabinet ministers and sympathetic to the human situation in the country and full of good advice on how to deal with the Iraqi authorities.

Phase v of the Oil-for-Food Programme had been approved by Secretary-General Kofi Annan for the period 26 November 1998 to 24 May 1999. On 18 May 1999 the UN Security Council issued the Secretary-General's 180 Day Report for this phase.[155] It covered a turbulent period for Iraq involving the December 1998 air strikes and a clearly noticeable new US/UK Iraqi destabilisation strategy in general but for the two no-fly zones in particular. During phase v, my office recorded air strikes on fifty-six days up to 3 May 1999. This was on average one air strike every three days. On twenty-one occasions UN staff had been either at or near such incidents[156] during this period. The morale of the UN staff, both national and international, helping to implement the humanitarian programme in all parts of the country, was falling. My concern for the staff and our ability to carry out tasks efficiently and safely was increasing. For safety reasons I had to take a number of precautionary security measures which were detrimental to the humanitarian operations, including a temporary halt to overnight stays by UN personnel in all locations south of Baghdad except Basrah. UN

155. See S/1999/573 of 18 May 1999, p. 3, para. 10.
156. UNOCHI confidential report on Impact of Air Strikes on UN Operations in Iraq, Baghdad, March 2000.

humanitarian truck traffic on roads between Mosul and Dohuk in northern Iraq was stopped between 11 A.M. and 3 P.M., since air-strikes would usually occur in that area during these hours.

Assessing the Humanitarian Exemption

The UN Secretariat's report to the Security Council on this period did not show the additional problems which had arisen in the course of phase v. There were the deteriorating circumstances created by the US and UK air forces and the cumulative impact of the many obstacles the UN Security Council had put in place in the course of the four earlier phases, as well as during phase v operations. Behind a maze of statistics, intelligible only to 'insiders' within the UN Security Council and the UN Secretariat, were hidden details of the avoidable inadequacies of the Oil-for-Food Programme.[157]

A transparent presentation would show: a gross amount of $5.2 billion had been authorised by the UN Security Council[158] for phase v leaving, however, only a net amount of $3.4 billion for the humanitarian programme. It would, furthermore, disclose that due to extremely low oil prices ($8 to $9 per barrel) during several months of the phase v period and because of interruptions in oil production due to air strikes, the budget of phase v of the humanitarian programme had to be reduced from $2.7 billion to $1.9 billion. This constituted a cut of 30 percent. An inadequate budget had become an even more inadequate budget. For the six-month period the humanitarian supplies that could be purchased with such a budget had a value of $122 per person. However, the humanitarian supplies that actually arrived during these six months amounted to only $1.4 billion or $53 per person. The World Bank and the UN consider anyone living on less than $180 for six months or $1/day as living in abject poverty!

The UN Report should have provided a concise analysis of this stark reality instead of presenting financial figures which, on the surface, looked acceptable but, in reality, were of catastrophic dimensions. In addition, of course, this report like all others should have reflected genuine UN concern. Carefully and emphatically worded recommendations for change should have been a standard part of all UN reports on the Oil-for-Food Programme. This was not the case for phase v, nor for the standard reports of other phases. The phase v report, furthermore, did not make clear the dangers of the unpredictability of funding for the Iraqi people. The UN and the Government of Iraq had negotiated a phase v with a budget of

---

157. See Table 7.
158. See Annex S/RES/1153 (1998) of 20 February 1998, para. 2.

$2.7 billion and the UN Secretary-General had approved it. Such funding, however, depended on an erratic international oil market and a dilapidated Iraqi oil industry. The risk was carried by the Iraqi people. The Iraqi oil industry could at best produce 2.2–2.3 million barrels of oil per day for export. With an immense sense of irresponsibility, the UN Security Council allowed this 'Iraq survival programme' to be ultimately defined by an external force, the international oil market. There was no reliable revenue forecast, no reliable implementation mechanism and no safety net whatsoever for the Iraqi people. If the revenue was earned, the programme could procure; if the revenue was lacking, then approved contracts would be frozen or transferred to the next phase.

The final report on phase V[159] points out that 'the Office of the Iraq Programme (OIP), in consultation with the Government of Iraq, was forced to transfer from phase IV to phase V 166 applications valued at $414 million'. During consultations between the UN/OIP and the UN Security Council in February 1999, Executive Director Benon Sevan informed the Council that 'about $30 million of approved applications continued to await funds almost ten months after the end of phase III which was on 25 May 1998. Among those applications were pharmaceuticals worth $3.4 million, as well as medical supplies and agricultural inputs valued at $7.3 million and $1.3 million respectively. For phase IV the funding of $300 million of contracts for oil spare parts and equipment was also delayed as a result of the combined effects of processing delays and holds and the slow rate of reimbursement from the '13 percent account'.[160] This involved funds the Government of Iraq had advanced from its account to Iraqi Kurdistan for purchases of food and medicines. All of this underlines the extraordinary financial inadequacy, the problem of holds and the prevailing financial mechanisms – three issues for which the UN Security Council and no one else was responsible. This made the UN Security Council entirely accountable for the human misery which these factors created in Iraq.

It has been argued that the UN Security Council did not violate international law as there was no deliberate act of withholding humanitarian supplies such as food and medicines. This is not correct as far as medicines are concerned: there are examples where the UN Security Council did withhold medicines.[161] More generally, the UN Security Council's adoption of rules and regulations for the import of humanitarian supplies including medical supplies into Iraq had to lead to under-utilisation of already inadequate resources and inordinate delays

---

159. See S/1999/573 of 18 May 1999, p. 3, para. 10.
160. Internal Briefing Note, dated 25 February 1999.
161. An example is the import of Pentosam, a drug needed for the treatment of leukaemia.

in the arrival of goods essential for life and health. If not directly, certainly indirectly, the Security Council right from the beginning in 1996 became responsible for a poorly implemented Oil-for-Food Programme. But for Iraqis who were malnourished, who could not obtain a proper diagnosis and medical treatment, who suffered from gastroenteritis because of polluted water, who could not grow their crops because of lack of irrigation water, who were barred from a decent education, it made no difference whether the UN Security Council was directly or indirectly responsible for their plight.

It must again be emphasised that the UN Secretary-General's report should have addressed the structural and financial shortcomings of the humanitarian programme and the resulting effects on the civilian population. The phase v report could and should have offered concrete recommendations for remedial action. This was neither in general nor in specific terms the case. The persistent efforts of the UN system in Iraq to inculcate a sense of urgency into the debate at the UN in New York in order to bring about a more humane sanction regime had once again failed.

The Food Sector

The food sector, which for obvious reasons had to perform better than the other sectors, did so during all phases. During phase v it delivered 95 percent of the planned caloric requirement of 2,200 kcal to the population in central and southern Iraq as well as in Iraqi Kurdistan.[162] Thanks to the cooperation between the Government of Iraq, Iraqi Kurdistan, food agents in the eighteen governorates, and the World Food Programme as an intermediary, this massive feeding programme which involved the import and distribution of 440,000 tons of food during phase v, worked well as a system. This does not mean that there were no logistical or other problems. The World Food Programme and the UNOCHI office and, to a lesser extent UNICEF and WHO, faced daily challenges to assist Iraqi authorities in removing bottlenecks related to transport, quality control, flour milling and procurement. When international shipments were late, temporary replacement of awaited food items with supplies from Government's own limited stocks became necessary. One problem the UN did not face during my tenure, contrary to US/UK allegations and reports by the UN Human Rights Rapporteur, was that food was deliberately withheld from the population by the Government of Iraq. The World Food Programme representative, Jutta Burckardt, and her team, the

162. See the UN Secretary-General's Report S/1999/573 of 18 May 1999, pp. 7 and 18. The period covered in this report for the food sector is November 1998 to April 1999.

observers in my office, and others in the UN system in Iraq would have quickly come to know this and would have reported such serious wrongdoing to the UN Security Council. The same holds true for the accusation that Government was selling large quantities of food at exorbitant prices in and outside of Iraq. WFP did find minor quantities of food for sale on the open market. The amounts were so small that they gave no cause for concern. The food was, however, sold not by Government but by private individuals mainly because they were short of cash or they did not like specific items of the imported food, such as foreign lentils.

More sensitive were the complaints of the Kurdish authorities that the Iraq Government was often providing them with commodities 'unfit for human consumption'. During visits to Erbil and Suleimaniyah, Kurdish officials would show me crates of weevil-infested flour, rice with impurities, spoiled cheese, etc. It was again the World Food Programme which clarified matters by reminding all concerned of the unavoidability of some of the stored food indeed becoming unfit for consumption. Given the large volumes involved, the quantities of substandard food, however, were negligible at less than 1 percent. The Kurdish officials were not satisfied with this explanation since they were convinced that this occasional problem was a deliberate act against them by the Government in Baghdad. Regrettably, the US and UK Governments did not correct their own perception by using UN reports and continued to re-state the false accusation that food was being withheld, sold or used as a political tool.

Frequently visiting the large warehouses maintained by the World Food Programme in Mosul and Kirkuk, from where Iraqi Kurdistan was supplied, I was impressed by the high degree of professionalism of the national and international WFP staff. They knew exactly what food stocks they had, their condition, and what they could pass on to the population. WFP was fully in control. This does not mean that the food basket of phase v was optimal in terms of kilocalories, proteins and calcium: it was not. This was due to inadequate financial resources, the international procurement process and the decision of the UN Security Council to disallow local procurement of food. Some will point out that the Oil-for-Food Programme was never intended to be more than a supplementary source of livelihood and that Iraq as a country and a Government had a responsibility to make up shortfalls. The US and UK Governments would stress that this did not happen because Saddam Hussein and those in his leadership did not care and squandered resources on palaces, luxury goods and special perks for members of the Ba'ath party. There is truth in this assertion but it is vastly overstated. In any case, as far as food supply during phase v is concerned, Iraq experienced its first year of severe drought and, therefore, was not in a position to 'supplement' the imported food. The harvest Iraq could have had through irrigated agriculture was prevented, to a large extent, by the UN Security Council's blocking or putting on hold pumps, generators, and piping.

The total budget for food and food handling equipment which the Government of Iraq and the UN in Baghdad had identified for phase v was $1.2 billion.[163] The total value of all humanitarian supplies which arrived during phase v, however, amounted to only $1.4 billion. It is figures such as these which need to be appreciated to fully understand what the Iraqi population had to face phase after phase: $2.7 billion had been programmed by Government and the UN. The budget was approved at this level by UN Secretary-General Kofi Annan. Humanitarian supplies worth $1.4 billion had arrived in Iraq. This included $984 million worth of food, or 68 percent of the total value of arrived goods. The total value of arrived humanitarian supplies for health, water and sanitation, electricity, agriculture and education, therefore, amounted to only $461 million to sustain a population at that time of 22.5 million for six months![164]

Health

In the health sector, the arrival of medicines and medical equipment was nowhere near the rate for the food sector: $240 million had been included for the health sector, or five cents per person per day for a population of 22.5 million for the 180-day period. Yet only $155 million or $5.80 per person worth of health supplies had actually arrived in Iraq during this period. The three Kurdish governorates received $23 million worth of health supplies from their budget of $35 million. The comparable figures for Central and Southern Iraq were $102 million from their budget of $205 million.[165] This contrasts with complaints by the Kurdish authorities that they did not receive their fair share of the bulk purchases made by the Government of Iraq. A more correct observation is that neither the three Kurdish governorates nor the fifteen governorates under Baghdad's control ever received the full benefit of what was foreseen in distribution plans for the health sector. We did not prepare such sobering calculations at the end of phase v or, for that matter, for any other phase: they should, however, have been carried out by the United Nations in Baghdad, by the UN Secretariat and by the UN Sanctions Committee whose formal responsibility it was to monitor the implementation of the Oil-for-Food Programme. It should be no surprise that with this kind of health

163. See Distribution Plan/Government of Iraq, 28 November 1998, p. 5.
164. See also Table A.11, p. 290.
165. See DPV of the Government of Iraq approved by the UN Secretary-General on 11 December 1998.

protection, 'there has been no significant reduction in general malnutrition among infants or among children under five, previously rising prevalence rates have stabilised, albeit at an unacceptably high level'.[166] According to UNICEF, 20.4 percent of Iraqi children under five were chronically malnourished in 1999, during the time when phase v was being implemented.[167]

The arrival in Iraq of $155 million worth of health supplies did not imply efficient distribution to end-users. WHO, UNICEF and UNOCHI did raise the slow distribution of health supplies to district hospitals, rural health centres and pharmacies with Dr Oumid Medhat Mubarak, Minister of Health. We found the Minister and his officials equally concerned. The health sector faced genuine and complex problems: these comprised inadequate management tools, particularly the lack of computers to keep track of hundreds of different medicines. Kimadia, the Government's health supply organisation, had only a third of its pre-sanction warehouse capacity; there was not enough handling equipment and, as in all other sectors, there was also a severe shortage of transport. The difficult procurement process and the perennial 'holds' problem often led to delayed arrival of complementary items and explains, to a large extent, the stock situation.[168] Mention must also be made of the lack of motivation of the workforce and poor training.

The storage of $300 million worth of medicines and medical equipment in central warehouses during November 1998 to March 1999 was indeed a joint concern of Government and the United Nations. Unless there were to be fundamental changes in the way in which economic sanctions were handled for the health sector and the Oil-for-Food Programme in general, we knew little would change for the better. Our appeals to the UN Security Council in this regard failed. In fact, the volume of items including medical equipment put on hold increased steeply in subsequent phases,[169] the bureaucratic system became more fine-tuned and items took longer to arrive. Instead of recognising these realities in the health sector, the US State Department and the British Foreign Office continued to talk of the 'deliberate procrastination of the Iraqi regime' and maintained a hard-line approach in the UN Sanctions Committee.

As UNICEF stated repeatedly, malnutrition, an inadequate supply of medicines and polluted water were the three major causes of the high rate of child mortality in Iraq. There is no denying that sanctions were mainly responsible for the existence of these factors. In early 1999 we had little

166. See UN S/1999/573 of 18 May 1999, p. 9.
167. See *The Situation of Children in Iraq*, UNICEF, p. 21; the figure for acute malnutrition had risen from 20.4 percent in 1999 to 30 percent in 2000.
168. See also UN/S/1999/573, paras. 33–5.
169. See Table A.4, p. 289.

hope that this picture would change. Chronic malnutrition stabilised, but at the unacceptably high level of 30 percent. Medicines arrived in the country at an erratic pace and there were innumerable constraints to efficient distribution.

Water and Sanitation

The water and sanitation sector did not fare any better: on the contrary, the UN Security Council put large amounts of equipment and supplies, particularly chemicals, on hold for various spurious technical and alleged dual-use reasons. The UN Security Council, not the Government of Iraq, therefore, largely bears the responsibility for the very poor delivery situation during phase v.

As the figures below show, there was a distinct double standard on the part of the Council in implementing the water and sanitation programme in Central and Southern Iraq as compared to the Kurdish areas. Those responsible for this situation in the US and UK missions to the United Nations would argue that the UN, responsible for this sector in Iraqi Kurdistan, was preparing contracts better and there was no need to seek additional technical information. More importantly, in Northern Iraq, the dual-use danger did not exist. These contentions distract from facts. The Government of Iraq knew very well how to contract necessary water and sanitation materials. The dual-use argument also had no standing as a large team of UN monitors, including UNICEF, WHO and UNOCHI specialists in the area of water supply and sanitation, were serving in Iraq. They had no difficulty in verifying use and location of equipment and supplies in any part of the country.

Distrust of the UN in Iraq by certain members of the Council played a role. There existed a deliberate effort to derail the UN Oil-for-Food Programme: it simply was not meant to run well. This conclusion amounts to a hard accusation; repudiation will invariably follow. It is, however, the US and UK Governments who are answerable to the question: why did they not support changes in the sanctions regime despite their knowledge of the impact of UN Security Council policy? Only when the human condition in Iraq became even more desperate and the political pressure for change intensified did the US and UK authorities decided to drop their opposition and agree to a freer flow of humanitarian supplies. In 1998/99, however, these two Governments were not prepared to do so, as documented by the conditions in the water and sanitation sector.

Distribution plan v had included a water and sanitation budget of only $150 million.[170] What actually arrived in Iraq during this period, however,

170. See Goi/DPV, p. 5.

was even more grotesque: only $43 million worth of equipment and supplies reached Iraq during that period; this amounted to $1.6 per person.

The delivery for Iraqi Kurdistan was 70 percent of their budget of $22 million in the water sector, for Central and Southern Iraq 15 percent of the $12 million – a significant difference. It was good that the Kurdish areas fared better in terms of clean water and sanitation and were spared the delivery obstacles which the rest of the country suffered. When the US and UK Governments used the better implementation in Iraqi Kurdistan as 'evidence that the Government of Saddam Hussein did not care for its people', they chose to ignore the fact that it was they who were largely responsible for creating these differences in the first place. Iraqi Kurdistan on a per capita basis did get a larger slice of funds, was allowed to break sanctions, especially through the use of a cash component, and was not subjected to the perennial blocking of supplies by the US and UK.

The sector objectives to 'provide sufficient quantities of potable water to the population' and 'to dispose hygienically solid and liquid wastes'[171] were not met in Central and Southern Iraq during phase v. The situation on both accounts deteriorated even further. Kofi Annan's report[172] pointed out that 'in terms of water quantities available at the end-user level, coverage has decreased as a result of deterioration in the distribution network, illegal connections and misuse of water ...'. Furthermore, the report indicated that 'UN observers report large amounts of untreated sewerage being discharged into rivers as the treatment plants are either non-operational or operating at very low efficiency levels. Phase v once again showed the interdependence between various sectors such as health, water and sanitation and electricity: polluted water affected health, and lack of electricity affected the production of potable water. The Secretary-General's report observed: 'Continuing contamination in water reaching end-users is mainly caused by interruption in electrical power supply and the deterioration in the status of the water networks.'[173]

UN headquarters reports told the story even if they did not convey the magnitude of the dangers for Iraqi wellbeing; we, the UN community in Baghdad and elsewhere in the country, noticed it every day. We saw the many water main leaks, we smelled the refuse in the streets and saw the pollution of the Tigris. Often we ourselves were victims of these circumstances. Our gastroenteritis problems, however, were nothing compared to those who had no access to antibiotics as we did. The UN's medical services were well equipped to reduce our discomfort; the Iraqi

171. See Goi/DPV, pp. 18–19.
172. See UN S/1999/573 of May 1999, pp. 10–11.
173. Ibid., p. 11.

civilian population had to face chronic problems, often resulting in permanent health damage or death. Neither UN staff nor the average Iraqi civilian was unaware that the UN's well stocked dispensaries and Iraq's miserable medical facilities were both financed by the same source: Iraqi oil revenue.

Agriculture and Irrigation

At the end of his phase v report Secretary-General Kofi Annan had to announce that 'limited stocks of pulses, vegetable oil, salt and dairy items' prevented the distribution of the planned food basket.[174] In Baghdad we had agreed at the outset of phase v that a food basket of 2,200 kilocalories should be distributed during the phase. As a result of the emerging drought, there was little hope that wheat, rice, pulses and dairy products would become locally available to meet the shortfall from international procurement under the Oil-for-Food Programme.

The quality of the agreed food basket was never in accordance with international standards.[175] Fresh food items were not part of the general ration. There was no programme to encourage local production of vegetables and fruit, nor was there an attempt to promote beneficial food preparation practices. There was no distribution of vitamins and mineral supplements as part of the monthly food basket. Had there been a provision in sanction regulations to purchase fruit, vegetables and meat locally, the quality of the basket would certainly have improved. During phase v local purchase would not have been an option, since the drought conditions reduced the availability of Iraqi commodities to insignificant levels. This, however, did not lead to the disappearance of fruit and vegetable stalls in Baghdad and other urban areas; along Al Arasat Street or in Karada one could buy apples from South Africa, kiwi fruits from New Zealand, fine local oranges, imported bananas and all kinds of vegetables. But there were not many Iraqis who could buy them. A school teacher with a salary of 10,000 Iraqi dinars or about $5 per month, or a middle-level government civil servant with 16,000 Iraqi dinars or about $8 per month, could hardly afford to buy six oranges for 1,000 Iraqi dinars or 50 cents. What about the 60–70 percent of Iraqis out of work? Those who could afford to buy were privileged foreigners and a few affluent Iraqis. This sufficed for the traders to make good profits.

The Secretary-General's report warned of likely wheat and barley crop failures in Iraq. Driving out of Baghdad one wondered what the flocks of

---

174. See UN S/1999/573, p. 7.
175. See 'Food and Nutrition Needs in Emergencies', Guidelines issued by UNHCR, UNICEF, WFP and WHO, undated, p. 14.

sheep were eating: on the way south towards Samawa and Basrah, grazing under the best of circumstances was poor. In Tikrit and Mosul, which had suffered a lack of rainfall in late 1998 and early 1999, a landscape was created which reminded one more of a Braque painting than an area for grazing. The highway curled through a vast expanse of parched countryside along empty water channels interrupted occasionally by patches of vegetation showing evidence that some farmer still had the means for irrigation. This included a fairly large area occupied by the Mujaheddi Khalq, the Iranian opposition who had been given refuge in Iraq by Saddam Hussein's Government and settled in Al Khalis some 80 km from Baghdad.[176] From the highway one could see their houses in the distance; trees and foliage suggested the presence of water. For obvious reasons, these 'Muj', as they were called, kept a low profile and confined themselves mainly to their headquarters in the Al Karade area of Baghdad and in their settlement in Al Khalis within the Diyalla governorate. What gave away their presence on Iraqi roads were their new Hino green army trucks and jeeps with special green licence plates. No doubt these vehicles were the envy of the Iraqi army, which had to make do with a fleet of old and decrepit vehicles.

Drought conditions were not only noticeable by the absence of clouds: travelling over any of the numerous bridges in Baghdad, one noticed the decreasing water level of the Tigris by the emergence of more and more islands within the river that eventually became covered with reeds and grass. River traffic, negligible as it was, became hazardous. The Iraq/Syria/Turkey water commission was set up to regulate the flows of the Euphrates and Tigris rivers, both of which originate in Turkey, with the aim of regulating the sharing of water. The commission had their last meeting in 1992 in Damascus. Turkey had lost interest in discussing water apportioning with its neighbours, Syria and Iraq. As the 1998 drought continued into subsequent years, the release of water from the upper reaches of the two rivers in Turkey would have made an important difference for Iraq's agriculture. The double effect of holding back water in Turkey and holding back irrigation equipment in New York had a devastating impact on Iraq's agriculture at a time when the imported food basket badly needed local supplements.

Poor arrival rates for agricultural supplies during phase v further aggravated the Iraqi farmers' plight. The budget for agriculture which Government and the UN had agreed upon amounted to $180 million; $146 million for the fifteen governorates under Baghdad's control and $34 million for the three Kurdish governorates. The delivery pattern in the sector was similar to other sectors: while Iraqi Kurdistan utilised $32

176. The Supreme Command for an Islamic Revolution in Iraq (SCIRI) and their Badr Brigade were the Iraqi opposition equivalent in Teheran.

million or 94 percent out of the $34 million, Baghdad managed to use only 52 percent or $79 million of its agricultural budget of $146 million. This was a particularly unfortunate shortfall at this critical time of drought and resulting local food shortage.

During this period, Government and the UN Food and Agriculture Organisation (FAO) carried out a survey which showed that the prevalence of foot-and-mouth disease in the country was much more widespread than had been assumed prior to the survey. The Minister of Agriculture, Abdul Ilah Hamid, made an urgent appeal to FAO to bring specialists into the country to review the facilities of the Foot-and-Mouth Vaccine Institute in Al Dora, on the outskirts of Baghdad. The Institute had been destroyed by UN disarmament experts of UNSCOM in the early 1990s as a site which was thought to have produced botulinum toxin and possibly anthrax.[177] Government hoped that FAO could assist in the rehabilitation of this facility to produce some of the badly needed vaccines to combat foot-and-mouth disease.

The FAO representative and I went to see the Institute at Al Dora. What was shown to us by civil servants from the Ministry of Agriculture and the Director of the Institute was a facility which could not be a danger to anyone: only the remaining walls reminded one of a building; inside, we saw air vents which had been cut, wiring ripped out of the walls, incubators dismantled, laboratory glassware smashed and copious rat droppings. No one had been in this facility for a long time. It would have had to be completely overhauled and refurbished before it could function again as a scientific institute capable of producing vaccines. Had intelligence agencies really seen Al Dora they would have advised their governments not to cite this facility as a source for WMD-related evidence. Instead, US and British intelligence agencies made a false case to their governments for treating Al Dora as a 'facility of concern'.[178]

We could see from the face of the former institute's Director that he was shattered by this return visit to his old institute. UNSCOM had indeed done an excellent job of destruction and disarmament. Precursors for biological weapons manufacturing could not possibly be produced at the Al Dora Institute of 1999 and, hopefully, would never have another chance to be produced in these premises.

The FAO representative and I had come to Al Dora to find out whether, and under what conditions, the UN could help Iraq to protect itself against the serious outbreak of foot-and-mouth disease which had

---

177. See more in 'Iraq's Weapons of Mass Destruction', International Institute for Strategic Studies, London, 9 September 2002, p. 39.
178. See US Government 'A Decade of Deception and Defiance', Washington, 12 September 2000, p. 8, and UK Government 'Iraq's WMD', London, 24 September 2002, p. 22.

already caused fatalities. We had to decide if an FAO mission should come to Iraq to determine whether the rehabilitation of the Al Dora facility was possible. We had to identify the kind of monitoring which would be required to safeguard against illicit production of WMD related substances. We decided to recommend a mission. FAO/Rome and UN/New York agreed and a three-member FAO team eventually came to Baghdad in January 2000 for a ten-day period. In their subsequent report the FAO mission referred to various options for the supply of vaccines. These included importing vaccines via Amman. Due to refrigeration requirements this would have been a complicated undertaking: transport from Jordan had to be by road because of the existing air embargo. Partial or complete rehabilitation of the Al Dora laboratory with international scientific supervision were further alternatives.[179]

The picture which emerged towards the end of phase v of the Oil-for-Food Programme in the agriculture sector was that drought and animal diseases had decimated the production of wheat and barley and meat from goats, sheep and chicken. At the beginning of the phase, the distribution plan approved by the UN Secretary-General had once again conveyed the message that Iraq's 'agriculture sector has a vital role to play in the improvement of food security within the country. The Iraqi population relies heavily on domestic food production as a supplement to the food basket acquired'.[180] The final report on phase v submitted by the UN Secretary-General to the UN Security Council on 18 May 1999 failed, however, to convey the seriousness of the local food security situation.

Under drought conditions, food security from within Iraq could not possibly mitigate the impact of an inadequate Oil-for-Food Programme budget. Poor delivery of agricultural goods under the Oil-for-Food Programme and poor growing conditions within Iraq should have been highlighted in the UN report. At the same time, we should have challenged the UN Security Council to adopt a catalogue of special measures to overcome this serious situation. These should have included accelerated animal vaccine imports, the provision of additional transport, purchase of animal feed, local rehabilitation of the cold chains and the release of irrigation equipment from US/UK holds. This would have ensured at least a partial protection of the agriculture sector and prevented a deepening of the employment crisis, particularly in Iraq's rural areas. No such measures were suggested in the report. The uncompelling nature of the report made it easy for the UN Security Council to justify complacency.

179. UN/FAO Foot-and-Mouth Disease Assessment Mission in the Republic of Iraq, 13–23 January 2000 by Dr Y. Cheneav, Dr M.F. Lombard and I. Franks, Rome, January 2000, pp. 36–41.
180. See GoI Distribution Plan v, part 5, para. 50.

Electricity

The entire electricity sector had been severely damaged by the 1991 war. Since then there had been a reluctance on the part of the UN Sanctions Committee to facilitate speedy repair of the electricity grid and stations, particularly in central and southern Iraq. The UN Sanctions Committee considered the electricity sector a 'dual-use sector' and put it on a special watch list at the behest of the US/UK Governments. As a consequence, supplies and equipment for the electricity sector represented a high percentage of items put on hold not only for phase v but also for the entire life of the Oil-for-Food Programme. For phase v, the total value of holds amounted to $212 million. Holds, cumbersome procurement, uncoordinated arrivals and the fact that many items in this sector were not 'off-the-shelf' items but had to be custom made, explain the electricity sector's very poor delivery rate of $68 million against a budget of $409 million.[181] For Iraqi Kurdistan there were practically no holds in this or any other sector. Delivery delays in Kurdistan were due to other factors, including inordinate delays in the delivery of custom-made generators and faulty equipment which had to be returned to the supplier. As Figure 1.5 shows, in per capita terms, electricity items which arrived during phase v amounted to $2.5 per person only.

For Iraqi households and for public services, including hospitals and schools, such constraints meant long, disabling and not infrequent, life-threatening power cuts. Phase v saw no improvement whatsoever: in fact, the electricity supply situation became worse. In January 1999, one of the cooler months in Iraq, with less demand for electricity, average electricity cuts were ten to twelve hours per day in the capital, Baghdad. Cuts were even higher in urban areas in both the north and the south of the country. The UN Secretary-General's report summarises the situation in the electricity sector by pointing out that 'it is difficult to measure any notable improvement in electricity generation attributable to programme inputs'. This was an understatement of the disastrous supply situation, as well as of the lack of progress in increasing generating capacity. It was also a statement which downplayed an observation made earlier in the report that power outages had 'increased' during phase v as compared to phase IV. In retrospect, it is amazing with what nonchalance we described the critical situation in a key sector of the humanitarian programme. Busy members of the UN Security Council and the UN Secretary-General's

---

181. The UN Secretary-General's Report of 18 May 1999 shows the extreme slowness of implementation by indicating that at the time of phase v 'only' 87 percent, 72 percent, 50 percent and 4 percent respectively of ordered electricity items for phases I, II, III and IV had actually arrived in Iraq, see p. 14.

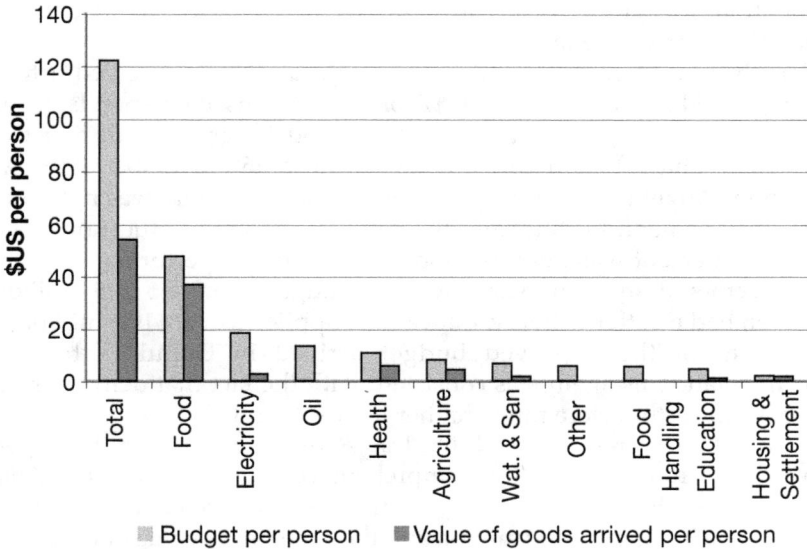

Figure 1.5   Phase v Budget and Value of Goods Arrived Per Person

Source: *Distribution Plan for phase v and Secretary-General's 180-day reports on the Oil-for-Food Programme, phases IV and V.*
Notes: *Food includes nutrition; health includes medicines; Wat. & San. denotes water and sanitation; KAR Specific includes various activities relevant only to the Kurdish Autonomous Region.*

Office could not possibly have been unduly concerned when reading reports which did not show the poor state of rehabilitation and repair of power plants between phase IV and phase V and electricity needs of a population of 23 million. The report missed the opportunity to review the causes for the slow arrival of items in the sector. There was not a single reference to either the poor delivery or the high volume of items blocked by the UN Sanctions Committee for the electricity sector.

Here was another grave example of the UN Secretariat's unwillingness to present to those responsible for sanctions policy a continuously updated and compelling picture of a truly failing Oil-for-Food Programme.

Education

This general statement, while applying to all sectors of the Oil-for-Food Programme, is especially relevant to the education sector. At the time of negotiation for phase v, I had noticed the particularly inadequate financial resource base in education.

For phases I to IV distribution plans, education had received a total amount of $181 million out of $7 billion.[182] This corresponds to an incredibly low 2.6 percent of the Oil-for-Food Programme during two years (four phases) from 10 December 1996 to 25 November 1998. An education budget of $100 million during phase v certainly was not much of an improvement. Additionally, the delivery rate in the education sector of only 25 percent was poor but consistent with low performance in the other sectors. Iraqi Kurdistan, with a budget share of $25 million, however, had a better delivery. Education supplies worth $10.5 million or 42 percent of the approved budget arrived in Dohuk, Erbil and Suleimaniyah. This again was consistent with the fact that delivery rates in nearly all sectors were much higher in Northern Iraq.

It cannot be overemphasised that Iraq's youth kept paying the largest share of the human costs for comprehensive economic sanctions. For them the red line of defendable 'sanctions damage' had long been crossed. The budgeted $100 million and the even lower value of the actual countrywide arrival of educational supplies largely explains the pitiful state of children's education. It also underlines the immense disregard by the UN Security Council and the Government of Iraq for the future of the country's youth. The final UN report on phase v does not even refer to this incredibly low allocation of funds for education and the even lower value of education materials that actually arrived. The report neglects to refer once again to the fact that 'the quality of teaching has been affected by the lack of basic educational means and materials', as stressed at the outset of phase v in the distribution plan.[183] Instead of evaluating the performance in the education sector, the report states that 'Phase v is expected to focus principally on the procurement of classroom furniture and to provide teaching aids for the Ministry of Higher Education'. It then proceeds to refer to the poor physical state of buildings and the lack of blackboards.[184] This, no doubt, was one aspect of the problem: it should have been raised together with issues of the content of education, curriculum development and the state of knowledge of teachers.

I felt very strongly about the poor condition of primary, secondary and university education and raised this repeatedly with the UN Office of the Iraq Programme in New York. I was told that the Oil-for-Food Programme was not a development but an emergency programme. Nine years of emergency? There was no understanding in OIP of what this

---

182. See Table A.7, p. 287. Iraq: The Oil-for-Food Programme Budgets: 1996–2003.
183. See DPV, part 6 of 26 November 1998.
184. See UN S/1999/573, pp. 15–16, paras 57–61.

policy was doing to Iraqi youth. I would go further and argue that this lack of concern contributed to severely disabling the young in their efforts to become adults who were ready to assume roles as responsible citizens. Of the three parties in the UN system concerned with education in Iraq under sanctions, the UN/OIP was short-sighted and uninterested, UNESCO was occupied with the physical aspects of education and only UNICEF tenaciously made the case for the quality of education and teacher training. It is unfortunate that UNICEF did not have more resources to make a major, countrywide difference.

In the spring of 1999 I began to have a deeper understanding of the humanitarian programme which I was managing and its myriad technical, logistical, financial, personnel and political problems. The UN/Baghdad team had to contend with the views of the Iraqi Government, the Kurdish authorities, the NGO community, the UN Security Council, the UN Secretariat, and permanent missions of countries represented in the Security Council. We were surrounded on all sides by hardliners defending their political and other interests which had little to do with our concerns: the welfare of the people of Iraq. There simply existed differing motivations among the various parties in New York and Baghdad which were not compatible with ours.

What I did not fully realise at the time was that separate reporting by the UN Secretariat on the implementation of the Oil-for-Food Programme in the Iraq under Baghdad's control and in Iraqi Kurdistan played into the hands of the US/UK and Iraq Governments. The US and UK, for example, would politicise UN reports about Iraqi Kurdistan by stating that better progress in sectors such as health and education, as reported by the UN, constituted evidence that Saddam Hussein could have achieved the same results but did not because he did not care for his people. The explanation, as has been discussed already, was quite different. The Iraq Government also used UN reports, such as UNICEF mortality surveys, to 'inflate' the findings and apportion blame for the poor state of health entirely on the UN Security Council.

Those responsible for the Iraq programme in the UN Secretariat in New York did not engage actively in the substantive Iraq discussion or played opportunistic balancing acts to please all sides. The UN Deputy Secretary-General, Louise Frechette,[185] who was the ranking official dealing with Iraq, delegated her involvement in the 1990s mainly to Benon Sevan, the Executive Director of the Office of the Iraq Programme. The Under Secretary-General for Political Affairs, Kieran Prendergast, did not want to play any active role in the Iraq discussion, or so it seemed

---

185. Frechette, prior to her appointment to the UN, served as Deputy Minister of National Defence in the Government of Canada (1995–8) and was Canada's Permanent Representative to the UN in New York (1992–5).

from the Baghdad vantage point: during my visits to UN headquarters I never had an opportunity to discuss Iraq issues with him. During 1998–2000 Sergio Vierra de Mello, the then Under Secretary-General of the Department of Humanitarian Affairs (DHA),[186] and his staff were, unfortunately, deliberately kept out of the Iraq discussion.[187] This left the Executive Director of the OIP as the sole authority for the running of the largest humanitarian exemption the UN had ever undertaken. This was a serious mistake with major negative implications for the Oil-for-Food Programme and its beneficiaries.

As phase v drew to a close in May 1999, I had accumulated six months of experience with a humanitarian programme meant to protect some 23 million people against the worst effects of comprehensive economic sanctions.

UN staff could be found, countrywide, on Iraqi roads every day of the week. Thousands of Iraqi civil servants, municipal workers and local government employees were involved in the management and distribution of the incoming humanitarian supplies. Close to 50,000 food agents alone ensured that every Iraqi in the eighteen governorates of the country would be connected to the lifeline 'food basket'. Additionally, the Iraqi Red Crescent, the Middle East Council of Churches and other religious organisations were actively engaged in reinforcing the Oil-for-Food Programme. Trucks arrived daily at Iraq's western and northern borders carrying supplies. Ships brought food and heavy equipment to Um Qasr, Iraq's only open sea port. UN bureaucrats and their Iraqi counterparts were inundated with contract-related paperwork. The dynamism of the routine looked and, in fact, was impressive. The tangible progress it afforded, however, was bleak and depressing as the preceding review of different sectors has made clear. Food quality was not what it should have been; medical protection was severely deficient; agricultural supplies were inadequate and local food security was impaired by irrigation equipment and pesticides put on hold by the UN Security Council's Sanctions Committee; electricity, water and sanitation supplies were similarly prevented, temporarily or permanently, from export to Iraq; the little resources available to the education sector allowed not more than minor improvements; housing, telecommunications and basic banking services were excluded altogether from any support. This was the state of the Oil-for-Food Programme at the end of its fifth phase in mid-1999. This was nothing less than avoidable deprivation. The UN

186. Renamed in 1997 as the UN Office of the Coordination of Humanitarian Affairs (UNOCHA).
187. A former DHA staff member pointed out to the author that even though the DHA offices in the UN Secretariat were only a few metres away from the Office of the Iraq Programme, contact was firmly discouraged: OIP was considered 'too political'.

Security Council could be challenged by the fact that at the end of phase
IV in November 1998, the overall human condition was such that Iraq
resolutions were increasingly in conflict with the UN Charter. Settlement
of international disputes, international law demands, were supposed to
be based on the principles of justice and in accordance with the purposes
of the United Nations. Was the human condition in Iraq based on justice
and phase V of the Oil-for-Food Programme consistent with the purposes
of the United Nations?[188] The Security Council could not plead ignorance
since UN and other reports had made it clear repeatedly that the UN
Security Council was failing the Iraqi people with irreparable costs to
their wellbeing. It also was not possible to put the blame entirely on the
Government of Saddam Hussein as some governments suggested.

What Figure 1.4[189] conveys in stark terms is that:

(i) payments to the UN Compensation Commission of $926 million up
to 1998 could have been frozen during phase IV/V revenue shortfalls,
without abrogating the rights of claimants, and the amount added to
the budget of the Oil-for-Food Programme;[190]
(ii) trusting the UN monitoring mechanism in Iraq would have
eliminated the need to block $212 million of humanitarian supplies
during phase V. This alone would have added a good amount to
purchase goods needed in Iraq;
(iii) a less bureaucratic procurement mechanism could have improved on
the poor delivery rates.

This aggregated data shows that the implementation of phase V was
not doing well. The sector descriptions and analyses underline this. And
yet the picture of misery remains blurred unless one goes one step further
and disaggregates to the level of individual Iraqis and the Oil-for-Food
Programme's phase V average contribution to their lives. What emerges
for planned and actual contributions to secure a livelihood as foreseen in
UN resolutions, reflects a truly horrific reality. Figure 1.5 provides the
details: during phase V, $5.80 worth of health supplies became available
per person, $1.60 for water and sanitation, $4.10 for agriculture, $2.50 for
electricity, $1.00 for education and $36.70 for food.[191]

The inadequate allocations of financial resources by the UN Security
Council and, to a much lesser extent, by the Iraqi Government, to keep a

---

188. See UN Charter, articles 1–1 and 24–2.
189. See p. 75.
190. Wealthy governments and commercial firms did not have problems of child
mortality, malnutrition and impoverishment; the Iraqis did.
191. It should be remembered that Iraqi oil revenue paid for both, the
'humanitarian' programme and UN salaries. UN staff working in Iraq
received a daily allowance of $100 in addition to their regular salaries.

population alive and healthy, even at minimal levels, had much to do with a lack of political will and sense of humanity among all the protagonists. To help the Iraqi people graduate out of their misery could be seen as an indirect way of strengthening the Iraqi regime and confirming it as a force that had successfully stood up against global powers. The Governments of the United States and the United Kingdom were not willing to uphold the provisions of international law for such a price.

Whenever I visited New York, members of the UN Security Council would be profuse in their expressions of concern for the welfare of the Iraqi people. Hardliners such as UK Permanent Representative Sir Jeremy Greenstock and, particularly his Deputy, Ambassador Eldon, as well as US Acting Permanent Representative Cunningham, would add a standard qualifier: 'the suffering of the Iraqi people is entirely due to Saddam Hussein'. I am not an apologist for the former Iraqi dictator but the Iraq story, as it unfolded before me during phase v, certainly was much more complex than that. Attributing misery to one side was simply false. The Government of Iraq could and should have done more to devote a larger share of the income they earned from sanction-breaking oil sales outside the UN mechanism to the direct benefit of the Iraqi people. Contrary to repeated US/UK claims, the Iraqi Government did not have large amounts that would have bridged the divide between ill being and wellbeing. The estimated $1.0 to $1.5 billion of 'extra' income would have made a difference, however.

The UN Security Council Enquiry on Conditions in Iraq

The UN Security Council could carry out required fundamental changes in sanction policy, particularly with regard to the funding mechanism. Further adjustments of the kind shown earlier in implementing phase v would have made a genuine difference for the people of Iraq. The state of destitution of the Iraqi people, however, did lead to increasing uneasiness and pressure for change among most members of the UN Security Council. One such voice of concern was that of the Canadian Foreign Minister, Lloyd Axworthy. In 1999, he repeatedly pointed out his Government's profound concern over the 'negative humanitarian impact' of sanctions. Most importantly, he had the courage to say in the UN Security Council:[192] 'It is imperative that the sanctions reflect the objectives of the international community, not just the national interests of its most powerful members'![193] It was ultimately at the initiative of Canada that the UN Security Council announced, on 30 January 1999, the

192. Canada was an elected member of the UN Security Council during 1997–9.
193. See David Cortright and George A. Lopez, *The Sanctions Decade, Assessing UN Strategies in the 1990s*, Boulder and London: Lynne Rienner, 2000.

establishment of an Iraq review. Three panels on disarmament, prisoners of war and missing Kuwaitis, and the humanitarian situation were appointed under the chairmanship of Ambassador Celso Amorim, Brazil's Permanent Representative at the United Nations in New York. This was good news for us in Baghdad.

My UN colleagues in Baghdad and I wanted to believe that our respective notes, reports, telephone conversations and visits to UN headquarters had contributed to this development. It was the first time that the UN Security Council had agreed to carry out a special assessment of the humanitarian situation in Iraq. Would this be a new and more responsible beginning for the Council's Iraqi oversight mandate, or just a one-off ad hoc review to meet the demands of an increasing number of governments and people in the Arab world, Europe, Africa and Asia who felt that the Iraqi sanctions had become intolerable? I would be able to convey to the Security Council panel the concerns over the flawed UN policy on the humanitarian exemption for Iraq. There was excitement in the UN community in Baghdad: who would serve on the panel? When would the hearings begin? How should we prepare for it?

One thing was clear: we would make a joint report with each UN agency concentrating on its mandate and special concerns within the context of the Oil-for-Food Programme. This unique opportunity to argue for change, to make the UN involvement less punitive had to be used to the best advantage. This news helped to ease the tension which we all felt following four nights of heavy bombing in December during Operation Desert Fox. Adding to the tension was the decision on 4 January 1999 by the Iraqi Government to ask the United Nations to withdraw all staff of US and UK nationalities since the Iraqi authorities would be 'unable to ensure the security of nationals from these two countries'.[194]

The group of senior UN staff in Baghdad was made up of highly interactive people. We met regularly and were quite at ease with each other, even though there was at times disagreement on the specifics of policy. The announcement of the establishment of a humanitarian panel in New York enhanced our gregariousness. We were eager to discuss a strategy for preparing our contribution. Shared meals, visits to each other's offices, meetings where all the UN representatives would come together characterised these days in early February 1999. It was clear to us in UNOCHI, FAO, UNICEF, WFP, UNDP, WHO and UNESCO that we would have to put together a persuasive document on the social conditions in Iraq. There was unanimity among us that we must assemble

---

194. About twenty American and British UN staff members – victims of politics following the December 1998 air-strikes – left Iraq on 3 February 1999. On that day, the UN system lost some of its most dedicated staff, e.g., Darlene Bisson of the World Food Programme.

material for which there had never been any space in the reports we normally were asked to prepare for New York. Excellent team work and an appropriate division of labour ensued. The surprising (and refreshing) absence of any 'guidance' from the Office of the Iraq Programme at UN headquarters allowed us a free hand in preparing this important compilation about the human situation in Iraq. In the preamble to the document we pointed out that we were 'guided by the basic principles of the universality and indivisibility of human rights and by our daily realisation of the grave problems the Iraqi people encounter and have to cope with'.[195] Despite the shortage of time, some lack of rigorously collected data of recent origin and, in some areas lack of competence, e.g., in judging the extent and strength of the parallel (illegal) economy, we were able to put together a compendium which covered most of the major and most serious social issues of concern to us. It was unfortunate that we did not have the capacity to present a picture of the life of the average Iraqi family. We knew anecdotally about poor living conditions and domestic violence due to unemployment; delayed marriages because of a lack of money; frequent illness because of malnourishment; poor sanitary conditions and a lack of medicines. All of these constituted major problems with which most Iraqi families had to cope. Besides time and a lack of adequately trained personnel which prevented us from presenting this subject to the UN Security Council, there would have been, most likely, objections from the Government for such an enquiry. Similarly, we knew that prostitution had been on the increase in Iraqi cities, particularly in Baghdad. The Ambassador of the Holy See, Archbishop Giuseppe Lazzarotto, for example, mentioned to me the fact that behind his apostolic nunciature a brothel had emerged. We were also told stories of female university students who were working as part-time prostitutes to finance their student life. This was such a sensitive subject in a Muslim society that little was known. Permission to carry out such research, in any case, would never have been given.

In my note to Ambassador Amorim, I conveyed to him[196] that the individual papers we had sent had several commonalities, among them:

• the inadequacy of available resources for the maintenance of minimum standards of physical and mental life for Iraqi citizens;
• the serious deficiency in life chances for Iraqi youth;
• the additive effect of years of shortage and severely restrictive conditions of life;

195. Special Topics on Social Conditions in Iraq, an overview submitted by the UN system in Iraq to the UN Security Council Panel on Humanitarian Issues, Baghdad, 24 March 1999, p. 3.
196. Ibid.; see p. 2 of note dated 24 March 1999.

- signs of depletion of abilities of average citizens to cope in honest and dignified ways.

All UN representatives in Baghdad signed the document and I despatched it on our behalf at the end of March 1999 to the Chairman of the UN Security Council Panel on Humanitarian Issues, Ambassador Amorim. We felt that we had made a solid case on behalf of the Iraqi people. No one, neither in the UN Security Council nor in the humanitarian panel, would be able to misunderstand or even underestimate the seriousness of the message we conveyed. It was a simple message: life for Iraqis had become catastrophic, funding was severely and unnecessarily inadequate to bring about a significant change, the young had become the most severely punished and were becoming handicapped for life as a result of sanctions and the dictatorship. In March 1999, Ambassador Amorim submitted his report to the President of the UN Security Council.[197] From his oral remarks to the Council, his statements to the Press and, most significantly, in the panel report itself, we realised in Baghdad that our message had been understood. Ambassador Amorim and panel members had become convinced of the seriousness of the human condition and were willing to share our concern. In many ways the report was a typical UN document with a tendency to be diplomatic: 'Although member States should not shun their collective responsibility in the face of acute Iraqi humanitarian needs, this does not exempt the Government of Iraq from its own responsibilities ...'.[198] The bottom line, however, addressed the core issues in plain language and with a clear warning which pointed to the UN Security Council: 'Even if not all the suffering in Iraq can be imputed to external factors, especially sanctions, the Iraqi people would not be undergoing such deprivations in the absence of the prolonged measures imposed by the Security Council and the effects of war.' The report continued: 'but even if all the humanitarian supplies were provided in a timely manner the humanitarian programme ... can admittedly only meet a small fraction of the priority needs of the Iraqi people. The gravity of the humanitarian situation of the Iraqi people is undisputable and cannot be overstated.'[199]

The panel's recommendations were totally in line with the perceptions and demands for change made by the United Nations team in Baghdad. We asked that the UN Security Council, *inter alia*, should agree to additional funding; lifting the oil ceiling and concurrently allowing the rehabilitation of the oil industry; supplementary funding outside the Oil-

197. See UN S/1999/356, 30 March 1999.
198. Ibid., p. 45, para. 45.
199. Ibid., pp. 45–6, paras 45–9.

for-Food Programme; borrowing from Iraq's allocations to the United Nations Compensation Commission (UNCC) or better, reducing the percentage of funds allocated to the UNCC; releasing of frozen assets; direct procurement of basic medical, agriculture, pharmaceutical, food and educational items without UN Sanctions Committee's approval; agreeing to a cash component for areas under Baghdad's control; allowing local procurement; no restrictions for hajj-related travels. The Government of Iraq was called upon to improve its capacity for speedy distribution of humanitarian supplies, particularly medicines, to provide better assistance to the internally displaced in areas under its control and to improve its care for vulnerable groups such as the elderly, mentally ill and street children. Prior to the release of the panel report I had gone to New York to appear before the panel.

I arrived at UN headquarters on 21 February 1999. This was my first return visit to New York since I left UN headquarters in early November 1998 for Baghdad. Much had happened during the subsequent four months. The Oil-for-Food Programme was extended at the end of November for another six months. UNSCOM personnel had been asked by the Iraqi Government to leave Iraq in late October but had been allowed to return in mid-November. December had seen four nights of heavy Anglo-American air-strikes. US/UK nationals working for the UN in Iraq had been asked by the Iraqi Government to leave the country in January. The UN Security Council decided to convene three panels on weapons of mass destruction, missing Kuwaitis and the humanitarian situation in Iraq.

During my stay in New York there would be much to discuss. First and foremost it would be an occasion to make the strongest possible case for fundamental changes in carrying out the UN's humanitarian mission in Iraq under sanctions. Meeting the panel would be the obvious priority.

In early February, the Chairman of the panels Ambassador Amorim, had announced the composition of the humanitarian panel. It included Sergio Vieira de Mello, Undersecretary-General of the Office of Humanitarian Affairs; Joseph Stephanides, Director of the Security Council Affairs Division; Benon Sevan, Executive Director of the Office of the Iraq Programme; and Staffan de Mistura, at the time Director of the UN Information Centre in Rome. They all knew the sanctions dilemma well. Staffan de Mistura had served in Iraq as the UN Humanitarian Coordinator before the Oil-for-Food Programme had been established. I had hoped that the panel would include not just UN insiders but some 'outsiders' as well. There were many knowledgeable individuals in organisations such as OXFAM, Save the Children/UK, and Care, who could have provided a broader and most likely bolder perspective. UN officials were not as free in their assessment as persons participating from outside the system. After all, they could not ignore the fact that they had a subordinate relationship with the UN Security Council, the very institution which was one of the parties whose policies were under scrutiny.

I appeared before the panel on 24 February 1999. We met in one of the smaller, windowless conference rooms in the basement of the UN Secretariat. This added a sombre note to the sombre topic that would occupy us for much of the afternoon. There was something unreal and clandestine about this meeting. Some 8,000 miles away from Iraq and behind closed doors, we were reviewing the plight of a nation and the role a dictatorial government and the United Nations had played in creating these conditions. I summarised the content of the UN Baghdad report to the panel: 'Without more funding, measures to de-bureaucratise the procurement of humanitarian supplies, greater confidence in the ability of the UN team in Iraq to monitor the distribution of these supplies, and the concurrent reduction of the high volume of items blocked by the UN Security Council, human suffering in Iraq will further intensify. The United Nations cannot escape the sharing of the blame!'

As I spoke, the panel members' body language, the Chairman's encouragement for me to amplify, and the type of clarifications sought made me confident that most of the panel members really wanted to get to the bottom of the story.

The panel's final report, which was forwarded to the Security Council by Ambassador Amorim on 7 April 1999, showed that UN insiders' restraint did not preclude strong observations on the intolerable human situation. The report conveyed a clear political message, mainly to the UN Security Council, but also to the Iraqi Government: people are suffering; something at long last must be done about it by all parties. I was relieved to realise that my reservation on the panel's insider composition had been unfounded, at least to a large extent.

It would be many months before the UN Security Council finally acted on some of the panel's specific recommendations, especially on the issues of more resources and easing the flow of humanitarian supplies. In October 1999, the Security Council belatedly authorised a one-time additional sale of Iraqi oil of $3.04 billion[200] to make up the shortfall of revenue which had occurred in phases IV and V. A severely under-funded humanitarian programme further curtailed by lower than expected oil revenue during 1998/1999 was allowed to generate additional resources a year after phase IV had ended in November 1998.[201] For whatever

200. See UN S/RES/1266 (1999) adopted by the UN Security Council to make up for what they called the 'humanitarian deficit' in revenue in phases IV and V.
201. For phases IV and V, the respective distribution plans had foreseen $3.1 billion and $2.7 billion respectively; based on the oil revenue earned only $1.8 billion and $1.6 billion had become available. This led to a worsening of the humanitarian situation because many contracts had to be frozen during these two phases.

reasons, political, bureaucratic or both, this was an expensive procrastination in terms of the human cost. Had the UN Security Council wanted to have an early warning system, it would not have waited a year.

It was not until the UN Security Council adopted the controversial Resolution 1284 on 17 December 1999,[202] just before ending the 54th General Assembly, that some of the humanitarian panel recommendations were accepted and reflected in the resolution. Instead of adopting these recommendations outside a formal resolution and implementing them with the urgency they deserved, the UN Security Council had waited a long time. The recommendations were then politicised by including them in a successor resolution to Resolution 687 of April 1991, which once again linked economic sanctions and disarmament. The Iraqi Government was quick to condemn the resolution. In a Press Release entitled 'Why we reject SCR 1284', the Foreign Ministry criticised that 'Iraq's legitimate demand to lift the embargo' was not met; the resolution constituted a 'rewriting of Resolution 687 (1991) in a tendentious and illegal manner'; the resolution was aiming 'at bringing back a special commission (UNSCOM) in a new disguise ... to resume its intelligence activities' and 'Iraq will not be offered anything other than "suspension" (of economic sanctions)'.[203] Dr Hans Blix, the head of the UNMOVIC, must have been relieved that Resolution 1284 made it clear, in contrast to earlier resolutions,[204] that UN inspectors would be 'international civil servants' of his choice and paid for by the United Nations from its overhead allocations out of Iraq oil revenue. There would be no more inspectors on loan from and paid for by governments. This would reduce the opportunity for bilateral 'intelligence piggy-backing', as he called it.

An Iraqi professor at Baghdad University summed up the general rejection in Iraq of this resolution by quoting a proverb well known in the Middle East: 'The mountain went into labour and then a mouse was born!' The Iraqis simply saw 1284 as a step backwards in defining conditions for ending economic sanctions. While Resolution 687 had stated in paragraph 22 that sanctions would end once Iraq had 'completed all actions contemplated ...', Resolution 1284 specified[205] that sanctions would only be 'suspended' for a period of 120 days and renewable by the Council if Iraq had proved not to have acquired prohibited items in the meantime. Inclusion in Resolution 1284 of humanitarian panel

---

202. See UN S/RES/1284 of 17 December 1999. This resolution was adopted by eleven 'yes' votes and four abstentions (China, France, Russia, as permanent members and Malaysia as an elected member).
203. A Press release handed to the author on 26 February 2000 by an Iraqi delegation at a conference in Brussels.
204. For example, Resolutions 687 and 699 of 1991.
205. UN/S/RES/1284 (1999), 17 December 1999, para. 33.

recommendations again deprived the Iraqi people of an immediate improvement of their condition.

Dr Blix felt 'quite happy' with this resolution because 'sanctions could be suspended rather than lifted ...' in return for cooperation evidenced by 'progress in "key" – rather than all – remaining disarmament issues'.[206] From his vantage point as a disarmament expert I could understand his reaction. My conclusion, however, was quite different. Comprehensive economic sanctions and disarmament remained inextricably linked in Resolution 1284 and all recommendations for improving human conditions made by the Amorim panel and us in Baghdad were on hold until the Government of Iraq satisfied the Council with regard to weapons of mass destruction. It was for this reason that I could not share Dr Blix's position. This resolution was definitely not in the interest of a population badly in need of help.

Not just the Amorim panel hearings kept me busy during the week in New York. There was a long list of persons I had to meet. It included the Under Secretary-General of the Office of Internal Oversight Services, Dr Karl Paschke, with whom I discussed the complex issues of audits of the Oil-for-Food Programme. I strongly felt that there had to be periodic integrated audits of this multibillion dollar programme involving all the participating UN entities in addition to reviews of individual components. Such integrated audits did not exist, making it impossible to have an audited overview of the Oil-for-Food Programme as a whole. Additionally, I was not satisfied with the quality of external audits: the time these auditors would spend with us was much too short and their reports superficial.

The Government of Iraq, at fairly regular intervals, thought it had cause to declare members of the UN staff *persona non grata* for a variety of alleged offences. These ranged from taking photographs of presidential palaces to the export of alleged antiquities, computer hacking or coming too close to off-limit areas, including military installations. The UN Assistant Secretary-General for Legal Affairs, Ralph Zacklin, and his staff were helpful in suggesting ways of how best to respond in such circumstances. The UN Treasurer, Suzane Bishopric, was the person with whom I had to find a solution to our monthly 'moment of scare'. In the absence of normal banking services in Baghdad, every thirty days we had to transport, overland, between $1 and 2 million in cash to meet our local payroll and other costs. For security reasons we would change the routes bringing in the money either via Kuwait and the UNIKOM offices at the line of control between Iraq and Kuwait or via Amman. It was an impossible situation which was eventually acknowledged by the US Foreign Assets Control Office (FACO) in Washington. To the surprise of

206. See Blix 2004, pp. 39 and 54.

both the UN Treasurer and I, they ultimately did agree to the formula which I had negotiated with the Iraq Central Bank. The UN in Baghdad would request the Iraqi Central Bank to let us have the amount we needed in cash: 'If you ask us for $20 million we need a few days. Anything less you can have at any time. We will be glad to transport these funds to your offices at the Canal Hotel in one of our armoured vehicles', Dr Abdul Munaiam Rashid, Deputy Governor of the Central Bank, told me. Given the hard-line approach that the US Government had followed, the United States Treasury in Washington could have blocked this agreement. In fact, we did not think they would go along with it. The Treasury in Washington, however, did agree, even to the payment to Iraq's Central Bank of a 1.5 percent commission for this service. The US thereby helped to end the UN cash transport saga.

A myriad of implementation problems needed to be discussed with the Executive Director of the Office of the Iraq Programme (OIP), Benon Sevan, the Department of Peacekeeping Operations (DPKO), responsible for OIP recruitment and personnel management and the Office of the UN Security Coordinator (UNSECCORD). For reasons that made little sense to me, the Executive Director of the OIP served concurrently as the head of the office that backstopped security management in some 140 countries with UN programmes.[207] My main concern in my meeting with Sevan was over the erratic quality of staff proposed for UN assignments in Iraq and conditions of service for UN staff in Iraq.

In retrospect, I realised that despite promises by both OIP and DPKO officials to scrutinise applications of candidates more thoroughly and to remove anomalies in conditions of service for mission personnel, nothing changed. Poor reference checks or worse, deliberate 'placements of convenience', continued as before. Anomalies of service conditions, including the fact that the majority of UN staff did not have medical insurance for their family members back home, remained, much to my annoyance. This was truly irresponsible: I made no secret of my views. Neither did I withhold my concern over the existing management structure. 'I cannot see any logic for having half the United Nations observers reporting directly to New York', I argued; 'This is not an issue we can discuss since the Security Council has made it clear that it wants a direct channel of contact between the UN in Baghdad and New York'. We should also have discussed the fact that all key administrative units (finance, personnel, logistics) reported directly to UN headquarters. These were two topics I would raise again and again in the course of my tenure in Baghdad. On this occasion, I asked Sevan: 'Do you know what it means

207. This ended only in May 2002 when the United Nations appointed Tun Myat as the UN Security Coordinator in New York. Myat, a national of Myanmar, had been my successor in Baghdad in 2002.

for the management of the humanitarian programme if half the staff in my office report directly to UN headquarters?' He shrugged his shoulders, thus ending this part of our meeting. Later in the year, during another visit to UN headquarters in June of 1999, I found that Secretary-General Annan had not been made aware of this state of affairs.[208] He reacted with disbelief and a promise to rectify this serious anomaly.

During my meeting with the UN Secretary-General on 1 March 1999, we discussed other issues. I briefed him on my meeting with the Amorim panel, particularly on our concern in Baghdad about the additive effects of prolonged deprivation on the Iraqi civilian population. Kofi Annan shared my concern. Unlike Benon Sevan's rejection of my initiatives to promote confidence-building measures between the Government in Baghdad and the local autonomous administration in Iraqi Kurdistan, the Secretary-General listened carefully to the 'one Iraq approach' I outlined to him. It was indeed a sensitive subject that required careful handling. As a contribution to a local peace process he was willing to let me attempt to bring central government and Kurdish administrations together in the implementation of the Oil-for-Food Programme. That this ran counter to policies in Washington and London was as clear to him, I am sure, as it was to me.

When one steps out of the lift on the top floor of the UN Secretariat building, or the '38th floor' as it is called by UN staff and diplomats, a UN security guard, similar to a traffic policeman, ensures that you 'drive' in the right direction – left to the Office of the Secretary-General or right to Louise Frechette, the Deputy Secretary-General. My meeting with Mrs Frechette involved the same issues which I had discussed with Kofi Annan, the Amorim panel hearings and my concern over the social deterioration in Iraq, the situation in Iraqi Kurdistan and the security situation in the no-fly zones after the December 98 US/UK Operation Desert Fox. I had briefly raised the no-fly zones issue with Kofi Annan but discussed it more extensively with Louise Frechette, since security issues were part of her brief. It was a friendly exchange but lacked the warmth that existed during my meetings with Kofi Annan. The picture which I painted for her of conditions in Iraq did not evoke in her the expression of concern which I had expected. Similarly, my reference to the rising number of civilian causalities in the two no-fly zones, termed by the US Central Command in Saudi Arabia as 'enlarged rules of engagement', did not give me the impression that she questioned, as did I, the legality of these incursions into Iraqi airspace. She did not seem willing to grasp the fact that besides the Dictator Saddam Hussein, the UN itself, with its sanctions policy, was playing a major and negative role in this human

208. See Fig. 3: UNOHCI Management Structure, p. 25. This Chart was handed to the UN Secretary-General by the author in June 1999.

drama. 'What is needed is hard core evidence!' I wondered what she meant by 'evidence'? Rigorously carried out reviews of the education and health sectors? Interviews with US and UK pilots about the defensive or offensive nature of their missions? Anecdotal evidence combined with surveys, whenever these were possible, seemed to me adequate options for 'evidence' of unacceptable circumstances. The United Nations Secretariat had, in the interest of human rights and the protection of the Iraqi population, an obligation to bring these realities to the attention of the Security Council. I returned to the Middle East with mixed feelings. The Amorim panel and the sensitivity of Kofi Annan encouraged me to believe that there was at least a chance for change in UN Iraq policy. At the same time, I felt uneasy over the inability of some senior colleagues in New York to fully comprehend what was happening in Iraq and the unparalleled challenges this posed for the United Nations. Had the UN become used to human misery, as do some doctors, to the suffering of a patient? Perhaps. It probably had more to do with the all-pervasive proximity of the United Nations to the tentacles of a superpower. The weight of bilateral authority was on multilateral shoulders.

I used a brief stopover in Amman to brief the 'Iraq watch group' of Ambassadors on developments in Iraq and my visit to New York. Klas Gierow, Swedish Ambassador to Jordan and a friend from the days of a joint posting in Islamabad, was hosting this event and would continue to do so during future visits. For me, it was a further opportunity to discuss the impact of sanctions and convey my knowledge about Iraq's internal situation. We also discussed the alleged pockets of unrest in Baghdad and Southern Iraq. The meeting was attended at the ambassadorial level, except for the UK, which was represented by the Deputy Chief of Mission in Amman. The United States Embassy decided to send no one. I noticed this, but did not think much about it. Later, when my strong reservations concerning US sanction policy had become better known, the absence of US and UK diplomats at various briefings became the norm. I understood that the earlier absence had not been accidental.[209]

The ninety-minute meeting with diplomats who were eager to receive first-hand information about Iraq was lively. Most of them had no representations in Baghdad. Invariably, the issue of who was to be blamed for the suffering of the Iraqi people, figured prominently. It was difficult to convey that the socio-economic plight could not simply be apportioned to one party only. Of course Saddam Hussein was responsible for this situation, but so were some of the governments whose ambassadors or

---

209. Not listening to those who had Iraqi views different from theirs seemed to be a US habit. In 2001 in Geneva, I watched the Head of the US delegation to the UN Human Rights Commission demonstrably take off her earphones the moment Mohamed al Sahaf, Iraq's Foreign Minister began to address the Assembly.

representatives were attending this briefing. A black-and-white picture simply did not represent the reality in Iraq.

A few days later I had a similar meeting at the UN offices in Baghdad with the diplomatic corps accredited to Iraq. The topics were the same as in Amman but the focus was quite different. Diplomats in Baghdad wanted to know how I perceived the chances that the UN Security Council would consider the recommendations of the Amorim panel to improve the delivery of the humanitarian programme. They were less interested in the politics of sanctions and more concerned with humanitarian issues resulting from sanctions and, of course, with trade opportunities.

The reactions to these diplomatic briefings, one in Amman with predominantly Western diplomats who had never been in Iraq and the other in Baghdad with a majority of Arab, Asian and other non-Western diplomats, could not have been more different in perception and attitude. Had the Baghdad group lost its objectivity? Not impossible. Yet, the majority of diplomats and UN officials living in Iraq certainly could distinguish between the impact of a dictatorial regime and the impact of externally imposed sanctions. A discussion about the Oil-for-Food Programme, whether in Baghdad or New York, would invariably refer to the resources situation. At the time of phase v (November 1998 to May 1999) enough experience existed, certainly within the UN Sanctions Committee and the UN Secretariat, to know that even the inadequate financial allocations permitted by the UN Security Council during any single phase could not be fully utilised because of the cumbersome procurement process. The volatility of the resources for the Oil-for-Food Programme was extremely high and predictability of use impossible, even though the only permitted income for this humanitarian programme came from the sale of Iraqi oil. Oil prices fluctuated significantly[210] and the state of Iraq's oil industry was precarious at all times.

Every UN mission coming to Iraq to review the state of the oil industry reported back to the UN Secretary-General and the Security Council that Iraq's oil industry was in a 'lamentable state'. More explicitly, the reports all stated that 'the developed oil fields have had their productivity seriously reduced ... the oil processing and treatment facilities, refineries and storage terminals ... have been severely damaged and continue to deteriorate'. The Security Council removed the oil ceiling in 1999. This was a political trick, as it was well known in the Security Council that in view of the condition of its oil industry Iraq was not in a position to produce more oil. The financing of the humanitarian exemption, upon which an entire nation depended, rested on an extremely precarious foundation.

The early March briefing which I had given to the diplomatic community in Baghdad identified an additional source of danger for

210. See Fig. 1.6, p. 112.

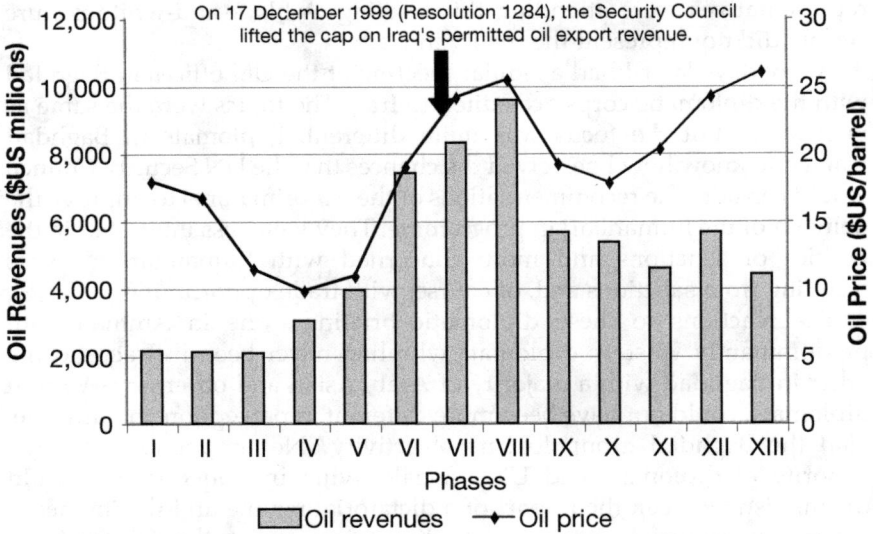

Figure 1.6 Oil Revenues and Oil Prices

Source: *Office of the Iraq Program 'Basic Figures' on the Oil-for-Food Programme (http://www.un.org/Depts/oip/background/basicfigures.html).*
Notes: *The oil price calculated are the phase averages, using volume and revenue information from the Office of the Iraq Programme.*

Iraq's only licit source of income: forced interruption of the oil flow through sabotage, military action or deliberate shutdowns by the Government of Iraq for political reasons.

While I was at UN headquarters, US planes had hit Iraqi oil installations in the northern no-fly zone on 28 February and again on 7 March 1999. Until then we had recorded twenty-six air-strikes since the beginning of the year, none of which, however, had disabled any oil installation in either the southern or northern no-fly zones. On 2 March 1999, the United Nations in New York had issued an extremely carefully worded statement by Executive Director Benon Sevan that he was 'deeply concerned at recent "incidents" which have resulted in an interruption in the flow of oil for export ... any extended stoppage will aggravate further the lack of funding available for humanitarian supplies'.[211] UN language in Baghdad referring to these air-strikes was significantly more to the point: 'On 28 February 1999 at 14.30 hrs. a communication centre of oil repeater station number six some hundred and twenty kilometres south of Zakho was hit by allied missiles. One person was killed and two others

211. UNOIP/New York statement dated 2 March 1999.

injured. On 1 March 1999 at 14.30 hrs. – the same hour as on the previous day! – a second oil control system near Aim Zala (Mosul) was hit. One civilian was killed and nine injured.'[212]

Were these strikes illustrations of enlarged US/UK rules of engagement? No doubt. Evidence of concern for Kurds? Acts of pilots' self defence? Hardly. UN oil overseers carried out site inspections and verified the damage.

Briefings on the Oil-for-Food Programme, whether for the Baghdad diplomatic community or for visiting delegations, were rarely occasions during which 'good news' could be reported. The allied air attacks on oil installations at the end of February and early March 1999, however, represented particularly bad news: it constituted an intensification of confrontation at the expense of the people of Iraq. The meeting with ambassadors at the UN Canal Hotel offices in Baghdad in early March 1999, therefore, ended on a sombre note. We all foresaw continued trouble of this kind; as events unfolded during 1999 we were to be proven correct.

The UN Secretary-General's Review and the Reactions of the UN Security Council

The Office of the Iraq Programme in New York had conveyed to the Security Council in January 1999 that the UN Secretariat would carry out a two-year assessment of the Oil-for-Food Programme for 1996–8. At first I thought that this would be an unnecessary duplication of the work of the Amorim panel; on reflection, I changed my mind. Amorim had had the opportunity to present his conclusions at the political level; we in Baghdad and New York would review and report the specifics of the programme at the operational level. These reviews, coincidentally, complemented each other in presenting a convincing case to the Security Council for fundamental policy changes. Ambassador Amorim's report had been presented to the UN Security Council in early April, the UN Secretary-General's report reached the Council on 28 April 1999.

At the outset, the Secretary-General's report reiterated Ambassador Amorim's strong concern and criticism of available funding levels. 'Even if all supplies arrived on time, what was being provided ... would be insufficient to address, even as a temporary measure, all the humanitarian needs of the Iraqi people ... I recommend that the Council ... re-examine the adequacy of the revenues ... to meet Iraq's priority humanitarian requirements.'[213] Ambassador Amorim rightly did not go into such

---

212. UNOHCI/Baghdad spokesman's statement dated 2 March 1999.
213. See UN/S/1999/481, 26 April 1999, p. 3, para. 10.

details. It was important that the Secretary-General, on the other hand, should do so. He stressed the multi-sectoral nature of the humanitarian crisis, for example, the links between water and sanitation, electricity and health conditions. While he recognised the inadequate allocation by the UN Security Council, he questioned the capacity of the oil industry to generate higher levels of production, should this be allowed by the Council.[214] He reminded the Council of his repeated recommendations to simplify the cumbersome process of contracting, processing, approving and procuring humanitarian supplies.[215] No one was better placed than the UN Secretariat in New York to assess staffing strength in the Office of the Iraq Programme in relation to the high volume of work required to administer a multi-billion dollar Iraq supply programme. The Secretary-General's report pointed out what a shortage of staff meant for timely processing of humanitarian contracts. Iraqis who depended on humanitarian supplies from abroad had to wait and suffer because of an inadequate number of UN personnel in New York.

The Secretary-General also criticised the inordinate volume of holds put on vital supplies by the UN Sanctions Committee. The procedures adopted by the UN Sanctions Committee were likewise identified as a serious bottleneck, even though the Secretary-General observed 'considerable improvement'. This may have been a tactical observation since at the time we in Baghdad observed no improvement at all in the Sanctions Committee bureaucracy: on the contrary, the volume of holds was on the increase.[216]

We appreciated the references in the report to the 'urgent need for training' and the equally urgent need for 'accurate data'.[217] UNICEF Representative Dr Anupama Rao Singh, other UN colleagues and I often reminded Government and the UN that training, institution building and the collection of reliable data had been severely neglected in all the humanitarian distribution programmes. To ignore these would constitute an extreme disservice to the Iraqi people.

The report of the Secretary-General showed sector by sector the inadequacy of the Oil-for-Food Programme. This revelation was what we in Baghdad had encouraged. A lack of funding had forced scaling back the caloric value of the food basket. The overall health situation had not improved, in part, because of the 'inefficiency' in the ordering, processing

214. See Fig. 1.8, p. 133.
215. Ibid, p. 4, para. 15.
216. At the end of the assessment report, the UN Secretary-General made a reference to the need for improvement when he wrote: 'I wish to invite the [Sanctions] Committee to review its procedures further with a view to expediting the processing of applications and reducing the number of applications on hold.'
217. Ibid., pp. 14–15.

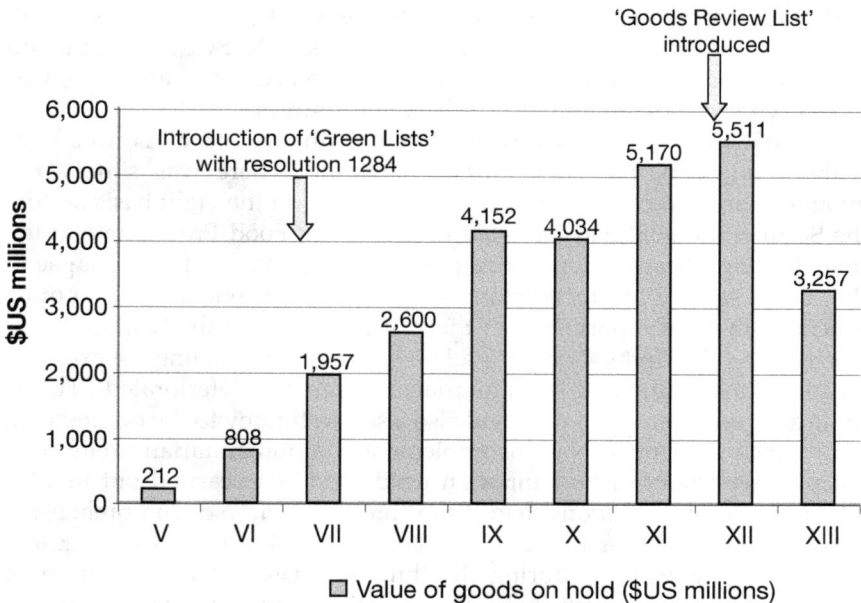

Figure 1.7 Balance of Holds in Phases V to XIII ($US millions)

Source: *Secretary-General's 180-day reports on the Oil-for-Food Programme, phases IV–XIII.*

Notes: *No data are available on holds before phase V. Data for phase V refers to contracts from phases IV and V only and might therefore understate the total number of holds. Also, the definition of holds is different in phase XIII, owing to the introduction of new procedures for the approval of contracts.*

and delivery of medical supplies. Some improvement could be seen in the volume of treated water available in urban areas. Yet there was no 'clear reduction in the incidence of water-borne diseases'.[218] While the report did not mention drought as a factor, it concluded that local food production should have met a larger part of food needs than it actually did. It reported that 'a severe shortage of essential inputs occurred as well as a continuous deterioration of basic infrastructure and support services'. The FAO representative had rightly insisted that the Secretary-General's report include a reference to the fact that wheat imported under the Oil-for-Food Programme had 'significantly undermined the demand for locally produced wheat leading to a sharp fall in wheat prices in the local market'.[219] Not allowing local cereal purchases had been a particularly irresponsible decision of the UN Security Council. The

218. Ibid.
219. Ibid.

electricity supply situation, the report pointed out, remained poor in all parts of the country. The report confirmed what UNESCO, UNICEF and UNOCHI had stressed repeatedly: the education sector, at all levels, was in a very poor state, mainly due to lack of resources.

The red thread of the assessment of the situation in all sectors was, without question, the poor funding situation. There was simply not enough money to cover minimum requirements in the eight basic sectors the Security Council had included in the Oil-for-Food Programme at the time. It is significant for an understanding of the causes of the collapse of the Iraqi society under dictatorship and comprehensive economic sanctions that the report stresses that 'At the outset of the [Oil-for-Food] Programme, the United Nations had no information detailing the extent to which infrastructure and humanitarian services had deteriorated'. This is quite an important admission, and also a sad testimony to the carelessness with which the United Nations implemented a humanitarian exemption. No pre-assessment of humanitarian needs had been carried out in 1990 when economic sanctions had been pronounced. No comprehensive quantitative review was made either before the Oil-for-Food Programme started, in late 1996, or during the thirteen phases of this programme which lasted until March 2003. This deficiency will professionally and morally haunt the United Nations for a long time to come.

The recommendations contained in the Secretary-General's report linked in well with Ambassador Amorim's panel's report. Both stressed the need for raising the level of funding. The Secretary-General's report, however, made an important amplification to this recommendation by suggesting 'complementary assistance'[220] from the international community to ensure that in future at least minimum needs could be met in case earnings from the sale of Iraqi oil would be insufficient.

The Security Council should have considered such a formula since the very beginning of sanctions. Yet even with this belated proposal the Council never adopted such a mixed financing during the entire Oil-for-Food Programme period. Financial uncertainty, with all the complications for the Iraqi people, continued throughout the sanctions. The Secretary-General also made the point that the supply and distribution approach severely curtailed the impact of the Oil-for-Food Programme. He called – as the UN in Baghdad had repeatedly asked – for funds to cover installation, training and logistics costs for commodities and equipment arriving in Iraq. Hospitals, schools, municipalities, farmers and others often benefited from arrived supplies and equipment only after considerable delays because there were no funds for transport, training and installation. This was, of course, also attributable to the Government of Iraq. They could and should have planned for such expenditures. But it was mainly a problem created

220. Ibid., p. 27, para. 119.

by the sanctions methodology adopted by the UN Security Council. This should have been foreseen and removed at an early date when the negative effects of this policy manifested themselves.

The Secretary-General ended his report with a plea to the UN Security Council and the Government of Iraq – a plea only he could make: 'Depoliticise the humanitarian programme and ... ensure that its distinct identity from other activities undertaken under the sanction regime is maintained.'[221] In plain language, he was asking to de-link economic sanctions and disarmament. The US and UK representatives in the Security Council would never go along with this justified demand, even though they were acutely aware that disarmament was a demand only the Government of Iraq could meet while the burden of economic sanctions fell squarely on the shoulders of the Iraqi people.

The two-year assessment the Secretary-General had submitted to the UN Security Council in April 1999 reflected the UN's and also his own personal concern over the humanitarian crisis in Iraq. The report contained a large number of implementable proposals which, together with those concurrently identified by Ambassador Amorim to the Council in his humanitarian panel report, could have made a substantial difference for the Iraqi people. There was, however, something missing in Kofi Annan's report: an assessment of conditions of life as a result of the immense difficulties in the health, food, water and sanitation and electricity sectors among others. The report focused on supplies and distribution, unfortunately not on the recipients. The human face was absent.

Something had gone terribly wrong at the time. The UN team in Baghdad had been asked by the Office of the Iraq Programme at UN headquarters in New York to comment on the reporting structure suggested by the OIP. We did so with care as we wanted to ensure that the UN Security Council would get a chance to 'see' this Iraqi face.

Detailed proposals for a reporting structure. including sectoral assessments of the implications of inadequacy of medical services, water supply and sanitation, electricity services, nutrition and education, were forwarded to New York. These proposals were never taken into account because they mysteriously 'got lost'. My strong protests to both Deputy Secretary-General Louise Frechette and Executive Director Benon Sevan resulted in a request to come once again to New York. This I did in June of 1999. At a large UN inter-agency meeting called by the UN Deputy Secretary-General, the reports of the Secretary-General and Amorim were reviewed. There was agreement among all those present that these reports showed political courage by criticising in strong terms the inadequacy of the UN humanitarian exemption in Iraq. Everyone recognised the need for fundamental changes. This was the moment

221. Ibid., p. 29, para. 127.

to raise the issue of the 'lost' reporting structure. Following my intervention on the proposals the UN team in Baghdad had recommended on the structure of the report to take account of the human condition in Iraq, Frechette agreed that the disappearance of our submission was 'most unfortunate'. This ended what I perceive as one of the most troubling incidents I had experienced within the United Nations in my then thirty years of service. I felt a tremor rocking the very foundations of the United Nations.

The Amorim panel and the UN/OIP assessment reports compelled the UN Security Council to at least review their approach on Iraq. New York's sense of urgency regrettably did not tally with ours in Baghdad. The recommendations on increased funding, reduction of the volume of blocked humanitarian supplies, on broader rehabilitation of the oil industry, on the provision of cash for national administration and for training were all looked at in the context of the negotiations of a new Iraq resolution as an update to Resolution 687 of April 1991. Improvements of the Oil-for-Food Programme for the sole purpose of making life better for the Iraqis had no chance to be adopted on their own in the summer of 1999. The politics in the Security Council had once again taken precedent over the need to preserve life and dignity in Iraq. The one tangible exception in response to the two reports[222] was the one-time approval of $3.04 billion in October 1999 to make up for the revenue shortfalls in earlier phases. Had there been any real appreciation of conditions in Iraq, this should have happened in April rather than five months later.

It is difficult to understand why, despite the evidence before the UN Security Council, this was not considered an urgent issue for immediate action. The UK representative on the Council, Sir Jeremy Greenstock, in May 1999 referred to 'adjusting the ceiling for Iraq's oil revenue to fund the humanitarian programme, if necessary'. Why did he add 'if necessary'? He knew, as did everyone else in the Council, how desperate the situation was in Iraq and, as his Russian colleague Ambassador Granovsky observed, 'With regard to the humanitarian programme the steps being taken ... are barely sufficient to ensure the physical survival of the population'.[223] It was indeed, once again, a case of 'politics before people'.

In the meantime, the UN Security Council approved a further extension of 180 days of the Oil-for-Food Programme to cover – as phase VI – the period from 25 May to 20 November 1999.[224] For this phase the pattern of implementation remained the same as for the previous phases as well as the subsequent seven phases: the value of humanitarian goods arriving in Iraq during any phase often was significantly less than the

222. See UN SC Resolution 1266 of 4 October 1999.
223. UN Security Council Iraq Debate, 21 May 1999.
224. See UN SC Resolution 1246 of 21 May 1999.

budget approved by the UN Secretary-General.[225] In order to understand the seriousness of this situation it must be remembered that these proposed allocations themselves were always much less than existing minimum needs of the sectors included in the Oil-for-Food Programme. The one welcome exception was phase XI (1 December 2001 to 29 May 2002). The value of goods that arrived during that phase was much higher.[226]

The main reason for this delivery spike was the belated impact of more revenue and therefore more contracts due to the doubling of oil prices from an average of $10 per barrel in late 1998/early 1999 to an average of $21 per barrel in mid/end 2000. It had nothing to do with the introduction of the so-called 'Green List' on 1 March 2000, even though this 'Green List' in principle constituted an improvement in the implementation of the Oil-for-Food Programme and belatedly responded to the repeated calls of the United Nations Secretariat to de-bureaucratise and streamline the procurement of humanitarian supplies. This list, identifying humanitarian supplies such as food, certain medicines and a range of non-dual use items in other sectors for unrestricted import into Iraq, had been proposed in Resolution 1284 adopted by the UN Security Council in December 1999.[227] Ultimately, the 'Green List' did not lead to better delivery of needed supplies.[228] This was acknowledged by the demands from within the Security Council to come up with a better system.

The concept behind the 'Green List' had been to identify and release those items included in distribution plans which were unquestionably of a civilian nature having nothing to do with possible military use. The UN Security Council continuing with its humanitarian 'experimentation' two years later, introduced a revised approach replacing the 'Green List' with a 'Red List'. This so-called 'Goods Review List' or 'GRL' was a 'negative' list identifying those supplies which needed to be cleared by the Sanctions Committee or UNMOVIC/IAEA on behalf of the Sanctions Committee. All humanitarian supplies not on this list no longer had to be cleared by any authority except the UN Secretariat. It was the exact reverse of the earlier Green-List approach, a better alternative which came much too late.

In contrast to the delivery in all the earlier phases (I–X), including those phases which were supposed to benefit from the 'Green List' (phases VII–X), the Goods Review List approach did have a positive impact on the

---

225. For example for phase VIII (9 June – 5 December 2000), the approved budget was $7.1 billion, the value of arrived goods $ 763 million or 10.7 percent.
226. The value of arrived goods amounted to $6.1 billion exceeding the budget of $4.4 billion by 32 percent, as Table 1 shows.
227. See UN SC Resolution 1284 of 17 December 1999, para. 17: 'directs the Committee ... to approve ... lists of humanitarian items; supplies of these items will not be submitted for approval ...'.
228. See Table 1.

flow of humanitarian supplies into Iraq. Delivery during the last two phases (xii and xiii) was indeed better.[229] It is not unreasonable to argue that if the UN Security Council had wanted to base its approach on Iraqi needs and had translated these into quantified targets, namely goods and services, and furthermore adapted procedures to meet these needs and targets, the goods review list approach could have been introduced in the early 1990s. It did not have to wait many years before it was finally adopted in May 2002. Instead the UN Security Council chose to politicise a humanitarian programme using Iraq as a veritable economic and social sanction experimentation chamber.

Following the transmission in 1999 of the reports of Ambassador Amorim, the UN Secretariat's two-year assessment of the Oil-for-Food Programme and the UN/Baghdad's only multi-sectoral review of social conditions in Iraq, the UN team in Iraq watched from a distance with awe and disbelief during the rest of the year the awkward wrangling within the UN Security Council to come up with a new Iraq sanction policy.

Finally, on 17 December 1999, the last day of the 54th General Assembly, Resolution 1284 was passed by the UN Security Council. The suggested improvements for the Oil-for-Food Programme[230] were made dependent on Iraq's cooperation in disarmament. They were thus kept in the 'steel case' of this resolution for which the Iraqi people did not have the keys: these were in the hands of only the United States and Iraq.

Ambassador Alain Déjammet, Permanent Representative of France to the UN, in his statement to the UN Security Council in 17 December 1999 explaining the reservation of his Government to Resolution 1284, echoed UN views in Baghdad when he said: 'We would have wished that the recommendations (of the Amorim panel) had been implemented by the (UN) Secretariat since April 1999'.[231]

In the absence of air traffic,[232] all travellers to Iraq had to use the Amman-Baghdad highway. Not far from Baghdad, they would pass on the right side of the motorway the high watchtowers of Abu Ghraib, the best known of Iraq's notorious jails. There, heavily armed guards made sure that no inmate would even attempt to escape. Visitors in my office would question me about this jail. How many inmates? Are Kuwaitis kept there? Other foreigners? Is the US pilot allegedly captured during the

---

229. Delivery amounted to 82 percent of the revenue available during these phases. In contrast, during the first phases (i–iii), the value of arrived humanitarian supplies came to only 58 percent of the finances available during this period.
230. This involved a cash component for local purchases, increased revenue, 'fast-track' procedures for the flow of humanitarian supplies, etc.
231. Press Release, Mission of France to the UN, New York, 17 December 1999.
232. Due to the embargo, only occasional humanitarian flights were permitted into Iraq by the UN Security Council.

1991 Gulf War still there? What about executions in Abu Ghraib? I could not answer any of those questions: no one within the UN community could, except possibly the UN Human Rights Rapporteur Max van der Stoel. He, however, had not been in Iraq since 1991 but found the information received from Iraqis living abroad compelling enough to include it in his reports to the UN Human Rights Commission in Geneva.

Many individuals and groups from abroad came to the UN complex at the Canal Hotel in Baghdad to be briefed. I had little to say about the nefarious ways of Iraqi intelligence and the prevailing judicial system but much about the humanitarian situation, the Oil-for-Food Programme and the impact of economic sanctions. 'Can we record what you are saying? What about statistics on health, nutrition, food, education? Can you brief us on the no-fly zones and the casualties resulting from the air-strikes?' Secretary-General's Chef de Cabinet, Iqbal Riza, had repeatedly cautioned me to confine such briefings to factual issues. He was right; I tried to do so. I was convinced that the facts on child mortality, malnutrition, school dropout rates, unemployment, polluted water, electricity shortages, and poor animal health due to lack of veterinary services would speak for themselves. A detailed description of the working of the UN Iraq Sanctions Committee and the procurement process involved in getting humanitarian supplies into Iraq would also allow the visitors to draw their conclusions as they would after hearing about civilian casualties in the no-fly zones resulting from air strikes by the US and UK air forces. I did not have to carry out assessments, they could do it themselves. And they did quite successfully as I would learn from their reports whenever I got these in Baghdad.

What I overlooked was the fact that journalists were not infrequently 'embedded' within these groups of visitors. The articles which they ultimately published, mostly in Europe and North America, would often mix facts which I had presented with their own interpretations, making it look as if I had been openly accusatory of the UN Security Council's sanctions policy. This did not remain unnoticed in Washington, London, New York and elsewhere. Towards the end of 1999 a 'media leash' was put around my vocal cords: on 23 November 1999, the Secretary-General's Chef de Cabinet conveyed to me, in a note, press guidelines which the Secretary-General wanted me to observe. Among these were that it was not 'within the Humanitarian Coordinator's mandate to report on matters of a political or military nature unless these impact directly on the implementation of the humanitarian programme', and that 'in relation with the media, the Humanitarian Coordinator will limit his statements to factual matters pertinent to his responsibilities and not make comments which may have policy or political implications without prior clearance from headquarters'. This was quite acceptable to me; I could live with these 'restrictions', at least so I thought. The timing of this somewhat justified censure had less to do with my briefings of visiting peace groups and others interested in the substance of the Oil-for-Food Programme and more with my interaction with the international Press. I realised that I had created difficult moments for the Secretary-General's Office because of interviews I had given in Baghdad to mainstream US and international media.

Douglas Jehl's piece in the *New York Times* of 21 September 1999 reflecting an interview he had with me irked many sanctions hardliners, wherever they were located. 'UN official calls for end of sanctions against Iraq' was the provocative heading the *New York Times* had given to this article. I was quoted as having warned of 'the dangers of using "the human shield" in hopes of "coaxing" Iraqi concessions on arms issues' and recommending to 'remove the humanitarian discussions from the rest in order to end a silent human tragedy'. I cannot deny that this article was a fair reflection of what I had said. It was not long before Iqbal Riza was on the telephone expressing his concern and making me aware that his office had received many calls seeking clarification. The first caller apparently had been Kuwait's Permanent Representative to the UN, who facetiously wanted to know whether the position I had taken in the *New York Times* interview 'reflected a new UN Iraq policy'. In the confines of my office in Baghdad, far away from the battlegrounds of world politics in New York, I could not help but chuckle when I heard this. But I also began to realise then that crossing the threshold from being an 'obedient civil servant' to following my conscience entailed costs.

Among those who came to Baghdad at regular intervals were groups from Spain, Italy and France. In 1999 they would come in busloads – 160 Spaniards, over a hundred Italians, smaller numbers of others. They would set up camp across the highway in front of the UN offices at the Canal Hotel. 'Down with sanctions', 'lift the unjust embargo', 'UN leave Iraq alone', their banners read. They were of all ages, with the young in the majority. We could see them distributing leaflets, trying to engage UN staff entering or leaving the UN compound in a discussion about UN policies. The Iraqi police let them be and did not interfere: they seemed bemused at these foreigners intervening on behalf of Iraqis. I often wondered to myself what Iraq would be with all its wealth of human, cultural and financial resources if the freedom of expression displayed by these groups from abroad were also be granted to Iraqis.

I took time to meet with these groups and was always amazed by the diversity of their backgrounds. There were doctors, priests, ministers, professors, retired civil servants, students, housewives – a true cross-section of their societies, united in their reaction to what they perceived as a seriously wrong international policy.

Apart from curious journalists who had been fortunate to get Iraqi visas, there were few other visitors from Europe, hardly anyone from Scandinavia, and a sprinkling from the Benelux countries, Germany and the United Kingdom. The country from which more peace groups came than from any other country was the United States. They were often led by Kathy Kelly, the dainty, middle-aged woman from Chicago who headed a peace activist group known by peers as 'VitW', or 'Voices in the Wilderness'. Under her leadership a social movement for peace and justice at home and abroad had evolved in the United States ever since the 1991 Gulf War. Year after year she and her group came to Iraq on humanitarian missions, helping in their small way poor families to survive and raising awareness back home of the conditions international politics had created in Iraq. Jail sentences for taking medicines to Iraq, fines, threats to close her small office in Chicago by the FBI – nothing prevented this strong woman from persevering and carrying on with her mission.[233] She became a true icon of the international conscience. The humanity shown by Kelly and her compatriots and their call for an end to the tragedy in Iraq stood in stark contrast to the official position of their government. In the words of Ambassador Peter Burleigh, Acting US Permanent Representative to the UN: 'The United States has a deep and enduring interest in the welfare of Iraqi citizens … we note with satisfaction the demonstrable success of this important humanitarian effort … it has brought about a significant improvement in living conditions for Iraqi civilians.'[234] This is what the 'official' Washington argued in the UN Security Council.

How could anyone come to such conclusions when report after report from the UN system and from non-governmental organisations documented the catastrophic conditions created by UN economic sanctions? There were hardly any US visitors in Iraq from the 'official' Washington. Those who came believing in the justification for sanctions and then saw for themselves conditions under which people lived often went away with views much closer to ours in the United Nations in Baghdad. In this context I remember vividly the visit of a five-member US Congressional aides delegation.[235] Four of them came with ambivalent positions on their Government's sanction policy; the fifth, Amos Hochstein, representing Sam Gejdenson, a Conservative Democrat in the US Congress from Connecticut, did not hesitate to state at the first of a series of meetings we had in my office that he had come to Iraq to squarely defend the hard-line position of both Congress and the White House.

After a week of visits to schools, hospitals, water and sanitation works, and meetings with government officials including Deputy Prime Minister

233. In 2005 Kathy Kelly's Chicago office was closed by the FBI.
234. See UN Security Council, 4008th meeting, New York, 21 May 1999, p. 3.
235. The US Congressional delegation included Brian Sims, Amos Hochstein, Jack Zylman, Peter Hickey and Danielle Leclair representing Danny Davis (D-IL), Sam Gijdenson (D-CT), Earl Hillard (D-AL), Cynthia McKinney (D-GA) and Bernard Sanders (I-VT) respectively.

Tariq Aziz, as well as detailed briefings from UN and NGO staff, the four were seemingly depressed by what they had seen and heard. According to their trip report, the visit had been planned 'out of increasing concern in (the US) Congress and among the American people about the humanitarian impact of US policy in Iraq'.[236] Amos Hochstein remained convinced that economic sanctions had to remain but, to my surprise, conceded that there was a need to 'humanise' these sanctions. While I did not think that this was likely to happen, I was encouraged by the impression that conditions in the country had made on him and the rest of the US delegation. What he did hide, as I subsequently found out, was that he had met 'on the side' with Under-Secretary Nizar Hamdoun of the Iraqi Foreign Ministry to discuss a 'hot' political issue: the possible resettlement of several thousand Palestinians in Central Iraq in return for the lifting of economic sanctions. I assume that this was an 'assignment' rather than merely raised out of his personal curiosity.

In meetings, following this visit, with the head of the US interests section in Baghdad, I raised the issue of such Congressional visits hinting that more aides and possibly US Congressmen and women, as well as US senators, should be encouraged to find their way to Baghdad. Unfortunately this did not happen as the official US position on Iraq became harder and harder in the months and years ahead.[237]

The profound dichotomy of perception between those in political office and members of the public was not just a characteristic of the situation in the United States.

During visits to the British House of Commons and the House of Lords, I sensed widespread uneasiness about the uncompromising stand that the Government of Tony Blair had been taking on Iraq. Two Labour MPs, Tony Benn and George Galloway,[238] were among the most severe critics of the British Government's Iraq policy. Benn, participating in an

236. Their report also refers to the letter written by forty-three members of the US Congress to President Bill Clinton in October 1998, the same month the US President had signed into law the 'Iraq Liberation Act'. The Congressional letter called on the US administration 'to de-link the economic sanctions which have been a complete failure, from the military sanctions'. See Iraq Trip Report, US Congressional Staff, 27 August to 6 September 1999.
237. In 2000 Tony Hall (D-Ohio) visited Iraq and on his return to Washington spoke out strongly against the impact of sanctions on children in a meeting the author had with him. He also criticised the blocking of contracts by his Government. Apart from him, there were four other congressmen, all Democrats, who in 2002 travelled to Iraq: Jim McDermott (Washington), David Bonior (Missouri), Mike Thompson (California), Nick Rahal (West Virginia).
238. Galloway has since been removed from the Labour Party because of his outspoken criticism of his party's foreign policy. He retains his seat in the British Parliament as an Independent.

Iraq debate in the House of Commons in January 1998, said that he 'hoped that the Prime Minister understands that the charge against British and American Governments is that they are applying sanctions that amount to genocide'.[239] In 1999 Galloway argued, during a similar debate: 'Please do not tell me that food and medicines are not covered by sanctions … if we subject a country to the tightest of mediaeval-style sieges, bankrupt its economy and freeze its international assets, how much food and medicine can it buy?'[240] This was extreme language; the assertions, however, were not wrong and shared by a majority of the British. Many activists' groups, of course, such as CASI,[241] a very committed and professional student group in Cambridge, Voices in the Wilderness (UK), and Friendship across Frontiers, were much more outspoken in their criticism of the UK Government's sanctions policy.

I recall the first of a series of briefings I had with members of the British Parliament in July 1999 in London. The International Development Committee, a committee of eleven MPs from the three major political parties (Labour, Conservatives and Liberal Democrats) chaired by Bowen Wells, a Conservative, had written to the UN Secretary-General's Office requesting that I be allowed to appear before this parliamentary committee to give evidence on the situation in Iraq. In this letter he pointed out that 'a number of groups – including a delegation sent to Iraq by the Archbishop of Canterbury – have recommended that we take evidence from the UN Humanitarian Coordinator in Iraq'. It was many weeks before I received clearance from the UN Secretary-General's Office in New York to travel to London, however, not without objections from the Executive Director of the Iraq Programme. He felt that such UN testimony was not necessary. I, of course, had the opposite view and was anxious to go since the UK Government had been such a staunch defender of an indefensible policy. UN Chef de Cabinet Iqbal Riza approved this briefing on condition that it would be held on camera and that no public statement would be made about the briefing, either before or after.

This was yet another clear indication of the pressure on the United Nations to tow the US/UK line, just like the recurring attempts by the US/UK missions to the United Nations to block briefing visits to the UN Security Council by myself and other UN staff in Baghdad,[242] or to change the reporting format from narrow technical supply accounts to broader reviews of the Oil-for-Food for Programme and its impact on the Iraqi civilian population.

239. House of Commons, London, 13 January 1998.
240. House of Commons, London, 29 June 1999.
241. CASI = Campaign Against Sanctions on Iraq.
242. This US/UK reluctance to hear Baghdad-based UN staff give testimony on conditions in Iraq eased somewhat in the course of 2000 under pressure from the rest of the UN Security Council.

The meeting at Westminster 'behind closed doors' was attended, in addition to the MPs, to my surprise by the Director of the UN Information Centre in London, Ahmed Fawzi. Maybe the UN Secretariat felt that not only the Committee should have a witness but the UN Secretariat should have one as well. I had known Fawzi for a good number of years; his presence did not disturb me. In any case, I had nothing to disclose to the Committee that I had not already brought to the attention of the UN Secretary-General and other colleagues in New York or to the UN Security Council or, for that matter, to Ambassadors Greenstock and Eldon of the UK mission in New York. In conveying to the Parliamentary Committee my account of the severe impact of economic sanctions and the damage that was being inflicted by the air forces of the UK and US, I also referred to the illegality of the establishment of the two no-fly zones. The Committee had been dealing with Iraq for several years and knew what I was talking about.

Before my departure for London, the security unit in my office in Baghdad, in cooperation with my British-Canadian spokesman, George Somerwill, had handed me a copy of the latest air-strike report that we had prepared with photographs of the damaged sites in Basrah, Mosul and other locations. These were places where particularly gruesome air-strike incidents had taken their civilian toll. The Committee, including Ann Clywd, a Labour MP known to be a sanctions supporter, appreciated the effort on my part to shed light on one of the less well known aberrations of US/UK heavy handiness condoned by the UN Security Council, even though international law and Iraq's sovereignty were being violated.

The Committee gave me all the time I needed to present an overview of social conditions, as I had done earlier in the year to the Amorim panel in New York. I spoke at length on the fateful bureaucratisation of the Oil-for-Food Programme, the lack of oversight on the part of the UN Security Council, the patriarchal manner in which the UN Sanctions Committee dominated the implementation of the humanitarian programme, and the unfortunate support role played by the UK authorities in reinforcing the US Government at the United Nations in their appetite for blocking billions of dollars worth of much needed supplies in the water, sanitation and electricity sectors as well as the oil industry. The ensuing questions of the MPs reflected not only their interest and concern, but also their knowledge of Iraq's plight. Seven months later, the House of Commons published their report entitled 'The Future of Sanctions'.[243] In the course of a year, the Committee had called twenty witnesses of all backgrounds and persuasions, from Kurdish political groups to British Intelligence,

243. UK House of Commons (session 1990–2000), International Development Committee, The Future of Sanctions, London, 27 January 2000.

diplomats, Her Majesty's Treasury, academics, and non-governmental organisations with long experience in Iraq such as Save the Children/UK. Present, of course, was also a major defender of British sanction policies, Peter Hain, Minister of State in the Foreign and Commonwealth Office. I was truly elated when I read the Committee's conclusions on sanctions against Iraq: 'We find it difficult to believe that there will be a case in the future where the UN would be justified in imposing comprehensive economic sanctions on a country ... [as] such sanctions cause significant suffering.'[244] This perception was good news. The non-partisan approach of the report set an example to other parliaments in Europe and elsewhere to conduct similar hearings. It ultimately failed to change the British Government's Iraq policy because Whitehall stubbornly argued, as Minister of State in the Foreign and Commonwealth Office Peter Hain consistently did, 'it is not right to blame sanctions for that suffering, nor would the situation necessarily improve if sanctions were lifted'.[245] This is an insight into the rigidity of the Iraq approach of the British Labour Government. Neither the British public nor the United Nations team in Baghdad could comprehend how anyone could possibly come to such a false conclusion. No wonder then that Peter Hain became one of the targets of the UK anti-sanctions movement. For us in Iraq the British Government's recalcitrant attitude was demoralising because we thought, ultimately wrongly, that the mountain of evidence against the prevailing sanctions policy had to lead to genuine changes for the benefit of an exhausted and paralysed society.

Instead, 1999 remained a year of contradictions. There were some hopeful signs for change, spearheaded by China, France and Russia, the P3 Group in the UN Security Council, and by signs of sanctions fatigue in the Middle East, particularly among neighbouring countries. Jordan, Syria and Turkey felt they had long been deprived of their pre-sanction lucrative trading relationships with Iraq, and were therefore increasingly enlarging the holes that had appeared in the sanctions regime by trading with Iraq outside the framework of the Oil-for-Food Programme. At the same time they were evoking their rights for compensation for loss of trade as a result of the UN imposed sanctions.[246]

During travels in and out of Iraq, I myself witnessed the increase in the number of trucks at the Jordanian/Iraqi border which bypassed the goods inspection post that Cotecna, the UN-appointed Swiss agency, had established.

244. Ibid., p. XVII.
245. House of Commons Hansard Debates, 8 February 2000, p. 4.
246. The UN Charter in Article 50 establishes that countries 'confronted with special economic problems arising from carrying out those measures shall have the right to consult the Security Council with regard to a solution to these problems'.

Besides sanctions fatigue and sanctions breaking there was also intensifying sanctions anger among human rights groups across the globe. Never had a single issue such as the Iraq sanctions brought so many people in so many countries on to the streets. The public conscience, or the emerging second 'superpower', as some optimistically called it, certainly rose to the occasion and encouraged us in the UN in Iraq.

The churches were other allies. The World Council of Churches repeatedly called on the United Nations 'to lift immediately all sanctions that have direct and indiscriminate effects on the civilian population of Iraq'. The General Secretary of the WCC, Dr Konrad Raiser, referring to statements made by the WFP representative in Iraq, Jutta Burckardt, and myself on conditions in Iraq in a public letter to Secretary-General Kofi Annan, wrote in early 2000: '[Iraq] sanctions are tantamount to violations by the United Nations itself of the fundamental rights inscribed in international law'.[247] Pope John Paul II, throughout the years of sanctions, spoke in strong words about the Iraq situation: 'I must call upon the consciences of those who, in Iraq and elsewhere, put political, economic or strategic considerations before the fundamental good of the people, and I ask them to show compassion. The weak and the innocent can not pay for mistakes for which they are not responsible.'[248] The Archbishop of Canterbury, Dr George Carey, who had been a vehement critic of the international sanctions policy on Iraq all along, observed: 'We have had eleven years of sanctions and there is no doubt they bite. Unfortunately, they have bitten the wrong people … ordinary Iraqis.'[249] The Church of England, in May 1999,[250] sent a delegation of Anglican Bishops to Iraq with the full support of the Archbishop of Canterbury. The Bishop of Coventry, John Bennett, the Bishop of Kingston, Peter Price and the Bishop of Cyprus and the Gulf, Clive Handford, accompanied by Canon Andrew White, who had been in Iraq before, came to Baghdad well prepared. They had studied the documentation, had met, prior to their visit, with British Government officials and Church groups as well as the public. Their time in Iraq with UN agencies, NGOs and their site visits merely heightened their awareness of the humanitarian crisis[251] and how

247. See 'Iraq on the WCC Agenda: Recent Policy Documents & Statements, World Council of Churches', May 2004.
248. Political Council for Justice and Peace, John Paul II, and the Family of Peoples, The Holy Father to the Diplomatic Corps (1978–2002), Vatican City, p. 264.
249. *The Times*, 16 October 2001.
250. 3–10 May 1999.
251. The three bishops used the opportunity of their visit to hold an early morning mass in the ruins of the British cathedral in Baghdad. An old Iraqi caretaker and myself were the 'congregation', witnessing moving sermons from churchmen in their colourful and magnificent robes praying for peace and justice in an environment of destruction and suffering.

wrong Britain's Iraq sanctions policies were. Father Benjamin, the Jesuit priest whom I got to know well as an outspoken and courageous man of the cloth, wrote at the time I served in Baghdad: 'D'un côté l'ONU lutte, par ses programmes dans le monde, contre ce genre de fléaux et de l'autre la même ONU "sponsorise" un véritable fléau en Irak.'[252]

The world was increasingly divided in its response to the conditions in Iraq. The international public wanted to see an end to economic sanctions. Some governments within the Arab League, e.g., Lebanon, Syria, Jordan and Yemen, shared this position, as did governments within the Organisation of Islamic Countries (OIC), such as Malaysia and Pakistan, as well as the Organisation of the African Union, particularly South Africa. Neither the European Union nor any of its members were prepared to go as far as that: they were content with 'tinkering at the edges' of the sanctions regime but not questioning the continued existence of economic sanctions as such. There was, however, an additive effect of various degrees of anti-sanctions attitudes which forced the hardliners in the UN Security Council to open up to proposals for change. The politicisation of all these attempts to make improvements in the Oil-for-Food Programme by maintaining the link between economic sanctions and the military embargo, as was the case in the run-up to the adoption of Resolution 1284 in 1999, made it a zero sum game for the Iraqi people. The art of procrastination in the UN Security Council had reached greater heights in the years 1999–2000.

The language of some UN Secretariat reports and the Amorim panel had been unambiguous and compelling, yet it was many months before the Council reached a consensus on revenue improvement, raising the level of funding for oil spare parts, adding at long last support for transport, communication, housing and construction – sectors which the UN in Baghdad had identified long ago as overdue priorities for Oil-for-Food Programme support. The political hourglass in New York had a timescale different from the human clock of deprivation in Iraq. The United Nations Secretariat had been fully aware of the dimensions of the human problem in Iraq. However, instead of strongly and persistently pressing for adoption by the Security Council of the recommendations they themselves had made, and those of Ambassador Amorim's panel, the Office of the Iraq Programme did no more than sheepishly remind the UN 'Iraq world' that 'the programme was never intended to meet all the humanitarian needs ...'.[253] Given the rigidity of the UN sanctions regime and the internal impoverishment, where was the 'balance' of the humanitarian needs supposed to come from? From smuggled oil income?

---

252. Benjamin 1999, p. 131.
253. See UN S/2000/208, 10 March 2000, p. 2, para. 10.

Hardly, since the amounts would not have been enough.[254] These resources, contrary to a common public misperception and persistent US/UK misrepresentation, were needed to a large extent for running the country, paying its civil servants, supporting a network of Iraqi embassies abroad and maintaining the remnants of a once state-of-the-art physical infrastructure. Unnecessary palaces and luxury goods absorbed only a small portion of these resources.

The backlog of much needed equipment and spare parts from earlier phases because of either lack of funding at that time or the horrendous sanctions bureaucracy was an equally urgent issue that needed resolution. The release of over $2 billion worth of supplies kept on hold[255] by the US/UK Governments during this period was a third issue that could have quickly been resolved if these two Governments had wanted to do so: they did so eighteen months later, in May 2002, when it was politically opportune. At once they released $800 million(!) worth of equipment Iraq had procured from Russia. This release by the US/UK was in return for Russian concurrence to UN Security Council Resolution 1409 introducing the Goods Review List (GRL) and setting up new 'procedures for the processing and approval of contracts for humanitarian supplies and equipment'.[256] This was political opportunism and had nothing to do with an adjustment of US/UK sanctions policy in favour of the Iraqi people.

Even though the United Nations Secretariat had demonstrated intermittently that it was concerned about the sorry state of the social and economic conditions in Iraq and had appealed to the UN Security Council to adopt more humane measures, the Secretariat failed to follow up with the fortitude that was required. Whatever the reasons were for this failure, shyness of a subordinate Secretariat vis-à-vis the political power house, the absence of a sense of urgency in the Security Council, pressure of day-to-day demands on senior officials of the world organisation they had all pervasive implications for the Iraqi population in the form of avoidable death and destitution. It was time for introducing fundamental changes in running the Oil-for-Food Programme. Instead, the UN Secretary-General provided breathing space to the UN Security Council by promising the Council yet another report 'on the progress in meeting the humanitarian

254. The Intelligence Unit of the Economist and others have estimated Iraq's income from extralegal and illicit sources as between $1 and $2 billion a year.
255. See UN SC Resolution 1409 (2002), 14 May 2002.
256. Not only were blocked humanitarian supplies a problem of ongoing phases, important consignments were at times kept on hold over a period of several phases. Many were permanently blocked or only eventually released from hold. In early 2000, to give just one example, 92 percent and 100 percent respectively out of $140 million worth of telecommunication contracts in phases V and VI were still on hold in phase VII.

needs of the Iraqi people and on the revenues needed to meet those needs'. These reports, of course, were important but the UN Security Council had already ample evidence of the damage their inaction had caused. UN Secretariat energies should have concentrated on creating the political will within the Council to introduce sanctions reform measures.

In March 2000, the Security Council adopted the 'Green List' approach through which some humanitarian supplies were meant to arrive in Iraq faster. During the same month, the Council agreed to raise the allocation for oil industry spare parts from $300 million to $600 million. These were positive steps, even though in practice, as it turned out, the 'Green List' approach did not lead to a significant acceleration of arrivals of humanitarian supplies. The increase in the allocation for oil spare parts resulted neither in corresponding increases in their arrival nor in large-scale rehabilitation of the oil industry. These measures fell far short of what the Security Council should have done. It was callous on the part of the Security Council not to act more decisively on the recommendations which Ambassador Amorim and Secretary-General Kofi Annan had put before them in the preceding twelve months. On 8 June 2000 the UN Security Council showed yet again that it was not prepared to act decisively.

During this 4,152nd meeting, the UN Security Council passed Resolution 1302[257] inviting the Secretary-General 'to appoint independent experts to prepare by 26 November 2000 a comprehensive report and analysis of the humanitarian situation in Iraq including the current humanitarian needs arising from that situation and recommendations to meet those needs ...'. The resolution once more reminded everyone that the Oil-for-Food Programme was a 'temporary measure' – after three-and-a-half years? – and that the Council was 'determined to improve the humanitarian situation in Iraq'![258] Following the 1999 Amorim panel report and its unequivocal recommendations, the two-year assessment by the UN Secretariat, the briefings the Security Council had had with senior Baghdad-based UN officials, the special reports by UNICEF, WHO, WFP and FAO on child welfare, public health services and nutrition, it was incomprehensible that the Council wanted yet another 'comprehensive report'. This was buying time at the expense of the Iraqi people, who clearly had no time to lose. Every month, in fact every day, a lack of fundamental improvements would mean more destitution, more death, and for the young, dimmer prospects for a proper education. Why did elected governments represented in the Council at that time,[259] being well

---

257. See UN S/RES/1302 (2000), 8 June 2000.
258. Ibid.
259. Apart from the permanent members (P5), China, France, Russia, UK and US, the group of temporary members in 2000 included Argentina, Bangladesh, Canada, Jamaica, Malaysia, Mali, Namibia, Netherlands, Tunisia and Ukraine.

aware of the conditions in Iraq, go along with such an approach? They could not possibly have believed that an additional review would bring new revelations.

Following this resolution, the UN Secretary-General found a suitable individual to lead this team of experts in Jan Stoltenberg, former Prime Minister of Norway, and was prepared to accept such an appointment. The Iraqi Government initially wanted to know the terms of reference for the experts. They then decided to reject such review as a delaying and costly redundancy. I sympathised with this reaction, as did many of my colleagues in Baghdad. Ultimately, this UN Security Council aberration did not materialise. Neither, unfortunately, did many of the recommendations for changes in the Oil-for-Food Programme which had been proposed over and over again during the preceding years.

The road for the Iraqi people remained rocky up to the completion of the Oil-for-Food Programme. The Programme concluded on 3 June 2003, fifty-five days after the end of 'Operation Iraqi Freedom', the US/UK led war against Iraq.

Following the peak in oil prices during 2000, when Iraq had earned more than $25 per barrel, Iraq decided to halt oil production on three occasions for a total of eleven weeks[260] at an estimated loss of $2.9 billion.[261] Revenue for the Oil-for-Food Programme fell sharply during the remaining phases.[262] It is important to emphasise that lifting the oil ceiling in late 1995 did not result in increased oil output, as Figure 1.8 shows.

Iraq's oil industry was in such a poor state that it could not do so. Lifting the oil ceiling was no more than a political ploy. The Council was informed about the state of Iraq's oil facilities through reports of UN oil missions who regularly visited Iraq.

The contention of the US/UK Governments that Iraq was not issuing enough contracts to utilise available resources was also false. Contracts for humanitarian supplies always exceeded available revenue.[263] This forced either the cancellation of some or the transfer of other contracts to subsequent phases, obviously with negative effects on the coherence of the sectoral distribution plans.

The volume of humanitarian supplies blocked in the UN Sanctions Committee by the US and UK Governments increased sharply between the adoption of the Green List and the replacement of this list by the Goods Review List. The upsurge of holds from $1.9 billion in 2000 to $5.5

---

260. 1–12 December 2000, over oil pricing disagreement with the UN; 4 June to 10 July 2001, in rejection of Resolution 1352; 8 April to 9 May 2000, in sympathy for the Palestinian Intifada.
261. See UN S/2001/321, 3 April 2001; S/2001/1842, 5 September 2001 and S/2002/1261, 29 May 2002.
262. See Table 9.
263. See Table 2, p. 16.

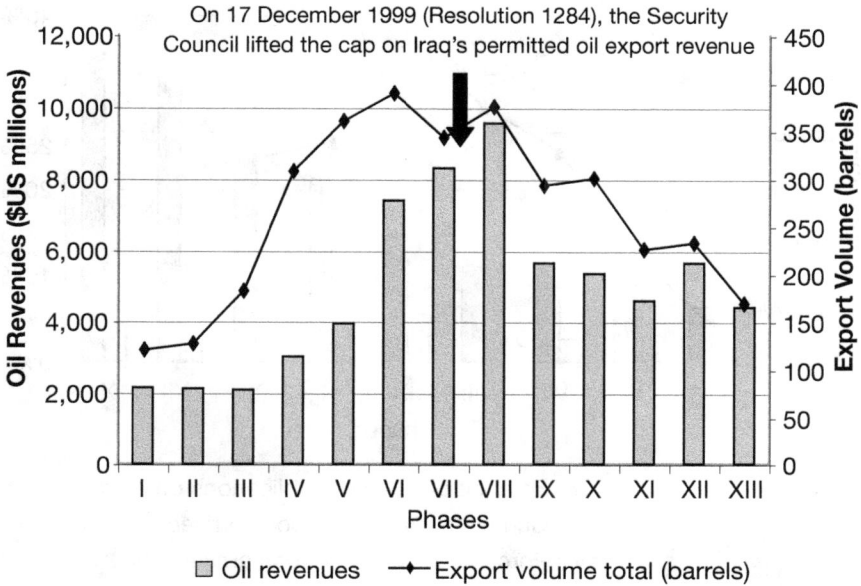

Figure 1.8   Oil Revenues and Oil Exports

Source: *Office of the Iraq Program 'Basic Figures' on the Oil-for-Food Programme (http://www.un.org/Depts/oip/background/basicfigures.html).*

million in 2002 created havoc within the Oil-for-Food Programme.[264] The US/UK position was that the Green and Goods Review Lists had facilitated the flow of humanitarian supplies. This was correct only with regard to some sectors, but not at all with respect to the overall volume of goods arriving in Iraq: 'The effectiveness of the humanitarian programme has suffered considerably, not only because of shortfalls in the funding levels for earlier phases … but also because of the very large number of applications placed on hold, in particular those concerning electricity, water and sanitation, transport and telecommunications, … the same applies also for the very large number of holds placed on applications for spare parts and equipment in the oil sector.'[265]

The positive effects of the fast-track procedures were, in fact, offset by the steep increase in the volume of holds levied on the Oil-for-Food Programme by the US and UK authorities. No other member of the UN Sanctions Committee blocked contracts during this period.

264. See Table 8, p. 132.
265. Briefing of the UN Security Council by Benon Sevan, Executive Director of the Iraq Programme, on Thursday 20 April 2000.

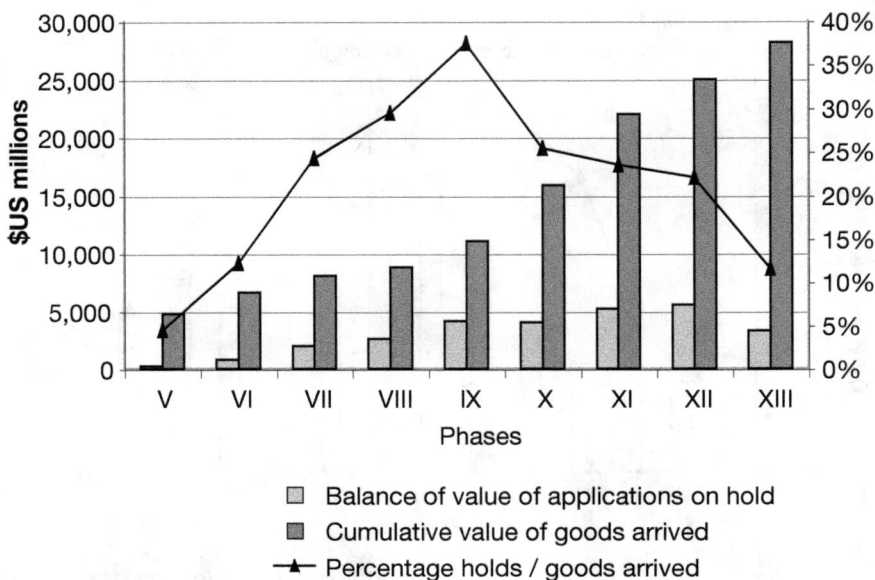

Figure 1.9 Holds and Goods Arrived

Source: *Secretary-General's 180-day reports on the Oil-for-Food Programme, phases IV–XIII.*

Notes: *No data are available on holds before phase V. Data for phase V refer to contracts from phases IV and V only, and might therefore understate the total number of holds. Also, the definition of holds is different in phase XIII, owing to the introduction of new procedures for the approval of contracts.*

In order to fully understand this extraordinary level of items blocked by the US/UK authorities, it must be recalled that the amount of $5.5 billion of blocked humanitarian supplies was higher than the entire humanitarian revenue available at any of the individual phases except for one.[266]

Thirty percent of the Iraqi oil revenue was deposited in the accounts of the UN Compensation Commission (UNCC) in Geneva in the years 1996–2000. In late 2000 the Security Council reduced this amount to 25 percent. The savings of 5 percent were added to the budget of the Oil-for-Food Programme humanitarian programmes in Central and Southern Iraq, the part of Iraq under the control of the Government in Baghdad. In so doing the UN Security Council responded belatedly to years of pressure from various quarters, including a majority of the members within the Council. The US and UK Governments, in the face of opposition to their hard-line approach, yielded.

266. See Tables 1, p. 12 and 8, p. 132.

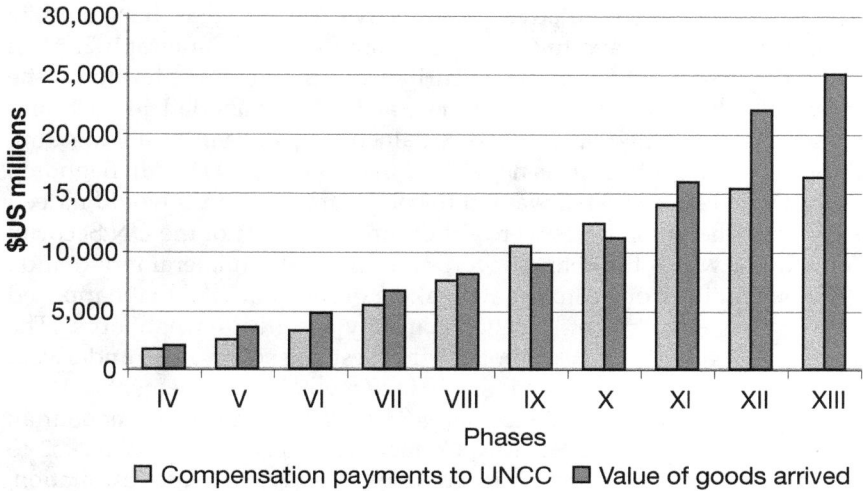

Figure 1.10 Compensation Payments to UNCC and Humanitarian Supplies Arrived

Source: *Secretary-General's 180-day reports on the Oil-for-Food Programme, phases III–XIII.*
Notes: *No data are available for the amount of goods arrived per phase before phase III.*

What is not readily known is that the prevailing sanctions system of apportioning Iraqi oil revenue provided the UN Compensation Commission in Geneva with a steady income while the humanitarian programme was subjected to the vicissitudes of a highly bureaucratised and politicised procurement programme.

As a result, payments into the accounts of the UNCC for the benefit of non-Iraqis, most of the time, amounted to nearly the value of goods arriving in Iraq for the benefit of Iraqis and on two occasions even exceeded the value of humanitarian supplies.

Proper oversight by the Security Council and appropriate analysis by the Sanctions Committee and the Secretariat in New York should have led to early corrective measures. However, only following the March 2003 war, was the percentage of transfers to the UNCC further reduced from 25 to 5 percent.[267] Such a reduction, if carried out in the preceding years, would have much improved the humanitarian resources base and brought more benefits to the Iraqi population.

At the initiation of a new phase of the Oil-for-Food Programme, the Government of Iraq, in the media and in conversations between its

267. See UN S/RES/1483 of 22 May 2003.

officials and UN representatives, was always adamant that this would be the last phase: 'We have fulfilled the requirements of paragraph 22[268] of Resolution 687 of 1991. The UN Security Council, therefore, has to lift the embargo!' This was said at the time I arrived in Baghdad in 1998 and repeated in the following years. It remained Iraq's wishful thinking until phase XIII, the last phase, was negotiated in December 2002.[269] In Baghdad, senior United Nations staff wanted to believe that sanctions would indeed disappear. The possibilities were either through an act of the UN Security Council, for which the chances were slim, through unilateral repudiation of UN resolutions, or by informal breaking of sanctions. All that happened was limited breaking of sanctions, mostly by Iraq's neighbours. The comprehensive economic sanctions regime, established in 1990, underwent much 'cosmetic surgery' and some incremental improvements. These included limited 'fast-track' clearances of certain groups of humanitarian imports. There were five Security Council decisions during 2000–2002 to grant such fast-track status[270] to supplies, mainly for water, sanitation, electricity and housing programmes.

US and UK officials would dispute this assessment, pointing to changes to which they had agreed in authorised levels for oil production, the unblocking of humanitarian supplies and the enlarging of the sectoral scope of the Oil-for-Food Programme, to include housing, telecommunications and transport. All of this is correct. Despite ample indications that such improvements were urgently required from the very beginning of the Oil-for-Food Programme in 1996, it took years of deliberate delays and wrangling within the UN Security Council for these changes to be introduced. The disagreements between the UN Security Council and the Government of Iraq cannot be considered an excuse for the poor preparation of the UN Security Council in implementing comprehensive economic sanctions against Iraq in 1990, or for the years of UN experimentation in the implementation for the Oil-for-Food Programme.

A tug of war on sanctions and the human condition between the United States and the UK as the hardliners in the Council and France, China, Russia and most of the elected members continued until 23 May 2003, when the Security Council pronounced the lifting of economic sanctions against Iraq.[271] That this act of lifting economic sanctions against Iraq was in violation of international law has gone largely

---

268. UN S/RES/1687 (1991), para. 22, 3 April 1991: 'decides … that Iraq has completed all actions contemplated in paragraphs 8 to13, the prohibitions against the import of commodities and products originating in Iraq and the prohibitions against financial transactions related thereto contained in Resolution 661 (1990) shall have no further force or effect.'
269. See UN S/RES/1447, 4 December 2002.
270. UN/OIP, Chronology from 2 August 1990 to 18 March 2003.
271. See UN S/RES/1483 of 22 May 2003, para. 10.

unnoticed in public discussion. The UN Security Council should have confirmed in such a resolution that in accordance with the conditions identified in Resolutions 687 of 1991 and 1284 of 1999 Iraq had fulfilled its obligations for disarmament and was considered free of weapons of mass destruction. This would have proven wrong the US and UK claims that Iraq did possess such weapons, and therefore it would have constituted a serious political defeat for Washington and London. The UN Security Council was therefore pressured into taking the (positive) step of removing economic sanctions from Iraq without concurrently confirming that the military intervention against Iraq was carried out based on false assertions. In doing so, the UN Security Council, for reasons of political expediency, violated its earlier legal pronouncements, i.e., the very laws it had created in the form of resolutions defining the basis for economic sanctions. In the history of the United Nations this must be considered a low-point.

The Government in Baghdad and the UN Secretary-General in New York both wanted to maintain a dialogue on the myriad issues which needed to be resolved. These issues could have been resolved had there been honesty of intention by all parties involved in the conflict. The US and UK were not prepared, however, to support such a dialogue, let alone engage in bilateral exchanges with Iraq: 'The United States rules out direct dialogue with Iraq on the grounds that Iraq's level of compliance does not justify talks'.[272] This was the defiant position of the US Government in 2002. The authorities in Baghdad conveyed in a message to the UN Secretary-General that 'the Council could continue the dialogue with Iraq to reach a balanced, equitable agreement in harmony with international law'.[273] The unwillingness of the US Government to engage with Iraq in direct discussions did not come as a surprise. However, had they wanted a de-escalation of the conflict they could have used the multilateral context of the United Nations to have indirect contact with Iraq. The US administration chose a different path and attempted to prevent all contact between the world body and the Government in Baghdad.

The US and UK authorities managed to ensure that the UN Security Council 'was seized of the matter'. This awkward UN language signified that even the UN Secretary-General could not engage in direct dialogue with the Iraq Government unless the Council agreed. However, other members of the Council, particularly Russia and France, favoured such contacts. The discussions Kofi Annan had in February 1998 in Baghdad

272. Iraq: Weapons Threat, Compliance, Sanctions and US Policy. Issue brief for US Congress/US Congressional Research Service, 27 September 2002, p. 11.
273. 'Presentation of the Delegation of the Republic of Iraq in the Dialogue with the Secretary-General of the United Nations', New York, 26–27 February 2001, p. 10.

with President Saddam Hussein and his Government resulted in improvements of the humanitarian programmes. This fruitful meeting had not been forgotten by the United States: US Secretary of State Albright had not favoured this initiative.

The deteriorating circumstances in Iraq, the moral outrage of international public opinion and the mounting sympathy for ending sanctions by many governments, particularly in the region, had its influence on the atmosphere in the UN Security Council.

Following the adoption of Resolution 1284 in December 1999, the 'lame-duck' resolution, because it did not lead to the return of the UN arms inspectors to Iraq or the implementation of envisaged changes in the running of the Oil-for-Food Programme, the voices in the Council calling for fundamental new approaches became louder. Russian Ambassador Serge Lavrov spoke for the majority of his colleagues when the Security Council met in March 2000, saying that: 'The report of the Secretary-General shows clearly that the scale of the humanitarian catastrophe in Iraq is inexorably leading to the disintegration of the very fabric of civil society there'. Ambassador Lavrov spoke of 'total impoverishment', 'serious employment problems', 'the poor education system', an issue which was rarely mentioned in the Council and concluded by saying the Council was confronted with 'a situation where an entire generation of Iraqis has been physically and morally crippled ...'. Such views were echoed by French Ambassador Alain Déjammet, who referred to the 'very serious humanitarian crisis in Iraq'.[274] These were strong words which we welcomed in the United Nations in Baghdad.

The US and UK Governments never conceded easily. Whatever concessions they were ultimately compelled to make were then unscrupulously portrayed as something they themselves had all along desired to implement, out of concern for suffering Iraqis. Had Saddam Hussein's Government cooperated, they claimed, the Iraqi people in any case would long ago have reaped the benefits. 'The United States is at the forefront of UN efforts to enable Iraq to use its resources to acquire goods needed to improve the lives of ordinary Iraqis. These international efforts initiated by the United States ... have prevented a potential human catastrophe in Iraq ... unfortunately the UN effort is hampered by Iraqi non-cooperation.'[275] The US State Department did not hesitate to issue such a statement in December 2002, following years of wilful obstruction on the part of the US and the UK authorities of initiatives by the Council

274. UN Security Council, S/PV. 4120, 4120th meeting, Friday, 24 March 2000, pp. 5 and 14.
275. US Department of State, Fact Sheet, Office of the Spokesman, 20 December 2002, The Oil-for-Food Programme, p. 1.

intended to bring about the fundamental changes in the humanitarian programme. Kofi Annan, the P3 Group of France, China and Russia, and elected members of the Council such as Malaysia, Tunisia, Bangladesh, Syria and others, had repeatedly demanded these changes. This is not a derogatory statement but a fair and critical assessment of the heavy handedness of the US/UK approach in the UN Security Council during those hard years for the Iraqi people.

For many UN officials, particularly those on 'the front lines' in Iraq, the United States Iraq policy seemed to cling unequivocally to a 'disarmament at all costs' approach The human costs incurred were clearly of secondary importance.[276] They never did share our sense of urgency for changing UN Iraq policy. The US Government defended the status quo and thereby stood in the way of implementing the many recommendations which had been proposed by the Council and the UN Secretariat and others.

At the outset of the Oil-for-Food Programme in 1996, a financial base was established that was far too low. In the ensuing years, efforts to increase revenue levels were opposed more often than not. The blocking of large amounts of goods badly needed by the Iraqi people was, to an overwhelming degree, due to the US authorities, and to a lesser extent, to the United Kingdom, the only other Council member deciding to put humanitarian items on hold.

Although the UN Security Council had severely neglected its mandate for overseeing the impact of its Iraq policies, the awareness level among the P5 members of the Council had risen in early 2000. Fundamental questions over the maintenance of comprehensive sanctions surfaced at practically every Security Council meeting on Iraq. The Government of Iraq followed these 'temperature' changes in the Council and in early 2001 managed to agree with the United Nations to meet with the Secretary-General on 'all outstanding issues between the UN and Iraq'. Given the build-up in the Council against the prevailing humanitarian conditions in Iraq, the US Government had no choice but to relent and to agree to this meeting. Asked about the dossier the Iraqi delegation, led by Foreign Minister Mohamed Al Sahaf, responded: 'There's nothing new in it! In almost 100 pages the Government in Baghdad defined its position on

---

276. See Statement for the Record of Ambassador John D. Negro-Ponte, Permanent Representative, United States Mission to the United Nations before the Committee on Foreign Relations, United States Senate on the Oil-for-Food Programme, second session, 108th Congress, 7 April 2004, p. 2: 'Although the flow of humanitarian and civilian goods to Iraq was a matter of strong interest to the US Government, it should be emphasized that an even greater preoccupation throughout the period of sanctions was to ensure that no items were permitted for import which could in any way contribute to Iraq's WMD Programs or capabilities. ... We concentrated our efforts on this aspect of the sanctions.'

disarmament, the no-fly zones, compensation, the humanitarian programme, the demarcation of boundaries, prisoners of war, the return of Kuwaiti property and a critique of the UN Security Council'.[277]

In 2001, the Foreign Minister of Iraq brought a delegation of seasoned negotiators, among them Dr Riyadh Al Qaysi, Under-Secretary in the Foreign Ministry in Baghdad. Al Qaysi was an experienced international law expert who had been involved in the 1988 Iran-Iraq armistice agreement. Ambassador Dr Samir Al Nimah, Permanent Representative of Iraq to the United Nations in Geneva and formerly Director of the Office of Deputy Prime Minister Tariq Aziz, was a member of this delegation, as was Ambassador Dr Saeed Al Musawi, Permanent Representative of Iraq to the UN in New York, a diplomat thoroughly familiar with the intricacies of the Oil-for-Food Programme. On the UN side, Secretary-General Kofi Annan was joined by the Under-Secretary-General for Political Affairs, Kirain Prendergast, a former UK Ambassador to Turkey who had accompanied Kofi Annan on his mission to Baghdad in February 1998, Hans Corell, the Swedish Under-Secretary-General for Legal Affairs who had negotiated and signed the Memorandum of Understanding establishing, in 1995, the Oil-for-Food Programme, Iqbal Riza, the Chef de Cabinet in the Secretary-General's Office, Benon Sevan, the Executive Director of the Office of the Iraq Programme, Ralph Knutssen, the Deputy to the Chef de Cabinet who had a long association with Iraq (and later to become the Executive Director of the UN Compensation Commission in Geneva), and Vladimir Grachev, a Russian colleague in charge of the Iraq file in the Secretary-General's Office.

The Iraqis emphasised that 'the Government of Iraq has cooperated fully with the UN agencies in discussing and determining the key elements of the sectors covered by the distribution plans in the hope that these requirements will be made available within the time limit of each phase in order to meet the urgent needs of the people of Iraq'.[278] The UN side could not but agree with this general contention of the Iraqi side.

The list of specific Iraqi grievances in connection with the economic sanctions was long. It included complaints about the apportioning of oil revenue between the humanitarian programme and the UN Compensation Commission and within the humanitarian programme itself. The Iraqi authorities objected to the high level of 25 percent (formerly 30 percent) of compensation deductions, and also the distribution of revenues between the northern (Kurdish) governorates under the administration of the United Nations and the rest of the country under control of the

---

277. 'Presentation of the Delegation of the Republic of Iraq in the Dialogue with the Secretary-General of the United Nations', New York, 26–7 February 2001.
278. Ibid.

Government in Baghdad. The perennial problems created by the volume of items kept on hold or being permanently blocked by the US and the UK Governments was, of course, raised by the Iraqi side. There was a slate of other complaints over various aspects of the financing of the Oil-for-Food Programme, including the long lead time for opening letters of credit and the allocations for UN overheads. The Government felt that a 3 percent deduction for the humanitarian and disarmament administrations was too high. Reference was made to 'excessive squandering and irrational expenditure'[279] on the part of the UN. The commercial clause issue which two years earlier Sevan and I had tried to solve, unsuccessfully, because of US/UK rejection, was brought up again. Another standard item on the Iraqi agenda involved the demand of the Iraqi Government finally to be allowed to pay arrears of its assessed contribution to the UN budget,[280] in order to become again a member country in 'good standing'.

For Kofi Annan these talks and his role were obviously very sensitive. The UN Security Council had divided views of their value. The Iraqis had justified grievances concerning economic sanctions and outstanding obligations in the areas of disarmament, missing persons and Kuwaiti property. The international public expected that the UN Secretary-General would succeed in bridging the gap between the Security Council and the Government of Iraq for the benefit of the Iraqi people. This was unquestionably Kofi Annan's wish as well. In all meetings with him, I was convinced that he had a deep compassion for the Iraqi people and wanted to bring about improvements for them. One could see that he was frustrated because of the obstacles confronting him. Given the complexity of the Iraq discussions and the controversy surrounding them in New York and in various capitals, the Secretary-General was guarded in his interaction with the press at the beginning of the talks as well as at their conclusion. On 26 February 2001, when arriving at UN headquarters early in the morning, he stated to the Press that he was 'encouraged that the Iraqi delegation is here and [was] looking forward to a frank and constructive dialogue … [to] breaking the current impasse'. At the end of the talks, on 28 February 2001, he told the Press: 'it became clear … that the Iraqis … saw three priority areas: the no-fly zones, the disarmament issue and … economic sanctions … I think these are the three key areas for them.' These were guarded responses indeed!

As far as the humanitarian issues were concerned, US Secretary of State Colin Powell had been absolutely right in referring to the Iraqi presentation

---

279. Ibid.
280. The US Government, year after year, had blocked the use of available Iraqi assets abroad for the purpose of payment of these dues and also refused the use of oil revenue. As a result, Iraq lost the rights that come with UN membership.

at the 2001 talks as 'nothing new'. The fact was that they had become standard items on the Security Council's agenda. For many years the UN Security Council had debated the inadequate revenue situation, the intractable holds of humanitarian supplies, the bureaucracy of sanctions management, compensation payments, and so on. The UN Secretariat, both in New York and Baghdad, had continuously raised the long lead times needed for the arrival of humanitarian supplies and the resulting disjointed implementation of humanitarian programmes. We pleaded for more revenue to meet sectoral needs. We tried our utmost to convince the Security Council that the UN in Iraq had the means to monitor the deployment of equipment and supplies without a danger of misuse by the Iraqi Government for dual use purposes. It was the Iraqi people, not the Iraqi delegation that had come to New York in February 2001, who were forced to pay the price for the excruciatingly slow process of improvement. The February 2001 dialogue between the Iraqi Government and the United Nations was the last involving Foreign Minister Al Sahaf.[281] It also was one of the last meetings in which the two sides had the freedom to consider all the unsettled humanitarian issues. One exception was an appearance by Iraqi Under-Secretary Dr Riyadh Al Qaysi in the UN Security Council on 3 July 2001 during which he, in forceful legal language, reiterated his Government's stand on all outstanding issues. In March 2002 the Iraqis, this time led by their new Foreign Minister Dr Naji Al Hadithi, presented the UN Secretary-General with a list of nineteen highly political questions. Among them: 'How do you explain the case of a permanent member of the Security Council who officially and openly calls for invading Iraq and imposing a puppet regime, in violation of Security Council resolutions themselves ... and the rules of international law ... while this permanent member ... demands Iraq to implement these resolutions?' 'The United States has declared once again that economic sanctions on Iraq will remain in place as long as the national Government remains in Iraq. What is the attitude of the Security Council towards such a policy which is in violation of relevant Security Council resolutions?' 'Can the United Nations guarantee the elimination of the two no-fly zones and also guarantee that the proposed inspection formula will not be a prelude to an aggression against Iraq as in 1998?'[282]

Kofi Annan told the Iraqi delegation that he would forward these questions to the Security Council. This he did. The Council never provided a reply. The two subsequent meetings between the UN and Iraq

281. In 2001 Al Sahaf was replaced as Iraq's Foreign Minister by Dr. Naji Al Hadithi, previously Iraq's Ambassador to Austria.
282. The informal document with the nineteen questions was handed to the United Nations by the Iraqi delegation.

in May and July 2002 in New York and in Vienna would be about avoiding war, not about improving life for the average Iraqi.

During the time I served as the Humanitarian Coordinator in Iraq the Oil-for-Food Programme's phases V, VI and VII were being implemented. The main and interlinked concerns of the UN agencies in Baghdad at the time were the implementation of the programme in Iraq and the policies of the Security Council. The former involved constant logistical and technical bottlenecks of all kinds, and the latter perennial political procrastination of decision making. This was the reality faced by each UN humanitarian coordinator before, and would continue until the Oil-for-Food Programme ended in May 2003.

It is no surprise that the largest humanitarian programme ever untaken by the United Nations would face recurrent implementation bottlenecks. In the food sector alone there was ample scope for distribution problems. To move 400,000 tons of food every month in a country of 437,000 km^2 to ensure that some 50,000 food agents could distribute the much-needed rations in a timely manner was quite a challenge. The Government of Iraq and the World Food Programme faced transport, storage and quality problems, but ultimately managed this vital aspect of the programme well. Purchase, quality control and distribution of medicines was another key area of the programme wrought with difficulties. The goal was that hospitals, health clinics and pharmacies should be stocked with the medicines which the Oil-for-Food Programme could afford to buy. Within the constraints of funding, the Government of Iraq and the World Health Organisation did achieve their objectives. However, the health sector was in no way ever adequately covered: funding was much too low and blocked medical supplies proved a major constraint, as did the slow pace of arrivals in Iraq. The same assessment applied to the agriculture sector where distribution of seasonal inputs, equipment and spare parts proceeded adequately with the cooperation of the Government of Iraq and the Food and Agriculture Organisation. At the same time, however, poor funding and the putting on hold of supplies for the agricultural sector impeded meeting even minimal needs of that sector.

Water, sanitation and electricity sectors, so important for the health and welfare of the Iraqi people, faced innumerable and avoidable constraints, just as the other sectors did, with a lack of resources and significant amounts of temporarily or permanently blocked items. The complexity of the needs in these sectors was aggravated by the state of poor roads, warehouses and transport. The Iraqi infrastructure was largely debilitated by the 1991 Gulf War and by years of forced neglect. Despite these bottlenecks, the Government of Iraq, together with UNICEF, WHO and UNDP, managed to deploy what became available under the Oil-for-Food Programme in quite an acceptable way. The same can be said for the telecommunications and housing sectors, which were added to the programme in 1999/2000. ITU, the UN's telecommunications agency, and UNCHS, the UN's housing and settlement organisation, cooperated with the Government and the Kurdish authorities to solve many technical and input difficulties.

Faced with totally inadequate funding, UNICEF, UNESCO and the Government made good use of imported and locally available resources to achieve a minor difference in the education sector. The available resources, inadequate as they were throughout the thirteen phases of the Oil-for-Food Programme, were deployed as best they could, despite inordinate obstacles.

The general conclusion that resources available to the UN system for this humanitarian exemption were adequately used should not be misunderstood. At no time during the years of comprehensive economic sanctions were there adequate resources to meet minimum needs for human physical and mental survival either before, or during, the Oil-for-Food Programme. The foregoing accounts have made this clear. The socio economic indicators for the period before 1989, during 1996 and 2000 and at the end of sanctions in 2003 confirm this.[283]

It is often said by those who defended economic sanctions that the Iraq Government had choices and could have ended the human drama in Iraq through early compliance in disarmament. One can discuss the choices the Government had and the extent of Iraqi cooperation or non cooperation with the disarmament agencies UNSCOM and its successor UNMOVIC. This, however, is a moot point: the fact remains the people of Iraq should not have been made to account for their Government's failure to act.

Iraqis, as often stated by Tariq Aziz, the country's Deputy Prime Minister and best known Iraqi link to the outside world, claimed until March 2003 that they had fulfilled the requirements of Resolution 687 of 1991 and therefore sanctions should be lifted. The US and UK Governments, on the other hand, vigorously contested this claim and, on that basis, justified the continuation of the sanctions regime.[284] The two Governments also maintained that the US and UK had been instrumental in making changes to the provisions of the Oil-for-Food Programme, thereby ending international contribution to Iraqi suffering. On 26 June

283. See Iraq, The Oil-for-Food Programme: 1997–2003, (as submitted by the Government of Iraq and approved by the UN Secretary-General, Table A.3, p. 282 and Table A.6, p. 286.
284. US Vice-President Dick Cheney told the Veterans of Foreign Wars Annual Convention on 26 August 2002: '... there is no doubt that Saddam Hussein now has weapons of mass destruction. There is no doubt he is amassing them to use against our friends, against our allies, and against us.' See 'US House of Representatives, Special Investigation Division, Iraq on the Record, the Bush Administration's Public Statement on Iraq, p. 7.

2001 US Ambassador Cunningham made the preposterous point in the UN Security Council that: 'During these past six years, the nature of the Oil-for-Food Programme has changed even though the name has not. But a better name today would be "Oil-for-Development", because such a term would more accurately reflect that even today the Iraqi regime could redevelop the country using the Oil-for-Food Programme, if it chose to do so.'[285] If this indeed had been an option, then the Iraqi economy should have been allowed to restart with the help of local and foreign direct investment, the oil industry would have been rehabilitated, new oil fields would have been opened, institutional renewal and training would have started, the Iraqi Central Bank would once again have resumed a role. None of this occurred or could have done so, given the tight control the Security Council maintained on Iraq's economic activities under the watchful eyes of the US and UK. The pillars of control were carefully guarded by these two governments throughout the years of sanctions. There was no foreign investment, no resumption of industrial entrepreneurship within Iraq on any scale, no overhaul of the oil industry, and certainly no role for Iraq's Central Bank.

The US and UK authorities were, however, right in insisting that the Iraqi Government, even within these comprehensive restrictions, could have done more throughout the years of sanctions. But as has been stated previously, even if the entire income that Saddam Hussein's Government acquired outside the sanctions framework had been invested for the benefit of the civilian population, Iraqi suffering would not have ended. The approximately $1–1.5 billion[286] which the Government obtained as an average per year from surcharges on commercial transactions and the income from illegal export of oil via the Gulf, Turkey, Jordan and, during the last three years of sanctions, Syria, would not have returned the Iraqis to a normal life. Dictatorships do not allow people to lead normal lives; neither do sanctions of the kind imposed upon Iraq. The question that must be asked here is whether a different approach by the UN Security Council with regard to its sanctions policy would have made a difference. With a knowledge of the human conditions in Iraq, it is pertinent to ask: did the UN Security Council have options for implementing sanctions in a humane and legally correct manner? A cursory review of the Security Council debates during these years would make it obvious that there were indeed clear policy options. My own, and limited experience, with the Security Council nevertheless gave me a first-hand indication that the Council had these options but chose not to exercise them. In 1995, at the time when the Oil-for-Food Programme was negotiated with Iraq,

285. S/PV.4336, UN Security Council, 4336th meeting, 26 June 2001, p. 8.
286. Much of this money was transported to Baghdad in cash from various collection points in the Middle East.

Ambassador Li Zhaoxint of China stated that 'the main purpose of the mechanism proposed is the easing of the situation in Iraq and that this is merely a temporary measure'.[287]

In fact, all delegations acknowledged the seriousness of the human situation that prevailed in Iraq at the time when the Oil-for-Food Programme was negotiated in 1995. During the first year of this humanitarian programme, in 1996–7, the Council members reiterated this seriousness. 'The humanitarian situation in Iraq ... gives rise to deep concern',[288] were the words of Swedish Ambassador Anders Lidén. His Polish, Portuguese, French and other colleagues in the Council agreed. There was a distinct sense of sympathy for the Iraqi people in the Security Council as a whole. It is important to note that at this early stage of the Oil-for-Food Programme there were already voices critical of its structure and mechanism. Ambassador Zbigniew Wlosowicz of Poland conveyed to the Council his Government's concern over the implementation of the programme as well as its procedures and working methods. More specifically, he referred to 'the level of necessary cooperation of the Iraqi authorities; the unsatisfactory pace of the arrival of humanitarian supplies in Iraq; the operating difficulties of the distribution system; the nutritional value of the current food basket ... and the adequacy of revenues'. His Russian counterpart in the Council, Ambassador Serge Lavrov, raised the issue of blocking humanitarian contracts and made the important observation that 'a situation in which the import of humanitarian goods lags far behind the export of oil is unacceptable'.[289] During phase I the UN Security Council was thus already fully aware of the gambit of constraints. And yet, they would remain with the programme for the following twelve phases: inadequate revenue, sanctions committee bureaucracy, operating problems due to lack of transport, storage and managerial incapacity and the blocking of humanitarian supplies.

In 1998, the Council met yet again to discuss the situation in Iraq. Individual members spoke out once more – often with great eloquence – about the human condition. Ambassador Hans Dahlgren of Sweden, referring to the Secretary-General's report on Iraq, indicated: 'It is worrying reading. In almost all sectors – food/nutrition, health, electricity ... the situation is described as grave and deteriorating.' Ambassador Déjammet of France made an important amplification by saying: 'After

---

287. S/PV.3519, UN Security Council, 3519th meeting, 14 April 1995, p. 3.
288. S/PV.3840, UN Security Council, 3840th meeting, 4 December 1997, p. 7.
289. Ibid., p. 2 and p. 11. Holds of humanitarian supplies in 1997 certainly disabled the programme but at a level far below that which prevailed later during phase VII (1999/2000) and phase XI (2001/2002) when the value of blocked items peaked at between 24 percent and 33 percent of the value of arrived goods (see Fig. 8).

seven years of embargo, the humanitarian situation in Iraq can no longer be treated like a natural disaster: sending medicine and food is not enough. Iraq must have a minimum of agricultural production; the population must have drinking water; and children must be able to go to school.'[290]

The Oil-for-Food Programme obviously had not succeeded in making a distinct impact in key areas of Iraqi life at that time. During this 1998 meeting there were renewed calls for specific changes in how the humanitarian programme should be revised. It is important to realise that individual members of the Council, to their credit, did not relent in raising these issues over which the Council did have jurisdiction. They had the power to bring about early changes for the benefit of the Iraqi people. As always, Ambassador Déjammet came well prepared to the Council. He made the French case for change with strong language and in the detail which the situation demanded. With regard to revenue, he expressed satisfaction that the Council seemed finally ready to act by doubling the existing allocation from $1.3 billion to $2.6 billion per phase as of phase IV. Such a step was obviously welcome. Nevertheless, it had taken a year to reach this stage. The amount was based on an earlier UN proposal in 1991 to cover what then was perceived to be a short-lived emergency-type humanitarian exemption. This figure was used to establish the revenue levels for the first three phases of the Oil-for-Food Programme five years later. In retrospect this constituted a truly unfortunate approach, since the financing formula did not represent the outcome of an in-depth, rigorous needs assessment. The UN Security Council and the UN Secretariat should not have allowed this to happen: it resulted in a detrimental ripple effect for subsequent phases. Had the earlier review of financial needs been done by the UN more professionally, the ceiling for these phases would undoubtedly have been higher.

The Security Council was not in the habit of pursuing basic analyses of this kind. Given its oversight mandate, it should have or at least ensured that its Sanctions Committee did so. Instead, the Council relied on the UN Secretariat and others to do so.

Apart from the oil income issue and the need for oil industry rehabilitation, members reminded the Council of the problem of approval procedures, the overall streamlining of the sanctions bureaucracy and the state of infrastructure. The issues agenda had not changed from the previous year, nor had the Oil-for-Food Programme been able to have a higher level of impact. By December 1999 phase VII had begun and the Council held another review of the conditions in Iraq and the Oil-for-Food Programme. On this occasion the Permanent Representative of Kuwait to the UN in New York, Ambassador Abulhasan, had requested the

290. S/PV.3855, UN Security Council, 3855th meeting, 20 February 1998, p. 7.

President of the Security Council, Ambassador Sir Jeremy Greenstock of the United Kingdom, to be allowed to attend this Security Council meeting and address the Council. Ambassador Abulhasan conveyed his Government's 'complete empathy with the fraternal people of Iraq in its suffering'. He added the customary qualification: 'the persistence of which [the suffering] is the sole responsibility of the Government of Iraq'.[291] Ambassador Qin Huasun of China did not hesitate to criticise the situation in Iraq by emphasising that there was 'an urgent need to relieve the Iraqi people of their tremendous inhumane suffering ... and that the nine year old sanctions had inflicted untold physical and psychological suffering on the Iraqi civilians, especially women and children'. The Ambassador of Malaysia, Tan Sri Hasmy Agam, made the point that 'nine years of punitive sanctions are far too long for any country to bear'. The alleged sympathy for the Iraqi people remained in the Council if for no other reason than political expediency; so did the calls for change.

It is interesting to see the evolution of concern for higher revenue levels. In 1996, the Council had agreed to the initial level of $1.3 billion for the humanitarian programme. About a year later the Council debated the doubling of this amount. In December 1999 the Council agreed to lifting altogether the ceiling for oil exports since it again became apparent that even the double amount of oil revenue would not suffice to keep a minimum programme alive. This measure was considered, or at least proclaimed by many, to be the panacea for the Iraqi people living under sanctions. 'Now Iraq can pump as much oil as it needs' was a common, albeit wrong, conclusion. The US and UK politicised this perception by adding that 'Saddam Hussein and his Government still do not care for their people'. There were, of course, others in the UN Security Council who had a more honest grasp of the situation in which the Iraqi oil sector found itself and they came to quite a different conclusion. Ambassador Serge Lavrov was one such representative. He pointed out that 'lifting the oil ceiling is welcomed but is limited in its impact by the severely debilitated oil infrastructure ... clearly no real improvements are possible if urgent oil spare parts and equipment continue to be placed on hold. We continue to believe that nothing short of massive rehabilitation of the entire economy ... will enable the situation to improve in a fundamental way.'[292] Throughout the lifespan of the Oil-for-Food Programme this rehabilitation of the economy did not happen. There was never a basic overhaul of the oil industry. This made the lifting of the oil ceiling a clever political gesture rather than a decision with genuine financial implications. Oil output did not increase as a result of this decision; in fact, the decision to lift the ceiling would not have been taken if there had

---

291. See S/PV.4084, UN Security Council, 4084th meeting, 17 December 1999, p. 3.
292. Ibid., p. 7.

been a genuine prospect that it would increase. OPEC and others would have objected.

For three years running the UN Security Council had modified the financing formula for the Oil-for-Food Programme. This showed a worrisome absence of knowledge of the basic financial requirements for implementing a sanction-based humanitarian programme in Iraq, a deliberate act of procrastination, or both. The lifting of the oil ceiling certainly was a key issue in December 1999 as far as the humanitarian programme was concerned. Other standard Iraq Oil-for-Food Programme concerns of previous years, such as the efficiency of the sanctions committee and the impact of holds, were also raised by many delegations. However, disarmament and weapons of mass destruction and the return of UN inspectors dominated this Council debate. This showed that despite a distinctive awareness of the human conditions in Iraq, the Security Council could not be easily moved to act in accordance with the UN Charter and international humanitarian law. When finally changes were introduced, for example, to increase the budget for the purchase of oil spare parts from $300 million to $600 million or to lift the oil ceiling, it was after a long delay. The consequences were borne by the Iraqi people.

The debate in the UN Security Council remained the same during the following year. Ambassador Saeed Hassan Al Mosawi, Iraq's Permanent Representative to the United Nations, told me that his Government had rejected UN Resolution 1284 in 1999 'because it was considered a step backwards'. Iraq's main objection had been that it did not confirm that economic sanctions would be lifted once Iraq had agreed to the return of UN inspectors and the installation of UNMOVIC in Baghdad. At the same time, the Government had quietly accepted all improvements suggested for the Oil-for-Food Programme in Resolution 1284. These included at long last the purchase of locally produced goods, exemption from the air embargo flights to Mecca, free imports for some sectors, (food, education material, standard medical and agriculture equipment, etc.), a cash component to be used for installation of equipment, training and other local needs of the programme, and the lifting of the oil ceiling.

The Security Council met on 24 March 2000 in the presence of the UN Secretary-General. Kofi Annan had joined the Council to present his report on Iraq's humanitarian situation. His message could not possibly be misunderstood during this fourth year of the UN's humanitarian programme in Iraq: the UN has brought some relief. It is not enough. The programme as devised cannot be enough 'even if it is perfectly implemented'.[293] Among the first to react was Ambassador Serge Lavrov of Russia, who agreed with the Secretary-General's presentation, saying that 'the scale of the humanitarian catastrophe in Iraq is inexorably

293. S/PV.4120, UN Security Council, 4120th meeting, 24 March 2000, p. 2.

leading to the disintegration of the very fabric of civil society there'.[294]
Canadian Ambassador to the UN Robert Fowler reminded the Council of
the importance of first-hand information, stating that a recent mission of
Canadian diplomats to Iraq 'came away with a vivid impression of just
how much more needs to be done'.[295] The Ambassador of Poland,
referring to the humanitarian situation, insisted that 'we [the Security
Council] should accept our share of the responsibility for the disturbing
situation in such sectors as health, water and sanitation and
electricity ...'.[296] As during previous Iraq debates in the Security Council,
the Ambassador of France[297] used similar stark language, blaming the
Council for much of the human disaster in Iraq: 'Admittedly, the Iraqi
Government bears a heavy share of the initial blame ... but the Security
Council can no longer disregard its own responsibility in the matter
which is indisputable and increasingly condemned by international
public opinion.'[298]

Once again, the Council showed its awareness of the conditions on the
ground and the negative role the Security Council had played in creating
such conditions. The Council's mistakes were emphasised. Russia spoke
of the 'paralyses of the Sanctions Committee as "unacceptable"'.[299] China
supported this position and additionally criticised the slow contracts
approval and the volume of holds, and furthermore called for 'enhancing
the observation and monitoring mechanism of UNOCHI'[300] as a way to
reduce the volume of holds put on humanitarian supplies by the US and
the UK. In March 2000 the issue of holds raised in all previous Security
Council meetings occupied the minds of a great many delegations. Apart
from China, France and Russia, the Ambassadors of Canada, Mali and
even the Netherlands, which more often than not aligned itself with the
US and UK position, voiced their concern. Dutch Ambassador van
Walsum, who also headed the UN Sanctions Committee at the time,
pointed out that 'we consider the current amount of applications placed
on hold intolerably high'. Intolerably high it was indeed: $1.9 billion of
much-needed goods were on hold during this period when distribution
plan VII was under implementation. All these warnings made no
difference. In subsequent phases even more items were placed on hold. In
2002 the level of holds would reach $5.1 billion, the peak during the six-
and-a-half years of the Oil-for-Food Programme.

294. Ibid., p. 5.
295. Ibid., p. 19.
296. S/PV.4120, UN Security Council, 4120th meeting, 24 March 2000, p. 24.
297. Ambassador Jean-David Levitte had replaced Ambassador Alain Déjammet
     on 20 March 2000.
298. S/PV.4120, ibid., p. 15.
299. Ibid., p. 18.
300. Ibid., p. 4.

Despite all the evidence of the devastation international policy had brought upon the Iraqi people, William Wood, a senior US State Department official maintained, three days after Washington's Iraq policy had been strongly criticised by the Council, that countries represented in the Council 'had been misled, that the Oil-for-Food Programme is inadequate'. Malaysian Ambassador Agam Hasmy retorted by saying: 'How ironic is it that the same policy that is supposed to disarm Iraq of its weapons of mass destruction has itself become a weapon of mass destruction …'.[301]

Concern and evidence of the damage that was inflicted on the Iraqi people still did not translate into changes which the Security Council should have introduced on legal and moral grounds. The US and UK hard-line approach on this issue resulted in inaction by the rest of the Council. Russia, China and France were always strong rhetorically yet, in terms of concrete follow up, ineffective. Politically, this was the easy way out. The cost for evasion, however, was borne by the Iraqi people.

The eleventh year of Iraq sanctions, 2001, saw more of the same as far as the Security Council was concerned. Phases IX and X were implemented, with considerable revenue problems. The high oil prices in 2000 of $25 per barrel during phase VIII had come down in 2001 to an average of $15 per barrel. In phase IX this was aggravated further by lower oil exports of about 1.4 million barrels per day instead of the expected 2.1 million barrels. This was due to a deliberate and irresponsible stoppage in production by the Government of Iraq from 4 June to 10 July. This five-week stoppage was a protest by the Iraqis about the pricing formula that the UN wanted to introduce to stop illegal oil surcharges.

The value of humanitarian goods that actually arrived in Iraq in 2000/01 was less than 50 percent of available revenue, a rate much lower than during previous phases. Humanitarian supplies kept on hold during the year had reached $4 billion, the highest level since the start of the Oil-for-Food Programme. It was in this context that the UN Security Council met on 26 June 2001. The agenda of issues was a familiar one, particularly to the P5 Group. In 2000 (phase VII) the high level of blocked items – almost 2 billion then – was criticised by many members of the Council. In 2001 (phases IX and X) this level had risen even higher, to an average of $4 billion.[302] Ambassador Kassé of Mali, supported by his Ukrainian colleague and others, referred to the 'excessively high number of contracts kept on hold …',[303] concluding that 'this is one of the main obstacles to proper implementation of the humanitarian programme'.[304]

301. See Reuters, 27 March 2000.
302. See Fig. 1.7, p. 115 and Table A.4, p. 284.
303. A year later, in June 2002, the number of holds stood at 2002 applications valued at over $5.4 billion, an absolute record – see Fig. 9.
304. S/PV.4336, United Nations Security Council, 4336th meeting, 26 June 2001, p. 19.

The United Nations in Baghdad certainly noticed the manifestations of this policy. There were delays in implementation of water and sanitation projects, the repair of central electricity facilities and the restoration of diagnostic facilities in hospitals. Instead of acknowledging this serious problem and supporting immediate and major remedial action, the US and UK delegations preferred to discuss the perceived inadequate utilisation of funds by the Government of Iraq – a clear case of detraction. Norway, which earlier had been critical of much lower volumes than this deflected from the holds discussion by citing that '$2.2 billion of the funds destined to meet ... humanitarian objectives remain unused in the United Nations ESCROW account'.[305] This gave the wrong impression that the Iraqi authorities were not interested in procuring humanitarian supplies. At the time when Ambassador Ole Peter Kolby of Norway made this assertion, phase IX had just been completed. It showed that $6.04 billion worth of contracts had been approved during this phase yet only $5.6 billion worth of oil revenue were available.[306] In addition, as Chairman of the UN Sanctions Committee Ambassador Kolby should also have known that there had been a serious backlog of contracts from previous phases which had to be transferred to the following phases because of the lack of resources. Members of the Council in 2001 were as 'ready' to 'consider ways of improving the humanitarian situation in Iraq under the devastating sanctions'[307] as they had been in prior years. The rhetoric was once again what the international community expected, but follow-up action, if it came at all, came excruciatingly slowly. At times I felt the UN Security Council had become a stage on which a tragedy of epic dimensions was enacted, with the Iraqi population performing the role of spectators, uninvited, yet forced to pay for the tickets.

The cumbersome flow of goods to Iraq,[308] the no-fly zones, sovereignty and territorial integrity, the importance of Iraqi cooperation, the cash component, the smuggling of Iraqi oil, and the capacity constraints of the Iraqi oil industry were all part of the 2001 debate, as they had been before. Since the humanitarian conditions in Iraq had not changed fundamentally, some members of the UN Security Council rightly wanted a much broader debate: 'The current status quo is not satisfactory ... For

305. Ibid., p.14.
306. See Fig. 1.2, p. 15.
307. S/PV.4336, United Nations Security Council, 4336th meeting, 26 June 2001, excerpt of statement by Serge Lavrov, Ambassador of Russia.
308. Ibid., p. 16. To cite an example that came up in the June 2001 Iraq debate in the Security Council: the Ukrainian Ambassador, Valery Kuchinsky, referred to 'new arrangements that would significantly improve the flow of commodities and products into Iraq'. The fact is that it took from March 2000, when the 'Green List' approach was adopted – which made little difference in the flow of goods – to May 2002, when the 'Goods Review List' replaced the Green List, a period of over two years, for an improvement to be seen.

more than three years we have been proposing significant reforms of the Oil-for-Food machinery' (Singapore and France); 'This type of collective punishment has to end' (Jordan); 'The sanction reviews must be focused effectively, targeted and of limited duration' (Jamaica); 'The least that can be expected from members of the Security Council is that we comply with our own resolutions' (Colombia). Following the resumption of talks between the UN Secretary-General and the Government of Iraq earlier in the year, many members of the Council stressed the importance of dialogue (e.g., China, Colombia, France, Malaysia, Mauritius, Tunisia).[309] These were all pertinent and important issues for which the international community, UN staff and most of all the Iraqi people had a right to expect serious follow up. Unfortunately, a UN/Iraq dialogue on how to end the double punishment for the Iraqi people would not take place. The ensuing months saw a hardening of the US/UK position and a gravitation toward military confrontation.

The year 2002 saw the end of phase XI in May, the completion of phase XII in November and the beginning of phase XIII, the last phase of the Oil-for-Food Programme, in December. Oil prices climbed during this period to over $25 per barrel, yet the volume of oil exports from Iraq hovered around 1.2 million barrels per day, a significant decrease from earlier peaks. Capacity bottlenecks in Iraq's oil industry increased and the recently reopened and illegally supplied oil pipeline to Syria, as well as the deliberate interruption of Iraqi oil exports in sympathy with the Palestinian *intifada*, explain this decrease.

This, of course, did not augur well for the implementation of the 2002/3 distribution plans. However, there was some acceleration of approvals of humanitarian supplies. The Security Council had introduced the Goods Review List approach in May 2002. The reduction in the backlog of approved and paid-for supplies and the sudden release of blocked goods led to a welcome upsurge in the arrival of humanitarian supplies during phase XI.[310] The opening of a fifth border crossing at the Iraqi/Saudi border at A'rar helped to increase the inflow of goods into Iraq. It was an important development following the improvement of political relations between the two countries in the wake of the preceding Arab League summit of March 2002 in Beirut.

None of this made a significant difference at the receiving end in Iraq: much more was required. It was not enough to just strengthen the crutches; major surgery was needed, but unfortunately the 'doctors' were increasingly preoccupied in another theatre. The UN Security Council invested more and more of its energies in acrimonious debates on the extent to which Iraq posed a threat to the international community.

---

309. Ibid., pp. 2–32.
310. See Fig. 1.1, p. 12.

The shock of 11 September 2001 converted the hidden determination of US leaders to remove Saddam Hussein's Government by force into an increasingly open plan. A year later proved to be a fateful time. US President Bush conveyed his intentions on 12 September to the UN General Assembly[311] when he said: 'Saddam Hussein's regime is a grave and gathering danger. To suggest otherwise is to hope against the evidence … and this is a risk we must not take'. Prime Minister Blair did likewise two weeks later when he wrote in his foreword to what has become known as the 'Blair dossier': 'I am in no doubt that the threat is serious and current, that he (Saddam Hussein) has made progress on WMD, and that he has to be stopped'.[312] 'A brew of many ingredients, currents and counter currents was simmering.'[313] In the UN Security Council this was the year when the focus of the Iraq debate shifted from improving the sanctions regime to preventing military confrontation.

On 8 November 2002 the Council unanimously approved Resolution 1441, which redefined the relationship between the UN Security Council and the Government of Iraq following Saddam Hussein's sudden decision in September to allow the unconditional return to Iraq of UN arms inspectors.

The report Kofi Annan submitted four days later to the Security Council on the Oil-for-Food Programme and its contributions to survival in Iraq did not evoke much of a discussion of the humanitarian situation, as had been the case in previous years. The entire Council was preoccupied with the WMD issue, the resumption of UN weapons inspections and preparations for the monitoring of Iraqi compliance.

In late June 2000 the number of holds stood at over 2,000 applications valued over $5.4 billion, an absolute record. All of this was recorded in the books of the UN Security Council but did not register in the minds of those concerned with Iraq policy: they were travelling on a track that had nothing to do with the immediate needs of the Iraqi people or efforts to bring about a reduction in their misery. At the time, the urgency of preventing a war provided the veil behind which the UN Security Council was hiding a colossal failure in implementing economic sanctions with a human face. The Oil-for-Food Programme was in its final round, not because sanctions were about to be lifted and Iraqis could begin to rebuild their country, but because a war would bring about new and more troubling circumstances; it was a war. It was not a 'conflict' or a 'crisis', as the report of the UN Secretary-General published two months later[314]

311. United States, Statement by President Bush, UN General Assembly, 12 September 2002, New York, p. 3.
312. 'Iraq's Weapons of Mass Destruction', an assessment of the British Government, London, 24 September 2002, p. 3.
313. Blix 2004, p. 69.
314. United Nations Security Council, S/2003/576, E.G., pp. 1, 6, 11 and 15.

euphemistically described it. This asymmetrical military confrontation resulted in thousands of civilian deaths.[315] The exact number will never be known, since neither the incoming coalition forces nor the Iraqi authorities kept casualty records.

On 23 May 2003, the UN Security Council unanimously passed Resolution 1483 ending six-and-a-half years of the most comprehensive economic sanctions ever imposed on a country and with it, the UN Oil-for-Food Programme. The review of this period, using official and private sources and taking into account personal experience, make it profoundly clear that the Iraqi people were subjected to two forms of undeserved punishment: heavy restrictions on their freedom and their fundamental human rights by the Iraqi Government, and severe deprivation of their lives through externally imposed economic sanctions.

The protagonists, those responsible within the Iraqi Government and those who had the political power within the UN Security Council to shape the international Iraq policy during the period 1990 to 2003, cannot escape the historic debt which they have jointly accumulated and owe to the people of Iraq.[316] The Government of Iraq and the UN Security Council had distinct and early policy options, but both chose not to exercise these in the interest of the Iraqi people, at least not to the extent which could have made a genuine difference in their lives.

They clearly share the heavy burden of responsibility for what has happened in Iraq. Permanent members in the UN Security Council did not use the power of veto when humanitarian considerations called for it and only rarely opted to abstain, even when it became obvious that the UN Security Council began to disregard the UN Charter and other international law. The wider international community, including the non permanent members during those years, must also shoulder responsibility for having been largely acquiescent while a human catastrophe was in the making. Good rhetoric cannot be a substitute for good action.

What were these policy options the UN Security Council had but did not take? In August 1990 when the first Resolution (661) was adopted to impose economic sanctions against Iraq, an assessment of basic needs

---

315. Ibid., p. 2: one can only wonder about the mindset of the authors of the UN report when they wrote, *inter alia*, that just before the war there had been a 'distribution of toys ... to primary school children to keep them occupied during the conflict'.
316. A letter dated 13 April 1995 from the permanent representatives of China, France, the Russian Federation, the United Kingdom and the United States to the President of the UN Security Council on the humanitarian impact of sanctions made it clear that the P5 Group had a full understanding of the implications and dangers of sanctions as policy instruments. In the context of Iraq they chose to ignore this understanding. See Appendix B, doc UN S/1995/300, page 299.

should have been carried out to determine the scope of the humanitarian exemption. While this was not done in 1990, there was a further opportunity to do so following the 1991 Gulf War and the adoption of a second fundamental Resolution (687) in April 1991.

The United Nations Secretariat solicited the international community for donations to prevent a human catastrophe during the years 1991–5 but the Government of Iraq and the UN Security Council were locked into disagreements over the details of a humanitarian programme. The UN Security Council had the option to unfreeze all the Iraqi assets it had abroad. This did not happen. When the Council realised that donated funds were a far cry from what the UN had identified as minimum requirements, it could have made a sustained effort with member governments and the wider international community to find these resources. Had there been the political will to do so, resources could have been found. At the time when the Oil-for-Food Programme was agreed, a sound resource base could have been established. The amount of $1.3 billion had no realistic basis, as was recognised by a string of subsequent Security Council amendments. The level of oil production could have been synchronised with identified needs of the civilian population.

Neither the needs nor the resource levels required to meet those needs were established. The distribution plans the Government of Iraq and the United Nations negotiated were considered as 'supplementary' and 'temporary'. This was done without knowledge of the locally available resources. When these resources became identified as marginal, the UN Security Council realised the predicament it had created for the Iraqi people. The Council could have responded at that time by agreeing to more realistic resource levels. There was the option to supplement oil revenue with funds from international appeals and contributions from those governments which insisted on tight, comprehensive economic sanctions. This was proposed by the Secretary-General but not considered by the Security Council.

As it became clear that the sanction provisions were anything but temporary, the UN Security Council could have restructured sanctions in such a way that the costs for running a nation would have been met. Instead, the Security Council continued for many years with the implementation of what essentially amounted to an 'emergency' supply programme. It was not only financing of recurrent costs that was required. The UN Security Council could have broadened the scope of the Oil-for-Food Programme in order to ensure that institutions in such sectors as public utilities, health, agriculture and education were maintained to function for the people.

It was not long before the UN Security Council became fully aware that the bureaucratisation of the procurement of humanitarian supplies and the inordinate resorting to putting oil equipment and spare parts, equipment for health and agriculture programmes, chemicals and testing equipment on hold had devastating effects on the running of the Oil-for-Food Programme. The Security Council had the option to ease these restrictions and entrust the monitoring of the deployment of these supplies to the UN team in Baghdad. The Security Council chose not to do so.

Throughout the sanctions period all members of the UN Security Council expressed their dismay over the plight of the Iraqi people. They were increasingly aware of the inadequacy of the resources they had made available. Their concern could have translated into special protective measures for the most vulnerable groups, particularly Iraqi youth in such areas as education, training and health. The slow implementation of the special targeted nutrition programmes by the Government of Iraq became politicised by members of the Security Council. The reasons for the delays were technical and not a deliberate attempt by the Government of Iraq to promote suffering. The Council knew this because UN agencies had conveyed the facts. Members of the Council, however, chose to argue otherwise. Due to war and neglect, the poor state of the infrastructure, including roads, bridges, rail networks, water, sanitation and electricity made it next to impossible to return Iraqi life to normality. The Security Council frequently discussed infrastructure needs but moved slowly before making allowances for some rehabilitation. A sense of justified urgency and speedier changes could have made a difference to the welfare of the people.

Despite awareness of the seriousness of the human conditions in Iraq, there was no genuine sense of urgency in the UN Security Council. Calls made by the UN Secretary-General for ending the misery of the Iraqis were heard regularly during the decade yet more often than not remained either unanswered or resulted in requests for more studies and reports. Timely acceptance of UN assessments of conditions in Iraq, including the specific proposals of the Amorim panel of 1999, could have prevented much death and destitution. Instead, procrastination prevailed leading to years of delay in implementing agreed changes, e.g., of the level of allowable revenues or in the rules concerning the flow of goods. Had these changes been carried out earlier they could have made a substantial difference.

In the early 2000s the international discussion on 'intelligent sanctions', sanctions that were focused on the perpetrators rather than a whole nation, began to intensify. A UN inter-agency working group on sanctions in New York, made up of representatives of various UN agencies, the NGO community and members of the Iraq and other UN sanctions committees, issued a series of working papers.[317] These papers showed a perceptive understanding of the needs for basic reforms to improve the focus and administration of economic sanctions and to reduce unintended harm to

317. E.g., Non-Paper (Rev. 7), dated 31 January 2001.

the civilian community. The UN Security Council repeatedly discussed the targeting of sanctions. It took more than five years to adopt, in 2002, Resolution 1409,[318] which became known in UN circles as the 'smart sanctions' resolution because it introduced a more reasonable processing of civilian supplies. An earlier sense of urgency within the UN Security Council combined with more confidence in the capacity of the UN in Iraq to monitor distribution unquestionably would have had a positive impact on the humanitarian programme.

The UN Security Council was aware of Iraq's excessively high unemployment. Under sanctions civilian industry and commerce could not be resuscitated to reduce this. The Council had the option to facilitate the resumption of private sector activities along with appropriate UN monitoring. This option was discussed in the Security Council on several occasions, but ultimately not pursued.

Throughout the sanctions period members of the Security Council referred to the negative effects for the Iraqi population and criticized the status quo that often characterised the Iraq debate in the Council. Key UN resolutions governing comprehensive economic sanctions against Iraq lacked the precise language, the specificity of objectives and the time-frames to allow an objective Iraq debate. Invariably this played into the hands of those who dominated the Iraq discussion in the Council. The Security Council could have tried much more persistently to overcome this weakness and in so doing 'act in accordance with the interests of the international community' – especially the people of Iraq – rather than in the interests of powerful members of the UN Security Council.

During more than twelve years of sanctions, the Security Council certainly did not do justice to its oversight responsibilities. Periodic assessments of the Oil-for-Food Programme were usually initiated by the UN Secretary-General, not the Security Council. Ambassador Wang Yingfan of China referred to this in the Security Council when he said in March 2000: 'Unfortunately, to date the UN has not been able to launch comprehensive reviews of the negative impact of the ten years sanctions on Iraq in the economic, social, cultural, religious human rights ...'.[319] With one notable exception, chairpersons of the Iraq Sanctions Committee never came to Iraq to gain first-hand information. Neither did any other members of this Committee or of the Security Council itself.[320]

318. See UN S/RES/1409 (2002) adopted by the UN Security Council on 14 May 2002.
319. S/PV.4120, UN Security Council, 4120th meeting, 24 March 2000, p. 18.
320. Ambassador Antonio Monteiro, Permanent Representative of Portugal to the United Nations and Chairman of the Iraq Sanctions Committee, visited Iraq briefly in 1998.

The option of regularly inviting UN officials serving in Iraq to brief the UN Security Council in New York was not chosen. In fact, it was often discouraged and even blocked by the United States and the United Kingdom against the preference of the majority.[321] Only towards the end of the sanctions period did briefings by Baghdad-based UN officials become more frequent. Apart from increasing such briefings, the format for UN reporting on the Oil-for-Food Programme was scandalously inadequate, as it did not provide for regular reporting on the human conditions in the country. Adding this important aspect the UN Security Council would have been in a better position to exercise its oversight mandate. That such reporting never became a standard feature must be considered as one of the major neglects of the Council's and the UN Secretariat's responsibilities.[322] The UN Security Council certainly had the option to request this. Just as briefings by Baghdad-based UN officials and reporting by the UN team in Iraq on the conditions in the country were discouraged, so was the political dialogue between the United Nations and the Government of Iraq. For this reason, the meetings between the UN Secretary-General and Saddam Hussein's Government were scarce and interaction between the Government in Baghdad and the UN Security Council was practically nonexistent.

In 2000, Ambassador Dr Tono Eitel, who had been Germany's Permanent Representative to the UN in New York, and due to that position had also been the Chairman of the UN Iraq Sanctions Committee, presented in his personal capacity a report[323] that was highly critical of sanctions-related developments in the Security Council. 'It is ... necessary for the targeted state ... to be able to interact with the [Security] Council already in the decision-making process', he pointed out and reminded of

321. On several occasions my predecessor in Baghdad, Denis Halliday, and I were asked by members of the UN Security Council to give the Council special briefings. The US and UK argued against their usefulness. On one occasion they went as far as writing to the UN Secretary-General to say that Halliday and I had only served in one sanctions circumstance and therefore could not be considered 'experts' on sanctions issues. In plain language: meeting two former officials with first-hand comprehensive sanctions experience was a waste of Security Council's time. They chose to overlook the fact that there was no precedent: Iraq was the only country ever to have received comprehensive economic sanctions.

322. A British student very familiar with UN affairs and sanctions against Iraq once observed to the author: 'For a $60 billion programme a horrifically poor reporting system and continuously changing parameters, the political side seemingly had no interest in accuracy nor in comparability!' The phase-by-phase review and difficulties in compiling comparative data certainly confirm this!

323. Ambassador Tono Eitel, UN informal report to the UN Security Council Working Group on General Issues on Sanctions, New York, 14 November 2002.

the Council's Provisional Rules of Procedure,[324] which confirm that 'unless it decides otherwise … [the Council] shall meet in public.' This had been the case in the past, allowing any interested party, particularly states affected by Security Council policies, to participate. 'Due to a grave change of procedure it is now the other way around: the Council meets daily in so-called 'informal consultations' behind closed doors, inaccessible to those who may have a vital interest in the sanctions project discussed'.[325] This is exactly how I experienced the Security Council. Just before an Iraq debate would begin, I would see Iraqi diplomats talking to some of those about to go into the Council chambers. When the meeting was called to order and the doors were closing, representatives of the Iraqi mission to the UN had to stay outside: they were not allowed to join. Incredible as it was, the Iraq situation would be reviewed without them.

This is not what the founders of the United Nations in 1945 had in mind. 'The United Nations shall place no restrictions on the eligibility of men and women to participate in any capacity and under conditions of equality in its principal and subsidiary organs' is what the UN Charter pronounces.[326] This was in 1945. Half a century later, the reality at UN headquarters looked different.

The UN Security Council certainly had many opportunities for linking up with the UN team in Baghdad, for receiving UN reports dedicated to conditions in the country and for interaction with representatives of the Iraq Government. It opted not to make use of these opportunities and gave in to those who preferred the isolation of Iraq to communication with Iraq.

The gamut of options which the UN Security Council had at its disposal was wide indeed. It contained the ingredients for a much more humane handling of economic sanctions. The Malaysian Ambassador to the UN in New York Tan Sri Hasmy Agam put it well when he said at the end of 1999 in the UN Security Council: 'Improvements … are essentially selective humanitarian measures which will only lead to incremental improvements and only address a small fraction of the needs of the Iraqi people'.[327] This would have been an equally valid observation four years later, at the end of sanctions in May 2003.

Whoever the members of the UN Security Council were, as individuals and the countries they represented during the twelve years of sanctions, they – individually and collectively – had the knowledge of all the aspects of the human catastrophe that was unfolding in Iraq. They could all have

324. Ibid., p. 1.
325. Ibid.
326. See UN Charter, chap. III, article 8.
327. See UN S/PV.4084, UN Security Council, 4084th meeting, 17 December 2000, p. 7.

contributed much more to bringing to an end that part of the punishment of the Iraqi people for which the international community was responsible. Instead of joining hands with like-minded governments and using their combined strength to insist on changes, they were satisfied with lip service.

The hard-line approach prevailed, with the result that practically an entire nation was subjected to poverty, death and destruction of its physical and mental foundations. Defenders of this approach will angrily reject this conclusion as false, biased or even 'nonsense' and point to the improvements that they had helped to introduce to the humanitarian programme in Iraq. Yes, there were improvements, incremental improvements, but not more than that.

The protagonists will not readily admit that even these changes for the betterment of the Iraqi people came about haphazardly, immensely slowly, and ultimately only because of the mounting pressure from the general UN membership, selected members of the Security Council and the international public. They did not come about because of a genuine will to reduce the suffering of a people living under sanctions and in the hands of a dictator.

The hardliners will also argue that the plight of the Iraqi people was entirely due to Saddam Hussein: 'It had all along been in his hands to end his people's misery'. That he chose not to do his part does not absolve the UN Security Council for failing to do its part. The United States and the United Kingdom, as the main and permanent hardliners in the UN Security Council throughout the twelve years of economic sanctions, insisted on the linkage of disarmament and economic sanctions. They were absolutely determined not to accept that more intensive humanitarian monitoring on the part of the UN in Iraq to prevent the arrival of possible WMD-related dual-use supplies would have been feasible and would have allowed a de-linking of the military embargo from economic sanctions. This could have allowed a broad reduction in the scope of economic sanctions. Those who were incapable of seeing beyond their own agenda insisted that there was no realistic approach in dealing with Iraq other than to maintain this linkage. 'It is preposterous to suggest that disarmament of Iraq could be done without economic sanctions', I was told by Ambassador John Dauth of Australia following an open debate on Iraq between Charles Duelfer, formerly with UNSCOM,[328] and myself in the Canadian mission to the United Nations in May 2002. This was one example of the uncompromising approach of those who were not able to strike a balance between their political objectives and humanitarian principles.

328. Charles Duelfer had been Deputy to Ambassador Richard Butler, Executive Chairman of UNSCOM. In 2004 Duelfer headed the US Iraq Survey Group charged by US President Bush to find Iraq's weapons of mass destruction.

A review of US and UK statements in the UN Security Council during the lifespan of the Oil-for-Food Programme (1996–2003) reveals an impressively consistent, albeit exceptionally rigid, stand on Iraq, summarised as: 'we do not want to see Iraqis suffering, we have no choice, however, to maintain economic sanctions and corresponding controls, since Saddam Hussein remains a serious threat. All he has to do is to cooperate, show evidence of complete disarmament and sanctions will be lifted.' In the words of Sir Jeremy Greenstock of the United Kingdom: 'There are two principles which have guided us and must continue to guide us … to prevent Iraq from posing a threat … ensure that Iraq is fully and verifiably disarmed' and 'alleviate the suffering of the Iraqi people and take whatever steps we can from outside to ensure that their needs are met'.[329] The message from the United States delivered by Ambassador Burleigh was the same: 'The United States has demonstrated a sincere and enduring interest in the welfare of the Iraqi citizens living under the tyranny and misrule of Saddam Hussein … Iraq has not fulfilled its obligations under the previous resolutions, sanctions must and will remain unchanged until Iraq does so …'.[330]

This was stubbornness, hypocrisy and callousness, with a high price tag for the Iraqi people and the UN's institutional integrity. It did not occur to them that to act 'in conformity with the principles of justice and international law' and 'in accordance with the purposes and principles of the United Nations' and out of 'universal respect for and observance of human rights and fundamental freedoms for all …'[331] was as binding for the US and the UK Governments and the UN Security Council as a whole as it was for the Government of Iraq.

Whether adherence to the status quo or adjustment to evolving circumstances in Iraq was the more appropriate approach for the UN Security Council to take will be discussed for a long time to come. The unravelling of the Iraq picture during the preceding review facilitates the conclusions on what would have been more acceptable approaches of the UN Security Council towards the Iraqi people and the international peace-building machinery. The UN Security Council bears the full responsibility for the international Iraq policies of the years 1990 to 2003. The question of whether the UN Secretariat as a subsidiary body had any margin of freedom to influence the policies of the UN Security Council is not easy to answer. In the light of the human catastrophe that resulted early on from the comprehensive economic sanctions measures, an answer to this question must, however, be given.

The UN Secretariat, from the beginning in 1990, neither structurally nor professionally established itself in a way that would have allowed it

329. UN SC/S/PV.4336, 4336th meeting, 26 June 2001, p. 4.
330. UN SC/S/PV.4084, 4084th meeting, 17 December 1999, pp. 18 and 21.
331. See UN Charter, articles 1(1), 24(2) and 55(c).

to run in an optimal manner the largest humanitarian programme that it had ever undertaken until then. The word 'establish' is used here because the UN Secretariat did have choices and it chose what turned out not to be in the best interests of a humanitarian undertaking. Until 1995 all humanitarian affairs were handled by the Office for the Coordination of Humanitarian Affairs (OCHA), headed at the time by Under-Secretary-General Yasushi Akashi, followed by Sergio Vieira de Mello in 1997. During that year the UN Secretary-General agreed to create the Office of the Iraq Programme (OIP) as an entity totally separate from OCHA. This was a serious mistake, since it deprived the new Iraq Unit from benefiting from the OCHA's experience with humanitarian exemptions in different parts of the world. To further aggravate this situation, the OIP and OCHA were openly discouraged from cooperating and, within the wider UN Secretariat, the OIP was not brought into the interdepartmental structure in a way that would have allowed continuous policy interaction with the departments for peacekeeping, political, legal, disarmament, humanitarian, social and economic affairs.[332] The Oil-for-Food Programme basically led a life of 'splendid isolation'. A UN Office of the Iraq Programme, well integrated into the Secretariat structure, could have significantly raised the quality of backstopping for the Oil-for-Food Programme, since a much broader access to UN sanction experience would have become available. More relevantly trained and experienced staff could have helped to run the humanitarian exemption and provide the United Nations Office of the Iraq Programme with better tools and also better arguments to influence the UN Security Council debate on Iraq. The immediate beneficiaries would certainly have been the Iraqi people.

The question of 'why' the UN Security Council did not follow through on the options it had to humanise economic sanctions cannot be fully explained by the heavy handedness of two of its members. A limited time of two years on the Council for the ten elected members and the resulting lack of Iraq knowledge, accentuated for many by lack of financial and human resources available to their permanent missions to go into depth in the Iraq discussion, has something to do with lack of forcefulness and lack of weight of their stands in the Council or with their ambivalence vis-à-vis the Council's Iraq policies. The more important factor is, no doubt, the pressure relentlessly applied to weaker countries in the Council by the US and the UK Governments for compliance in return for political, economic and military favours in other areas. In this regard, China, France and Russia, the P3 Group were in a similar situation, as they too were continuously subjected to such pressure politics.

---

332. A former UNOCHA staff member with solid experience in sanctions matters was told to stay away from the Office of the Iraq Programme across the hall on the same floor of the UN Secretariat 'because they are too political'.

The Security Council was fully aware of the financial limitations of the Oil-for-Food Programme from its beginning in December 1996, as the Council had been of the financial shortages of international humanitarian assistance in the preceding years. The inadequate levels of revenue for the humanitarian programme remained a subject of concern to many members of the UN Security Council throughout the thirteen phases of the programme. The financial basis of $1.3 billion for the initial period of six months of the Oil-for-Food Programme in 1996/7 had been established by the UN Security Council without a rigorous assessment of needs. Removing the oil ceiling in 1999 did not and could not lead to adequate revenue levels for the humanitarian programme, given the state of Iraq's oil industry. Even though the UN Secretary-General did repeatedly introduce proposals for supplementary financing beyond earned oil revenue, as did Ambassador Amorim in 1999 (unfreezing Iraqi assets abroad, voluntary international contributions, revival of the private sector economy, etc.), the Security Council never took decisions in this respect. The Iraqi people were simply left to the whims of a volatile international oil market and to an ailing Iraqi oil industry rather than to a careful and continuously updated assessment of needs of the Oil-for-Food Programme, resulting in adequate financial allocations and policy adjustments.

On the eve of the March 2003 war, some thirteen years after economic sanctions were imposed by the UN Security Council on Iraq and the Oil-for-Food Programme had been operational for six-and-a-half years since December 1996, the picture which emerges of the conditions of life of the Iraqi people shows a stark reality:

Child malnutrition

Prior to 1990 chronic[333] and acute malnutrition rates[334] in Iraq were modest and similar to those of a well-nourished population. The Iraqi Ministry of Health reported that from January 1989 to August 1990 approximately 1 percent of hospital admissions were due to malnutrition. Between 1991 and 1996, there was a sharp increase in malnutrition, particularly child malnutrition. As of 1997 – the beginning of the Oil-for-Food Programme – these rates levelled off at moderately high levels. Nevertheless, one out of five children under five in Central or Southern Iraq was chronically malnourished.[335] In Iraqi Kurdistan malnutrition

---

333. Stunting/height for age.
334. Wasting/weight for height.
335. 1996 Multiple Indicator Cluster Survey: A survey to assess the situation of children and women in Iraq. Final report with results from south/centre governorates/Iraq. UNICEF Ref. IRQ/97/288, August 1996.

levels had been moderate prior to 1990; these levels rose through 1994, then gradually declined.[336]

Child mortality

Iraq, like many Arab states, had high levels of mortality among children under five relative to the country's per capita income during the 1960s and 1970s. Infant mortality fell in the 1980s to an all-time low which, however, was still about 20 percent higher than in neighbouring Jordan.[337] It rose more than twofold during and after the 1991 Gulf War. Instead of declining after 1997 with the introduction of the Oil-for-Food Programme, it plateaued at unprecedentedly high levels: between 100 and 120 deaths per 1000.[338] In Iraqi Kurdistan, better access to health services, lower rates of malnutrition, higher levels of humanitarian assistance, and higher levels of employment contributed to falling mortality rates that reached historic lows in the late 1990s.[339]

Calories per capita

Up to August 1990, approximately 3,375 calories per capita per day were available for Iraqis. Within the region, only Turkey had higher calorie availability levels. In 1991, calories available via subsidised rations had fallen to about 1,300. As of 1997, the beginning of the Oil-for-Food Programme, calorie levels improved and remained up to the end of economic sanctions in 2003 at levels between 2000 and 2215 calories or about 65 percent of the pre-sanction levels.[340] In Iraqi Kurdistan the same rations were distributed, but most people had access to additional foods through self-production or purchase of additional supplies.

336. Ibid., Final report with results from the northern governorates, UNICEF, Iraq, May 1997; R. Garfield, 'Changes in Malnutrition Levels in Iraq, 1990–1999', (US) Nutrition Reviews 58(9) (2000); 269–77.
337. M. Hurwitz and P. David, The State of Children's Health in Pre-war Iraq, London: Centre for Population Studies, London School of Hygiene and Tropical Medicine, August 1992.
338. According to J. Blacker, G. Jones and M. Ali, 'Annual Mortality Rates and Excess Deaths of Children under Five in Iraq, 1991–98', Population Stud (Camb.) 57(2) (2003): 217–26, the number of excess deaths of children under five during 1991–8 was between 400,000 and 500,000.
339. Ibid.
340. FAO/WFP Crop, Food Supply and Nutrition Assessment Mission to Iraq, 5 June to 14 July 2003, September 2003, FAO, Rome.

Adult literacy

The Government of Iraq did not permit international organisations to carry out regular assessments of the state of literacy in the country. Limited studies indicated that literacy among adults declined during 1990–2003 from around 81 percent to 74 percent. Literacy was lower for women and people in rural areas, reaching a low of about 50 percent among rural women.[341] In Iraqi Kurdistan, literacy increased in the 1990s to around half of all adults.[342]

Per capita income[343]

Iraq's annual income expressed in per capita terms peaked in 1980 at about $2,450. It rapidly declined in 1990 to a low of about $250. Due to higher oil prices it began to recover from 1998 onwards, maintaining a level of about $1,000/year, but never reached the pre-war (1989) level which at that time was double the regional average.[344] Jordan, a country without oil reserves and traditionally a poor neighbour of Iraq, increased its per capita income during the period 1990 to 2001 from $1,235 to $1,725.[345] Iraq had fallen from being prosperous to one of the poorer countries in the region. The decline was far less in Iraqi Kurdistan after 1993, due to local rain-fed agriculture, remittances from families in other countries, development funds, and smuggling.

Primary and secondary school enrolment

Total school enrolment remained stagnant through the 1990s despite a 3 percent annual rise in the population. The percentage of children attending primary schools gradually declined throughout the period 1990–2003. Nearly twice as many girls as boys dropped out of secondary school. In Iraqi Kurdistan primary and secondary school enrolment increased by 50 percent from 1995–2002.[346]

---

341. The 1996 Multiple Indicator Cluster Survey: A Survey to Assess the Situation of Children and Women in Iraq. Final Results from South/Centre Governorates, Iraq, UNICEF Ref. IRQ/97/288, August 1996.
342. The 1996 Multiple Indicator Cluster Survey: A Survey to Assess the Situation of Families in Iraq. Final Report with Results from the Northern Governorates, UNICEF, Iraq, May 1997.
343. In constant (2002) US dollars.
344. Coalition Provisional Authority. An Historic Review of CPA Accomplishments on http://www.iraqcoalition.org and El-Guindi T. The Extent and Geographical Distribution of Chronic Poverty in Iraq's Centre/South Region, UN-WFP, May 2003.
345. UNDP Human Development Report, 2004.
346. UN Development Group. Iraq Watching Brief.

Per capita production of water per day

During the 1980s piped water reached most Iraqis, especially those in cities. The system deteriorated severely throughout the 1990s. Deterioration of the system reduced the amount and quality of water produced far more than the number of connections to water networks. For Baghdad alone, there was a 55 percent decrease from 330 litres/day in 1989 to about 150 litres in 2003.[347] Both coverage and quality increased from very low levels in Iraqi Kurdistan, but were still less than in the Centre and South. Increase was due to greater levels of investment and better local administration.

Sanitation

Most people in Iraq had piped connections for waste disposal increased in the early 1990s. Waste connections receiving sanitary treatment was small at the beginning of the period and approached zero[348] by 1996. Piped connections rose in Iraqi Kurdistan, but still only reached about half of households.[349] The percentage of the population with piped connections for waste water disposal increased in the early 1990s. However, the proportion with treatment of that water was small in the beginning of the period and approached zero by 1996. Little recovery occurred during the Oil-for-Food period.

Professional disagreement exists among the protagonists and in the international community as to whether comprehensive economic sanctions led to a violation of international law or not. There are even disputes among those who agree that sanctions did cause such violation. Some will maintain that the breaking of international law on the part of the UN Security Council was premeditated, while others will not be willing to see more than violation of law through negligence and questionable priorities.

There cannot be any disagreement that the economic sanctions imposed by the UN Security Council on Iraq in August 1990[350] in response to Iraq's invasion into Kuwait were legal. Iraq had violated international law and the UN Security Council had decided that this violation constituted such a serious 'threat to peace' and was an 'act of aggression' to which the international community had the right to respond with military action and with economic sanctions.[351] Whether the 1991 Gulf War could have been avoided through further negotiations

347. http://Inweb 18.worldbank.org.
348. Ibid.
349. Ibid.
350. See UN S/RES/661, August 1990.
351. See UN Charter, Chap. VII, articles 39 and 42.

can be discussed, but is not an issue here. Of paramount importance, however, are the questions of how this right to impose economic sanctions on Iraq was used to implement such sanctions, and whether and when the application of sanction law became itself a violation of international law and the cause of a human catastrophe. In raising these questions I side with those who argue that the UN Security Council failed to carry out its policies within the limits prescribed by the UN Charter.

The evidence of the correctness of this assertion is simply overwhelming, as we have seen. First of all, comprehensive economic sanctions were implemented by the United Nations without careful predetermination of needs of the civilian population. The accompanying UN resolutions were imprecisely formulated, and therefore open to interpretation and political exploitation. Objective and controllable sanction implementation for the protection of the Iraqi population was thus not possible.

A date during the 1990–2003 sanctions period at which the UN Security Council had crossed the boundary between acceptable inconvenience for an innocent population or 'collateral damage' and unacceptable or illegal treatment of the Iraqi population cannot be defined precisely. I would argue that the first step in the direction of violation of international law was taken when the UN Security Council did not respond adequately in its humanitarian policy to the warnings of UN Under-Secretary-General Athisaari and the UN Executive Delegate, Prince Sadruddin Aga Khan in 1991 that a human catastrophe of extraordinary proportions was in the making.

A second major step towards illegality involved the manner in which the UN Security Council carried out its oversight mandate. Loosely formulated resolutions, an absence of needs assessments and neglect of continuous oversight and the resulting inadequate resource base paved the road on which the UN Security Council travelled from a legal start to an illegal destination. The humanitarian protection of the Iraqi people was quickly overwhelmed by the weight of economic sanctions in the early years of the 1990s.

It will be left to experts in international law to provide the details. Suffice it here to reiterate the disregard by the UN Security Council of fundamentals and the profound impact this had upon the people of Iraq. Can one in good faith maintain that Article 50 of the Hague Convention and Regulations of 1907 (No general penalty, pecuniary or otherwise shall be inflicted on the population on account of the acts of individuals for which they cannot be regarded as jointly or severally responsible.) was taken into account when devising comprehensive sanctions for Iraq?[352]

---

352. See Convention IV, Respecting the Laws and Customs of War on Land and its annex: Regulations Concerning the Laws and Customs of War on Land, The Hague, 18 October 1907.

Are the indicators for child mortality, malnutrition and illiteracy during the years of sanctions and their causes not evidence of the violation of Article 50? At the time when phase VIII of the UN Oil-for-Food Programme had just started in June 2000, the UN Commission on Human Rights heard the legal assessment of UN sanctions on Iraq by Professor Mark Bossuyt. An eminent lawyer who serves as a Judge in Belgium's Court of Arbitration, Bossuyt suggested the adoption of a six-prong test for evaluating the legality of sanctions.[353] This test relates to the validity of the reasons for sanctions, the targeting, the time-frame, the effectiveness and the acceptance of sanctions by the international community. In the course of the years of sanctions their initial validity vanished: Iraq retreated from Kuwait, a disarmament process started, the regime in Baghdad benefited from the 'hothouse' existence of international isolation and the people of Iraq felt the brunt of dictatorship and sanctions.

While there was a continuing justification for a military embargo, there was none for comprehensive economic sanctions. This is also the response to the question of whether economic sanctions were targeting the proper parties, goods or objects. An old man in Erbil who died because the battery of medicines he needed for his heart condition was not available, or the child that passed away in Basrah because the hospital had no rehydration fluids for the treatment of cholera, or the young woman in Hillah that grew up as an illiterate because her parents did not have the money to send her to school, or the twins in Baghdad who were permanently disabled due to severe stunting in early childhood since the parents could not feed them properly – were they the proper targets of economic sanctions?

The fact that the UN Security Council, in imposing sanctions on Iraq, had not included any time-bound termination clauses in this unique case of sanctions had a particularly detrimental effect on the people of Iraq. Professor Bossuyt's reference to the 'undue future burden' effect is of special importance in the Iraq context. An Iraqi boy or girl aged six at the beginning of sanctions in 1990 was nineteen at their end in 2003. In contrast to their parents, these children will have had a 'poor' education at best. Badly trained, sometimes even untrained teachers, limited teaching aids, outdated or no textbooks at primary and secondary-school levels, and certainly no state-of-the-art access to knowledge at tertiary level – these were the characteristics of education under sanctions. During my visits to different parts of Iraq I not only saw the collapsed education system, the run-down classrooms, the empty libraries, the broken-down sanitary facilities, the sewerage in schoolyards, I heard the complaints of

---

353. See UN Economic and Social Council, E/CN.4/Sub.2/2000/33, 21 June 2000, The Adverse Consequences of Economic Sanctions on the Enjoyment of Human Rights.

headmasters and parents alike. I discussed with students and realised their fears about a tomorrow for which they knew they were not well prepared. What an 'undue burden' indeed for innocent youth that are expected to play their future role in Iraqi, regional and global communities.

The economic sanctions imposed by the UN Security Council were not free from international protest. The global outcry against these undiscriminating sanctions grew stronger and stronger in the course of the thirteen years, and did affect national attitudes towards international sanctions policy, regrettably not in those countries that took the uncompromising and hard-line approach in the UN Security Council.[354]

If Professor Bossuyt's sanctions test had been part of the Security Council's toolkit, its application would have shown failure on all counts early on in the implementation of sanctions. Early redress and resorting to targeted sanctions would have helped protect an innocent population. The international community can not but insist that the UN Security Council as a whole, and individual member governments represented in the Council during these years, had the knowledge and the options to forestall this catastrophe. The default, however, is even more serious than simply ignoring options. Knowledge and adherence to the Iraqi policies that led to this immense suffering of a people invariably establishes a casual relationship and points to 'intent'. Evidence of intent[355] in turn leads to evidence of conscious violation of human rights and humanitarian law on the part of governments represented in the Security Council, first and foremost those of the United States and the United Kingdom.[356] There will be those who will reject this hard conclusion as an untenable anti-American/anti-British bias. This is not so. However, those

354. The Hague Convention of 1907 (referred to also in the Geneva Convention of 1949) includes the so-called 'Martens Clause' – named after Professor von Martens, the Russian delegate at the Hague Peace Conferences in 1899 - which establishes *inter alia* the legal value of the public conscience. The international protest against economic sanctions therefore strengthens the conclusion that Iraq sanctions violated international law.
355. The Sanctions Assessment Handbook published by the United Nations in October 2004 states: 'Establishing intent does not prove that "sanctions caused children to die". Instead, one has to ask, "what did they die of? Did the lack of crucial supplies contribute to a higher death rate? Did sanctions reduce access to those supplies? If all of this can be shown, evidence of intent can form the first link in a chain of causation".' This chain of causation existed in the case of Iraq.
356. In the report Professor Marc Bossuyt presented to the UN Economic and Social Council in 2000 came to the grave conclusion that 'the sanction regime against Iraq has as its clear purpose the deliberate infliction on the Iraqi people of conditions of life (lack of adequate food, medicines, etc.) calculated to bring about its physical destruction in whole or in part', i.e., that member governments of the UN Security Council violated article 2(c) of the UN Genocide Convention of 1948. See E/CN.4/SUB.2/2000/33, p. 18.

who confuse the reality of US/UK Governments as well as Security Council wrongdoings with the wrongdoings of dictator Saddam Hussein and his Government are out of order. Similar reasoning can be applied to the adopted humanitarian exemption measures. The Oil-for-Food Programme could and should have been equipped by the UN Security Council to indeed 'exempt' the civilian population from lack of medicines, absence of diagnostic equipment, education materials, etc.[357] The fact that the UN Security Council had the options to do so but chose not to leads again to the issue of 'intent' and confirms that inadequacy of humanitarian supplies under sanctions also constituted violation of international humanitarian law. The correctness of this assertion is not called into question by the fact that inadequacy of humanitarian supplies at times was also due to the improper handling of imports by the Government of Iraq. Even the full utilisation of revenue as permitted under sanctions by the UN Security Council would not have led to adequate protection of the civilian population in Iraq, especially not in the initial six phases (1996–9) of the Oil-for-Food Programme. The conclusion that, *inter alia*, the UN Convention on the Rights of the Child, the Genocide Convention, the Covenant on Economic, Social and Cultural Rights was violated by the UN Security Council from the beginning of the Oil-for-Food Programme in 1996 by, for example, severe limitations of rights of children to health, development of their personalities and education is therefore sound.[358]

357. The frequent contention of the US and UK Governments that the welfare of the Iraqi people depended on the cooperation of the Government of Iraq detracted from the key issue. It was the obligation of the UN Security Council, in the very interest of the Iraqi people, not to depend on such cooperation. Dr L. Oette, a humanitarian law expert, writes: 'The [UN] Security Council has the duty to shape economic sanctions in such a way that, independent of the comportment of the party against whom sanctions are pronounced, they do not lead to an extensive infringement on human rights.' See L. Oette, 'Die Vereinbarkeit der vom Sicherheitsrat nach Kapitel VII der UN Charta Verhängten Wirtschafts – Sanktionen mit den Menschenrechten und dem Humanitären Völkerrecht', *European University Studies*, series II, vol. 3689 (2003): 274.

358. Article 6 of the UN Convention on The Rights of The Child of 1989 states: '(1) States parties recognize that every child has the inherent right to life; and (2) states parties shall ensure to the maximum extent possible the survival and development of the child.' Yet, the states parties in the UN Security Council allocated only $1.3 billion for phase I of the Oil-for-Food Programme (December 1996 to May 1997) of which $817 million had to be allocated for food and nutrition. This left $504 million only for all other sectors (water, sanitation, electricity, agriculture, education and health). Even if the amount of $220 million for health had been doubled at the expense of other vital sectors such as water and sanitation, it would not have been sufficient to 'ensure to the maximum extent possible the survival and development of the (Iraqi) child'. The Security Council did have the option to make available adequate funds.

Years of sanctions and humanitarian assistance, including the Oil-for-Food Programme, ended in a political victory for the hard-liners in the UN Security Council and a defeat for the Security Council as an international conflict resolution instrument, a rejection of prevailing humanitarian law, an affront to the international public and the destruction of a people who had nothing to do with the political and disarmament conflict.

Chapter 2

The UN Compensation Commission: Benefit for Some, Deprivation for Others

The European headquarters of the United Nations is located not far from the shores of Lake Geneva. The UN took over the buildings of the League of Nations in 1946. It gradually expanded across an immaculately landscaped estate that has been on loan first to the League of Nations and subsequently to the United Nations by the City of Geneva. The north-east wing of the United Nations houses the headquarters of UNCTAD, the UN body that deals with trade and development issues in low income countries, the UN Economic Commission for Europe (ECE) and most of the larger conference rooms where, year in, year out, the issues of the world are debated by the 191 UN member countries. It is also here where each year in March the UN Human Rights Commission meets and, since 1991, has received the reports of the UN Special Rapporteur on the gruesome human rights situation in Iraq and indications by delegations and NGOs of the deteriorating conditions in Iraq due to economic sanctions.

Delegates looking out of windows facing the lakeside would most likely notice the old cedars, the fine lawns, the magnificent lake in the distance and, on clear days, the outline of Mont Blanc. Few will be curious about the nineteenth-century patrician villa, if they notice this building at all. Villa 'La Pelouse', as it is called by insiders, has served a variety of special purposes. For many years it was the official residence of the Secretary-General of the League of Nations. I got to know it in the late 1980s, when it housed the Humanitarian Programme for Afghanistan. Since the early 1990s it has been occupied by one of the least-known and most secretive UN entities, which has budgets bigger than most UN agencies. Here is the Secretariat of the UN Compensation Commission (UNCC), the low-profile body which handles claims of individuals, firms and governments who are seeking compensation for losses they have allegedly have as a result of Iraq's 1990 invasion into Kuwait.

The UN Compensation Commission for Iraq was established in May 1991[1] as a subsidiary body of the UN Security Council. This happened a few months after Saddam Hussein's occupation force was evicted from Kuwait by coalition forces led by the United States.

Demands for compensation had been made soon after Iraq's invasion of Kuwait. Foreign workers in both Iraq and Kuwait who were forced to leave the area during the August 1990 invasion and again during the 1991 Gulf War asked for compensation, as did commercial firms and government enterprises, particularly those from Kuwait.

The UN Security Council held its first informal consultations on the issue of compensation in the autumn of 1990. It became clear at that time that the UN would urgently deal with the question of compensation when the Security Council passed a resolution in October 1990. The resolution reminded Iraq that under international law it was liable for 'loss, damage or injury'[2] as a result of the invasion. It also asked states to compile data 'regarding their claims, and those of their nationals and corporations, for restitution or financial compensation by Iraq, with a view to such arrangements as may be established in accordance with international law.'[3] Between these first signs in the autumn of 1990 that the UN Security Council intended to set up a compensation mechanism and the establishment of the UNCC in mid-1991, there was a gradual build-up as reflected in various resolutions,[4] promoted by the US representative in the UN Security Council, towards such a mechanism as was finally established in Resolution 692 of 1991. In the same resolution the Council also decided to 'create a fund to pay compensation for claims' and to ask the UN Secretary-General to outline an administrative mechanism for determining the level of Iraq's contribution to the fund 'based on a percentage of the value of its [Iraq's] export of petroleum and petroleum products ... taking into account the requirements of the people of Iraq ...'.[5]

The fact that the future Oil-for-Food Programme, established to mitigate the effects of sanctions on the Iraqi people, would also include provisions for reparation payments to external parties would become a serious obstacle in the subsequent negotiations between the Government of Iraq and the United Nations. It explains to a large extent why the

---

1. See UN S/RES 692 (20 May 1991), para. 3, which reads: (the UN Security Council) decides to establish ... the United Nations Compensation Commission ... and decides also that the Governing Council of the Commission will be located at the United Nations in Geneva ...'.
2. See UN S/RES 674 (29 October 1990).
3. Ibid., paras. 8 and 9.
4. See UN S/RES 686 (1991) and 687 (1991).
5. See UN S/RES 687 (1991), paras 18 and 19.

Government of Iraq rejected in 1991 the oil export mechanism within the proposed humanitarian exemption. The Government felt that Iraq's sovereign right to determine freely the use of its natural resources would be impaired. It was four more years before the Iraqi Government modified its original position and accepted an Oil-for-Food formula in the light of the deteriorating human conditions in Iraq.

The US and UK Governments over the years again and again cited the Government of Iraq's refusal to accept the UN Security Council's offer of an oil-for-food programme in 1991[6] as proof that Saddam Hussein's Government did not care for its people. The two Governments failed to mention that the major reason for this refusal related to the inclusion of provisions for a UNCC-type compensation mechanism.

The beginning of the Oil-for-Food Programme in December 1996 was also the start of payments into the Compensation Fund managed by the UNCC. Initially, at the recommendation of the UN Secretary-General, 30 percent of each oil dollar earned by Iraq was transferred into the UNCC accounts.[7] As of December 1999[8] the amount was reduced to 25 percent through phase XIII in 2003. Following the March 2003 war, the lifting of economic sanctions in the following May further reduced it to 5 percent.[9] Among the fourteen countries on which the UN Security Council had imposed sanctions between 1945 and 2004,[10] Iraq stands out as a unique case. No other country has been subject to comprehensive economic sanctions of comparable scope and duration: economic sanctions here were tied to disarmament and a military embargo, and total disarmament of weapons of mass destruction constituted a precondition for ending the all embracing economic sanctions. Such an integrated package of measures was meant to promote disarmament, compensate victims of Iraq's aggression, and encourage political change within Iraq. The Oil-for-Food Programme as a humanitarian exemption under these circumstances was ill-equipped to protect the Iraqi people.

A compensation payment and claims processing mechanism formed part of this unique sanctions arrangement. A Governing Council of the UNCC constituted its main organ.

6. See UN S/RES 706 and 712 (1991).
7. See UN S/22661, 31 May 1991, para. 7
8. See UN S/RES 1330 (5 December 1999).
9. See UN S/RES 1483 (22 May 2003), para. 21. Whether the UN Charter (Article 39) provides a legal basis for such a decision is open to debate.
10. Angola, Afghanistan, Cambodia, Haiti, Iraq, Liberia, Libya, Rhodesia, Rwanda, Sierra Leone, Somalia, South Africa, Sudan and Yugoslavia.

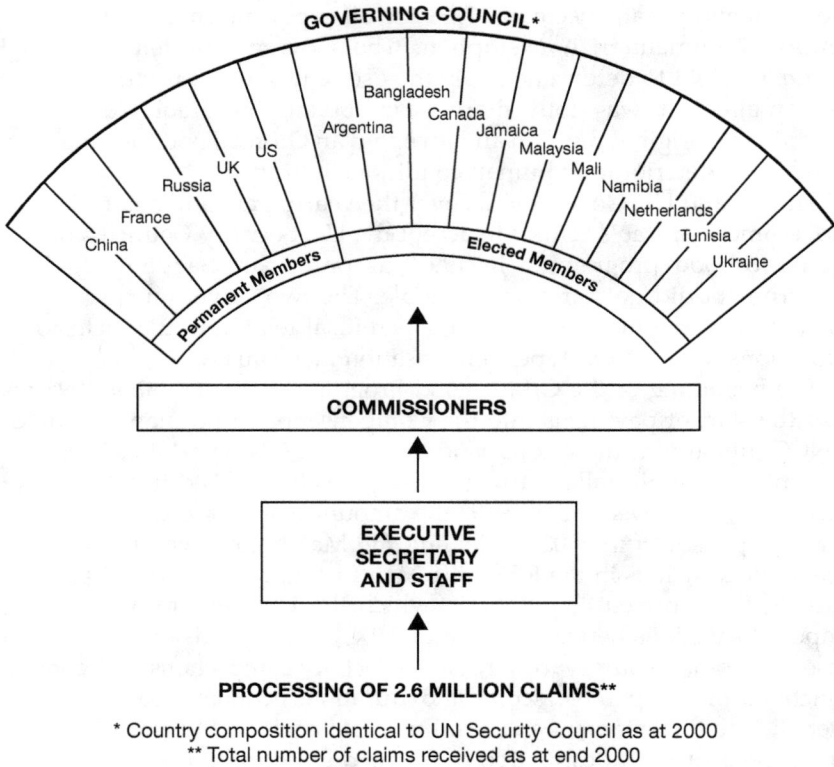

Figure 2.1 United Nations Compensation Commission (UNCC)

It was this Council which determined compensation policy, rules and procedures for entertaining claims against Iraq. The UNCC Council consisted of representatives of the fifteen Security Council member countries who presided over the UNCC as governors. The Council held sessions in Geneva four times a year and on these occasions made decisions regarding claims payments proposed by panels of commissioners assigned to specific claims categories. Governing Council meetings were closed to the public and to states that were not members of the UN Security Council. Iraq, as the compensating party, was also barred from participating in the Council's proceedings. The Governing Council approved the UNCC's annual budget which derived its resources from the payments made to the UNCC by the Oil-for-Food Programme out of earned Iraqi oil revenue.[11] An Executive Secretary appointed by the UN Secretary-General and assisted by over two hundred UN staff was responsible for the day-to-day management of the UNCC.[12]

The verification and evaluation of claims against Iraq was made by a college of commissioners. These were chosen by the Executive Secretary and approved by the UN Secretary-General. Among them were jurists, experts in finance, insurance, accountancy, engineering and other claims-related fields.[13]

Since the establishment of the UNCC in 1991, the Commission had received more than 2.6 million claims with a total value of $348 billion.[14] In mid-2004, the UNCC had finalised 2.604 million claims, awarded $48.2 billion and paid out $18.4 billion to claimants.[15] The Commission identified these claims in six different categories: A, B, C and D for claims made by individuals, E by corporations (private and public) and F by governments.

The Commission decided to expedite claims from individuals (categories A, B and C) since the majority of claimants were foreign workers in Iraq and Kuwait from low-income countries, particularly in Asia, Africa and the Middle East.[16] A copy of one's passport showing the date of departure from Iraq or Kuwait, or airline ticket stubs and a statement from the individual that he or she had suffered personal loss or injury, or a certificate of the death of a family member, were sufficient for processing such claims and payments of compensation from Iraqi oil revenue.

Claims ranging from $2,500 to $10,000 coming from individuals or families in categories A and B were approved and paid out to a total of

---

11. The administrative budget of the UNCC has amounted, on average, to about $50 million per annum.
12. In 2004, Rolf G. Knutsson, formerly Deputy to the Chef de Cabinet in the Office of the UN Secretary-General, served as the Executive Secretary of the UNCC. He replaced Jean-Claude Aimé in 2001, who earlier on had been UN Secretary-General Boutros Boutros Ghali's Chef de Cabinet in New York. Michael F. Raboin has been Deputy Executive Secretary since the beginning in 1991. An American national, he came to the UNCC with relevant experience having served as the Deputy US agent at the Iran-US Claims Tribunal. He was to ensure that the US experience in the Iran Tribunal would be helpful in shaping the Iraq Compensation Commission in the interest of the United States. Most key positions in the UNCC Secretariat, in addition to the post of Deputy Executive Secretary, have also been held by US nationals. These included, in 2000, the Head of the Oil Sector Claims, the Head of the Environmental Claims, the Head of the Financial Division and the Head of the Legal Services Branch.
13. Between fifty and sixty commissioners or about 3 per compensation category were involved in reviewing claims.
14. UNCC documents, Press Releases, Panel Reports refer.
15. See also summary table at end of chapter.
16. Prior to Iraq's August 1990 invasion into Kuwait, the expatriate population in Iraq was estimated at 1,162,000, and for Kuwait at 2,142,600.

$3.2 billion.[17] Individuals claiming compensation up to $100,000 for damages such as personal injury, mental pain and anguish, loss of bank accounts, stocks, income and business were grouped in category C. Until mid-2004, a total of 634,376 C claimants were awarded $5.01 billion[18] and were paid. Those with claims of more that $100,000 for similar losses as individuals in category C were classified as category D claimants; $2.1 billion were awarded and paid to 8,717 applicants in this category.[19] Claims involving corporations were considered category E claims.[20] The UNCC received 5,800 such claims asking for a total of $80 billion in compensation. The commission accepted 3,842 E claims and awarded a total of $26.22 billion, of which $3.4 billion were for Kuwaiti corporations outside the oil sector and $18 billion for Kuwaiti oil companies.[21]

The Commission had received 225 category 'F' claims, submitted by forty-three governments and six international organisations, seeking a total of US $150 billion in compensation. The type of losses in these claims were for those incurred in connection with the departure and evacuation of individuals and for damage to property belonging to governments and to international organisations such as embassies and governmental buildings.

A special subcategory was allocated to sixty-three claims of US $113.8 billion by the Government of Kuwait. The Commission resolved most of these claims and awarded US $8.8 billion out of which US $8.2 went to the Kuwaiti Government.[22] In addition, the Commission had received 167 claims seeking a total of approximately US $81 billion for damage to the environment and the depletion of natural resources in the Gulf region. As of mid-2004 the Commission had resolved 140 claims in this category and awarded US $2.3 billion.

It does not come as a surprise that among the hundred governments which have submitted claims in any category A-F, Kuwait is the overall main recipient of compensation from Iraq oil revenue. Total compensation

17. See UNCC claims reports and Press Releases.
18. Ibid.
19. Ibid.
20. The UNCC subdivided these claims into four 'E' categories: E1 = non-Kuwaiti oil sector claims; E2 and E3 = non-Kuwaiti corporations; E4 = Kuwaiti oil sector claims.
21. Compensation actually paid to date (2004) to these 'E' claimants came to $4.9 billion – see UNCC Press Releases.
22. The UNCC subdivided these claims into four 'F' categories: F1 = damage to individual and government property; F2 = claims by the Governments of Jordan and Saudi Arabia except claims for environmental damage; F3 = claims by the Government of Kuwait; F4 = damage to the environment and depletion of natural resources in the Gulf region.

worth $34.7 billion had been approved by 2004 and out of this amount $9.2 billion have actually been paid to the Government of Kuwait.[23]

The total of 2.6 million claims submitted to the UNCC with a value of $340 billion constitutes an immense amount, even for the largest economies. For Iraq, a potentially rich country with the second biggest known oil reserves in the world after Saudi Arabia, it would, even under normal circumstances, still be an unmanageable compensation burden for decades to come. Iraq has barely begun national reconstruction and has to embark upon a full-scale rehabilitation and modernisation of its oil industry, as well as the opening up of new oil fields. Compensation even at 25 percent of the $348 billion would severely limit the extent of national rehabilitation and development for many years to come. This period would be even longer if multi- and bilateral debts (including interest payments) incurred prior to 1990, amounting to not less than $100 billion, had to be repaid.[24]

The capacity of Iraq's fragile oil industry during the years of sanctions allowed it to produce at best 2.1/2.2 million barrels per day for export. At the end of 2004 such a level had not been reached since the March 2003 war. Therefore, even if Iraq did succeed in 2005 to rehabilitate its oil industry and obtain the OPEC oil quota of 3,140 barrels per day that it had prior to the Gulf War in July 1990, and the oil price stabilised at $30 per barrel, it would take Iraq many decades to settle about a quarter or $85 billion of the total claims of $348 billion received. The issue here, however, is not to speculate about the ultimately agreed total level of compensation, the future of the oil market and the ultimate amount of finance Iraq could afford to settle UNCC claims and its international debts. The issue is to discuss the UNCC in the context of the sanctions regime and the humanitarian exemption. The decision of the UN Security Council in 1991 to accept the UN Secretary-General's recommendation to deduct 30 percent of Iraq's permitted oil income for compensation payments severely reduced the humanitarian revenue available to the Oil-for-Food Programme. Pérez de Cuéllar made this fateful calculation at the very time when humanitarian revenue was most urgently needed in Iraq itself.

During the first three phases of the Oil-for-Food Programme, the UNCC received its 30 percent share or $1.7 billion of Iraq's oil revenue. During

23. The three major recipients other than Kuwait, Egypt, India and Jordan had been paid at mid-2004 $1.8 billion, $1.0 billion and $1.1 billion respectively. Of the P5 group, the UK received $279 million, the US $260 million, Russia $103 million, France $64 million, China $113 million. Of countries in the region, Israel received $114 million, Iran $205 million, Saudi Arabia $317 million, Syria $315 million.
24. Former US Secretary of State James Baker, asked by US President George W. Bush to negotiate debt forgiveness with Iraq's creditors, has obtained promises towards reducing the volume of Iraq's debts but by no means eliminating them altogether.

this period (1996–8) child mortality in Iraq was at unprecedentedly high levels, between 100 and 120 deaths per 1000.[25] $1.7 billion would have constituted a significant additional amount for the purchase of food and medicines. If these funds had been available for humanitarian supplies in Iraq, the Oil-for-Food Programme would have had $5.1 billion. Given the profound decline in living conditions, these funds could have made a substantial difference in mitigating harm.[26]

In the course of the thirteen phases of the Oil-for-Food Programme (1996–2003), the UNCC received a total of $17.9 billion from Iraq's oil revenue, an amount that corresponded to more than half the value of $28.1 billion of humanitarian supplies that actually arrived in Iraq during the same period.

Figure 1.10 on page 157 shows the financial flows for compensation (UNCC) during individual phases of the Oil-for-Food Programme and contrasts these with the value of humanitarian goods that arrived during the same period.[27]

More funding for the humanitarian exemption would have meant that more goods could have been procured and distributed in Iraq. The fact that a large sum of money went to the UNCC instead of the humanitarian programme, however, does not explain human destitution in Iraq during this period. The inadequacy of the total resources available was simply too large to guarantee the civilian population an acceptable standard of living. These resources would, nevertheless, have made a difference to a good number of Iraqis. There would have been fewer deaths, less disease and malnutrition and a reduced number of impoverished.

Iraq's invasion of Kuwait in August 1990 resulted in many Kuwaiti casualties.[28] Property was destroyed in Kuwait and the environment, including both the waters of the western Gulf and large tracts of land were damaged. A big foreign workforce in Iraq and Kuwait lost their jobs and often their savings. International demands for compensation from the Iraqi Government were, therefore, fully justified. The UN Security Council's pronouncements to this effect[29] as early as 1990/91 reflected

25. J. Blacker, G. Jones and M. Ali, 'Annual Mortality Rates and Excess Deaths of Children under Five in Iraq, 1991–98', *Population Studies (Cambridge)*, 57(2) (2003): 217–26.
26. While for Iraq the figure for child mortality (under five) was between 100 and 120 per 1,000, for the UK and US the corresponding figures in 2001 were 7 and 8 respectively. (See UNDP Human Development Report 2003, Oxford University Press, p. 262.)
27. To demonstrate how significant UNCC deductions were, see also Table A.8, p. 288 and Table A.17, p. 293.
28. The British Foreign Office refers to '1000 Kuwaiti Muslims' that were killed – see: Saddam Hussein – Crimes and Human Rights Abuses, London, November 2000, p. 22.
29. See UN S/Res. 674, 686, 687 and 692.

international sentiments. The surprise, however, was that the UN Security Council departed from the usual condemnation of a country's violation of international laws and norms of behaviour. In addition, there was a call for compensation of the aggrieved party by establishing a compensation fund administered by the United Nations and by quantifying the amounts to be paid into this fund.

The UN Security Council had never done this before. Judicial court functions and executive authority for implementing a general verdict had hitherto not been seen as part of the Security Council's mandate. UN Secretary-General Boutros Boutros Ghali confirmed the unique nature of the UNCC when he said in Geneva on 14 January 1994: 'This is, in fact, an unprecedented project. For the first time in history the international community shall bear by itself the responsibility for securing a processing of claims of compensation for war victims and taking decisions thereof.'[30]

The compensation process reminds one of the harsh measures included in the Treaty of Versailles against Germany in 1919 at the end of the First World War and the influence this had on the direction of German politics and extremism leading up to the next war of 1939. The details of compensation, just like the question of debt liabilities, should have been left to Iraq and the country or party seeking redress.

UN Secretary-General Pérez de Cuéllar stated in 1991 that the UNCC is 'not a court or an arbitral tribunal before which parties appear; it is a political organ that performs an essentially fact-finding function of examining claims, verifying their validity, evaluating losses, assessing payments and resolving disputed claims'. He added 'Given the nature of the commission, it is all the more important that some element of due process be built into the procedure.'[31]

Reviewing the time and the manner in which the UNCC has carried out its functions, it becomes clear that the governors of the UNCC saw it differently. The UNCC staff, the commissioners and an army of experts reviewing and assessing claims were indeed involved in 'fact-finding', and did discover highly inflated and even fraudulent compensation demands, and in that sense protected Iraqi interests. The UNCC governors, nevertheless, acted not as neutral arbitrators but as judges of claims.

Ultimately, UN Secretary-General Pérez de Cuéllar and the UN Security Council accepted the 'essential elements of the institutional framework – which would become the United Nations Compensation Commission and the Compensation Fund', as proposed by the Government of the United

---

30. Compare to the UN Security Council's reaction to Portugal's invasion into Guinea in 1970, South Africa's incursion into Lesotho in 1982 and Israel's destruction of Iraq's Tamuz Nuclear Research Centre in Baghdad in 1984.
31. See UN S/22559, 2 May 1991, para. 20.

States.[32] 'Providing for the payment of claims by a percentage deduction from the value of Iraqi exports of petroleum ... seemed ... a secure source of funding' for compensation.[33] No one was concerned at that time about a secure source of funding for Iraqi survival.

The claims revue picture reveals a number of distinct challenges for the UNCC. Firstly, there was the enormous caseload of 2.6 million claims. Determining the propriety of such a volume of claims was a formidable task for the UNCC. The magnitude of alleged losses presented was huge. The wider context of sanctions within which compensation funds were allocated had to be taken into account.

The following four examples of claims underline how immensely difficult it was for the UNCC to be 'fair' and how 'tempting' it was for the commission to be political:

Example 1

The Government of Jordan submitted twenty compensation claims on behalf of various ministries and other government offices.[34] The claims related to the provision of emergency relief for about 865,000 non-Jordanian nationals who had fled Kuwait and Iraq during the 1991 Gulf War and at the time were in Jordan in transit to their home countries. The Government of Jordan demanded expense reimbursement of $8.1 billion. The UNCC panel of commissioners reviewing the submitted documentation judged that the costs amounted to less than 1 percent of the claimed amounts and therefore awarded only $72 million.[35]

In 2001, the UN Office of Internal Oversight Services (OIOS) in New York, responsible for internal audits including the accounts of the UNCC, discovered 'deficiencies' in the Government of Jordan's estimation of camp preparation and health services and concluded that costs estimated at $43.2 million had not been correctly evaluated. What the UNCC and the OIOS conveyed in polite language, in order not to offend a government, was a stark message: you claimed $8.1 billion of Iraqi revenue for your costs and in the end the OIOS considered that no more than $28 million or 0.3 percent of the original claim as a reasonable amount of

---

32. Ronald J. Bettauer*: *Establishment of the United Nations Compensation Commission – The US Government Perspective, Thirteenth Sokol Colloquium*, ed. Richard B. Lillich, Irvington, NY: Transactional Publishers, 1995.
   (*Bettauer served in the early 1990s in the US State Department as Assistant Legal Adviser for International Claims and Investment Disputes.)
33. Ibid., p. 43.
34. These were category F2 claims.
35. See Report and Recommendations of the (UNCC) Panel of Commissioners concerning the first instalment of category F2 claims, S/AC.26/1999/23, 23 September 1999.

compensation. The OIOS in New York asked the UNCC in Geneva to take appropriate action and reduce the claim award further to $28 million. The UNCC refused to do so, stating that its decisions were final and the OIOS had no right to impose its findings on the Commission. The UN Security Council should have intervened but did not. The Government of Jordan was paid an amount of $72 million.

Example 2

The Kuwaiti Government submitted a claim on behalf of its national committee for prisoners of war and missing of war affairs.[36] The amount of compensation sought was $111.5 million to reimburse the Government of Kuwait for payments it had made for salaries of missing Kuwaitis and payments in support of their families. The UNCC, instead of approving the amount of $111.5 million, decided to award $177.1 million, or $66 million more than the amount of compensation the Government of Kuwait had expected.

Example 3

The UNCC awarded $324,358 in compensation of a claim[37] submitted by the Government of Israel on behalf of a tourist company owned by four kibbutzim. These settlements carried out tourism operations located in the Golan Heights (Al-Hamma/Hammat Gader), the Syrian territory occupied by Israel since 1967.

The UNCC approved this claim and payment of the awarded amount was made. Syria objected and demanded that the money be returned to the UN Compensation Fund. The Syrian Government, moreover, pointed to a series of UN Security Council resolutions[38] relating to the occupied Syrian territories. The UNCC agreed to seek advice from the UN Office for Legal Affairs. The UN Office for Legal Affairs recalled earlier UN Security Council pronouncements that the establishment of settlements of a foreign state in Syria constituted a violation of the fourth Geneva Convention and that the existing settlements should be dismantled. The UN Office of Legal Affairs furthermore confirmed that the UNCC, as a subsidiary body of the UN Security Council, should not contribute to either the establishment or maintenance of such settlements. Just as the UNCC had ignored advice from the UN Office of Internal Oversight (OIOS) in New York to reduce a Jordanian claim (see example 1), the

36. UNCC Claim No. 500169; see S/AC.26/1999/24, 9 December 1999, pp. 76–80.
37. UNCC Claim No. 4000 246 (E/2); See S/AC.26/2001/19, 28 September 2001.
38. For example 446 (22 March 1979), 452 (20 July 1979), 465 (1 March 1980), 497 (17 December 1981), 672 (12 October 1990) and 681 (20 December 1990).

UNCC also ignored advice from the UN legal office and refused to reconsider this claim case even though it was confirmed that through this award, the UNCC had violated international law.[39]

Example 4

Immediately after the ceasefire of the 1991 Gulf War, Australia, Canada, Germany, The Netherlands, the UK and the US responded to appeals by Kuwait and other Gulf countries for help in efforts to clean and restore the environment which had been affected by oil spills and oil fires resulting from war and sabotage.

Following the establishment of the UNCC, these countries submitted claims in 1995 and 1996 demanding compensation amounting to some $45 million.[40] Australia sought compensation for the expenses of an oil spill specialist. Canada was seeking compensation for a team of experts, also in the field of oil spill rehabilitation. Germany wanted reimbursement for 'the abatement of risks to people, the environment and navigation' due to oil pollution. The Netherlands asked for cost recovery for two tug boats that had been provided for 'emergency fire fighting, rescue and salvage services in 1991'. The UK sought compensation for expenses involving the purchase and transport of oil skimmers, a portion of its contribution to the International Maritime Organisation (IMO) that was used for Gulf clean-up operations and a contribution the UK had made to the International Council for Bird Preservation for a study of oil-spill impacts on migratory wading birds in the Gulf. The US submitted nine claims amounting to $9.1 million for expenses of technical personnel travelling in the area, for participation in Iraq-related meetings in the US and Europe, for the collection and analysis of air quality data in the region, and an assessment study of health risks posed to military personnel by exposure to emissions of oil fires in Kuwait.[41]

Some of these claims had legitimacy but at a time of extreme suffering in Iraq, it was inappropriate for the UNCC to entertain them.

39. UNCC Internal document dated 26 June 2002.
40. Report and Recommendations of the Panel of Commissioners – see Claims S/AC.26/2002/26, 3 October 2002. None of these countries received the compensation they asked for: Australia asked for $20,099 and received $7,777; Canada received $529,923 instead of $1,252,325; Germany $2,038,256 instead of $28,717,109; Netherlands wanted $1,974,055 and received no compensation; the UK received $1,891,857 instead of $2,219,315 and the US $3,885,835 instead of $9,199,329. The UNCC paid a total of $8,353,648 or 18.7 percent of the total of $45 million these six countries had wanted from Iraq for immediate post-war services.
41. See also footnote 23, p. 179, outlining compensation for permanent members of the UN Security Council.

The review of UNCC decisions leaves a profound feeling of uneasiness, if not contempt, for the overall claims approval process. Scarce Iraqi funds were awarded to governments and corporations to compensate them at a time of undisputed human misery in Iraq. As some of the reviewed claims cases show, the justification was often questionable, certainly in terms of urgency of payment and the amounts requested. UN Secretary-General Pérez de Cuéllar rightly referred to the need for 'due process', yet the 'due' seems to have been often forgotten in the process. The Government of Iraq repeatedly pointed out to the UN Secretary-General, to the UNCC and to the UN Security Council that it had accepted, in principle, its liability[42] as required by the UN Security Council resolutions, but that it refused to accept the specifics of the compensation formula. The Iraqi Government argued that there was no provision in international law for such a compensation commission and, even if there had been such a provision, Iraq was given no rights to participate in claims discussions, let alone claims decision making. It also had no right to see the documentation on which claims decisions were based. The UNCC commissioners met behind closed doors and Iraq was allowed to attend proceedings only on rare occasions involving isolated cases. The Iraqis were particularly upset that the Commission did not agree that the Government could access Iraqi funds held by the UN Commission for its legal defence and its right of appeal.[43]

The Government of Iraq protested against the use of Iraqi money for the payment of the annual administrative costs of the UNCC, as it did for all the other sanction-management related costs of the UN humanitarian and disarmament programmes of the UN/OIP and UNSCOM/UNMOVIC.[44] In 1992, the Iraqi Government requested a five-year grace period to meet financial obligations to the UNCC in view of 'the humanitarian situation of its people'.[45] 'The compensation scheme ... will run short of the ability to pay, impede reconstruction in the aftermath of the destructive use of force by the coalition forces and impoverish Iraq's coming generations to the extent of reaching a regime of economic slavery', was the conclusion reached by Iraq's Foreign Minister, Mohamed Al Sahaf, when he met UN Secretary-General Kofi Annan on 26 and 27 February 2001 in New York.[46]

---

42. See Iraqi Ministry of Foreign Affairs, 'Presentation of the Delegation of the Republic of Iraq in the Dialogue with the Secretary-General of the United Nations, New York', 26–7 February 2001, p. 42.
43. An exception was made by the UNCC for environmental claims where Iraq was allowed to use UNCC (Iraqi) funds for preparing its defence.
44. 3 percent of Iraq's oil revenue was reserved for these administrative costs.
45. See UN S/23687, Report of the UN Secretary-General to the UN Security Council, 7 March 1992, para. 16.
46. See op. cit. (note 42), p. 43.

The approach to dealing with Iraq at the UNCC in Geneva was comparable to the way in which the Iraq debate proceeded over the years at the UN Security Council in New York. Iraq's representatives in both places were rarely allowed to participate in the deliberations involving Iraq.

This approach certainly was not in the spirit of a world body which proclaims in its Charter that it wants to see a Security Council discharge its duties in accordance with 'appropriate measures to strengthen universal peace' and 'respect for human rights and for fundamental freedoms'.[47] The same applies to the secretive manner in which the UNCC carried out its affairs, blocking participation by all countries not current members of the Security Council, including Iraq, who was the financier and a main party in the compensation process. Iraq should have been allowed to attend claims meetings and been given sufficient time[48] to prepare responses to specific claim reports which often involved billions of dollars of Iraqi money. 'Due process' without adequate legal defence is hardly possible, especially when the cases involved were often of a highly technical nature. Iraq should have had this opportunity and should have been allowed to use its own resources for such purposes. At a time when the UN Security Council severely limited the sale of Iraqi oil, especially during the initial phases of the Oil-for-Food Programme, the diversion of 30 percent of these inadequate resources was tantamount to purposely mistreating an innocent population.

Whether the UN Security Council had the right under international law to define compensation amounts and determine the timing of deductions is the subject of continuing debate among jurists. I would argue that the Council, given existing UN Charter law and international humanitarian law, did not have the right to go beyond general pronouncements of the rights of aggrieved parties to seek compensation for damages and losses resulting from Iraq's invasion into Kuwait. Details of compensation constituted until then 'bilateral business'. The International Court of Justice could have played a role, if so requested by Iraq and the aggrieved state party. Whatever the outcome of the legal debate on the lawfulness of the UN Security Council's handling of the compensation issue, the Council cannot deny the fact that it had options at a time of human crisis in Iraq which it chose not to consider. The few examples included here of claims cases the UNCC approved are quite representative of the absence of urgency for payments to the claimants. Many of the corporations and governments could have waited; for many

47. See UN Charter articles 1(2), 24/2) and 55(c).
48. At the request of both the UNCC in Geneva and the Iraqi Government, the UNOHCI Office in Baghdad provided its vehicles for trips between Baghdad and Amman to transport in UN diplomatic bags claims documentation requiring the Iraqi authorities to respond to voluminous technical reports, often within totally unrealistic time periods of a few weeks.

Iraqis, on the other hand, the lack of funds made a difference between survival or death and destitution.

The most humane option would have been to recognise a grace period for the payment of compensations until such time as the Iraqi people had been given a minimum of support for their survival. Iraqi oil revenue levels and procedures for the procurement of humanitarian supplies should have been geared to an assessed minimum needs level. The UN Security Council and the UNCC could have defined, without difficulty, a package involving compensation for foreign workers in Iraq and Kuwait who had become victims of Saddam Hussein's expansionistic moods. This amount added to the budget needed for the humanitarian exemption in Iraq and paid out to individual claimants would have amounted to no more than about $3 billion.[49]

Accountability for basing compensation on resources which were urgently required in Iraq lies with the UN Security Council. Responsibility for spurious claims and fortuitous settlements rests with individual governments and the UN Compensation Commission. The moral debt of silence has to be shouldered by the UN Secretariat. If nowhere else, it is in the UN Secretariat where voices should have been raised over the compensation mechanism, some of the claims and the level of resources taken away from an Iraqi population that badly needed them. The UNCC Secretariat also had the responsibility of objecting to many more of the claims which the commissioners presented and the governors approved at the very time when child mortality was increasing in Iraq and destitution was rampant.

From the time when the UN Compensation Commission became fully operational in December 1996, simultaneous to the beginning of the Oil-for-Food Programme, and until the US/UK war started against Iraq in 2003, the UN Security Council rarely made mention of the work of the UNCC. The UNCC was shrouded in secrecy: public documents, aside from periodic press releases, were rarely issued. No insight was allowed into the UNCC claims operations. Press releases would identify aggregate payments made to claimants in the six categories, and tables would list the recipient countries. What exactly these payments were for was not disclosed. The examples given above are indications of why such information was withheld. Had the public and governments not represented in the UNCC known of claims details such as those outlined above there would have been an immediate outrage over both the content and timing of payment. Efforts would have been undertaken to disqualify many of the claims, freeze others and change much earlier the '30 percent formula' until the human conditions in Iraq had improved.

49. 'A' and 'B' category claimants were awarded between $2,500 and $10,000 per person or family.

A tight-lipped UNCC and a Security Council that had delegated full authority to the Commission prevented the kind of analyses that would have shed early light on this component of the Iraq sanctions mechanism.

This raises a wide range of fundamental questions: why, in the case of Iraq, did the UN Security Council set a precedent for new ways of handling international compensation in the context of comprehensive economic sanctions? Why was the claims process structured as it was, with no provision for legal defence of the defendant state? Why were compensation details not left to be worked out in bilateral negotiations? Why were claims payments for firms and governments carried out at a time when funds were sorely needed in Iraq by a suffering population? Why did the UNCC entertain claims for which there was little justification? Why did the Security Council yet again fail to exercise its oversight mandate, just as it did in the case of the Oil-for-Food Programme? Why did individual governments represented in the UN Security Council and the UNCC not protest and go public with their objections? Why did UN Secretaries-General Boutros Boutros Ghali and Kofi Annan, recognising the inaccurate forecast their predecessor de Cuéllar had made of Iraq's national income, not press for a downward revision of the level of compensation payments? Why did the UN Secretariat, privy to all the details of compensation, decide to remain mute?

These questions should have been discussed and answered in the UN Security Council. The UN Secretary-General had the responsibility to press for such answers, if for no other reason than in the name of the protection of the Iraqi people.

Answers will also be necessary for defining the role of the Security Council vis-à-vis the International Court of Justice in future compensation programmes. Ways must be found of preventing the heavy-handedness of individual member countries in the Security Council in determining future policy. Just as there is now recognition of the need for 'smart sanctions', there must be a corollary for 'smart compensation'.

Table 2.1 United Nation Compensation Commission Claims Processing as at Mid-2004

Category	Claims still under consideration		Resolved claims		Resolved claims with compensation awarded		Compensation paid ($US)
	No of claims	Amount ($US)	No of claims	Amount ($US)	No of claims	Amount ($US)	Amount ($US)
"A"	0	0	919,704	3,451,526,000	856,170	3,190,864,000	3,204,243,985
"B"	0	0	5,734	20,100,000	3,941	13,450,000	13,450,000
"C"	40,896	2,410,139,000	1,662,500	8,901,795,990	634,376	5,011,886,012	5,006,878,904
"D"	3,346	11,010,000,000	9,948	7,605,969,310	8,717	2,513,831,531	2,147,002,595
"E1"	0	0	105	44,624,122,170	67	21,520,820,521	667,648,817
"E2"	0	0	2,445	13,658,348,403	954	916,054,517	818,334,128
"E3"	0	0	398	8,104,766,051	159	402,562,327	343,358,173
"E4"	0	0	3,160	11,560,795,212	2,662	3,369,084,194	3,039,874,150
"E/F"	0	0	123	6,122,977,002	57	311,282,668	180,071,703
"F1"	0	0	100	18,607,934,491	70	291,171,423	253,987,026
"F2"	0	0	63	17,573,716,993	46	264,422,123	256,121,518
"F3"	1	0	62	113,897,315,769	60	8,261,985,226	2,146,955,723
"F4"	27	69,200,000,000	140	11,862,730,448	95	2,103,023,715	317,383,653
Total	44,270	82,620,139,000	2,604,482	265,992,097,839	1,507,374	48,170,438,256	18,395,310,375

Sources: *UNCC documents, Press releases, panel reports and other related documents.*
Notes: *Figures refer to the status of claims as at 7 May 2004.*

The Fateful Breakfast.
Courtesy of Matthias Schwoerer.

Chapter 3

The No-Fly Zones,
the Humanitarian Programme
and Changed Security in Iraq
following Operation Desert Fox

Thursday 16 December 1998 had indeed been a fateful day for Iraq and the United Nations. It was the day on which the Government of US took a big step beyond its declared Iraq containment policy. The October 1998 Iraq Liberation Act of the US Congress was no longer just an intention. Not long before midnight, US and UK war planes began their attack of Iraqi installations within and outside the no-fly zones. 'Operation Desert Fox', as it was called, lasted for four days during which about two hundred civilians lost their lives and seventy regime buildings in Baghdad were wholly or partially destroyed.[1] This included the Ba'ath Party headquarters, the Iraqi intelligence services building, state radio and television, the biological research centre at Baghdad University, the Ibn Al Haytham Missile R & D Centre, the Directorate of General Security (near the UN offices), the Special Security Organization (SSO) headquarters, the Special Republican Guards (SRG) headquarters and the SSO Communication and Computing Centre. No one knows the number of military personnel who perished in this attack.

As mentioned earlier, Iqbal Riza, the Chef de Cabinet of Kofi Annan, had called me in the early hours of that day to warn us of a possible full evacuation of UN international staff in Iraq in the event that an attack would happen. Following this call I rushed to my office at the Canal Hotel on the outskirts of Baghdad to convene a meeting of all senior UN officials who formed the security management team. As the designated official for security, I was responsible to the UN Secretary-General for UN staff security in Iraq. The United Nations Special Commission (UNSCOM) and

1. See UNOCHI/Baghdad Press Clippings dated 19 January 1999, p. 9.

its disarmament personnel, located in the same Canal Hotel offices as the rest of us, decided not to be part of this mechanism and made its own security arrangements. UNSCOM had its own call signs and security checks as well as its separate evacuation plan. Even at critical moments, as on 16 December 1998, there was no contact between the UNSCOM administration and the rest of the UN community. Under one blue and white UN flag flying over the Canal Hotel offices in Baghdad were two distinct United Nations – a remarkable anomaly.

While I had developed friendly relations with UNSCOM's officer in charge at the time, Colonel Jaako Yiitalo from Finland, it ultimately made no difference in terms of unifying our security systems. Much later I understood why: it was due to the mindset of UNSCOM's Chairman, Ambassador Richard Butler. For him, the nature of UNSCOM's disarmament mission was so unique that, in his opinion, it had to insulate itself. This included times when all UN staff, regardless of their assignments, were facing identical threats to their well-being. UN Secretary-General Kofi Annan was more than unhappy about Butler's imperial style. We in Baghdad could see that his insular approach had permeated the 'ranks' and created unnecessary acrimony in the daily lives of the UN humanitarian and disarmament communities. It was symptomatic of Butler's approach that he met with the Acting Permanent Representative of the US to the United Nations, Ambassador Peter Burleigh, in the US mission in New York on 15 December rather than with UN Secretary-General Kofi Annan prior to presenting his report to the UN Security Council a day later.

There has been much speculation about the content of this discussion and earlier meetings between Butler and US diplomats. Had these influenced the wording of his transmittal letter to the UN Security Council, the content of UNSCOM's report and his eventual presentation of the report to the UN Security Council on 16 December?

While Butler reported to the UN Security Council, Bill Clinton, the US President had given the order to attack Iraq. As the UNSCOM Chairman was speaking and the UN Secretary-General listening to the presentation in the Council he was handed a note which broke the news that the United States, joined by Britain, had begun the attack on Iraq. The UN Security Council and the UN Secretary-General could do no more than to take note of this grave violation of international law and the belittling of the United Nations that resulted from this US/UK unilateral act. There was a justified sense of helplessness in the corridors of the United Nations, not only in New York but wherever there was a UN presence around the world. In Baghdad we were devastated.

In terse language a US government document records for 16 December 1998: 'Following Iraq's recurrent blocking of UN weapons inspectors, President Clinton ordered four days of air strikes against military and security targets in Iraq that contribute to Iraq's ability to produce, store, and maintain weapons of mass destruction and potential delivery systems.'[2]

While Chef de Cabinet Iqbal Riza had alerted me on 16 December of the possibility that UN staff might have to be evacuated out of Iraq, Richard Butler had already ordered the evacuation of UNSCOM's staff. My UN colleagues and I tried to make arrangements for establishing the Canal Hotel as a 'safe-haven' area where our staff would have to await further instructions. UNSCOM staff were leaving.

Just before the departure of the UN disarmament personnel, I became more aware of the division between UNSCOM and other members of the UN family in Baghdad. We had two immediate reasons to ask UNSCOM for help. I wanted to secure two or three seats in UNSCOM's large aircraft for staff with special medical conditions. Secondly, I hoped UNSCOM would take some of the cash our administration had in its possession which might fall into the wrong hands in case of turmoil during the crisis. In the absence of any banking services, the UN system had to bring its entire monthly payroll in cash into Iraq. On 16 December 1998 the finance unit in my office held about $1 million in cash.

I personally went to the second floor of the UN building to talk to UNSCOM's administrative officers. The appearance of non-UNSCOM staff in their premises was a rare event: we seldom had reason to go there. Now that they were about to leave, such a visit was even more unexpected and less welcome. The answers to my requests were brief and curt: 'We have no extra seats in the aircraft and cannot take cash that does not belong to us!' I left UNSCOM premises disappointed and again wondering why they did not want to accept that in these difficult moments 'we' should be part of 'us'. On the same day, I wrote to the Chef de Cabinet of the Secretary-General, Iqbal Riza: 'UNSCOM personnel left us yet again without any hand-over.' I ended the communication to Riza with the conclusion that 'the entire history of behaviour of UNSCOM that I have seen while here is a shameful chapter in the UN book for Iraq'.[3]

'It would be prudent to take measures to ensure the safety and security of UNSCOM staff presently in Iraq', Butler had been told by US Ambassador Burleigh on 15 December in the US mission in New York. 'I told him that I would act on this advice and remove my staff from Iraq', Butler recounts.[4] One can only wonder why UNSCOM staff were singled out by the United States Government for 'early' protection. Only in a later 'advisory' were Secretary-General Kofi Annan's office and the UN Security Coordinator in New York encouraged by US authorities to evacuate the 'other' staff.

2. GAO–04–651T.
3. Fax to Iqbal Riza, Chef de Cabinet, Executive Office of the Secretary-General, 16 December 1998.
4. Butler, 2000, p. 224.

The 'I would act' and 'remove my staff' was not the language of a senior United Nations civil servant involved in a complex political crisis. Even though Ambassador Butler travelled, as we all did, with a UN 'laissez-passer', in spirit he never was an international civil servant: he made no secret of the fact that the UN Security Council and not the UN Secretary-General had appointed him to his post. This was another unfortunate 'first' created by the Security Council. Butler thus considered informing, briefing and exchanging views with the UN Secretary-General as 'discretionary' and not part of his formal terms of reference. It is not surprising, therefore, that he was not seen as a 'welcomed colleague' on the UN Secretary-General's floor at UN headquarters in New York.

On the evening of 16 December 1998, all 200 UNSCOM personnel had left Iraq and all 450 'other' UN international staff were in Iraq, half in Baghdad, the other half in Iraqi Kurdistan. The UN offices at the Canal Hotel had been converted into an international 'refugee' camp with staff, and a few dependants, from all over the world awaiting uncertain developments. 'Would there really be an attack?' was the question in everyone's mind. The UN security management team and I had a host of immediate concerns: would 250 people really fit into the hallway on the ground floor?

We had identified this location as the best place for our safety, since there were no windows and only an exit glass door. Would there be enough water and food for up to a week? Markus, the cafeteria manager, an Iraqi Christian, had left us with a good stock of fruit, vegetables, bread, rice and meat, but we had no idea how long these supplies would last. The UN offices had previously been a hotel training school. This was fortunate for us since practically every office had been a bedroom and therefore had adjacent bathrooms. However, what would happen to the sanitary facilities if there was a breakdown in water services? How would the Iraqis react to us in case of an attack? There was the Iraqi public who could turn their anger against us and there was also the Iraqi military – 159 officers and soldiers – who had been assigned by the Government to protect our compound. We had good relations with them through regular contact: they were given a meal a day, but how would we be able to feed them under such circumstances? Would they change their friendly attitude toward us? Adjacent to the eastern side of the UN building was an Iraqi military psychiatric hospital.[5] Could we expect problems from that direction? What could we expect from the Iraqi Government?

5. This was the 'soft spot' in the security of the UN offices at the Canal Hotel since only a thin wire fence separated the UN premises from the open area in front of the military hospital. It was here, not surprisingly, that a suicide bomber had chosen to hit the UN building on 29 August 2003, killing 22 persons. Among them was Sergio Vieira de Mello, the Special Representative of the UN Secretary-General.

Uppermost in my mind was the question of how we would cope should there be a hit on our building. Near to our 'bunker floor' was the UNOCHI health unit. This proximity was good, but was the unit really equipped to handle a large number of potential cases?

Our Romanian doctor's more immediate concern was the mental preparedness of the staff for the looming crisis. At a staff meeting I convened in the late afternoon of 16 December Dr Gilda Mukungu pleaded with us to drink as much water as possible, since this would 'have a good effect on your anxiety level ... and avoid alcohol as much as possible'. This was important advice. During the lunch I had had a few hours earlier in our cafeteria, I sat briefly with four colleagues who had decided to 'enrich' their meal with a bottle of campari. Twenty minutes later, when I left the dining hall, I saw the empty bottle. In difficult missions, particularly in conflict areas, the UN did face problems of this kind; Baghdad was no exception. We were aware of such problems but alcohol consumption was not easy to control, especially at times of acute crises. For these four difficult days and nights of Operation Desert Fox the doctor's reminder was, therefore, timely.

A second question that troubled me greatly was the possible interruption of food distribution and medicines to hospitals and health centres should there be an attack. The majority of Iraqis depended on the food basket, but neither our international nor our Iraqi staff, nor the 50,000 food agents in the eighteen governorates would be able to help under conditions of war. WFP food trucks would not move, the food warehouses would be unattended, and no new humanitarian supplies would enter Iraq.

During the late morning of 16 December, after the departure of the UNSCOM staff, I joined Ambassador Prakash Shah, the special envoy of the UN Secretary-General,[6] to meet Deputy Prime Minister Tariq Aziz at his office along the Tigris River near the Al Jumhuriya Bridge.[7] As we entered his spacious office on the top floor of the Planning Ministry, we found ourselves opposite two stern-looking Iraqi officials, Tariq Aziz and Dr Riyadh Al Qaysi, Under-Secretary in the Foreign Ministry. After a tirade of angry words about Richard Butler, Tariq Aziz conveyed to us that the report Butler had submitted to the UN Security Council in no way reflected the progress that had been made by Iraq in eliminating weapons of mass destruction. He said that the report had exaggerated the conflicts

6. Prakash Shah, in mid-1990 India's Permanent Representative to the UN in New York, had been appointed to this post following Kofi Annan's February 1998 visit to Baghdad. Shah was to be the 'diplomatic bridge' between the UN in New York and the Iraq Government in Baghdad. This was a genuine effort of the UN Secretary-General that in practice, however, made little difference in the relations between the Government of Iraq and the UN.
7. 'Bridge of the Republic'.

that had arisen between groups of UN weapons inspectors and Iraqi officials in the weeks before UNSCOM's withdrawal. Aziz made a reference to an incident in which a team of UN inspectors had been refused entry into the Ba'ath Party headquarters in Baghdad. 'We expected nothing else – Butler is a liar and a tool of the United States.' Defiantly, he added 'We are prepared for an attack.' Under-Secretary Qaysi remained silent but his face showed agreement and deep concern. It was a short meeting at the end of which I reminded Tariq Aziz that it was Iraq's responsibility, as the host country, to protect the UN mission in Iraq during this crisis. I wanted to make the point that the military guarding the UN compound should be vigilant to possible public anger against the United Nations Security Council and by extension the UN's presence in Baghdad. 'We will do all we can, rest assured', were Tariq Aziz's parting words as we left his office.

When the Baghdad sun had set and the sun in New York began to rise, our telephones started to ring as they had during the previous evening. Everyone wanted to give us advice and words of comfort and encouragement. This made us feel good but also reinforced our conviction that they knew more than we did. Just after 6 P.M., the Executive Director of the Office of the Iraq Programme in New York, Benon Sevan, called to tell me that the Secretary-General had decided to carry out an evacuation of the UN international staff in Iraq, except for a small group of my choosing which should stay behind. This was what I wanted to hear. I had feared that there would be an UNSCOM-type departure leaving no UN presence in the country. I was truly relieved that Kofi Annan felt the same and had taken the wise decision not to evacuate the entire UN community; Heffinck's and my plan could be shelved. (Earlier in the day, after another security management team meeting, the UNICEF representative Philippe Heffinck, a Belgium colleague, and I agreed that the two of us would remain, even if a full evacuation had been agreed upon. That this would have disciplinary, insurance, legal and personal implications did not concern us at that time.) I did remember how uncomfortable I had felt as UN Resident Coordinator in Islamabad in the early 1990s when the UN evacuated all staff from Afghanistan to Pakistan in the last days of the Najibullah regime. The ICRC and *Médecins Sans Frontières* had remained in Kabul.

The telephone conversation with Benon Sevan who called me in both his capacity as the senior official in the Iraq programme in New York and in charge of worldwide security for UN offices and missions, turned to practical aspects of the evacuation. Washington, he pointed out, wanted a pre-dawn evacuation. 'We cannot be responsible for the safety of UN staff on the road after 9 A.M.', was the conclusion of the American officials who had contacted Sevan's office. I told Sevan that we were prepared for the evacuation and that six buses had been hired from an Iraqi company and were parked in our compound. The drivers had been instructed to report for duty at 8 o'clock the next morning. With telephone lines in Baghdad down we, however, would not have any way of contacting them at this time to prepare for such an early departure. The time of departure demanded by the Americans could, therefore, not be met. Sevan was indignant and I was insistent.

A gloomy atmosphere permeated the UN family huddled together at the Canal Hotel. Would air-strikes really occur? We continued to hope that they would not until just before midnight when the Russian liaison officer of UNIKOM received a call from General Esa Tarvainen, a Finnish colleague and Force Commander at UNIKOM headquarters in Um Qasr on the Iraq-Kuwait border, to inform us that 'a large formation of foreign aircraft has just crossed the border into Iraq at high altitude'.

The UNIKOM officer's prediction that they would reach Baghdad within an hour proved to be right. First Baghdad was awoken by local sirens, followed soon after by Iraqi anti-aircraft batteries and the incredible noise of the impact of bombs. The US and UK air forces were above Baghdad. With a bullhorn, UN staff in the building were alerted to go immediately to our 'bunker', the hallway on the ground floor. In retrospect, had there been a direct hit on the building, the location we had chosen would not have protected us very much. But we had little choice: this was the best available alternative. The effect of sounds which many colleagues had never heard in their lives was profound. We were all frightened. To my surprise, male colleagues were much more affected than female staff. It was difficult to ease this atmosphere. I attempted it by making jokes and teasing staff so that they could laugh. Some did and this reassured others. We had distributed narrow foam mats for each staff member. In one of the earlier staff meetings I announced that it would be against the rules to have two persons on one mat. In the middle of the night, when most people were half-awake and worried, I noticed a husband and wife – she with an opera singer's opulence and he, diminutive and resembling Woody Allen, were lying together on one of these mats. 'Two people lying on one mat is a punishable offence', I said in a loud voice. A hundred heads went up and there was an explosion of laughter. It improved the mood in the 'bunker'.

After four long hours of heavy bombardment we received the message from the border that the formation had left Iraq and returned to their bases in Kuwait, Saudi Arabia and other locations in the Gulf. The sudden silence had a palliative effect; the UN compound in Baghdad had at last found sleep. I decided to spend this long night mostly in my office on the first floor – slightly against the rules, since everyone else had been told to be in the 'bunker'. Periodically, I returned to the ground floor, however, to make sure everything was in order. My assistant, Srini and I would alternatively sleep in our adjacent offices so that one of us would be available at all times to respond to incoming calls … and they came, some from UN headquarters, others from UN agencies in Europe and elsewhere, and many from media around the world competing for the latest news from an embattled Baghdad. I had told my spokesman, George Sommerwill, to tell journalists, if they asked when we would be leaving: 'The UN does not run when it gets hot!'

The subsequent coverage was uneven. It was sober from the *Christian Science Monitor* and *Le Monde Diplomatique* and ridiculous from the boulevard press. The *Bild Zeitung*, a widely read tabloid in Germany, had a front page article with a bulky headline which read: 'Baghdad is Burning', allegedly based on an interview with me which I had never given.

The reality which I saw the following morning looked quite different. Wanting to assess the damage that had been done during the night, I drove with my Iraqi driver, Abu Laith, through Baghdad. The precision of laser-guided bombs and cruise missiles could be seen without difficulty. From a distance some buildings which had been hit looked almost unharmed: only at close range did I realise that the frame was intact but the inside destroyed. Where the 2,000-lb bombs had impacted on the General Intelligence building near the UN offices, the picture was different. Here the bombs had left more immediately visible damage. Since this building was so close to our own, the impact of such a powerful device felt like an earthquake. The Canal Hotel was shaking and so were we when this particular government building was attacked.

After another night of heavy bombing of targets in Baghdad and sleeplessness, it took several hours during the morning to assign 300 staff to the six buses. We had to prepare accurate lists of who was sitting in which vehicle and who would remain. The Jordanian authorities at the Trebil border crossing had agreed to process the entry of this large international group on the basis of these lists. The buses were finally on their way at about 9.30 A.M., leaving behind the twenty-eight colleagues which I had identified as 'essential' staff. These were the UN doctor, members of the security management team, colleagues from various administrative services, the UN security guards unit, and a few others. This evacuation exercise went smoothly with one serious exception: totally against the rules, two senior colleagues with their families decided to quietly leave the UN compound while the evacuation exercise was under way and use their official vehicles to drive on their own to Amman. This was an unfortunate sign of dangerous indiscipline. It delayed the departure of the convoy until we had established mobile telephone links with the prematurely departed colleagues and could adjust our lists accordingly.

As soon as the buses left the Canal compound, the hustle and bustle that had prevailed when there was a full house gave way to a calming silence.

In the early afternoon of 18 December, UN colleagues in Amman called us to give us the good news that after a gruelling eighteen-hour overland journey the six buses had safely reached the Jordanian capital. Many hours had been spent at the border. The lists which the Jordan immigration authorities had asked us to prepare to facilitate easy entry had apparently made little difference.

Around the same time Secretary-General Kofi Annan contacted us. 'Thank you for holding out. I appreciate very much what all of you are doing to keep the UN flag flying high. Please convey my best wishes to everyone, including our Iraqi staff.' This call was a morale booster which came at a good time. On a more personal note, the UN Secretary-General wanted to know from me whether he had fulfilled his promise to give me a more exciting assignment than the one which I had had in Geneva. Now it was my turn to laugh since his question was a reference to our accidental meeting half a year earlier when I saw him in the corridors of the Palais des Nations in Geneva. He had asked me then whether I enjoyed my assignment as Director of the UNDP European Office and I told him that I found it boring!

After four days of Operation Desert Fox the damage to our building, fortunately, was minor. Some windows had been shattered and four of our rooftop water tanks were leaking since they had developed cracks, probably due to the bombs that were dropped on the Am Al Amn building a few hundred meters away and the resulting air pressure.

Besides wanting to assess the damage to buildings, I was anxious to get a sense of human casualties. In fact, after each night of bombing I drove to various parts of Baghdad in the mornings to visit the Al Yarmuk and Al Jumhuriyah hospitals as well as to Medinat al Tib, Baghdad's medical city. I wanted to see the wards where bomb victims were being treated. These wards were pitiful sights of civilian suffering, with doctors and nurses trying their best to save the lives of badly hurt civilians. Such images are hard to forget. There were two young men in one of the wards with open burn wounds: protective gauze and strong pain killers were not available. In their painful condition they sat upright in their beds, hoping that in spite of the scant medication they had been given a healing process could begin.

Outside the same hospital, on the morning of 18 December, I passed a young man wearing a sweatshirt depicting a large star-spangled banner, the US flag, on his chest. Inside the hospital were victims of the US bombing, outside a display of the national flag of the country that had just attacked Iraq. I wondered how people in my own country would have reacted under similar circumstances. Again and again I came across this remarkable ability of Iraqis to make a distinction between a country and its policies and its people, goods, symbols and music. Some time later a high-school student in Baghdad was asked where he would like to go if he could travel. He spontaneously replied 'to the United States to hear a Dr Dre concert'.

Damage to civilian areas had been limited since only a few of the missiles and bombs had gone astray. Nevertheless, over two hundred

Iraqi men, women and children had lost their lives; figures of military casualties were never made available.

Apart from signalling a more aggressive Iraq policy, 'Operation Desert Fox' had achieved little in Iraq, except to add a further dose of trauma to the Iraqi people. As Tariq Aziz, the Deputy Prime Minister had indicated to me when the bombing started, the Government indeed seemed well prepared for the strikes. The seventy buildings belonging to the Ministries of Defence and Foreign Affairs, the military industrial complex, intelligence services, the Republican Guards and the Ba'ath Party had been emptied of their furniture, files, equipment and staff. The missiles destroyed little more than abandoned buildings.

I had witnessed these preparations. Before Operation Desert Fox on 16 December, after my visit to Tariq Aziz, I drove to the Foreign Ministry to see Ambassador Adnan Malik who was responsible for the multilateral department, to discuss the possibilities of a UN evacuation and what steps the Government intended to take to keep the Oil-for-Food Programme operational. As I entered the building, I saw workmen carrying cartons of books, files, tables, chairs, TV sets and other office items to waiting trucks. The Ministry was preparing for the evening. CNN had been useful since it had repeated over and over again speculations that Washington was about to attack Iraq. While the people could not view CNN but only controlled programmes broadcast by the three Iraqi TV news channels, senior officials in all ministries had their individual TV sets with access to CNN, BBC, Al Jazeera and other international channels. Many ministers had two TV sets in their offices. Trade Minister Mohammed Mehdi Saleh and Education Minister Dr Fahad Al Shagra, for example, had both sets switched on simultaneously, watching BBC, CNN or Al Jazeera whenever I visited them. The Iraqi leadership was in little doubt about the seriousness of the situation, and the Iraqi people were no less so since the streets of Baghdad were full of rumours. Downtown traffic was worse than usual. Al Karade, Al Rashid, Al Adamiya and, of course, Sadoun Street were crowded with people who hurried through the markets to stock up on essentials and to hear the latest news.

During the period of air-strikes I convened daily meetings with staff who had stayed behind. It was important that there should be good communication among us. When I told them that the Secretary-General had called to enquire about their welfare, I could see from their faces how much they appreciated this gesture. We were all proud to have such a compassionate Secretary-General.

On the surface, conditions in Baghdad appeared fairly normal during the daytime; at night it was quite a different picture. The streets, usually full with vehicles as soon as the sun had set, were suddenly deserted and an uneasy silence lay over the city. Stories abounded about the feelings of

Baghdad's citizens during these difficult days. There was the family in Al Mansur who had seen better days before the embargo. The holy month of Ramadan had started and they invited me for 'Iftar', the breaking of the fast after sunset.[8] After dinner the teenage daughter suddenly asked her parents whether she could play some pieces of music on the piano. She played classical European music with great skill and passion. When she finished she looked at me with her big, brown eyes and said 'when the bombs came, I went to my piano and played to hear only my music, not the explosions'.

Then there was Dr Sadik Alwash, the Head of the Iraqi Red Crescent, who recounted how his daughter would go to their living room each time the bombing started and sit in the middle of the room, covering herself and his granddaughter with a big piece of cloth 'to create a tent and within it a little world of peace for her and her child'.

At lunchtime on 19 December, after the third night of bombing, I looked out of my office and saw on the other side of the fence a young, emaciated looking Iraqi soldier wearing a torn uniform. He was one of the 159 men who kept vigil for us throughout the crisis. He was praying, putting his head on the hot, hard cement floor in deference to his god. It was the *thuhur* or midday prayer, the second of the five daily prayers. At this moment I felt very humble.

There was no public reaction to the few of us who had remained at the UN compound in Baghdad. This happened despite Iraqi radio and the one TV station that was still functioning condemning the US/UK bombings in vitriolic language and criticising what they called 'Butler, the dog' and the United Nations for having facilitated Operation Desert Fox. I was not sure whether the public mood could alter and become more aggressive, or possibly be made more aggressive by the Iraqi authorities. This prompted me to step outside my authority for a brief moment: I asked the UN administrative officer to remove two prominent signs, one displayed at the gate, the other over the entrance to the Canal Hotel offices. In bold lettering both signs identified the 'United Nations Special Commission' (UNSCOM) , the disarmament unit, as one of the UN entities housed in this complex. Since UNSCOM was a focus of Iraqi anger, I felt that these signs might attract violence.

It was not long before I realised that I had taken a wrong decision. According to the UN Security Council, UNSCOM was still in existence. No one but the Council had the authority to remove UNSCOM 'insignia'. The next morning I asked the same colleagues who had removed the signs the day before to quickly put them back. This they did immediately but not, however, without smirks on their faces.

8. Ramadan had started on 20 December, a day after 'Operation Desert Fox' ended.

Nevertheless, both the Iraqi Press and the relatively small international Press corps in Baghdad had noticed my sign tampering. References to this appeared in some of their articles. New York, usually quick in reacting to whatever the UN in Baghdad was doing, kept silent. The justified reprimand never came.

Contact with New York throughout the four days of Desert Fox was continuous and mainly concerned with the security situation in Baghdad. There were no UN international staff in any other location during this period. Contact with Iraqi authorities was kept to an absolute minimum. We knew that they had little time for us; they probably felt, that barricaded as we were at the UN Canal Hotel, we could look after ourselves. This we did with difficulty since we did not know for how long we would have to face this crisis.

During the day we received damage reports from Iraqi and other sources. We knew that some schools, health facilities, and ministerial buildings such as the Ministry of Health, had been hit. Among ourselves time was spent discussing how we could assist in the days following the military strikes. This kept us occupied and ultimately helped speed up the special 'clean-up' programmes that UNICEF, WHO, UNOCHI and others would carry out in cooperation with NGOs who had also remained in Iraq. These included the French Première Urgence and Enfants du Monde, Care International, the Italian Bridge to Baghdad, the Middle East Council of Churches and, of course, the ICRC and the IFRC. The UN worked well with all of them.

We discovered on 20 December that the previous night had been our last night of fear. On that last evening, as on each previous one, my Russian UNIKOM colleague stood with me for long moments outside the entrance of our building and looked at the illuminated night sky. He explained with great patience to the layman the spectacle over Baghdad. He pointed out, for example, that what looked to me like uncoordinated fireworks were, in fact, Iraqi anti-aircraft batteries. 'They have no chance to hit any of the incoming scuds and other missiles', he told me. The US and UK aircraft dropped their ordnance from high altitudes: 'No hope for the Iraqis to shoot one down'. In any case, the remnants of the once respectable Iraqi air force wisely gave way to such superior technology and remained on the ground throughout the four nights of military operations. The Iraqi generals knew they could only lose against such mighty opponents. It was, nevertheless, quite a spectacle over the Baghdad night skies.

On international television screens it looked far more serious and all embracing than it actually was. The families of UN staff serving in Baghdad, including mine in Geneva, were naturally deeply worried. We were all relieved when the news reached us in the morning of 20 December that Operation Desert Fox was over at last. US Secretary of

Defence, William Cohen, had made an announcement to this effect at a news briefing pointing out that 'Saddam Hussein's ability to deliver chemical, biological and nuclear weapons had been degraded.'[9]

Again, the UN Secretary-General acted wisely and swiftly. He ordered those UN staff we had evacuated to Jordan to return immediately to Iraq to resume their duties. Those of us who had stayed behind hardly had time to reconvert our 'bunker' building back into offices before the six buses reappeared at the gates of the UN offices at the Canal Hotel. This time it was an arrival accompanied by smiles and obvious relief rather than the departure filled with tears and fear.

Operation Desert Fox had become part of history. For a long time, however, these painful days in December of 1998 remained in our collective memory. We debated what this unilateral episode of air-strikes had actually achieved. Years later, Robin Cook, the then former British Foreign Secretary indicated during a conversation with me that Desert Fox, in his opinion, had been of 'limited significance'. Cook added that he had pressed the British military to give evidence of the destruction of WMD facilities. 'I did not get a satisfactory answer.'

Of course, buildings had been destroyed in Baghdad and elsewhere in Iraq. These had to be rebuilt at a cost to the Iraqi people and to the international community. Schools and hospitals had to be repaired with funds provided by the NGO community and the UN system from their regular (non-Iraqi oil revenue) resources. This money could have been spent on humanitarian programmes. The energy and time of Iraqi and international personnel had to be invested in the post-strike clean-up rather than in helping to run the Oil-for-Food Programme. For weeks senior UN staff were involved in these repair efforts on a daily basis.[10] In addition to the physical damage, there was the shock effect of the heavy strikes on the minds of the Iraqi people. As WHO, UNICEF, IPPNW, Caritas the ICRC and many others had repeatedly observed and reported, the Iraqi population had been under extraordinary stress for many years as a result of the dictatorship and the punitive sanctions programme. Operation Desert Fox was a 'stress bonus'.

How much, we wondered at the UN in Baghdad, could a people take? US/UK air-strikes against Iraq, as an international issue of concern, were

---

9. US Department of Defence, News Briefing, 19 December 1998.
10. The UN Human Rights Rapporteur at the time, Max van der Stoel, erroneously reported that no damage assessment by the UN in Baghdad had been allowed, 'especially any direct or collateral damage to facilities of the UN Office for the Iraq Programme (OIP)'. First of all, there were only very minor damages to our premises. Secondly, the Government did allow UN/NGO assessments of damages to civilian facilities. What Iraqi authorities did not want was an assessment of total damage as they feared that this would have intelligence value: (see: E/CN.4/1999/37, 26 February 1999, p. 9).

quickly put aside by most governments and a large part of the public. Current affairs other than those of Iraq competed for their attention.

This was not so within the UN community in Iraq. We remained acutely aware that the United Nations had been sidelined, that the UN Security Council and the UN Secretary-General had been left out of the decision-making process and international law had been discarded and broken. The UN, as a conflict resolution and peace-building institution, had been further weakened. More Iraqis had died.

On 26 December 1998, the Government of Iraq announced that following 'Operation Desert Fox', UNSCOM would no longer be welcome to return its arms inspectors to Iraq.[11] The US/UK Governments had indicated that they had adopted 'enlarged rules of engagement' in the two no-fly zones, giving the pilots of their air forces greater freedom of action. This would significantly alter the security situation in large parts of the country. A first sign of what was to come was the attack on an Iraqi anti-aircraft base near the city of Mosul on 28 December 1998, nine days after the end of Operation Desert Fox. Baghdad, Washington and London continued to climb the ladder of confrontation.

The two no-fly zones had been established by the US, the UK and French Governments in 1991/92 to implement 'Operation Provide Comfort' in northern Iraq north of the 36th parallel and 'Operation Southern Watch' in areas south of the 32nd parallel.[12] The three governments maintaining these two no-fly zones argued at the time that this would help to protect the Kurdish population in the north and the Shi'ite population in the south against attacks by Saddam Hussein's air force.

Travelling in Iraqi Kurdistan in late November/early December 1998, I witnessed the daily afternoon visits by US and UK aircraft flying at high altitudes in the northern no-fly zone. After a few over flights in the Dohuk, Erbil and Suleimaniyah areas and the repeated breaking of the sound barrier to remind everyone that they were in the area, they would return to the Incirlik airbase in south-eastern Anatolia. The Turkish Government had assigned this base to US and UK forces for this purpose.

One could almost set one's watch by this display of presence. It would repeat itself day after day at exactly the same time in the afternoons. The pattern was similar in the southern no-fly zone. The incursions into Iraq's airspace prior to the air-strikes of December 1998 had been as benign as was Iraq's reaction.

11. The US/UK Governments and much of the media, the latter either innocently, or deliberately, later reported that the Government of Iraq had 'expelled' the UNSCOM arms inspectors. The fact is that they were voluntarily withdrawn by UNSCOM on 16 December 1998, the day 'Operation Desert Fox' began.
12. In 1996 the southern no-fly zone was extended to include areas up to the 33rd parallel.

Map 3.1 The Northen and Southern No-fly Zones

Source: *Country boundary data from Digital Chart of the World 1:1,000,000 digital data. Prepared by NIMA (US Military) and publicly available from http://www.maproom.psu.edu/dcw/.*

'Enlarged rules of engagement' abruptly ended the period of mere 'over-flight reassurance' for Kurds and Shi'ites and converted most of the areas in these two no-fly zones into combat areas, places of 'destabilisation' and 'destruction'. The pilots were increasingly free to determine their actions and where to strike. The new policy had little to do with the original pretension of protecting ethnic and religious groups. The containment policy of the United States during the last days of the Clinton administration had begun to crumble and under the incoming administration of George W. Bush in January 2001 was speedily substituted by an aggressive 'regime replacement policy'.

The key manifestation of this new policy in the no-fly zones was the destabilisation of conditions in Iraq. The official US/UK explanation for air attacks on Iraq targets under these enlarged rules of engagement was always the same: US and UK pilots flying their protective missions in the no-fly zones had been locked into Iraqi radar screens, thereby endangering the safety of the pilots. In the words of the US State Department: 'The air-strikes are not targeted at the Iraqi people. They are the direct response for self-defence of the forces that protect the Kurds in the north and the Shia in the south from the regime's civilian repression.'[13] What the State Department did not disclose was that each time the US/UK air forces crossed into Iraq it was no longer by a lone plane that made its rounds over the Kurdish north and the Shia south. The operation had become an armada of electronic jamming planes, tornado fighter bombers, jaguar attack planes, F-15s and F-16s and refuelling tankers, all assisted by AWACs on watch in the border areas.

Over-flight reminders in Iraq of a coalition presence in neighbouring countries before December 1998 did have reassurance value. In Erbil, I was told that people in Iraqi Kurdistan welcomed this 'aerial reassurance' of their international protection. I assume that similar sentiments existed in the Shia south. The 'protective' value of the presence of the US and UK air forces, however, was doubtful. It was more a case of appeasement of critical governments and the international public who were increasingly less convinced of the justification of having no-fly zones in the first place. Until there were civilian casualty reports of US/UK air-strikes, the issue of legality of the no-fly zones and what was happening there was rarely evoked in the international discussion on Iraq.

Gruesome pictures of mangled bodies of civilians and destroyed schools, rural health centres and warehouses alerted members of the UN Security Council, parliaments, anti-war and anti-sanctions movements around the world, as well as the UN community in Iraq. The US State Department's spokesman in 1999–2000, James P. Rubin,[14] repeatedly tried to justify these air-strikes by stating that 'the purpose of the no-fly zones is to prevent Iraq from using its airspace to kill and maim its own citizens'.[15] A few months later he claimed: 'They [the US/UK aircraft] never target civilians or civilian facilities … these aircraft … are carrying out a humanitarian mission …'.[16]

---

13. The US State Department, Bureau for Near Eastern Affairs, 'Myth and Facts about Iraq', August 2000, p. 5.
14. James P. Rubin was the US State Department's Spokesperson when Madeleine Albright served as Secretary of State. In 2004 Rubin was Foreign Policy Advisor to Democratic presidential candidate John Kerry.
15. US Department of State, Daily Press Briefings, 29 February 2000.
16. See Washington Post, 'US Defends Air Strikes in Iraq's No-Fly Zones', 17 June 2000, A.M.

The governments in Riyadh and Ankara became increasingly uneasy about the US/UK shift from benign takeover of Iraqi airspace to an intensifying confrontation between Iraqi ground forces and coalition air forces. The Saudi and Turkish Governments kept reminding Washington and London that their airbases were available but for 'peaceful' rather than 'hostile' forays into their neighbour's territory. Ankara was particularly concerned, repeatedly reminding the US/UK command at Incirlik airbase that they did not want to see an escalation in the no-fly zones of Iraq.[17]

It should be remembered that the US/UK air forces had begun flying under 'enlarged rules of engagement'. There were a few who thought that the US/UK air forces were deliberately 'targeting civilians'. There were many who doubted the 'humanitarian mission', and there was an increasing number of Iraq watchers who began to ask the key questions: whose 'rules' were these 'enlarged rules' following and what was the legality of the no-fly zones?

The US and UK Governments tried to avoid a discussion of these questions in and outside of the UN Security Council. When pressed for a position, they invariably would make the general contention that existing UN resolutions had already given them the authority to maintain the two no-fly zones and that they were acting in self-defence. If this did not satisfy the enquirers, they would refer to a string of UN resolutions which, in their opinion, gave them mandate and legality.

The resolution, evoked more than any other by the two Governments, is UN Security Council Resolution 688 of April 1991. This resolution, in article 5, requests the UN Secretary-General 'to address urgently the critical needs of the refugees and displaced Iraqi population' and appeals to member States 'to contribute to these humanitarian relief efforts'.[18] There is no reference anywhere in this resolution that would empower member States 'to take forceful measures like those necessarily associated with the establishment and enforcement of no-fly zones'.[19] This short

17. These observations are based on numerous conversations the author had in 1999/2000 with Turkish diplomats in Baghdad.
18. See UN S/RES 688 (1991), 5 April 1991. This resolution, it is important to point out, was adopted by the UN Security Council, under Chapter VI of the UN Charter. This chapter deals with 'Pacific Settlement of Disputes' and not Chapter VII, which is entitled 'Action With Respect to Threats to the Peace, Breaches of Peace and Acts of Aggression' and includes article 42. This article gives the Security Council the right to take 'action by land, air, sea … as may be necessary to maintain or restore international peace and security'. All other key resolutions on Iraq make specific reference to Chapter VII. See also UN Charter, pp. 24–8.
19. See Rex J. Zedalis, 'The Quiet, Continuing Air War Against Iraq: An Interpretive Analysis of the Controlling Security Council Resolutions', in *Zeitschrift für Öffentliches Recht*, 2000, p. 188.

resolution has not even implicit references to a military protection role, let alone the use of force in these two areas of Iraq. It only deals with the UN's role in meeting specific humanitarian needs in Iraq. UK Ambassador Jeremy Greenstock was out of order when he stated in the UN Security Council that 'the action we take in the no-fly zones is following Security Council Resolution 688 (1991), to protect the civilian population of Iraq from repression by the Iraqi Government.'[20]

Other Security Council resolutions referred to by the US and UK Governments as legitimisation[21] also contain no enabling wording for the establishment of the two no-fly zones, and certainly not for the type of engagement perpetuated by the coalition air force in the zones. Resolutions such as 678 (1990) and 687 (1991), both passed under chapter VII of the UN Charter, did contain such phrases as 'use all necessary means'[22] and 'take further steps as may be required to secure peace and security in the region'.[23] The former, however, relates only to Iraq's invasion of Kuwait; wording of the latter was incorrectly, and without legal base, taken by the US and UK Governments as an indirect consent of the UN Security Council to do anything that they thought would 'secure peace and security'. This included the delineation of no-fly zones and the offensive acts which were increasingly carried out by their air forces.

It is more than doubtful that this is what the Security Council had in mind when it passed Resolution 687. Had the UN Security Council been of the opinion that strong measures should be included, as foreseen in chapter VII of the UN Charter, should be included they would have done so. In the subsequent Resolution 1441 of 8 November 2002, for example, in which the Council referred to a 'material breach of its (Iraq's) obligations' and that 'Iraq ... will face serious consequences as a result of its continued violations ...',[24] this was done. Had the Council wanted to establish no-fly zones, it could have included a specific reference in Resolution 688 or in any other Iraq resolution. The Council, however, had no such intentions.

Throughout the years the no-fly zones were not a standard topic of the Iraq debate by the Security Council. They, however, were raised periodically by various permanent and non-permanent members who questioned the legality of the zones and the attacks that were carried out by the air forces of the US and the UK. While such references were made, the Council regrettably never discussed the zones. Nevertheless, at no time did the Security Council even implicitly support the existence of the no-fly zones. In 1999 the Russian representative, Ambassador Granovski, expressed his Government's position very clearly when he said: 'we

20. UN/S/4152nd meeting, S/PV.4152, 8 June 2000, p. 4.
21. For example, Resolutions 678 (1990) and 687 (1991).
22. See UN S/Res/678 (1990), 29 November 1990, para. 2.
23. See UN S/Res/687 (1991), 3 April 1991, para. 34.
24. See UN S/Res (2002), 8 November 2002, paras. 1 and 13.

condemn in particular the continuing aerial bombing of Iraqi civilian and military facilities by the United States and the United Kingdom under the illegal pretext of the no-fly zones which were created unilaterally in circumvention of the Security Council.' Throughout the years other governments have echoed this Russian position in the Security Council. Ambassador Babaa, representing the Libyan Arab Jamahiriya (Libyan Government) at the United Nations, criticised the Security Council during an open meeting on Iraq on 28 June 2001, saying that it 'had not even initiated a debate of [the no-fly zones] which flagrantly violate[s] international law ...'.[25] On the same occasion, India's Deputy Permanent Representative Satyprata Pal reiterated this position by pointing out that 'the no-fly zones are not sanctioned by any aspect of the Council's resolutions'.[26]

The Government of Iraq, of course, did not restrain its anger over the existence of the no-fly zones. During a February 2001 visit to UN headquarters, Foreign Minister Mohamed Al Sahaf told Kofi Annan that 'the United States and the United Kingdom bear the full international responsibility for their illegal actions' and submitted a detailed statement on the no-fly zone to the United Nations.[27]

The Iraqi Press made news about the 'US/UK evil crows' and their armed sorties into Iraq a standard piece of reporting. Whenever civilian sites had been hit, Iraq and the US/UK would engage in another battle, a 'battle of words'. The Iraqis would accuse, the US/UK would refute. For example, Iraq claimed that a warehouse in Southern Iraq that had been destroyed contained food supplies, but the US/UK Governments insisted that it had held anti-aircraft weapons.

In the UN offices in Baghdad, we read these news items and were confused since we were not able to verify the reporting. Following Operation Desert Fox, the frequency of incursions into Iraqi airspace increased. I was determined to better understand this emerging security issue. For me this was not only an issue of general concern. It had implications for the security of a large number of UN staff who were using Iraqi roads while overseeing the Oil-for-Food Programme and was endangering the lives of Iraqi civilians living in these areas.

Given my responsibilities for the security of UN staff in Iraq, I discussed the enhanced security risks with Abraham Mathai, the Chief of the Security Unit in the UNOCHI office and his staff. There was unanimity among us that we had to create a much more reliable information base than the one we were given by the national and international media. We

25. UN Security Council, S/PV.4336, 4336th meeting, 28 June 2001, p. 2.
26. Ibid., p. 4.
27. See 'Presentation of the Delegation of the Republic of Iraq in the Dialogue with the Secretary-General of the United Nations', New York, 26–7 February 2001, pp. 31–41.

wanted to devise a format for the collection of data concerning incidents in the no-fly zones. This would entail keeping a record of the air-strikes reported by the Iraqi media, with full awareness that they may contain false or inflated information. At the end of December 1998, all UN staff travelling in Iraq were instructed to include, as part of their back-to-office reports, air-strike information which they could obtain at the locations where they worked and, of course, report on air-strikes they themselves had witnessed.

Under the leadership of the UN Security Office in Baghdad, visits to selected air-strike sites were organised to verify what we read in the local media or heard from Iraqi Ministry of Defence spokespersons.

Quarterly reports and a consolidated annual report were to be issued. Such information in turn would be analysed to see whether we could discover any patterns in the timing and frequency of allied sorties involving incidents in civilian areas and to estimate the extent of civilian damage. Mathai and I agreed that we would then determine what the implications, if any, would be for the movement of UN personnel in Iraq. We soon realised that there was no pattern, but security incidents of a kind not occurring before Operation Desert Fox became a repeated aspect of life in Iraq. This was a worrying development for Iraqis and foreigners alike.

The air-strike report[28] which we eventually prepared and forwarded to the UN Security Coordinator in New York and the Office of the UN Secretary-General showed that in 1999 air-strikes occurred on average on every third day. Basrah in the South and Mosul in the North and their vicinities received the maximum of strikes, with thirty-three killed in the governorate of Basrah and fifty-seven in the governorate of Nineva (Mosul).

There was also damage to private houses, vehicles and civilian government buildings including a warehouse, a primary school, and a

Table 3.1 Iraq's No-Fly Zones US/UK Air Strikes (28 December 1998 – 31 December 1999)[29]

Total number of air strikes (days)	132	Total number of air strikes with civilian casualties (days)	56
No. civilian deaths	144	No. civilian injuries	446
Northern no-fly zone	57	Northern no-fly zone	133
Southern no-fly zone	87	Southern no-fly zone	313

Source: *Confidential report prepared by UNOCHI/Baghdad entitled 'Air Strikes in Iraq/Reported Civilian Casualties and Damages, 28 December 1998 – 31 December 1999'.*

28. Confidential report prepared by UNOCHI/Baghdad entitled, 'Air Strikes in Iraq/Reported Civilian Casualties and Damages, 28 December 1998–31 December 1999'.
29. Ibid.

mosque, as well as livestock in sixty-four different locations. These UN air-strike reports led to considerable acrimony within the UN secretariat.

While individual members of the UN Security Council used these reports extensively to argue the case against the no-fly zones, the UN secretariat was split over whether I, as the UN Security Coordinator in Iraq, had the right to produce such documents. The UN Security Coordinator and Executive Director of the Office of the Iraq Programme, Benon Sevan, was outraged that I had decided to produce such reports. The Chef de Cabinet, Iqbal Riza, wrote to me that these air-strike reports were 'very interesting and useful' for the Secretary-General's Office and should be continued.[30] There could be no doubt that this information was relevant for the UN team in Iraq and our humanitarian mission, as it allowed us to take protective measures for staff and humanitarian supplies. We decided, for example, that UN staff on duty travel outside of Baghdad had to return to the capital or specified nodal points elsewhere in the country by nightfall. UN staff resident in the locations of Basrah, Kirkuk and Mosul were withdrawn following continued heavy air-strikes there. We also halted UN truck traffic between Mosul and Dohuk in Iraqi Kurdistan between the hours of 11 o'clock in the morning and 3 o'clock in the afternoon because air-strikes tended to occur in this area during those hours. We became more sensitive to staff welfare by allowing staff members who were apprehensive about their safety while outside Baghdad to remain in the capital.

As the security value of the incident database and the air-strike reports became well established and the Secretary-General's Office welcomed the reporting, I was convinced that the UN in Baghdad was correct in continuing our record-keeping of this unfortunate situation. We issued the second quarterly report in July 1999. Shortly thereafter I travelled to New York and London for consultations and briefings on the Iraq situation. Soon after my arrival in New York I received a message from the UK mission to the United Nations that Ambassador Stewart Eldon wanted to see me. I assumed he was interested in hearing the latest from Iraq and discussing the status of the Oil-for-Food Programme. Accompanied by another member of the UK mission, Eldon met me at the UN Secretariat. He quickly came to the point and did not mince his words: 'Why are you compiling these no-fly zone reports? Do you realise that you are totally straying off your mandate? As the UN Humanitarian Coordinator you have no business dealing with issues outside your area of competence! In any case, all you are doing is putting a UN logo of approval on Iraqi propaganda.' Following this vehement introduction, Ambassador Eldon then conveyed with pride that he knew what he was talking about since he

---

30. Internal fax from S. Iqbal Riza, Chef de Cabinet to the author, dated 18 May 1999.

had been a Deputy Manager of Operation Desert Storm in the 1991 war against Iraq. 'You should know that British Intelligence received information in the early 1990s that Iraqi agents were planning to travel in Europe in possession of lethal substances.' Why did he tell me all this? It did not fit at all into the context of our 'no-fly encounter'.

Eldon had walked across from the Dag Hammarskjöld Plaza on Second Avenue to tell me what the UN should not do in Iraq rather than discuss with me what the UK could do to help in improving the human conditions in Iraq. I was disappointed but not entirely surprised. After all, a representative of a government which year after year invested its energies in the Security Council in maintaining the status quo, preventing dialogue and only as a last resort giving in to pressures for long overdue improvements in the economic sanctions regime and the Oil-for-Food Programme could not be expected to be eager to discuss ways in which sanction policies were implemented, especially with someone as critical of British sanctions policy as he knew I was. When he had finished his litany of rebukes, I told him that UN security staff, UN observers travelling in areas where air-strikes had taken place or I myself would verify what the Iraq News Agency (INA) and others had written. I gave him the example of a cruise missile which had struck the Al-Jumhuriya residential area of Basrah on 25 January 1999 when US/UK bombers were concurrently attacking Abu Flos in the Shatt-El-Arab, Abu al-Kaseeb south of Basrah, the infamous Al-Rumeila oil fields and Basrah airport. Iraqi media had spoken of eleven casualties, many injured and rows of houses destroyed. 'I had travelled to the area, Ambassador Eldon and could confirm the destruction of houses in this poor neighbourhood of Basrah and in Abu Kaseeb'. I mentioned to Eldon that Mathai, my Chief of Security, and I had spoken to residents who described to us their losses and told us of the many injured relatives and neighbours. 'We counted a total of seventeen coffins Ambassador Eldon, not eleven, as reported by the media. Iraqi propaganda?'

Eldon's response: 'We regret any civilian casualty but our pilots act only in self defence. The Iraqi military installs itself in civilian residential areas. Incidents are often caused by the Iraqi armed forces.' Considering this, I decided to say no more. It would have made no difference except to harden his resolve.[31] In any case, he repeated that I should refrain from writing such reports. For him they were out of order. For me they were evidence of serious wrongdoing.

---

31. John Pilger in his article 'The Secret War on Iraq', quoted NATO Secretary-General George Robertson who in 1999, as the British Minister of Defence, had remarked: 'We have to continue making these air strikes in order to carry on with our humanitarian work'.

While I spoke with Ambassador Eldon his assistant was engrossed in recording what was being said. The minutes of this meeting could not possibly have been flattering to the UN Security Coordinator in Baghdad. I did not mind: I wanted it to be known that I was not succumbing to unjustified pressure; the United Nations had a responsibility to keep such records.

The conversation ended fairly abruptly when I reminded Ambassador Eldon that I reported to the UN Secretary-General and not to the British Government and would, therefore, continue to monitor the no-fly zone incidents until instructed by the UN otherwise.

Perhaps I should have also told Eldon of the attack in the spring of 1999 by US/UK planes on a shepherd's family – the Jarjees family near Quban village, 30 km from Mosul. The shepherd, six members of his family and 101 sheep were killed, and a water bowser and a vehicle destroyed. I will never forget the stench that hung over the wide, open plain in April temperatures of 40°C[32] at the time of my visit there. Nor will I forget the immense sadness on the faces of those who showed us around. The human bodies had been removed. The mangled carcasses of sheep lay where they had been struck.

The US/UK military described this incident quite differently:[33] '30th April 1999 … Operation Northern Watch aircraft were fired upon by Iraqi antiaircraft artillery. Responding in self defence, US air force F-15E strike eagles and F-16C falcons dropped GBU-12 laser-guided bombs on Iraqi radar and antiaircraft artillery sites south and northeast of Mosul. In addition, US air force F-16CJ falcons launched AGM-88 high-speed anti-radiation missiles (HARM) at Iraqi radar and antiaircraft artillery sites south and northeast of Mosul.'[34] Referring to this incident, Robin Cook, British Foreign Secretary at the time, said to me five years later: 'I cannot understand how the US air force could not distinguish between an anti-aircraft facility and a shepherd's grazing ground. Yes, the US committed a lot of blunders' in the no-fly zones.[35]

USEUCOM did not even acknowledge this horrendous error. Truth was again sacrificed in order not to invite renewed criticism by many who felt that the US and UK Governments were acting illegally and brutally in maintaining the two no-fly zones.

The continuing air-strike reporting and the fact that I had not given in to Ambassador Eldon's intimidation efforts undoubtedly contributed to a build-up of the determination by the Foreign Office in London and the

32. This incident happened on 30 April 1999.
33. Statement by the US European Command (USEUCOM) near Stuttgart in Germany.
34. See www.eucom.mil.
35. Meeting with Robin Cook, former British Foreign Secretary, in Brighton, 29 September 2004.

State Department in Washington to encourage Kofi Annan to get rid of his obstinate UN official in Baghdad.

A few months later, in the autumn of 1999, on another visit from Baghdad to New York, I was made acutely aware of this. It was Wednesday, 27 October, when the Secretary-General received me in his office with the words: 'Are you aware that the US and UK Governments have asked me for your removal?' I replied in the affirmative since I had heard this from a colleague the evening before and as a consequence had passed a night full of reflection. The Secretary-General then looked straight at me and said: 'Your contract is hereby renewed.'[36] Vindication? A strong and principled Secretary-General? Relief? All of these came to my mind at this moment, but more than anything there was a feeling of pride to work with such a Secretary-General. 'Go and see the British and US Ambassadors. This will help', Kofi Annan suggested to me. I did, even though I was not convinced that it would. There did not seem any room for US/UK policy adjustment. Facts from Iraq were not needed. Important for them was that a UN official in their opinion had stepped out of line, did not see the bigger picture, constituted a nuisance, was not competent for the job.

Ambassadors Greenstock and Burleigh received me in a friendly way. We exchanged views on Iraq. I mentioned to both that UN no-fly zones reporting was done out of security concerns and not to antagonise their governments. I thought I had found at least some understanding by both ambassadors. This was apparently not the case since a short while later I received a note in Baghdad from Chef de Cabinet Iqbal Riza to tell me that both 'had reiterated their concerns' after our meetings.[37]

At this October 1999 meeting with Secretary-General Annan we spoke not so much about the no-fly zones as about the management of the humanitarian programme and my involvement with the media, another source of US/UK irritation. He advised me, in his gentle way, to refrain from criticising Security Council policies, 'even if you think there is justified cause to do so', and 'confine yourself to outlining to the press the factual situation in Iraq as you perceive it'. Kofi Annan was right. But for UN staff having to represent Security Council policies in Baghdad and to see the human consequences of such policies on the ground was quite another matter.

The northern no-fly zone only partially covered Iraqi Kurdistan, the area that the zone allegedly was meant to protect. Parts of Suleimaniyah governorate, including its capital, were below the 36th parallel and, therefore, outside this 'protection zone'. Why the coalition governments so decided remains a mystery. In the areas of the northern no-fly zone

---

36. Meeting with UN Secretary-General on 27 October 1999 in New York.
37. Letter from Iqbal Riza, Chef de Cabinet, to me dated 23 November 1999.

which were under the control of Saddam Hussein's Government, the security situation under 'enlarged rules of engagement' had progressively worsened. Insecurity in the Baghdad-held areas was predominately due to air-strikes. It was also less complex here than in the Kurdish areas across the line of control. Soon after the Gulf War ended on 28 February 1991 and members of the UN Security Council had agreed 'to bring their military presence in Iraq to an end as soon as possible',[38] Kurdish leaders sought international protection for their people. They feared that Saddam Hussein would repeat in Iraqi Kurdistan what he had done in the Shia South. There he had ruthlessly quelled resistance to his regime and to initiatives for local autonomy. After the enormous suffering of the 1980s, which was symbolised most dramatically by the carnage of the 1988 Anfal campaign, the Kurds were frightened.

Many left towns and villages and took to the rugged mountains of northern Iraq. A good number crossed into the Kurdish areas of Eastern Turkey and Syria. In 1991, the US/UK initiated 'Operation Provide Comfort', involving a large multinational defence force[39] that entered Northern Iraq, constituted the immediate response to reassure Iraqi Kurdistan of international protection and provide emergency assistance. Iraq's occupation of Kuwait, the suppression of opposition in both Southern and Northern Iraq by Saddam Hussein's military and intelligence and the volatile political situation created in the region by the large number of Kurdish refugees in Turkey, Iran and Syria all contributed to international acceptance of the crossing into Iraq by this multinational protection force. The fact that, in the absence of a UN Security Council mandate, Iraq's sovereignty and territorial integrity had been violated was ignored. The need to make the return of Kurdish refugees to their homelands in Northern Iraq possible was the immediate priority.

The UN Security Council did not authorise 'Operation Provide Comfort' but debated the security situation for Kurds and other ethnic and religious minorities in Iraq. The Council asked Secretary-General Pérez de Cuéllar to extend help to 'all those in need of assistance'[40] and report accordingly to the Security Council. Pérez de Cuéllar recognised that the deepening humanitarian crisis in all parts of Iraq called for bold and circumspect measures. In this spirit the UN negotiated, with the Government of Saddam Hussein, the Iraq-wide deployment of United Nations guards. The UN's first Secretary-General, Trygve Lie, had already proposed this method in 1945 to protect humanitarian missions in crisis

---

38. See UN S/RES/686 (1991), 2 March 1991.
39. There were two 'Operations Provide Comfort', the first ended on 24 July 1991, the second on 31 December 1996.
40. See UN S/RES 688 (1991), 5 April 1991.

areas.[41] The Government of Iraq accepted the presence of a contingent of up to five hundred persons of what became known as the 'United Nations Guards Contingent in Iraq' (UNGCI).[42] Its mission was to protect 'UN personnel, assets and operations linked with the humanitarian programme'.[43] These guards, who were authorised to carry sidearms provided by the Iraqi authorities, came from contributing countries' police and military forces.

Over the years the number of these UN guards was not only continuously adjusted downwards at the insistence of the Iraqi authorities but, as of mid-1992, their presence was confined to the three northern (Kurdish) governorates. Their presence in the early 1990s, small as it was, nevertheless helped to facilitate the return and reintegration of Kurdish refugees from neighbouring countries and the distribution of food, medicine and clothing.

At the time of the Oil-for-Food Programme, the UNGCI carried out important border-control functions, gave protection to UN civilians travelling in Iraqi Kurdistan in connection with the implementation of the Oil-for-Food Programme, monitored the general security situation in Iraqi Kurdistan,[44] performed rescue operations following not infrequent road accidents, and extended medical help to UN and non-UN persons travelling in their command areas.[45] The white UNGCI four-wheel drive vehicles plying the roads of Northern Iraq were welcomed by the local population as a sign of international concern for their welfare. UN staff,

41. The UN represented by Sadruddin Aga Khan and the Government of Iraq by its Foreign Minister Ahmed Hussein signed a Memorandum of Understanding (MOU) on 18 April 1991 on humanitarian assistance to which six weeks later, on 30 May 1991 an annex was added with details on the deployment of a 'UN guards contingent'. This MOU was replaced on 21 November 1991 by a second memorandum to refine the conditions of UN humanitarian assistance and the terms of the UN Guards Contingent in Iraq (UNGCI). The first ten guards arrived in May 1991 and were stationed near Zakho at the Iraqi Turkish border in Dohuk governorate. The full complement of five hundred guards, representing thirty-five nationalities, was deployed by October 1991.
42. The Government of Iraq changed its position on the number of guards soon after signing the annex to the April 1991 MOU. In August 1992 the Iraqi authorities insisted on a reduction to 150 guards. At the time of my tenure in Iraq there was a tacit understanding between the UN and Government that no more than sixty-nine guards would be allowed service in the country limited, however, to Iraqi Kurdistan.
43. See UN/Iraq MOU of 21 November 1991 in, 'UN and the Iraq-Kuwait Conflict, 1990–96', UN Department of Public Information, p. 362, para. 7.
44. In 1999, UNGCI conducted 1,695 escorts for UN personnel in the three governorates of Iraqi Kurdistan and carried out 1,494 security patrols – see UNGCI confidential report for 1999, dated 23 January 2000, p. 8.
45. UNGCI officers also assisted the humanitarian programme by placing communication repeater stations and car fuel depots in remote areas of Northern Iraq.

whether permanently assigned to the UN area headquarters of Erbil or Suleimaniyah, or travelling across the northern areas on the Kurdish side of the line of control, were also reassured by the presence of these experienced UN blue-clad security officers – and for good reasons.

The security situation in this part of the country was significantly more volatile than in areas under Baghdad's control. Located in the northern no-fly zone, with the exception of the south-eastern half of Suleimaniyah governorate, the area was outside the zone of direct influence of the Iraqi armed forces. Diplomats, intelligence personnel, foreign military, businessmen, NGO representatives, and even tourists would travel in and out of Iraqi Kurdistan from neighbouring countries without notifying Government and without visas. This free-for-all also made a mockery of UN Security Council resolutions which had consistently emphasised Iraq's sovereignty and territorial integrity.

The result was that Iraqi Kurdistan became the convenient meeting-ground of foreign intelligence organisations interested in playing the 'great game' in this part of the world.[46] Matters were further complicated by the fact that the Turkish army maintained a semi-permanent force with armed vehicles and tanks in the Dohuk governorate because of the Turkish Kurdish People's Party operations in the border areas of Turkey and Iraq.[47] In Suleimaniyah, MIT, the Turkish Intelligence and the Turkish Kurdish People's Party had for some time, in the late 1990s, 'semi-official' representations recognised by the PUK. There is little doubt that Western undercover agents had infiltrated some of the many non-governmental organisations carrying out their humanitarian missions in Iraqi Kurdistan. It was an absurd situation that certainly complicated the implementation of the Oil-for-Food Programme and the wider humanitarian exemption in Northern Iraq.

Each time my UN colleagues and I travelled across the line of control into Iraqi Kurdistan it was a trip into uncertainty. On the Kurdish side we were received by UN guards in two UNGCI vehicles, one to head the convoy, the other to provide protection from the rear. Colonel Sethsson, the Swedish chief of the UNGCI and his sixty-eight guards were indeed an important part of our humanitarian mission. Made up of eight nationalities from countries in Asia and Europe,[48] they were a well

---

46. MI6, CIA, MOSSAD, MIT, SAVANA, BND and, of course, the Iraqi Intelligence had their presence, if not their stations there.
47. At times there were long spells of absence of Turkish armed forces / PKK encounters. During these periods one could witness, as I did, entrenched Turkish contingents socialising with Kurdish villagers. On one occasion I saw Turkish soldiers in Al Amadiya (Dohuk governorate) playing netball across the barrels of their tanks.
48. As of 31 December 1999 UNGCI included guards from Bangladesh, the Czech Republic, Netherlands, Philippines, Greece, Nepal and Poland.

trained, professional and disciplined UN contingent – exactly what was needed under these fluid circumstances.

How unstable the situation was in the very area that the US and UK had designated for special protection and no-fly zones is reflected in the many security incidents that occurred in all three Kurdish governorates month after month. During the first year as Humanitarian Coordinator UNGCI recorded some 350 security-related incidents for Iraqi Kurdistan.[49] A good number of these had to do with the UN presence in northern Iraq. The UNGCI identified close to forty such incidents involving anti-UN street protests, shooting at UN personnel, vehicles and other property, explosions at UN warehouses, booby traps, rocket attacks, threatening telephone calls to individual UN staff, planting of anti-personnel mines and stone throwing. Several UN staff members lost their lives in these encounters and others were severely wounded.[50] Bands of Kürdistan Işçi Partisi or Kurdish People's Party (PKK) insurgents were seeking temporary refuge in Northern Iraq or had crossed the Turkish/Iraqi border to fight their ethnic brothers from the Iraqi Kurdish Democratic Party (KDP) for cooperating with Turkey. They also confronted the Turkish forces stationed in Dohuk, which added significantly to the volatility of the security situation in Iraqi Kurdistan.[51]

The introduction by the US/UK Governments of enlarged rules of engagement in 1998 for their air forces in the no-fly zones led not only to steep increases in the number of air-strike incidents in both the southern and northern no-fly zones, but also added a new dimension to the security situation in the northern no-fly zone. Confrontation between the US and British air forces with Iraqi ground forces at times spilled across the line of control into Iraqi Kurdistan. During a February 1999 visit to northern Iraq, I witnessed, for example, a series of missile hits in the Dohuk area. The Kurdish authorities accused Baghdad of indiscriminately firing into their areas of control. The Iraqi Government version was different. It argued that the damage was due entirely to foreign aircraft which had entered Iraq illegally. Our report to New York pointed out that 'a total of 33 ground-to-ground artillery shells/missiles (were) known to have hit Dohuk city and areas around six villages spread over approximately 250 square kilometres'.[52] These shells and missiles were undoubtedly of Iraqi military origin and were intended for the incoming US and UK aircraft.

---

49. The majority of these took place in Erbil and Dohuk – see confidential UNGCI report for 1995 dated 23 January 2000.
50. Ibid.
51. In 1999 UNGCI identified thirty-nine serious security incidents with many casualties involving the PKK – see UNGCI confidential report for 1999 dated 23 January 2000, pp. 13–1 to C–17.
52. UNOHCI crypto-fax dated 16 February 1999 to the UN Secretariat on 'Incidents of Missile Hits in the Dohuk Area of Northern Iraq, 2–12 February 1999'.

When they failed to reach their targets they at times fell upon Kurdish autonomous territory, causing more political than physical damage. Deliberately provoked incidents across the line of control did occur but were, fortunately, rare. Sometimes they bordered on the ridiculous: the Iraqi Foreign Ministry requested my presence to protest alleged UN collaboration with Kurds in releasing cobra snakes or planting locust eggs along the line of control. On another occasion, I was asked to instruct my office in Erbil to remove an anti-Saddam Hussein cartoon from the bulletin board. There were also isolated skirmishes between Iraqi soldiers and Kurdish Peshmergas[53] and, in Southern Suleimaniyah, outside the no-fly zone, Iraqi air force incursions and attacks in Kurdish-held areas. These, however, were extremely rare since the Iraqi Government knew the implications of sustained provocation in Kurdish areas.[54] In the late 1990s relations between the KDP and the PUK, the two main Iraqi Kurdish factions, had sufficiently improved. This made confrontation along their internal line of control dividing the governorates of Dohuk and Erbil (KDP) and Suleimaniyah (PUK) rare.

The Kurdish areas of the northern no-fly zone were anything but tranquil. The daily life of Iraqi Kurds and the many foreigners who had come with either honourable or dubious motives faced many uncertainties and dangers. This security reality obviously had its impact on the implementation of humanitarian programmes. These included the nineteen NGOs that were active in Iraqi Kurdistan at the turn of the century, and the UN system with its Oil-for-Food Programme. The nearly daily incidents of varied origin did restrict the freedom with which the humanitarian exemption could be carried out in Iraqi Kurdistan.

The balance sheet for the no-fly zones is not a good one, either for the Iraqi people or for the United Nations. To protect vulnerable groups against a ruthless regime cannot possibly be an objectionable goal. To establish two rigid exclusion zones and make these increasingly the practice ground for waging a war, however, was not the way of achieving this goal.

International monitoring of the human rights situation in Iraq by the UN Security Council and the UN Human Rights Commission could have constituted an adequate UN early-warning system.

Just as the UN Security Council had options for implementing comprehensive economic sanctions which could have reduced the harm to the Iraqi people, the Council had options on how to react to the unilateralist approaches of three of its permanent members in establishing

---

53. *Peshmerga* – literal translation from Kurdish = 'those who face death'. For Kurds these are their freedom fighters.
54. On 13 March 1999, for example, two GOI helicopters bombed an empty land cruiser in the Jabari district of new Kirkuk in Suleimaniyah governorate.

the two no-fly zones.[55] The issue of the no-fly zones, however, was intermittently raised in the Council by individual members but never debated as a specific agenda item by the Security Council as a whole. Never did the Council pronounce the illegality of the existence of these zones; it was simply not a Security Council topic.

As experts continue their discussion over the interpretation of various Security Council resolutions with respect to the legality of the establishment of the no-fly zones, it cannot be argued that Iraq resolutions contained explicit provision for such exclusion zones. They did not. It again points to the weakness of a Council that was willing to overlook the fact that two permanent members had maintained these zones for over ten years without a Council mandate. The implications of this neglect of Security Council responsibility were serious enough in the period leading up to 'Operation Desert Fox' in December 1998. The subsequent introduction by the US and UK Governments of enlarged rules of engagement for their pilots operating in the no-fly zones and their air-strikes resulted in harm imposed on Iraq's civilian population. The Security Council's connivance constituted guilt by omission.

The Security Council had access to the air-strike reports prepared by the United Nations in Iraq, and individual members did use these to present their objections to the strikes.[56] The Council was aware that it had never authorised these zones and that all three Secretaries-General (de Cuéllar, Boutros Boutros Ghali and Annan) had referred during their tenure to the problem of the no-fly zones. Yet, the Council did not have the capacity to get 'involved', even when the number of civilian casualties rose steeply in 1999 and during the provocation in 2002/03 of the US and UK air forces. Preparing for the March 2003 war, these air forces could no longer hide their intentions behind the need for self-defence. There were almost daily incursions into Iraqi territory by US and UK air forces and Turkish land forces. This all made a mockery of the Council's repeated reassurance in its Iraq resolutions of the country's right to sovereignty. The Council, as a council, had the obligation to take a clear stand rather than leaving it to a few members of the Council, notably Russia and China, to condemn the zones and the air-strikes. These individual protests made no difference whatsoever at the political level. Surveillance from neighbouring countries and respect for Iraq's land borders rather than air incursions could have prevented the security chaos in Iraqi Kurdistan:

55. The US, the UK and France. France decided in 1996 to opt out of this coalition.
56. Even though members of the Security Council made use of the UN/Baghdad prepared air-strike reports, none protected the UN designated official for security – nor did the UN Secretariat, which remained silent during harsh and unjustified criticism of his reports. The neutrality of the UN civil service was not defended.

they could have saved lives and facilitated smoother implementation of the Oil-for-Food Programme in both the northern and the southern no-fly zones.

Iraq's 1991–2003 no-fly zones constitute a powerful example of a UN Security Council in urgent need of reform, since it was structurally and normatively incapable of withstanding unilateralism and bilateral misuse in the name of the international community.

Chapter 4

The United Nations Special Commission and the UN Office of the Humanitarian Coordinator for Iraq: Two Units of the Same Organisation?

The UNSCOM Laboratory

At the best of times the cohabitation of UNSCOM (the disarmament office) and UNOHCI (the humanitarian programme) at the Canal Hotel in Baghdad was uneasy. More often the atmosphere was tense and at times outright confrontational. This was not surprising. After all, UNSCOM manifested tough and uncompromising expectations of the UN Security Council that Iraq disclose its WMD arsenals and facilitate their destruction. UNOHCI, on the other hand, was in Iraq to mitigate the effects of an embargo through the Oil-for-Food Programme. In local parlance, the UNSCOM disarmament personnel were considered the 'tough guys', whereas UNOHCI humanitarian staff were dubbed the 'softies'. In one part of these UN offices were the 'cowboys'; in the other, the 'bunny-huggers', as we were also known.

Soon after my arrival in Baghdad, I realised how different indeed were the two groups. At lunchtime, for example, one could see the 'UNSCOM tables' and the 'UNOHCI tables'. Of course, there was some socialising between us, but only very little: UNSCOM management did not encourage mixing. In any case, the mobility of UNSCOM technicians, highly specialised biological, chemical and nuclear scientists and warfare specialists, helicopter crews and others, was significantly greater than that of the Oil-for-Food Programme staff. There were other distinctions. While UNSCOM personnel had access to gym facilities it had built within the building, we, the 'other UN staff', were barred from using such facilities. The bar on the ground floor of our joint premises, on the other hand, was 'common ground' – all international staff had access, but not at all times: UNSCOM insisted that at certain times the bar should be restricted to UN disarmament staff only. 'Why?' I asked soon after my arrival in November 1998. Jaako Ylitalo, the Finnish Colonel in charge of UNSCOM during the absence of its Chairman Richard Butler, replied: 'UNSCOM personnel are working in Iraq under heavy stress. They need to "unwind" and not have to watch their words. This is only possible if they have time on their own.' This did make some sense to me even though I regretted the effect this had on the atmosphere in the building. However, when similar arguments were advanced to justify the existence of two UN medical services, I reacted more critically, particularly when I discovered that UNSCOM's medical unit was significantly better equipped than ours. They had, for example, access to life-saving equipment and two ambulances. We had none of these. It was an amazing double standard that could not be justified by the fact that UNSCOM personnel was dealing with hazardous materials and therefore more likely to be in need of specialised medical facilities.

An integrated medical unit open to all UN staff should have been in place. We never reached this point. Such a unit could have saved Iraqi resources without depriving those in need of special medical attention from receiving it. The only concession I obtained from UNSCOM, after heated exchanges, was that for seriously ill or injured UN staff other than UNSCOM – in other words – for 'stretcher cases' we would be allowed to have access to 'their' life-saving equipment and the ambulances. The ambulances, as I learned much later, had not only the customary radio communication equipment installed, but also sophisticated eavesdropping devices. This was in total violation of the neutrality of the United Nations[1] but may explain UNSCOM's reluctance towards having their ambulances used by others.

When UNSCOM left they decided to lock their ambulances, thus leaving UN colleagues who were about to face four days of air-strikes with no immediate access to these important UN vehicles.[2]

The world of UNSCOM was indeed a world apart from the rest of the United Nations in Iraq. Much has been written elsewhere about the misuse of UNSCOM by bilateral intelligence agencies working under cover or quite openly for national, rather than international, interests. Few UN officials, however, other than UNSCOM staff, knew of rooms 251, 253 and 254 in the UN building. These rooms contained highly specialised communication equipment. Even within UNSCOM they were accessible

1. Dr Hans Blix, Richard's successor as Executive Chairman of UNSCOM, refers to this as 'intelligence piggybacking' in his book *Disarming Iraq* (Blix 2004), p. 37.
2. See confidential facsimile dated 30 January 1999 from UNOHCI/Baghdad to the UN Secretary-General's Office in New York.

only to 'privileged' personnel. After UNSCOM had evacuated its staff on 16 December 1998, just prior to 'Operation Desert Fox', and the issue of UNSCOM's premises became a safety concern, I was told that these three rooms should be excluded from any inspection since 'a government remains the owner of equipment positioned there'.[3]

The December 1998 closure of UNSCOM offices in Baghdad was not, as we had hoped, the end of a complicated relationship between two UN entities.

One morning in early January 1999, driving into the compound of the Canal Hotel, I saw what looked like a small water tanker adjacent to the north wing of the building. It apparently had been there ever since the December air-strikes; I simply had not noticed it. 'This carriage belongs to UNSCOM. We do not know what it was used for', I was told. A little later, to our horror, we discovered that this was a mobile petrol storage container filled to the brim with gasoline: UNSCOM had left it behind without informing us. In a small shed ten yards away, into which we had to force our entry, we found an additional 250 jerrycans filled with petrol belonging to UNSCOM. I reported this to New York, pointing out that 'the shrapnel which landed in our courtyard during the air-strikes could have had serious implications for UN staff if it had hit the petrol container or the petrol shed.'[4] At that time none of us was remotely aware of how serious this negligence on the part of UNSCOM had really been. The following months would make this clear. While we understood the dangerous link between the stored petrol and the shrapnel pieces that had fallen on our compound, we did not make a connection at the time between the petrol, the shrapnel and UNSCOM's laboratory. The laboratory was situated on the second floor, facing the petrol container and the shed. The locked UNSCOM offices, nevertheless, prompted my request to the Secretary-General's Office in January 1999 to allow us entry into these offices for reasons of safety. In the absence of a response, I took the opportunity to visit New York to meet Ambassador Butler and to make arrangements with him for entering the premises of the Special Commission in Baghdad. Butler agreed to a single entry and confirmed four weeks later that Jaako Ylitalo, the Colonel from Finland, would contact me 'for the provision of [the] necessary keys and the access code' to the UNSCOM premises.[5] In his memo to me, Butler did not refer to what UNSCOM was keeping in storage in his offices.

During the second week of April I travelled to Amman to give a briefing to EU ambassadors on the humanitarian situation in Iraq.

---

3. Cryptogram from UNOHCI/Baghdad to the Office of the UN Secretary-General, 19 April 1999, p. 2.
4. Ibid.
5. Facsimile from Richard Butler to author dated 24 March 1999.

UNSCOM used my presence there to arrange for Colonel Ylitalo to travel from their Gulf headquarters in Bahrain to Amman and hand me the keys and code for access to their premises. This was something which, of course, should have been done at the time UNSCOM left Baghdad. Ylitalo and I met on 11 April in a downtown Amman hotel. He 'trained me' for the entry into the world of UNSCOM in Baghdad. We spoke in low voices that at times were drowned by an ambitious Russian quartet attempting to prove that they had received their Jordanian visas for the right reasons; it was a genuine John Le Carré atmosphere. In the end, I found myself with a pouch full of keys, an UNSCOM floor plan, the entry code and a reconfirmation that rooms 251, 253 and 254 should be excluded from any inspection. I got the message. It later occurred to me that again there had been no mention of the contents in the UNSCOM laboratories.

Soon after my return to Baghdad I wrote to Iqbal Riza asking to have permission to finally enter the UNSCOM premises.[6] In the meantime, I received the first expressions of concern about our safety from colleagues, particularly my UN Iraqi colleagues. Some seemed to know more about the laboratory than I did. Military colleagues from UNIKOM's liaison office in our building added to my determination to expedite this matter. They spoke of 'avoidable fire hazards' and the 'carelessness' with which UNSCOM personnel had left our joint premises. In my communication with New York I also indicated that I had informed the Iraqi Ministry of Foreign Affairs of our intention to enter UNSCOM premises. We had enough informants in our building making this an open secret. We did not want to subsequently be accused by the Iraqi side of collusion with a UN body which they saw as a symbol of partiality and international suppression.[7]

Rumours about the UNSCOM laboratory intensified in parallel with the rising summer temperatures of early 1999. The local staff association called on me to discuss their misgivings. They were right in doing so; I shared their apprehension. I convened a general staff meeting to reassure colleagues that I had obtained agreement from New York to enter the special commission offices and would do so soon.

'Soon' turned out to be two months later, much to my annoyance. The local staff association became more and more agitated, threatening staff refusal to come to their Canal Hotel offices. I decided to pass on their frustration and my irritation by calling and writing again to New York, reminding the Secretary-General's Office, UNSCOM and the Office of the Iraq Programme that the keys I had been given in Amman were ready to be used.

---

6. Cryptogram from UNOHCI/Baghdad to the UN Secretary-General's Office dated 19 April 1999.
7. Ibid.

The Ambassadors of France, Russia and China in Baghdad repeatedly called to be informed of developments. The Iraqi Foreign Ministry likewise was anxious to understand the UN's intentions. As so often in the Iraq debate, there was no common UN approach. Richard Butler had written in late April to the Secretary-General to take exception to my having informed the Iraqi Foreign Ministry of our intentions, stating that 'this matter [had] been blown out of proportion'.[8] He went on to say that, under the circumstances, he would ask me not to enter the Special Commission's offices for the time being, 'except in case of an emergency'. Had he told the Secretary-General in New York and me in Baghdad what he conveyed involuntarily to the Security Council on 1 June, I certainly would not have used the keys 'in case of an emergency'.[9] Butler informed the Security Council of 'the status of the chemical laboratory and the biological room'. It contained twelve samples of the chemical warfare agent mustard, 'with a total quantity of less than one kilo stored in the laboratory refrigerator'. In the biological room, Butler continued, one biological sample was stored which had been handed over to the coalition by the Iraqi authorities. The sample was labelled 'smallpox vaccine'. 'At the time of the departure', Butler pointed out, 'the commission had not been able to determine the content of this vial'.[10]

According to Butler, 'the issue of safety at the UN premises in Baghdad has always been of priority importance to the commission'. Such an assertion was simply untrue: UNSCOM left in December 1998. The very fact that UNSCOM had left its premises without determining the content of the vial in the biological room alone should have been ample justification for Butler and UNSCOM to be concerned and anxious to act quickly. It took Ambassador Butler six months to divulge what he had a responsibility to convey to his superiors, including UN Secretary-General Kofi Annan, as soon as UNSCOM had left Baghdad; it was three months before Butler confirmed his agreement that we could enter UNSCOM premises; a further two weeks passed before keys and code were given. The agreement to enter was withdrawn by Butler later in April[11] on spurious grounds. Ultimately, it was another ten weeks before the UNSCOM offices were finally opened. A truly concerned UN official should have acted within weeks, if not days, with a full disclosure of the contents of the Special Commission's laboratories and a plan for de-activation. Butler, if he did not have a technical knowledge of the dangers posed by what was left behind in the chemical laboratory and the biological room, should have sought counsel from expert members of his team.

8. Inter-office memorandum from UNSCOM to the Secretary-General's Office dated 21 April 1999.
9. Ibid.
10. Ibid.
11. See Butler facsimile to the author dated 24 March 1999.

Butler's assertion to the UN Security Council in his June memo that 'there were no immediate safety concerns' but 'that it was now appropriate to seek access to those areas in order to shut them down', *inter alia* because 'summer was approaching', is in sharp contrast to the view of a French chemical expert. This former UNSCOM employee went to see officials at the Quai d'Orsay in Paris to convey to the French Foreign Ministry that his conscience forced him to remain silent no longer out of fear for the safety conditions in the UNSCOM laboratory in Baghdad.[12] French Ambassador Alain Déjammet in New York was absolutely right in pointing out that 'the most troubling aspect was the fact that UN Special Commission Chairman Richard Butler had failed to alert the [Security] Council to the fact that toxic substances were left in Baghdad when his inspectors pulled out ahead of air-strikes in December'.[13]

I was greatly relieved when the Security Council insisted on receiving a report on UNSCOM's offices from the Executive Chairman. This brought the serious neglect of duty into the open, even if Butler's report to the Council on the laboratory was a masterpiece of understatement. That the media would get involved was clear to me. I had not expected, however, that this would happen as soon as Monday 1 June, the day on which Butler submitted his requested report to the Security Council. CNN reported at the time that 'Russia had called an emergency meeting of the UN Security Council ... to demand information about chemical materials left behind by UN weapons inspectors ...'.[14] AFP quoted Russian Ambassador Serge Lavrov as expressing shock that UNSCOM would keep 'dangerous poisonous substances in the very centre of Baghdad', charging that a crisis could have occurred if the office had been struck when Baghdad was bombed by US and British forces ...'.[15] British Ambassador Jeremy Greenstock told the Press, 'There is a smell of exaggeration in all of this.'[16] Politicisation of this issue and sensational reporting certainly could have been avoided through more responsible handling by Ambassador Butler.

In Baghdad UN staff welcomed the belated Security Council involvement. For the first time we could see light at the end of a long tunnel. During a meeting with the Press in Baghdad, intended to brief them on the serious drought conditions in the country that had prevailed for the second consecutive year, I had a difficult time keeping journalists 'on track'. The drought calamity had suddenly become an issue of

12. Conveyed by the French Ambassador in Baghdad to the author in the early summer of 1999.
13. AFP, United Nations, New York, 16 July 1999.
14. CNN, United Nations, New York, 1 June 1999.
15. Iraq News, UN Press Release, New York, 2 June 1999.
16. Reuters, United Nations, New York, 2 June 1999.

secondary importance. Everyone, Iraqi and foreign journalists, wanted details of the UNSCOM laboratory story.

This was indeed a very sensitive issue and at the time we had scanty information. I decided it was not timely to make a detailed statement for which, in any case, I had not yet been given authority. The Associated Press quoted me as saying, 'the safety of UN staff was a matter of concern but it would be left to experts to decide whether the chemicals found in UNSCOM's laboratory are hazardous'.[17]

During the month of June the UN Secretary-General, in consultation with the Security Council, requested the Director-General of the Organisation for Chemical Weapons Prohibition (OCWP), a non-UN agency based in the Hague, to despatch a team of experts to Baghdad. Their mission was 'to destroy the conventional laboratory chemicals, the chemicals standards and the biological samples, including the chemical warfare agent mustard, identified by Richard Butler, in addition to all other hazardous material that might be found. OCWP Director-General José Bustani responded quickly. On Sunday 14 July a high-powered team of scientists, experienced with chemical and biological warfare substances, arrived in Baghdad to perform what Richard Butler and UNSCOM should have done half a year earlier. Their team leader, Dirk van Niekerk, a chemist from South Africa, insisted that there could be no entry into the laboratories without full protective clothing. This posed a problem for those who had been identified to join the team from the Hague[18] when the UNSCOM offices were to be opened. The UN Secretary-General agreed that the team could be accompanied by representatives from the French, Chinese and Russian Embassies in Baghdad, the three permanent members in the Security Council with diplomatic representations in Iraq. Ambassador Prakash Shah, the special envoy of the UN Secretary-General, and I would complete the group. Where would we find enough protective clothing for ten people? Finally we succeeded, except for the slightly overweight number two in the Russian Embassy, who had to sign a statement that he entirely accepted liability for entering UNSCOM's premises without full protection. As all this unfolded I suddenly remembered that at one point earlier in the year Richard Butler's intention had been for me to enter Special Commission premises on my own, without protective clothing. I caught myself smiling.

In preparation for the 'momentous' occasion of entry it was agreed that van Niekerk and his team, Prakash Shah and I would meet with

17. AP, Baghdad, 2 June 1999.
18. The OCWP team consisted of Dirk van Niekerk (South Africa), chemist, Li Hua (China), analytical chemist, Sergei Orlov (Russia), analytical chemist, and Miroslaw Miklasz (Poland), medical doctor. Wolfgang Beyer (Germany), microbiologist, had joined the group since OCWP had no mandate for biological weapons issues so the UN had directly appointed Dr Beyer for this assignment.

representatives of the Government of Iraq. The Government of Iraq had as much right to know the full UNSCOM laboratory story as did the UN Security Council, UN staff and the public.

It eventually became clear that the laboratory not only contained UNSCOM equipment and calibration substances. Biological and chemical agents such as agent mustard were found. Agent mustard had been recovered not far from Baghdad at Al Muthanna, Iraq's principal chemical weapons research and production site, and from Al Fallujah III, a facility that at one time had produced chemical weapons precursors for Al Muthanna but had been disabled by UNSCOM in the mid-1990s.[19]

We were ever more aware of the importance of handling this unfortunate affair in as transparent a manner as possible. We had no intention of adding to the political dynamite that already existed.

The conference room adjacent to my office was normally used for reviewing the Oil-for-Food Programme, for receiving visiting delegations, and for our weekly senior staff meetings. On Monday 26 July 1999 it became the venue for a most unusual meeting involving the team from the Organisation of Chemical Weapons Prohibition; French, Russian and Chinese diplomats; UN officials and senior Iraqi military personnel as General Dr Amer al-Sa'adi,[20] President Saddam Hussein's scientific adviser, and General Hossam Mohammed Amin, the Director of the Iraq National Monitoring Directorate.

It was a sombre meeting. Ambassador Shah opened it by explaining the purpose of the OCWP mission. Then the South African team leader went into some detail concerning the planned inspection of the UNSCOM offices. He conveyed to us that the mission's brief confined the team to the destruction of all biological and chemical substances found in the chemical laboratory and the biological room. 'What about prior identification of the origin of the agents?' General Dr Amer al-Sa'adi asked. 'The United Nations did not include this in our terms of reference', Mr van Niekerk responded. The faces of the two generals expressed disbelief and amazement. General al-Sa'adi, in a composed manner, looking at all of us around the table and speaking in a low voice with an impressive mixture of firmness and humility, said: 'in this case the United Nations will deprive Iraq of the last pieces of evidence that the VX stored

---

19. The author visited Al Fallujah III in June 2002 accompanied by ARD, German State TV and, contrary to UK Intelligence, the castor oil plant once capable of producing the biological agent Ricin was found and filmed in a totally dismantled state. Compare with: 'Iraq's WMD', UK Government, 24 September 2002, p. 22, where Al Fallujah is identified as a 'facility of concern'.
20. Dr Amer al-Sa'adi would in 2002 become the main Iraqi counterpart to Dr Hans Blix, Executive Chairman of UNMOVIC. He remained in this position until March 2003 when the US/UK attacked Iraq. In April 2003 he voluntarily surrendered to the coalition forces.

in the UNSCOM laboratories is not of Iraqi origin but was brought into the country'. At this moment there was total silence in the room. Helpless looks were exchanged between van Niekerk and his deputy, Li Hua, a chemist on loan from the Chinese Academy of Sciences. The rest of us hoped that someone would respond. No one did, at least not immediately. Van Niekerk then apologetically repeated that he had to follow his brief and added that the destruction of the VX samples would, in fact, only mean a substance degradation. Even though this would make tracing of the origin technically more complicated it would still be possible. Neither Dr al-Sa'adi nor General Amin looked convinced. The meeting did not last much longer.

Today one has to question why the UN brief for the OCPW team had been so narrow. Why did the Secretary-General not anticipate the importance of the origin of the stored substances? Why did individual members of the Security Council such as Russia, China, Malaysia and others not demand information on the origin of the biological and chemical substances that were stored in the UNSCOM offices? In July 1999 no one did. Those of us 'at the scene' should have insisted that the UN expand the OCPW team's mandate and that the UN Security Council function as an arbiter interested in discovering the entire story. The onus of default should have rested with the Council and not been shared between the UN Secretariat and the Council. Again the UN Secretariat's neutrality was compromised. On Tuesday 18 July 1999, Ambassador Shah and I accompanied the OCPW team as they entered the UNSCOM offices. In protective clothing, everyone resembled astronauts going to a masquerade.

The first thing I noticed was the fine dust that had settled on the floors, furniture, wall decorations, filing cabinets and equipment during the previous six months. As the group made a first round of inspection, I detached myself from them for a moment to stay longer in one room. I saw a plate with what looked like petrified fruit lying on a table, obviously left behind when UNSCOM personnel had left in a hurry in December 1998. But what attracted my attention was a document lying on the same table as the shrivelled fruit – it was the evacuation plan which UNSCOM had implemented on 16 December 1998, the day 'Operation Desert Fox' began. The document, carrying the date of 16 December, was a meticulously prepared plan showing, name by name, who would be assigned to which vehicle, how these vehicles were going to proceed to the Habbaniyah military airport, what should be done in case there was a vehicle breakdown, etc. This was anything but a departure schedule prepared in a hurry in the early morning of an evacuation. This plan, carelessly left behind, was undoubtedly carefully worked out in good time and synchronised with the arrival and the departure of the C-130 aircraft that would fly UNSCOM personnel out of Iraq on 16 December 1999. It was not difficult to be convinced that Chairman Butler and his

UNSCOM colleagues in New York and Bahrain knew well in advance that 'Operation Desert Fox' would begin on the night of 16 December. The telephone conversations I had had on that day with the UN Secretary-General's Office made it clear that they did not have the knowledge Butler had at the time.

Once the OCWP team had finished their assignment and were ready to return to the Netherlands, I met Dirk van Niekerk on his own. I was eager to know the answer to one question: what would have happened if our building had indeed been hit during the four days of air-strikes? He looked at me and said: 'nothing!' but then he continued: 'except if there had been a fire'. The VX, tabun and sarin, in small and diluted quantities used for calibration, would not have been very hazardous for the surroundings. A more problematic situation could have arisen if agent mustard had been in contact with fire. UNSCOM, it must be remembered, had created the conditions for this by leaving significant amounts of petrol adjacent to their laboratory. While the quantity of 2.2 lb (1 kg) of agent mustard in its laboratory was relatively small, it could nevertheless have been a danger for those subjected to mustard gas fumes because of their carcinogenic properties. The vial labelled 'smallpox vaccine' for which, according to Ambassador Butler, 'the Commission had not been able to determine the content at the time of UNSCOM's departure', constitutes perhaps the most serious act of negligence. If indeed it had been smallpox vaccine, contagious virus material could have been freed, representing a real danger.[21]

The petrol dump and the mobile petrol container abandoned by UNSCOM directly under our office building and the shrapnel pieces that had landed in our compound came to my mind. Were Ambassador Butler and his team really unaware of what a precarious situation they had created for their UN colleagues and the Iraqis living in the area?

A day after the OCPW team had destroyed the VX, tabun and sarin samples, the kilogram of agent mustard and the vial labelled 'smallpox', Tariq Aziz, Iraq's Deputy Prime Minister dispatched a letter to Secretary-General Kofi Annan in which the Government of Iraq protested over the destruction of 'the seven specimens of VX nerve gas'. I was not surprised that the Iraqi Government had taken this step. Meetings in the Foreign Ministry, some late at night, involving Under-Secretary Dr Riyadh al Qaysi and, at times, Tariq Aziz revealed how concerned the Government had been at the UN's handling of the UNSCOM laboratory affair.

21. The author discussed in general terms the danger posed by a kilogram of mustard gas and various other biological and chemical substances in case of fire with specialists at OCWP in the Hague and Labor Spiez near Berne, and received helpful replies. He takes, however, sole responsibility for the description of the problem.

This sad episode, of course, is another insight into the disjointed and fragmented approach the United Nations pursued in the handling of the Iraq crisis. It is, however, much more: the UNSCOM evacuation, the lack of administrative handover by a UN unit leaving the country to a UN unit staying behind, the carelessness of leaving a petrol dump unattended, the lack of urgency in the removal of toxic biological and chemical agents in UNSCOM offices, in particular a vial containing a substance that had not been tested at the time of UNSCOM's departure – all of these are undeniable signs of considerable irresponsibility. This certainly added to the 'shameful chapter' of UNSCOM's behaviour to which I referred in the note to Kofi Annan's Chef de Cabinet, Iqbal Riza, on 16 December 1998.

The UN Security Council failed again to exercise timely oversight and to hold accountable those who had betrayed the neutrality of the institution which had appointed them to resolve a conflict.

Mesopotamia 2000.
Courtesy of Matthias Schwoerer.

Chapter 5

The Government of Iraq, Its People and Their Rights

Human Rights in Iraq

It was March 2000. I asked for an appointment with Iraq's Foreign Minister, Mohammed Al Sahaf. There was a long list of issues I needed to discuss. The Oil-for-Food Programme, inadequate as it was, had more resources at that time because of higher oil prices. As a result, implementation of the humanitarian programme needed to be accelerated to make better and more timely use of these additional funds. At the same time, sanctions fatigue had set in internationally, giving the Government of Iraq the false hope that an end to sanctions was in sight.

I wanted to discuss this and encourage the Government to cooperate more fully with the United Nations. This was not the time for the Iraqi authorities to be recalcitrant. Yet we did have difficulties in obtaining the required entry permissions for new UN staff, particularly those assigned to Iraqi Kurdistan. We also had problems receiving permission for the release of imported vehicles, equipment and supplies which the United Nations needed for its operations in Iraq. The UN was caught in the maelstrom of polarised Iraqi policies which were hardening on all sides. The protagonists believed vehemently in the correctness of their positions and defended these at all costs. The price of deadlock, of course, was paid by the Iraqi people. It was not an easy time to discuss changes in a humanitarian programme under a weakening international sanctions resolve with an Iraqi minister.

On the evening of 25 March, a Saturday but a work-day in Iraq, I received a call from Ambassador Kadhun al-Rawi, the Chief of Protocol of the Foreign Ministry, to confirm that I had an appointment with Minister Al Sahaf the following morning at 8.15. 'Do you really mean 8.15?' I asked. 'Yes' was the answer. This struck me as most peculiar since meetings with government officials would rarely start before 10 o'clock at the earliest. I contacted my driver, Abu Laith, at home to alert him to this early morning appointment. He was certain that I had misunderstood. The next morning we arrived punctually in Karadet Miriam where the Foreign Ministry is located. We were indeed expected. A special elevator normally reserved for the Minister took me to his reception room on the fourth floor of the Ministry. For a brief moment I waited in a room carpeted wall-to-wall and adorned, of course, with a large picture of President Saddam Hussein, flowers, and ceramics depicting Mesopotamian culture. It was not long before Al Sahaf emerged, in his green uniform,[1] from a door that connected the reception room to his personal office. This was a routine I had witnessed a good number of times, but on this occasion there was a different atmosphere. Al Sahaf looked somewhat tense and certainly did not seem prepared for the kind of conversation that I anticipated. We drank the obligatory cup of tea, exchanged some pleasantries, and then, with his eyes squarely fixed on me, Minister Al Sahaf informed me that 'Al Rais', the 'leader', President Saddam Hussein wanted to see me.

Now I understood why I was asked to come to the Ministry at such a special hour. Would I really be received by the man whose picture accompanied me each day in Baghdad, wherever I was, but who was never seen in person? This man dominated the conversation among diplomats in Baghdad; we could read his advice to the nation in every issue of the local Press. He had been at the helm of Iraq since 16 July 1979, the date President Ahmad al-Bakr had stepped aside as Chairman of Iraq's revolution command council. He never met with foreign ambassadors and had not received a UN official for a decade, with the exception of Secretary-General Kofi Annan in February 1998. This man was probably the most feared dictator the world had experienced in a long time.

There was not much time to think. It seemed that everything had been arranged for this visit. Before I could fully comprehend what was happening, I found myself following Minister Al Sahaf to a side-exit of the Foreign Ministry. There a heavy black limousine was awaiting us. We drove off with destination unknown, at least for me. I did not even have a moment to alert Abu Laith, who was waiting for me at the Foreign Ministry's main entrance, that he could enjoy a few more cups of tea with his ministry friends.

Ignoring traffic signals and saluted as we drove by submissive looking police who apparently recognised the licence plates, the car took us to the Al Zaqurah building, named after the tower-like structures or 'Zikkurats' which had been important temple buildings some four thousand years

---

1. After the 1991 Gulf War, all ministers had to wear military-like uniforms to signify that Iraq was in a state of war.

ago, for example, in Ur, the birthplace of Abraham. Foreign Minister or not, at the gate the car was inspected by armed guards and intelligence personnel in civilian clothes. Al Sahaf left our car and walked to another vehicle that apparently had been assigned to him. I was joined by two Iraqi officials, one of whom was a presidential protocol officer, the other a security guard. We obviously had not yet reached our destination. In convoy, we began to drive at a frightening speed, at least for me, through Baghdad and to the outskirts of the city. I had no idea where we were heading, nor did I feel like asking. I had only a few moments to prepare for the most unusual meeting I was to have during my stay in Iraq. After about twenty minutes, at times agonising minutes, particularly when crossing intersections, the two cars suddenly slowed down at a large, yet unpretentious, gate. It was opened from the inside by two military guards who obviously had been notified of our arrival: they did not even glance inside the two vehicles. We then drove slowly along an alley lined with massive four- to five-metre-high cement slabs and acacia trees. It was a long driveway, similar to a tunnel without roof. After a kilometre or so it suddenly ended in a wide courtyard. From there I was ushered into a small room where a rather stern-looking officer received me and asked me to be seated. He turned out to be General Abid Hamid Hamoud, the Tikriti personal secretary to President Saddam Hussein.[2] Minister Al Sahaf had been assigned to another room.

I cannot remember how much time passed before General Hamoud suddenly arose, saying 'The President of Iraq is ready to receive you'. Until this moment the General and I had been discussing the fierce battle of Al Fao which Iraqi and Iranian forces had fought at the southern end of the Shatt al Arab in 1988. Many lives on both sides were lost on this occasion, but Iraq managed to repossess the area.

As I stepped out of the office and into the hallway, I found myself opposite a tall individual dressed in elegant Western clothes. This was the man whose effigy I had seen a thousand times. It was Saddam Hussein. He extended his hand, looking with intensely piercing eyes at me and said in English: 'welcome'. This was exactly how an Iraqi friend of mine who had met Saddam Hussein had described meetings with him.

We entered a large reception hall furnished with the heavy gold sofas, chairs and tables so popular in affluent residences in the Middle East. Minister Al Sahaf was awaiting us at the far end of the hall. There were two other persons present: the President's interpreters. As President Saddam Hussein entered the room, everyone seemed to freeze. There was

---

2. A report published by the British Foreign and Commonwealth Office in London, in November 2002, entitled 'Saddam Hussein: Crimes and Human Rights Abuses' alleges that both 'General Hamoud and Saddam have signed death warrants for prisoners', p. 11.

total silence until the President motioned for us to sit. I was on his immediate right, the others a little further away. Scrutinising his visitor, he repeated his welcome, this time in Arabic. These were friendly words but his voice appeared cold and his face expressionless. I thanked him and then continued to see whether in turn I could pierce through this mask which my host seemed to wear. I said: 'I am aware, Mr President, that I have been a troublemaker in carrying out my responsibilities as UN Coordinator for Iraq!' I achieved my objective. He looked at me, surprised. Whose troublemaker had I been? A reference to this obviously had not been part of the brief the Foreign Ministry had given him. For a fleeting moment there was a faint smile on his face, followed by an invitation to explain to him how I saw the circumstances of the population in Iraq. This was a tall order. There was a lot to say to this Head of State about a population living under such inhuman conditions. Did I talk about the brutality of his regime? Human rights violations? Weapons of mass destruction? Extra-judicial killings? Halabja and the Anfal campaign[3] of 1988 in Northern Iraq or the plight of the marsh Arabs in Southern Iraq? The treatment of the Shi'ite clerics? No, I did not. Neither did I use the opportunity to criticise US/UK policies or the work of the UN Security Council. Perhaps such criticism would have released my frustrations, but I knew that it would have made no difference. Instead, I decided to address issues more immediately related to the survival of a people and the inadequacy of the Oil-for-Food Programme. This included the need to increase funding for education, the situation of the Iraqi youth who were the most severely damaged by this conflict, and the urgent need for the Iraqi Government and the UN to de-bureaucratise the programme.

I had heard that Saddam Hussein could be a good listener. Now I had the opportunity to confirm this. I noticed the intensity with which he followed what I had to say. The interpreters translated from English into Arabic and vice versa, taking turns after five minutes. Saddam Hussein frequently interrupted them to correct their translations. I was amused and wondered whether their presence was not superfluous. Hussein seemed to understand every word I spoke in English, or at least wanted no one to forget, even in this situation, who was the leader. The advantage for me was that I gained time to reflect on what to say next. When I had finished my review of the human condition and the humanitarian programme and its shortcomings, I was eager to make a point of much importance to me. Out of my suit pocket I took something that I always carry with me – the UN Charter and the Universal Declaration of Human Rights – and showed them to President Saddam Hussein: 'This, Mr

---

3. 'Anfal' is the name of the Sura of the Holy Koran, with the title 'The Spoils' or 'The Plunder of the Infidels'.

President, is the basis on which I have been carrying out my work'. I am not sure that he understood what I wanted to convey, namely that these were universal instruments to which all parties, including he himself, should abide.

Saddam Hussein responded by saying: 'What you have told me is not a small message, particularly since it comes from an individual rather than an institution.' This was followed by a long and detailed exposé by Saddam Hussein on the situation in the Middle East, and that he regretted that 'the governments of the Arab nation have been split by outside forces'. 'The people of the Arab nation, however, are squarely supporting the Iraqi struggle', he said. I was surprised when he then looked at me and said: 'I want to thank you twice, once for your conscience and the concern you have for the Iraqi people and secondly, for the hope you are giving to Iraqis that they are not alone in their struggle.' The President also referred to what he called the 'inner strength' of the Iraqi people and his conviction that they would overcome all obstacles facing them. In my communication to Secretary-General Kofi Annan on this meeting, which turned out to be a 90-minute conversation, I made the point that Saddam Hussein appeared increasingly relaxed, reflective and philosophical, often using soft and even humorous language.[4] At one point Saddam Hussein informed me that he had decided that 'you and your family will no longer require visas to visit Iraq', and, he continued, 'your luggage will not be inspected'. Duly expressing my thanks for this 'presidential magnanimity', I could not help but ask him how my 'intellectual luggage' would be handled. Foreign Minister Al Sahaf had not said anything up to this point. His face did not disclose whether or not he thought that with my somewhat sarcastic intervention I had gone too far. In any case, Saddam Hussein assured me, with a grin, that my intellectual luggage would also be left alone.

I cannot remember how the subject of obesity entered out conversation. President Saddam Hussein thought it important that I should know that he had given an order that no one among his Cabinet ministers – they were all men – could have a waistline beyond a certain size, 'and Tariq Aziz is barely making it!' he explained with a smile. I could think of others in his Cabinet who should be disqualified, for example, Taha Yassin Ramadan, one of the two Vice-Presidents whose distinctive features were his protruding stomach and a black pistol that menacingly adorned his military outfit.

There was no meeting in Iraq without coffee or tea. A side-door to the reception hall was opened at some point and two members of the presidential household tiptoed towards us, one in uniform, the other in civilian clothes, each holding a *dallah*, the beak-shaped Arab coffeepot, in

---

4. Cryptogram to the UN Secretary-General dated 28 March 2000.

their hands. Coffee was poured into delicate porcelain vessels. Before handing a cup to President Saddam Hussein, the man in uniform became a taster. Only after he had performed this duty did he pass the cup to the President. The civilian employee charged with handing the second cup to me seemed not to have reached the honourable position of Presidential Taster. I received my coffee straight with a gesture that conveyed 'taste it yourself'. I wondered what would happen if the two coffee cans had been mixed up. Weeks later I laughed at this episode; at the time I was intent upon observing this man next to me whom the world feared. He had become a mystical recluse about whom many speculated but few had actually met. It was a momentous occasion, at the end of which Saddam Hussein accompanied me to the palace's front door and then suddenly held my arm and said: 'We have to take pictures'. We returned to the hall we had just left and there was indeed a photographer who captured this incredible encounter. It was not the actual meeting that can be described as such, but rather the fact that I had met a man whom I would ultimately remember as gregarious and even congenial had I not been told of the horrendous and heinous crimes against humanity for which his own people and the world were holding him accountable.

This man did have the aura of a leader who spoke confidently about the ultimate victorious battle his people would fight. His analytical and incisive mind was evident when he conveyed to the visitor 'his' sense of history. This is the same man who stands accused of unimaginable atrocities and personal brutality. He did not look like a murderer who had caused the deaths of thousands, nor one said to have gassed his own Kurdish countrymen including women and children. We are told that he personally shot senior members of the Ba'ath Party whom he considered no longer loyal to him, ordered the torture of anyone who seemed to have violated 'his' laws, punished entire families of military deserters and committed untold other violations of human rights in Iraq, ably assisted by his sons Uday and Qusay. It did not occur to me at the time that the modern Western clothes Saddam Hussein was wearing covered up a man who had his origins in a small village, al-Awja, not far from the infamous Tikrit, and who had never abandoned his feudal connections. Even though he came from a humble background and a poor family, his drive and deep commitment to Iraqi nationalism and pan-Arab socialism saw him become, at the age of forty-two, Iraq's President in 1979. He was a leader who, for the following twenty-four years, would reign more like a feudal sheikh than a modern statesman.

A story is recounted which illustrates that the Saddam Hussein in Baghdad had always remained the man from the rural areas with a tribal mentality. In early 2003 he called his ambassadors to Baghdad from the fifty countries around the world which had diplomatic ties with Iraq. Two of them, Dr Mohammed al Dori, Iraq's Ambassador to the UN in New

York, and Dr Samir al Nima, who represented Iraq as Ambassador to the UN in Geneva, met with President Saddam Hussein in the presence of Iraq's then Foreign Minister, Dr Naji Sabri al Hadithi, and Ambassador Dr Mudafhar Amin, head of Iraq's interests section in the Jordanian Embassy in London. The two ambassadors to the UN told Saddam Hussein that Iraq's dues to the United Nations had remained unpaid for many years and that Iraq had, as a result, lost its voting rights. 'How much do we owe?' asked Saddam Hussein. 'Seventeen million dollars' was the answer. Saddam Hussein turned to his Foreign Minister and said 'Naji, pay it!'[5] For Saddam Hussein the issue was closed. The fact that Iraq had these resources and wanted to pay its dues to the UN and was blocked year after year by the United States Government in doing so was another matter.[6] Finally in December 2000, the Security Council with US and UK consent agreed that $15 million could be used from Iraq's oil resources for payment of its arrears. Ultimately, these two Governments nevertheless blocked the implementation of their resolution.

After the photographs had been taken Saddam Hussein took me to the waiting car, we shook hands; the piercing eyes freed me and the car sped away. The statues of Saddam Hussein which were strategically placed throughout Baghdad, were many times larger in size than normal human beings. This was meant to remind everyone, Iraqi and non-Iraqi, that he could not be compared to normal-sized human beings. His photographs were in every office, posters in all nooks and corners of the city, stone monuments, mosaics and paintings in front of every single government building from the entrance to the Baghdad trade-fair grounds to the Al Shaheed war memorial. His likeness watched us at the Al Rashid Hotel, the Al Yarmuk General Hospital, Al Mustansariyah University, Sharea Al Nahr Zuq – he was everywhere. Since our meeting these manifestations of a man who was no longer in touch with his people, a recluse who needed isolation for survival, suddenly had a face I had seen. The face haunted me, as did the question of whether this man, even after years of dictatorship, could not be swayed to change direction and follow all the international conventions, covenants and declarations which his Government had signed and ratified in order to lift the yoke of

5. This conversation, recounted to the author by a participant, took place at the Conference of Iraqi Ambassadors in Baghdad on 4 January 2003.
6. In 1995, the Iraqi Government had started to make requests to the UN Committee on Contributions to exempt Iraq from the provisions of article 19 of the UN Charter since its arrears were due to sanctions, a condition beyond the immediate control of Iraq. The US and UK blocked these requests in the UN General Assembly's Fifth Committee. When the Oil-for-Food Programme started in 1996, Iraq requested the UN Secretary-General and the UN Sanctions Committee to use oil revenue resources to pay its dues. This was also refused. See also UN S/RES/1330 (2000), 5 December 2000, para. 8.

suppression from his people. Had the international community tried hard enough? Should they continue to endeavour, despite the evidence of so much wrongdoing and the allegations of the worst crimes against Iraqi and other humanity?

In June 1991 the United Nations appointed Max van der Stoel, a former Dutch foreign minister, to be the first Special Rapporteur on Iraq for the UN Commission on Human Rights. Until he was replaced in 2000 by Andreas Mavromatis, a Foreign Secretary of Cyprus, van der Stoel unswervingly tried to bring about changes in the human rights situation in Iraq through his reporting and the resulting pressure for change. Unfortunately his approach failed, mainly due to his decision to strictly adhere to the limitations put on this difficult assignment by the UN[7] and the intransigence of the Iraqi authorities. Andreas Mavromatis viewed human rights in a context other than just government violations. He thereby avoided a confrontational relationship with Baghdad which van der Stoel had fostered and found Saddam Hussein's Government more receptive to cooperation. Mavromatis decided to go beyond the limited mandate which he had been given. He continually reminded the international community that economic sanctions also perpetuated the lack of human rights in Iraq. This reassured the Iraqis that he sought not to have a preconceived agenda.

It is, nevertheless, difficult to imagine that Saddam Hussein and his authorities could have been swayed by any Human Rights Rapporteur to fundamentally change the harsh and uncompromising control of Iraqi life. Serious human rights violations in Iraq were legalised by the promulgation of formidable decrees signed into Iraqi law by President Saddam Hussein. This was planned and transparent brutality ready to be applied to anyone who was considered an inconvenience or threat to those in power or who had, in their opinion, strayed from the correct path. Together with the punitive approach of economic sanctions, a terrible package of misery for the Iraqi people was perpetuated. Decree no. 96 of 28 July 1994,[8] signed by Saddam Hussein as Chairman of the Revolution Command Council, makes the gruesome point that 'the penalty of amputation (of hand or foot) shall be carried out at a public hospital' and be witnessed by an enforcement board. The decree further

---

7. UN Commission on Human Rights Resolution 1991/74 mandated Rapporteur van der Stoel 'to make a thorough study of the violations of human rights by the Government of Iraq ...'; Resolution 2003/84 reconfirmed for Mavromatis the mandate his predecessor had. In addition his report should focus 'on newly available information about violations of human rights and international law by the Government of Iraq over many years ...'. See also United Nations, General Assembly A/46/647, 13 November 1991, p. 59, para. 58.
8. See Appendix C, page 295.

specifies that 'In the case of a pregnant woman, enforcement of the penalty of amputation shall be deferred until four months after her delivery.'[9] The loss of ears, hands and feet for offences like theft, currency trafficking, desertion from military service or ridiculing the President were punishments defined by a large number of government decrees. Repeat offences would invariably carry the death sentence. Decree 59 of 4 June 1994 prescribes that 'the penalty shall be death instead of amputation if the theft is committed by a person carrying a visible or concealed weapon'.[10] A person sheltering or protecting anyone who evaded or deserted from military service had the auricle of one ear cut off and 'the auricle of the other ear shall be cut off' and 'a horizontal line one millimetre thick and no less than three centimetres and no more than five centimetres long shall be tattooed on the forehead of every person whose ear has been cut off'.[11] Medical doctors who refused to carry out penalties of amputation would face similar punishment of amputation in accordance with a separate decree to this effect which was published in the official Iraqi Gazette.

The death penalty was passed out without hesitation, not just to those accused of criminal activity or military desertion, but also to persons who 'misbehaved' politically, including those who 'deliberately concealed ... previous party-political links and affiliations'.[12] It seems that every possible situation was covered by inhumane legal 'provisions of punishment'.

Following the 1990 Gulf War there was a tightening of the rules to which the Iraqi people had to adhere. Ba'athists will readily admit this. They point out that Iraq, during the years of economic sanctions, the military embargo and the no-fly zones, was forced to live in a state of war. They describe this to hostile and peace-destabilising actions by Iraq's neighbours, especially Iran and Kuwait, and the United States. They argue that the resulting insecurity within Iraq, including rising crime rates, left the Government with no choice but to introduce harsh measures such as those reflected in presidential decrees. These decrees were implemented to warn the population that the Government of Saddam Hussein, in the wider interests of the nation, had to be tough. They further argue that Iraq's Sharia-type laws which included limb amputation or Falaqa, the beating of the soles of feet, did not differ from those applied by other Arab governments in the region, e.g., Saudi Arabia.

---

9. See United Nations, Economic and Social Council, E/CN.4/1995/56, 15 February 1955, p. 27.
10. See United Nations, General Assembly, A/49/651, 8 November 1994, p. 29.
11. Ibid., p. 32.
12. United Nations, Economic and Social Council, E/CN.4/1993/45, 19 February 1993, p. 66.

Emergency conditions in Iraq and the fact that other countries in the Middle East practised similarly inhumane laws, of course, cannot excuse the Government of Iraq from serious wrongdoing against its people.

It is too early to come to a final and measured understanding of the extent of the offences committed by Government against the civilian population. It is also premature to identify the number of victims, dead or still alive. In the years ahead, no doubt, research into the number of Kurds 'eliminated' or 'displaced', the number of Shiahs victimised, the number of Madan (Marsh Arabs) relocated or killed, the number of Turkomen evicted from their lands or executed, will be carried out as a necessary component of a difficult national reconciliation process.

There are, nevertheless, a number of conclusions one can draw. The first is that not only the people of Iraq lived in a constant state of fear; the Government of Iraq did, too. This is one major reason why it developed these harsh and cruel rules. The impression that they were applied to everyone but those of Sunni faith is, of course, wrong. Anyone who fractionally showed opposition to the Government of Saddam Hussein, including Sunnis, would face severe punishment. The refined and multilayer intelligence network[13] covered everyone who lived in Iraq including foreigners. Another consequence of this all-embracing policy meant that it was next to impossible to obtain concrete evidence of human rights abuses in Iraq.

We in the United Nations in Baghdad picked up fragments of rumours, often contradictory. It was not possible for us to get a coherent understanding of how Saddam Hussein's henchmen pursued their victims. Rare exceptions were the cases involving Iraqi UN staff who had been picked up by police or secret service, usually for minor violations such as traffic offences. In one such case one of our UN drivers who had ignored a traffic light was imprisoned. In his prison cell, I was told, lights, bed sheets, blankets and walls were all bright red, causing extreme discomfort during the ten days he was kept there. Our demarche with the Foreign Ministry, reminding the Iraqi Government that UN staff, local and international, enjoyed immunity from arrest until waived by the UN Secretary-General, had no effect: the driver was released when the authorities were ready to release him. This relatively small incident gave us an inkling of the prevailing justice system but not more than that.

We could not judge the validity of the reports the UN Human Rights Rapporteur Max van der Stoel presented to the Human Rights Commission, the UN Economic and Social Council and the UN General Assembly. What we read in these reports was gruesome, yet removed from our own 'Iraq world': closeness in distance did not equal insight.

---

13. See Outline of Intelligence Network, p. 255.

From 1991 until March 2003 the UN reports on the human rights situation in Iraq, reviewed the same range of alleged serious government violations These included the situation of ethnic and religious groups, the status of Shi'ite clerics, the prevailing draconian laws of Iraq and Iraq's international obligations as signatory to all international human rights conventions except the convention against torture,[14] arbitrary detention and inhuman treatment of imprisoned citizens, missing persons and disappearances, the existence of mass graves and the suffering of the Iraqi people because of inadequate supplies of food and medicines.

While van der Stoel ascribed the catastrophic conditions of life solely to the Iraqi Government, his successor, Andreas Mavromatis, was significantly more objective in reminding the UN Security Council of its own obligations. In November 1995 van der Stoel wrote: 'Among the most visible signs and disturbing policies of the Government of Iraq affecting virtually the entire population are those that concern the rights to food and health!'[15] Mavromatis, on the other hand, fully recognised that the plight of the Iraqis had two causes, when he observed in August 2000: 'humanitarian issues are not *stricto senso* within [my] mandate, they cannot be brushed aside or ignored when dealing with violations of not only the right to life, but also of rights under the international covenance on economic, social and cultural rights. Security Council resolutions are binding on the Government of Iraq as well as on all other countries.'[16] Van der Stoel also referred to economic rights, yet concluded that 'the Government of Iraq has violated its obligations regarding [these rights] both by its actions and omissions', and chose not to refer as Mavromatis did to the obligations of the international community to guarantee their adherence to such rights.

Mavromatis softened his observations, unfortunately, by always adding that the negative consequences of economic sanctions were 'unintended'. After years of implementing these sanctions, the UN Security Council could not plead innocence since it was fully aware of the consequences of its Iraq policies.

Neither of the two rapporteurs devoted much time to the Security Council's responsibility for the human rights situation in Iraq. They concentrated instead on the violations of human rights perpetrated by Saddam Hussein and his Government, as their mandate demanded.

Much of van der Stoel's human rights picture related to the Kurdish tragedy of eviction from their lands. This had resulted in either displacement of many into one of the three Kurdish governorates of

14. See *UNDP Human Development Report 2003*, Oxford: Oxford University Press 2003, p. 334.
15. See UN General Assembly, A/50/734, 8 November 1995, p. 4.
16. See UN General Assembly, A/55/294, 14 August 2000, p. 8.

Dohuk, Erbil and Suleimaniyah, or relocation to Southern Iraq into areas totally outside traditional Kurdish habitation. The 1987–8 attack by the Iraqi military against Kurdish towns and villages in what became known as the 'Anfal Campaign' was seen as a major example of Saddam Hussein's brutal treatment of this people. There can be no doubt of the atrocities that were committed against the Kurds by the Government of Iraq in the years preceding the imposition of economic sanctions. There are sufficient documents from the Government of Iraq which have been found as self-incriminating evidence.[17] This reference should in no way deflect from the brutality of the Government's handling of the Anfal Campaign, but highlight the need for much more research into this period of Iraqi history.

In a report on human rights abuses in Iraq the British Government quotes an Amnesty International estimate that 'over 100,000 Kurds were killed or disappeared during … the Anfal Campaign …'.[18] The Iraqi Government version as recounted in 2004 by a senior former Iraqi official acknowledges Iraqi brutality. 'Both sides used chemical weapons! The Anfal Campaign was part of Iraq's determination to liberate the northern territory of our country from Iran and to end an armed rebellion by the Kurds. Iranian revolutionary guards, while using chemicals, were the main victims in Hallabja because they had beards and therefore could not wear masks to adequately protect themselves against the chemical weapons they were using.'[19]

Assuming that these explanations are correct, they, of course, cannot serve as justification for the death of 100,000 or more Iraqi Kurds, many of whom were civilians, including women and children. The

17. Claims of forgery of documents have been made, but in the light of the volume of such documents, the authenticity of most cannot be convincingly questioned. Many of these bear the signature of Ali Hassan al-Majid, a Tikriti cousin of Saddam Hussein. He served during the years of the Anfal Campaign as the Secretary-General of the Northern Bureau of the Ba'ath Party, and became known as the infamous 'Chemical Ali' for his leading role in the use of chemical weapons during this campaign. The Iraq Government, in a memorandum received by the UN on 25 October 1991, referred to a 1990 study by the US Department of State which concluded that it was Iranian forces who had used chemical weapons filled with cyanide gas in Hallabja and other Kurdish villages, rather than Iraqi forces. The Iraqi memorandum quotes a Pentagon official as having said 'we know that Iraq did not use cyanide, we have a very good idea of the nature of the chemical agents which Iraq is developing, manufacturing and using. We know that Iraq has not used any types of such agents and we are convinced that Iran has used cyanide gas' – see UN General Assembly, A/46/647, 13 November 1991, p. 28.
18. See *Saddam Hussein: Crimes and Human Rights Abuses*, London: Foreign and Commonwealth Office, November 2002, p. 15.
19. Meeting with the author on 9 October 2004 in Damascus.

disappearance of thousands, the arbitrary arrests, the destruction of villages and the forced relocation programmes are not explained.

The Government of Saddam Hussein fought another battle on two other 'fronts', south of Baghdad. One was to keep Shi'ite clerics at bay and contain their religious outreach; the other to pursue military deserters into the marshes to prevent Iranian and Iraqi insurgents from using the swampy areas straddling the Iraq/Iran border as convenient hideouts and crossing points. The marsh tribal communities were punished if they cooperated with these groups and also because of their own opposition to the regime in Baghdad. Gone were the romantic days of tranquillity and serenity which had earlier attracted European travellers to Iraq's southern marshes.[20]

According to the UN Human Rights Rapporteur, the 1990s were tough years for the Marsh Arabs. Reports received by van der Stoel indicate that Marsh Arabs were harshly treated, deprived of food rations and medicines and faced indiscriminate bombardments and the use of 'chemical weapons during attacks in the region of Um al-Ghag and the Abu Zergi marshlands near Basrah at the end of September 1993'.[21] There was a perpetuation of arbitrary arrests, detentions and relocations 'from their traditional and ancestral marsh homeland to the urban centres in and around the marshes'.[22]

Human rights reports repeatedly provided vivid descriptions of life in marsh communities threatened by Baghdad. Documentation confirmed that the international community and the UN Human Rights Rapporteur had good reason to be concerned about the Iraq Government's harsh reaction to the insurgency that was growing in the marsh areas during and following the 1980–8 Iran-Iraq war. A document from the Iraqi Directorate of Security, dated 30 January 1989, puts into perspective what van der Stoel received as allegations in the mid-1990s. The document, entitled 'Plan of Action for the Marshes', outlines in some detail what hostile, anti-government groups were doing, according to Iraqi intelligence, in the marshes, 'under directives from Iran'. 'The groups', the report states, 'must inflict the greatest damage on the authorities ... Persons who collaborate with the authorities may be killed ... Foreigners working for foreign companies may be kidnapped and killed ... since they are working to strengthen the regime'.

In 1987 Saddam Hussein had already approved a plan on how to react to this insurgency. The plan recommended security operations which included poisoning, explosions and the burning of houses, recruitment of trustworthy deserters to assassinate hostile elements and the application

20. See Thesiger 1964 and Young 1977.
21. See UN General Assembly, A/48/600, 18 November 1993, p. 9.
22. Ibid., p. 12.

of an economic blockade (withdrawal of food supplies, banning the sale of fish, prohibiting goods traffic into the area). Among the guidelines was one stating 'action must be taken against hostile groups in the marshes commensurate with the threat they pose'.[23]

The plight of the Marsh Arabs was further exacerbated by Government's implementation of plans to drain part of the marshes to enlarge the area under crop cultivation. Van der Stoel, referring to information he had received, concluded that 'the true objective of the Government of Iraq is to destroy the physical and social environment which provides a "safe haven" for suspected criminals, deserters and infiltrators and "its desire to control"'.[24]

I travelled around Amara and witnessed the truly desolate conditions in which relocated Madan communities had to live. I never went, however, either east of Amara towards the Iranian border or to the 'heart land' of the Marsh Arabs between Amara and Nasariyah. We knew in the UN of the 'unwritten law' in Baghdad to avoid travelling in that area. In the late 1990s UN observers, however, did. The WFP representative at the time, Jutta Burckardt, made the important point that contrary to van der Stoel's repeated assertion, all areas of the marshes were included in WFP food monitoring and that during her tenure 'the distribution of food there was in order.'[25] Had there been large-scale exclusion of people in the rationing system, the WFP would have known of it. In 2002 when the new UN Human Rights Rapporteur, Andreas Mavromatis, met with the UN country team in Baghdad, he was told by his UN colleagues that 'the Oil-for-Food Programme provided the entire population with sufficient food' and that 'the Government of Iraq was complimented for its efforts in this regard'. I could confirm this for the time I had been in Baghdad. At that time the WFP and Government tried their best to keep Iraq fed as adequately as was possible.[26]

The Human Rights Rapporteur communicated extensively with those who knew the Iraqi marshes, had lived there and had become victims of the policies of the Government of Saddam Hussein. It is to the Rapporteur's credit that the international community became aware of a tragedy that was evolving in Southern Iraq in communities which had been allowed to lead their traditional lives as fishermen and cattle herders for centuries.

In his reviews van der Stoel, however, did not reveal the complexity of the Iraq situation. He left out, or made only scant, obscure references to,

---

23. See UN Economic and Social Council, E/CN.4/1993/45, pp. 94–7.
24. Ibid., pp. 18, 20.
25. This was conveyed to the author in a communication by the former WFP representative dated 19 September 2004.
26. See UN Economic and Social Council, E/CN.4/2000/44, 15 March 2002, p. 18.

factors other than the deliberate policy of intimidation and persecution of those whom the Government in Baghdad did not trust or found inconvenient. The draining of the marshes was not only a political act or an idea which had originated in a dictator's mind. The water dam in Kut, for example, had been built in the days of King Ghazi in 1934. Already in the 1950s American and British companies had been asked by the then Kingdom of Iraq to draw up plans for land reclamation in the marshes of Southern Iraq. In the 1970s the Majnoon oil fields, among the richest in Iraq, had been discovered in the marshes. The Iraqi Government signed a contract with Elf Aquitaine at the time and took initial steps to develop the area.[27] The traditional way of life of Marsh Arabs was to be sacrificed for economic and not political reasons.

What became known as the 'third-river project', an ambitious development scheme to have a large water channel besides the Euphrates and Tigris rivers, had not only to do with a president's ambitions of grandeur but also responded to the upstream water policies of Turkey and Syria. This van der Stoel largely dismisses.[28] Lower water tables, because of reduced inflows of water from Turkey and Syria, had created serious water shortages for agriculture and resulted in soil salination. The Iraq/Syria/Turkey Water Commission had not met since the early 1990s to attempt to resolve these water-sharing problems. Iraq responded with its own measures, one of which was the 'third river project' to help resolve desalinisation of agricultural lands.[29]

There is no question that Iraq faced a serious security problem at its border with Iran. An enemy country weakened by the Iraq/Iran war and failed invasion into Kuwait, as well as the war of 1991 and the subsequent economic and military sanctions, could be conveniently further destabilised by infiltration through the marshes shared by Iran and Iraq. These realities, however, can in no way serve as an acceptable justification for the Iraq Government's harsh treatment of Marsh Arab communities.

The third pillar of persecution and destruction in the human rights picture of Iraq under the Government of Saddam Hussein is linked to the Shiah community in Iraq. In day-to-day living there were no clear ethnic or religious divides separating Shiahs and Sunnies. Sunni/Shiah intermarriages were not uncommon in Iraq. There were also a good number of Arab/Kurdish families. Many Shiahs served in government,

---

27. The Majnoon oil fields, close to Iraq's border with Iran, had the potential to create problems with Iran similar to those which Iraq and Kuwait had over the Rumela oil fields at their common border.
28. See UN General Assembly, A/48/600, 18 November 1993, p. 80.
29. This was convincingly conveyed to the author by a member of the Iraq/Syria/Turkey Water Commission and corroborated by others familiar with this issue.

universities and other professional areas. Shiahs also actively participated in Iraq's political life, including the communist, royalist, nationalist and Ba'ath Parties prior to 1979 when Saddam Hussein became President of Iraq. Following the introduction of the one party state, many Shiahs continued as active members of the Ba'ath Party. They were not barred from high office.

During the period I served in Baghdad the Iraqi Cabinet included several Shiah ministers, among them the Minister of Foreign Affairs, Mohammed Al-Sahaf. Shiahs also assumed prominent positions in Iraq's military and foreign services. Nevertheless, even though the Shiah community made up 60 percent of Iraq's population, its political strength never equalled that of the Sunnies. It was the Sunni minority, 20 percent of the population, who had held the reins of power ever since King Faisal the second was toppled by Colonel Abdul Karim Kassem in 1958.

The relationship between the Shiah community and the Government of Saddam Hussein was always influenced by a number of factors. Firstly there was the 'Iranian connection', strong religious ties between Najaf and Karbala in Iraq and Shiah clerics in Iran. Before the Iraq/Iran war large numbers of pilgrims from across the border would come to visit the shrines of Imam Ali and Imam Hussain, his son, in Najaf and Karbala. After the war the pilgrims came in much smaller numbers, yet whatever their numbers they presented security risks. A good number of Iranian clerics had settled in Southern Iraq, among them Grand Ayatollah Al Sistani.

Van der Stoel points out in his reports that the 'Iranian origin' issue continuously occupied the Government in Baghdad and led to deportations and arrests. Persons classified as 'Iranian-Iraqis' often disappeared and were never heard of again. Decree 474 of 1981 even encouraged Iraqi husbands married to women of Iranian origin to divorce their wives and send them out of the country in return for financial compensation. Shiah communities, according to UN and non-UN human rights reports, faced many forms of discrimination. Among them was the seizure of religious sites, subsequently used for the construction of commercial buildings and the closure of theological schools such as Kulhiyyat al-Figh, a college of jurisprudence in Najaf. Shiah libraries and Husseiniyas, as well as religious community centres named after Imam Hussain, were affected. The destruction of holy shrines and restrictions in the curricula in Shiah higher institutions of learning took place.

In 1994 the UN Human Rights Rapporteur reported that 'the Shiah version of the call to prayer is ... still prohibited in a number of districts inhabited by Shiahs.'[30] They were also restricted in commemorating the

---

30. UN Economic and Social Council, E/CN.4/1994/58, 25 February 1994, p. 46, para. 134.

holy month of Muharram as fellow Shiahs did elsewhere. Flagellation or walking on highways for long distances to reach the holy shrines in Najaf and Karbala were not permitted. For us in Baghdad this reality was largely unknown. We did hear of occasional Shiah uprisings which were apparently quickly quelled by the Iraqi authorities. Among the religious taboos was the prohibition of distributing reproductions of Shiah shrines and religious sites. This I discovered when a Shiah friend in Europe asked me to find such pictures for him; there were none available in Baghdad.

A second factor affecting Shiah relations with the Government related to the decision of the Ba'ath Party that there should be a clear separation of religion and state. I am told that during public statements Saddam Hussein was often heard to say: 'Everyone is free to practise his or her religion. Government should not act as the Imam of the people.' It was clear that his Government wanted to maintain a strictly secular state. Shiah clerics, on the other hand, preferred a state based on religion and Sharia, the Islamic law of governance.

There was zero tolerance, according to van der Stoel, by Saddam Hussein's Government to any organised Shiah involvement in public life. Large-scale public meetings in Shiah areas were not allowed, with the exception of modest fatiha majlis, gatherings of mourning, to pay the last respects to a deceased person.

In 1994, the UN Human Rights Rapporteur concluded that 'Government policy systematically violates the rights to religious freedom guaranteed by article 18.[31] of the international covenant on civil and political rights'. He referred to an 'anti-Shiah prejudice' and 'to systematic threats to the Shiah clergy', and a 'continuous assault on the community's religious heritage'.[32] Five years later, van der Stoel informed the UN Commission on Human Rights of 'systematic assassinations, attacks and threats carried out against the Shi'ite leadership since the 1991 uprisings' and that 'the fate of more than 100 clerics and religious scholars … taken into custody by the Government … has not been clarified'.[33]

On all accounts, Saddam Hussein and his Government were deeply fearful of any attempt on the part of Shiah leaders, clerics or not, to be organised and become an anti-government political movement.

31. Article 18 refers to 'freedom of thought, conscience and religion', 'freedom to adopt a religion', 'manifest religion in worship' and 'liberty of parents to ensure religious and moral education of their children'.
32. See UN Economic and Social Council, E/CN.4/1994/58, p. 53.
33. See UN Economic and Social Council, E/CN.4/1999/37, p. 5. Among clerics who were murdered or lost their lives in the 1990s and later under dubious circumstances were prominent Ayatollahs such as Grand Ayatollah Shaykh Mirza Ali al-Gharawi, Ayatollah Shaykh Murtada al-Burujerdi, Ayatollah Sadiq al-Sadr, and Ayatollah Hussein Bahr al-Aloom.

The Ba'ath leadership had not forgotten the return to Iran of a Shiah cleric, Ayatollah Ruhollah Khomeine, who at one time had been living as an Iranian refugee in Najaf until he decided to leave Iraq in 1978. In 1979, after the overthrow of Reza Shah Pahlavi, he became the Supreme Leader of the Islamic Revolution. The title referred not only to Iran, but rather to 'the Islamic Revolution'!

This development gave a boost to the Shiah underground opposition in Iraq and to the clandestinely operating Daawa al Islamiya or 'Islamic Call' Party. This religious party was founded in 1969 and led by Ayatollah Muhsin and Muhammad Bakrai Hakim, first in Najaf itself and then later during their exile in Teheran.[34] It also intensified the Government's resolve to clamp down, with brutal force, on any Shiah leader thought to be involved in anti-government activities. Anyone belonging to the outlawed Daawa Party or its armed wing, the Shahid al-Sadr force which was established in 1979, or the Iran-based Faylaq Badr (Badr Corps), the armed wing of the Supreme Council for the Islamic Revolution in Iraq (SCIRI), if caught, would be executed.

Nine years of UN human rights reporting portrays a Government's ruthless pursuit of these groups by citing assassinations, arrests, disappearances, destruction of religious properties, prohibition of religious ceremonies and interference with religious teaching. Shiah leaders were carefully watched. Many were persecuted, even eliminated or forced to seek refuge abroad and prevented from actively participating in public life. What these reports fail to show is that the average Shiah could lead the same difficult life under dictatorship and sanctions as anyone else in Iraq if he chose not to speak out or act in any way against the regime.

This certainly was the impression I gained from talking to members of the Shiah community while living in Baghdad. Many Shiahs and Iraqis, living in exile abroad, would corroborate van der Stoel's assessments of brutality of the Iraqi regime towards the Shiah community. They became agitated with anyone who questioned whether the entire Shiah community was subjected to this brutality. Many of them had lost members of their families and had themselves suffered while living in Iraq. One could not be surprised about their deep-seated anger and hatred against the leaders in Baghdad.

I had a first-hand introduction to these feelings in London in October 2000. Abdel Majid al-Khoie was the Head of the Al-Khoie Foundation, a religious trust founded by the respected Shiah cleric Ayatollah Mohammed Taqi al-Khoie in Najaf in 1988. The Foundation had opened an office in London in 1989, which Abdel Majid had headed since his

34. For good background information on the Iraqi Shiah opposition inside and outside of Iraq see Hiro 2001.

escape from Iraq in 1991. Abdel Majid invited me to speak about my Iraq experience: he had brought together a sizeable group of Iraqis and some Iranians, I assume all Shiahs, living in London. In this serious looking group I noticed quite a few Shiah clerics in their black *amaim* or turbans.[35]

My presentation emphasised the impact of sanctions on the Iraqi people. I had little to say about the impact of Saddam Hussein's dictatorship because I knew much less about it than they did. The audience listened politely and then engaged me in a debate which, at the time, caught me by surprise. Emotions ran high. I quickly sensed how much suffering had been brought to the meeting room. There was not a remote willingness to recognise that the human drama in Iraq was parented not only by Saddam Hussein and his Government, but also by the UN Security Council. Their message was loud and clear: 'Our people will have to suffer until the dictator is gone'. It was not possible to make this group agree that the Iraqi people had become victims of a double punishment with two guilty parties. This one-sided logic was similar to that in Washington and central London. We parted in a friendly way and agreed to disagree.

Among themselves Iraq shiahs could not agree on the extent to which they were subjected to discrimination. While those in exile naturally held the view that the Government of Saddam Hussein was anti-Shiah, the opinions back home in Iraq seemed more diverse. In 2001 I witnessed an angry exchange in Geneva between a visiting Iraqi from Baghdad and another Iraqi living in exile in Europe. They were both Shiahs. After the refugee Iraqi had made an impassioned statement about the discrimination faced by all Shiah in Iraq, his countryman jumped up and told the audience at the United Nations European headquarters: 'I am Shiah too and like many other Shiah working in Iraq as civil servants, I face no discrimination!' Human rights reports, accounts by travellers, statements by members of the Shiah community in and outside Iraq and my own limited experience suggest that the reality in which Shiahs lived in Iraq in the 1990s meant for some a 'normal' life under dictatorship and sanctions, while for others it was a life of persecution, arbitrary detention, torture and possible execution.

Andreas Mavromartis, the former Cypriot Foreign Secretary who replaced van der Stoel referred very guardedly to alleged political killings in Iraq in his first two reports in March and August 2000.[36] They included

35. Abdel Majid al Khoie returned to Najaf on 7 April 2003, his home town, after thirty years in exile and was assassinated three days later in the Imam Ali Mosque, allegedly by followers of Moqtada al-Sadr because of a long-standing religious feud between the families of al-Khoie and al-Sadr.
36. See UN Economic and Social Council, E/CN.4/2000/37, 14 March 2000 and UN General Assembly, A/55/294, 14 August 2000.

the death of Ayatollah Sadiq al-Sadr and two of his sons[37] in February 1999 and groups of protesters who apparently had been indiscriminately fired upon. He made no mention of the fact that the victims all belonged to the Shiah community. Mavromartis, it seems, wanted to start his relationship with the Iraqi Government on a new footing after years of counter-productive stalemate between his predecessor and Baghdad. Mavromartis was a seasoned communicator, I observed each time we met. He wanted to go beyond his mandate, look at all aspects of the human rights situation in Iraq and, with that approach, achieve better cooperation with the Government.

Even though modern Iraq has had at least seven Shiah prime ministers out of a total of twenty-four,[38] political power remained at all times in the hands of the Sunni minority. Ambitions of Shiah clerics and the pressures from this religious majority for more adequate power sharing, however, was never absent in Iraq politics. The fear that the 1980–8 Iran-Iraq war would lead to a Shiah betrayal of Iraq was totally unfounded. Iraqi Shiah patriotism was stronger than sectarian affiliation. The war enhanced the fear for Saddam Hussein's Government that Iran may succeed in exporting its revolution to Iraq.

When economic sanctions were introduced following Iraq's 1990 invasion into Kuwait and reconfirmed after the 1991 war between a US-led coalition and Iraq, 'the security factor in Iraq assumed a paranoiac importance within the Iraqi Government', in the view of a former senior official in the Government of Saddam Hussein. 'My Government, as a result, made "huge mistakes" in dealing with Shiah clerics'. The same former official confirms that Government used extreme force against Shiah Ayatollahs and their supporters, as was reported by the UN Human Rights Rapporteur. He and others point out that the Iraqi population was 'upset', 'angered' and 'depressed' because of the 1991 Iraqi defeat in Kuwait. This, they contend, was partly the reason for the 1991 uprising in Southern Iraq and aggravated Shiah opposition to the Government in Baghdad. The outlawing of their Daawa and other political parties, the persecution of their leaders and the pruning of their religious practices provided the Shiah community additional ground for discontent and opposition.

The uprising and the Iraqi Government's response resulted in many casualties. When the military had retaken towns such as Najaf, Kut and Amara, 'the first priority was to bury the large number of dead, including Iranians.'

---

37. Moqtadar al-Sadr, the political activist in Najaf who rose to prominence beyond his community in 2003 as a leader of the Al Mehdi armed resistance to the US/UK occupation, is one of the surviving sons of Ayotalla Sadiq al-Sadr.
38. See Amir Tahiri, *Al-Sharqalawast* newspaper, London, 2 July 2003.

```
                    ┌─────────────────────┐
                    │  The President of Iraq │
                    │      Al-Ra'es         │
                    └─────────────────────┘
                       ↑              ↖
          ┌─────────────────────┐  ┌─────────────────────┐
          │ Presidency Secretary │  │  The Special Security │
          │   Serater al-Ra'es   │  │   (Al-Amn al-Khas)   │
          └─────────────────────┘  └─────────────────────┘
                       ↑
          ┌───────────────────────────┐
          │ The National Security Council │
          │   Majlis al-A'mn al-Qawmy   │
          └───────────────────────────┘
              ↗           ↑            ↖
┌──────────────┐ ┌──────────────────┐ ┌──────────────────┐
│ General Security│ │ The General Directorate │ │ The General Directorate │
│  Directorate   │ │   of Intelligence   │ │  of Military Security │
│ Muderiyat al-A'mn│ │ Muderiyat al-Mukhabarat │ │ Muderiyat al-Istekhbarat │
│   al-A'am     │ │     al-A'mah      │ │     al-Askariya    │
└──────────────┘ └──────────────────┘ └──────────────────┘
```

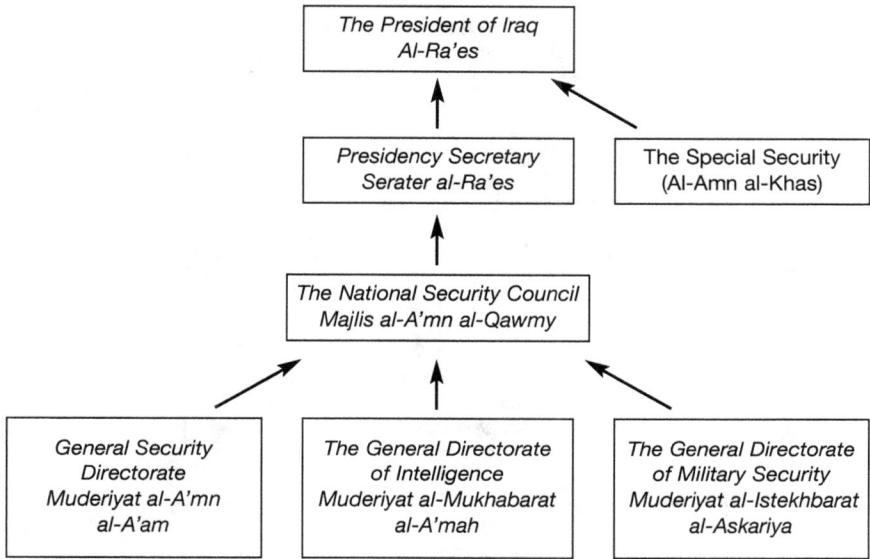

Figure 5.1   Structure of the Iraqi Intelligence Services

Iran, it is said, had sent soldiers, arms and wheat across the border in support of the uprising. An Iraqi source maintains that in 2002, when Iraq and Iran exchanged POWs, there were some sixty Iranian officers among them who had been captured by the Iraqi army during their battle against the uprising. The ICRC in Geneva was involved in this prisoner exchange but could neither confirm nor refute the authenticity of this assertion.

The picture that emerges from a review of UN documentation and conversations with both Iraqi and non-Iraqi sources of the 1991 uprising in Southern Iraq and the relations between the Shiah community and the Government in Baghdad during the following years is fairly clear. It confirms the conclusions that the uprising and subsequent military intervention produced many casualties. Persecution against Shiahs and their families as well as identifiable opposition groups was severe. The freedom of religious practice, at least in Southern Iraq, was curtailed.[39]

What is also quite apparent is that the prevailing surveillance machinery and the Ba'ath Party structure provided the Government means to control and influence Iraqi life in Southern Iraq and everywhere else, except in Iraqi Kurdistan (see Figures 5.1 and 5.2).

39. It is interesting to note that in 2002, some two years after Andreas Mavromatis had been appointed as the Human Rights Rapporteur, he points out, following his visit to Iraq that 'His general impression … was that Shiah as well as Sunni Muslims were free to visit the mosques and shrines in Karbala'. See UN E/CN.4/2002/44, p. 17.

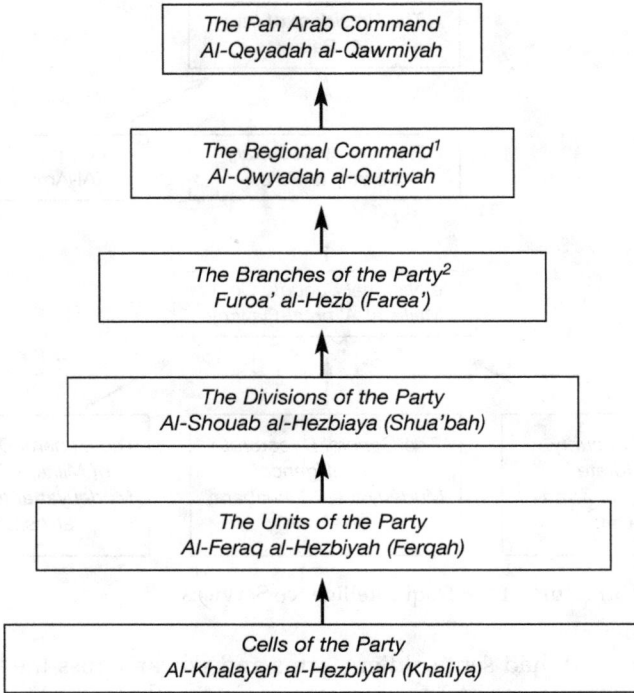

Figure 5.2 Structure of the Iraqi Ba'ath Party*

*Syria maintained a Ba'ath party of its own.
1. *The Ba'ath Party, led by Iraq, had four regional commands – Lebanon, Yemen, Sudan and Jordan.*
2. *In Iraq there were more than one hundred branches of the party, each branch consisting of five or more divisions, each division consisting of five or more units, each unit consisting of several cells.*

While intelligence services and the Ba'ath party did not have a formally defined interface, there was considerable interaction at all levels to implement 'the business of running' the country. The *bellediyes*, or municipal administrations, with their *mukdars*, the local representatives, provided 'services' of various kinds to both networks. In addition, they helped citizens with resident permits, marriage certificates, food ration card verification, etc.

It would be difficult to argue against the reference to Iraq as a 'republic of fear'.[40] Fear certainly permeated the Iraq that I encountered in the late 1990s. People were afraid to express their views, whispered or motioned

40. See Makiya 1989.

when they wanted to be critical. They preferred to talk to their families and friends somewhere in the open such as a garden, away from intrusive listening devices when something significant was to be exchanged. The years of economic sanctions, disarmament and foreign intelligence operations sometimes ... in the guise of multilateral arms monitoring intensified government paranoia. The Iraqi leadership feared the 'outside', while the population feared the 'inside'. Thanks to the extensive reports by van der Stoel and Mavromatis we know that crimes against humanity were committed by the Government of Saddam Hussein. The extent of such crimes will have to be subjected to more investigation and analysis of sources that are beginning to become available. To prevent the politicisation of such research will require immense professionalism: an example is in analysing mass graves.

More gruesome gravesites will be found and opened. They will certainly confirm the brutality of the Iraqi authorities and the extrajudicial killings in centres managed by the Mukhabarat, the Iraqi intelligence. There will, however, also be gravesites of Iraqis killed in 1991 by insurgents in Southern Iraq and gravesites as a result of the 1996 confrontation between Kurdish factions in Northern Iraq. There will be mass graves caused by US air attacks on retreating Iraqi troops in 1991. That area is known in Iraq as the 'Road of Death'. In saying this there is no belittling of the scale of human rights violations which occurred during the reign of Saddam Hussein.[41] The international community must insist that accountability in the context of Iraq should not overlook any perpetrator. This applies to any who participated in the persecution and the killing of innocent civilians, or the infringement of internationally recognised rights.

I take exception to van der Stoel's human rights reporting and recognise the efforts that Mavromartis made in bringing balance to the review of the human rights situation in Iraq. As an example, van der Stoel regularly mentioned the right to food and health, yet always saw these as rights for which only the Government of Iraq was responsible. Throughout his years of reporting he was not willing to analyse the role which the UN Security Council was playing in depriving Iraqis of their right for food, medicines and other necessities spelt out by the international covenant on economic, social and cultural rights. To argue that this was not part of his mandate cannot be an acceptable excuse. His successor Andreas Mavromatis, on the other hand, from the beginning of his tenure in 2000, paid close attention to the role played by economic sanctions in the lives of Iraqis. In his first report to the Economic and Social Council he emphasised that 'in examining allegations of violations of ... economic,

41. Human Rights Rapporteur Mavromatis rightly warns that 'investigation into mass graves will be difficult and time consuming, and presupposes the existence of necessary data ... required for DNA examination ...'. see United Nations Economic and Social Council, E/CN.4/2004/36, 19 March 2004, p. 3.

social and cultural rights such as the rights to food, housing, medical care, social services and education regard should be given to all situations ... including the effects of economic sanctions on the enjoyment of these rights'.[42]

Ambassador Saeed Hassan al-Mosawi, responsible for Iraq's Ministry of Foreign Affairs at the time of the visit of Mavromatis to Iraq in February 2002,[43] discussed with me the UN's human rights reporting on Iraq. He said: 'Mavromatis was much more acceptable to us. He seemed fair and a man with whom we could do business.'[44] This confirmed my own impression since meeting with him beginning in February 2000 in New York. Mavromatis requested my briefing on the humanitarian situation in Iraq. He listened carefully and showed convincing interest in the background information I gave him on the human conditions in the country and the status of the Oil-for-Food Programme and its shortcomings. Neither during this meeting nor subsequent ones in Geneva did I notice the aggressive tone which was so prevalent in van der Stoel's writings and the single telephone conversation I had with him.

During that conversation I offered van der Stoel our cooperation in an effort to allow him to more accurately interpret the humanitarian situation in Iraq. He did not seem interested, and made no attempt to follow up. The reports that van der Stoel issued were one-sided interpretations of the causes of suffering. He neglected to realise that non compliance with international covenants did not apply only to the Government of Iraq but also to the UN Security Council. The slow implementation of a special targeted nutrition programme was not a deliberate act of delay by the Government but a result of Iraq's complicated political relations and the difficulty in finding appropriate suppliers in countries which were not opposed to Iraq. The lack of adequate medicines certainly was not due only to 'poor procurement planning and stock management', but equally to the horrendously bureaucratic UN procurement and clearance processes. Had van der Stoel wanted to present more balanced reviews on the humanitarian exemption, he could have done so.[45] Balanced reporting by the UN Rights Rapporteur could have increased pressure on the UN Security Council to adjust its policies and emphasise targeted sanctions and accelerate changes in the management of the Oil-for-Food Programme. The people of Iraq as well as the United Nations would have been the beneficiaries.

Personality, cultural and academic backgrounds, knowledge of the Middle East and political affiliation influenced the manner in which

42. See UN Economic and Social Council, E/CN.4/2000/37, 14 March 2000, p. 3.
43. The UN Human Rights Rapporteur visited Iraq 11–15 February 2002.
44. Meeting in Damascus, 10 October 2004
45. See United Nations Economic and Social Council, E/CN.4/1999/37, 26 February 1999, paras. 29–43; see UN General Assembly, A/54/466, 14 October 1999, paras. 20–37.

Human Rights Rapporteurs in Iraq or elsewhere carried out their missions. A major impediment for the rapporteurs in Iraq, however, was the approach that the UN Commission on Human Rights had chosen. Mandates were lopsided since they neglected the international dimension of human rights in Iraq. The mandates were formulated in a politicised and confrontational manner and made Iraqi cooperation, right from the beginning, highly unlikely. The ultimate objective of human rights reporting was to make the Government of Iraq change its national decrees and laws and implement international covenants, conventions and UN Charter law in accordance with its legal obligation as a signatory. This was not achieved. The Iraq experience leaves the United Nations no defendable alternative but to make 'comprehensive' human rights reporting take all conceivable relevant factors into account. This should be the basis for its future work.

In October 2000 I was invited by the President of Iraq's National Assembly and former Prime Minister Dr Sa'doun Hamadi to speak to the 250-member Iraqi parliament about how I saw the situation in Iraq. I had left my post as Humanitarian Coordinator and was, therefore, free to decide how to respond.

After initial hesitation and several attempts by friends to discourage me from accepting this invitation, I decided to be loyal to the philosophy which I had followed in my UN life. I believe that dialogue is preferable to solitarian monologue and isolation. I had experienced this regarding Iraq-UN relations. Avoidance of each other complicated the situation. Therefore I decided to accept Dr Sa'doun's invitation and told my friends: 'Before you conclude that I am playing into the hands of a dictator, first hear me out.'

On the evening of 10 October 2000 I met Under-Secretary Dr Riyadh Al Qaysi in the Foreign Ministry in Baghdad. He had been asked to translate my presentation into Arabic. We spoke for a long time about the text. He understood, and I think appreciated, the balance I sought to show between the effects of economic sanctions and human rights violations within Iraq. What I intended to convey to the Assembly on the following day was not difficult to understand. My words, however, were chosen carefully. There was enough time between our meeting and that in the National Assembly the following day to clear the text with the Office of the President. As it turned out, there were no requests for changes. After a brief meeting in the Office of the President of the Assembly, he and I went into the Assembly Hall and the meeting was called to order. The fact that I faced one of the most unelected assemblies in the world and spoke in front of an oversized portrait of a President who in the annals of history would forever be identified as one of the fiercest dictators of the twentieth century, a man who had signed almost all international human rights treaties but followed none, did not disturb me. In fact, it encouraged me to speak out against measures the Government had introduced and which police and intelligence agencies were loyally protecting. I assumed that most of the parliamentarians were staunch supporters of the regime who did not often hear critical observations of their President's policies.

I first paid tribute to Iraq's proud heritage and its gifts to civilisation in the arts, sciences, law and philosophy. This awareness, I said, 'intensified the sense of sadness and compassion with which I had come back to Iraq.' I reminded members of the Assembly that 'during a time of suffering, parliamentarians had a formidable responsibility to feel with the people and to care for their troubled minds.'

I did not really wish to convey to the men and women listening to me my views on the harm sanctions had inflicted on the people of Iraq; they knew this better than I did. The core of my presentation related to the Iraq Government's failure to honour the 'contract with its people'. 'The Iraq perceived widely in Europe and elsewhere', I said, 'is not the Iraq of generous and capable but of tired people that I have come to know and appreciate …'.

It was very quiet in the Assembly when I pointed out that 'Iraqis in their country were facing many restrictions. These comprised travelling, that a multiparty system did not exist, that the judicial system was too harsh, that people could not speak as openly as they wished'. After this I purposely paused for a moment and then continued by saying: 'President Saddam Hussein and you – the parliamentarians – by introducing changes can prove those wrong who want to say this in future!' Present conditions facing the Iraqi people were 'making no allowance for justice, fairness, the right to live, the right to the full development of the human person and the wider application of international law',[46] I stated.

Iraqi TV, CNN and other TV and print media were present. The Iraqi TV showed the critical remarks I made on the impact of sanctions but left out what I said on human rights; CNN recorded the entire forty-minute event. I do not know which segment found its way into the international and US programmes. Iraqis later gave me a positive but guarded feedback. Some friends in Europe offered no comments. Regardless of this, I concluded that I had done the right thing.

It is important to point out that as serious research into violations of the Iraqi human rights during sanctions and dictatorship proceeds, credibility will be established only if the UN Security Council's own responsibility for what happened in Iraq is not obscured by the Government of Iraq's culpability.[47]

46. Included in author's presentation to Iraq's National Assembly, 11 October 2000.
47. This is a paraphrased conclusion to which Human Rights Watch came in a letter by Hanny Megally, Executive Director of Human Rights Watch, dated 4 January 2000 to US Ambassador Richard Holbrooke who served for that month as President of the UN Security Council. I entirely share this conclusion.

Chapter 6

The UN Sanctions Structure: Confrontation, Fragmentation, Conclusions

The UN structure for managing economic and military sanctions, set up in response to Iraq's invasion of Kuwait in August 1990, was not static but evolved over time. By 1996, however, it had taken a shape which would remain until the March 2003 war. The UN Office of the Iraq Programme (OIP) in New York and its Iraq-based outreach, the UN Office of the Humanitarian Coordinator, formed the last supporting walls of the UN sanctions edifice that was constructed in 1996. From then onwards changes involved bureaucratic fine-tuning. 1996 was also the year when the cost of managing sanctions-related programmes was increasingly shouldered by Iraq from its oil revenue.

The UN Security Council had built a large 'UN Sanctions House' using its own designs exclusively. It declared itself the owner and passed on most of the bills to Iraq. The Council decided that this was justifiable since Iraq had violated international law by invading Kuwait. Iraq threatened international peace and security because of its weapons of mass destruction machinery and its disturbing human rights record within the country.

The main occupants of the UN Sanctions House were those concerned with disarmament and the military embargo and those mandated to protect the civilian population against economic sanctions.

The United Nations Special Commission (UNSCOM) and the International Atomic Energy Agency (IAEA) had begun their mission in 1991 with large teams of highly specialised inspectors and support personnel in the fields of biological, chemical, nuclear and ballistic warfare. By the time UNSCOM left Iraq shortly before Operation Desert Fox in December 1998, Iraq had become the most 'x-rayed' country in the world. UNSCOM and IAEA teams had inspected every part of the country, ably assisted by national intelligence services. Manned and unmanned surveillance flights had photographed each and every corner of Iraq. Following an interruption of four years of on-site inspections, UNSCOM's successor, the United Nations Monitoring, Verification and Inspection Commission (UNMOVIC) and the International Atomic Energy Agency (IAEA) resumed their disarmament work in Iraq in November 2002. President Saddam Hussein, recognising that he had little choice, agreed to their return. This costly interruption could and should have been avoided through dialogue and diplomacy.

From the beginning in November 2000, Iraqi cooperation with UNMOVIC and IAEA appeared adequate and, in hindsight, must be considered satisfactory. For Iraq to prove to a justifiably suspicious international community that it had no active WMD programme turned out to be mission impossible. 'Absence of evidence' was not accepted as 'evidence of absence',[1] but used instead as a justification for going to war.

The UN Office of the Iraq Programme (OIP) in New York and the UN Office of the Humanitarian Coordinator (UNOHCI) in Baghdad moved into the UN Sanctions House much later than did the UN disarmament team. They followed a much smaller group from the UN Department of Humanitarian Affairs (DHA) at UN headquarters and in Baghdad. At this point, in 1996, the DHA ended its involvement in the Iraq emergency. UNOIP and UNOHCI were responsible for UN humanitarian activities in Iraq, in cooperation with other units of the UN system. Ultimately, this was to the detriment of a broad-based UN involvement. For a duration of seven years UNOIP and UNOHCI managed a budget of $43 billion available from the $64 billion that Iraq's oil sales had earned.

The United Nations Commission on Human Rights occupied some space in the UN Sanctions House, but made use of the Baghdad premises on only two occasions, in 1991 and 2002: these occurred when the two Human Rights Rapporteurs who reported on Iraq during the thirteen years from 1991 to 2004 each paid one visit to Iraq.

The assignment of Human Rights Monitors, which the UN Human Rights Commission and its rapporteurs wanted to station throughout Iraq, never materialised, since the Government of Iraq rejected this proposal.

The United Nations Compensation Commission preferred its Geneva facilities to the ones available in Baghdad. From 1992, when it was created, the UNCC never visited Baghdad. It performed its entire work from the UN European headquarters. By mid-2004, the UNCC had paid $18.4 billion from Iraqi oil funds to various claims parties. At this point total compensation claims were worth $48.2 billion.

---

1. This is a reference to a phrase used by US Secretary of Defence, Donald Rumsfeld, in building the case for war against Iraq.

The United Nations Guards Contingent in Iraq (UNGCI) maintained a small but important presence in the UN Sanctions House that was concerned with Iraqi Kurdistan. Since 1991 UNGCI was meant to have a presence in all parts of Iraq in order to monitor humanitarian assistance and extend protection to staff carrying out the UN's humanitarian mandate. The UN and the Government of Iraq ultimately agreed to reduce the planned contingent strength of five hundred guards for Iraq to sixty-nine guards, confined only to the three Kurdish governorates in Northern Iraq. The costs of their presence in the country were met by non-Iraqi sources.

All major UN Security Council resolutions dealing with Iraq under sanctions stressed the international community's determination to respect Iraq's sovereignty and territorial integrity. In reality this was not the case, due to the unauthorised movement in and out of Iraqi Kurdistan by various foreign parties, the restrictions put on Iraq's economic and financial activities and the existence of the two no-fly zones.

In 1991 the United Nations Iraq/Kuwait Observation Mission (UNIKOM) was charged with monitoring Iraq's southern border with Kuwait. It did little more than that. UNIKOM, consisting of military personnel from the five permanent members in the UN Security Council and individual UN member countries, had not sufficient force to protect state sovereignty. This was confirmed by nearly daily incursions of foreign air forces into Southern Iraqi airspace and by Operation Desert Fox. The cost of their presence in Southern Iraq, like that of the UN Guards Contingent for Iraq in the north of the country, was met from non-Iraqi sources.

The UN Sanctions House became more and more crowded and the rent, paid by the Iraqi authorities as absentee financiers, escalated. Little protection for those caught in the conflict between Iraq and the UN Security Council was provided, yet this very responsibility to extend protection had been used to justify the construction of the UN Sanctions House.

The UN Security Council, the 'landlord', well knew the activities of its tenants: it was briefed by those on the ground in Iraq, read the UN Secretariat's accounts concerning conditions in Iraq and listened to a committed UN Secretary-General. The Council occasionally verbalised its concerns, yet largely remained ineffective in averting an avoidable human crisis. Consensus in the Council was more important than dissent. The Council failed to take decisive action to prevent the United Nations becoming party to violations of human rights and international law, yet it sought to halt these violations perpetuated by the Government of Saddam Hussein.

Oversight is of little value if it does not lead to an adjustment of policy when new knowledge becomes available and conditions change. This holds true in any context. The UN Security Council, as the supreme body

Table 6.1   Main UN Entities

UNIKOM The United Nations Iraq-Kuwait Observation Mission (1991)[1] → *monitoring of the demilitarised zones*	UNSCOM The United Nations Special Commission (1991) *followed by:*
IAEA The International Atomic Energy Agency (1991) → *verification and destruction of Iraq's WMD (nuclear)*	UNMOVIC The United Nations Monitoring, Verification and Inspection Commission (1999) → *verification and destruction of Iraq's WMD (chemical and biological)*
UNCC The United Nations Compensation Commission (1992) → *claims – Iraq's invasion into Kuwait*	UNGCI The United Nations Guards Contingent in Iraq (1991) → *protecting UN personnel, assets and operations*
UNOHCI & OIP The United Nations Office of the Humanitarian Coordinator for Iraq & (UN) Office of the Iraq Programme (1996) → *implementation – Oil-for-Food Programme*[2]	**Special Rapporteur of the (UN) Commission on Human Rights** (1991) → *monitoring human rights in Iraq*
UNHCR[3] The United Nations High Commissioner for Refugees → *Iraq-based refugees*	

Notes:
1 *Date established*
2 *In cooperation with UN agencies/programmes.*
3 *No direct involvement beyond protection of refugees in Iraq under sanctions.*

of the United Nations seeking to uphold the spirit and legal dictates of its Charter, had an additional heavy responsibility: it was supposed to implement policies in the interest of the community of nations and not to succumb to special-interest groups. The UN Security Council did succumb repeatedly over the years, thus failing to effectively execute its oversight mandate. It was structurally and normatively unprepared to handle its responsibilities in the interests of world order, international law and humanity, even though it had the options of doing so.

UNSCOM/UNMOVIC, UNOIP/UNOHCI, UNCC – the main UN implementers of sanctions-related programmes – were subsidiary to the

UN Security Council. Constructive oversight, had it existed, should have included the assurance that these subordinate units cooperated fully in the interests of a coherent approach. There was no encouragement from the UN Security Council to do so: it was a true free-for-all for these entities. In fact, contact and consultation between these 'sanctions house tenants' and others within and outside the United Nations were discouraged; when they were attempted, demands to desist would often follow. The disarmament programme, the Compensation Commission and the Oil-for-Food Programme had clear and independent agendas, yet they had commonalities. All three had the obligation to stay within the boundaries of international law, having the same institutional base of the United Nations. They all were expected to implement their functions within the framework of the UN Charter and operate strictly independently of any party external to the organisation.

The UN Security Council should have been the guardian of these programmes but was not. The implementation of UN sanctions against Iraq was performed without Security Council protection and without the Council's insistence that the various UN entities cooperate with each other. What should such cooperation have entailed? Firstly, institutions such as UNSCOM/UNMOVIC, UNOIP/UNOHCI and UNCC should have continuously assessed the impact of their programmes on conditions in Iraq. The pooling of such information and joint reviews of such assessments could and should have led to a coherent UN approach for Iraq. At no time did this happen: neither the UN Security Council nor the UN Secretariat ever brought the various UN bodies concerned with Iraq into one room to discuss conditions in Iraq and to draw from this appropriate conclusions on how to deal with the country.

Even within the humanitarian programme, reviews of the consequences of UN Security Council economic sanctions policies were rare and never rigorous. The apportioning of scarce resources from limited oil sales between humanitarian and compensation programmes could have been synchronised with assessments of socio-economic conditions in Iraq. This could have allowed a much earlier downward adjustment of the high level of 30 percent of oil revenue awarded to the Compensation Commission and helped to reduce the magnitude of the disaster faced by the Iraqi population. It is not unreasonable to argue that the UN Security Council had the responsibility to promote cooperation within the UN system of sanctions organisations and to coordinate implementation. The people of Iraq would have benefited. Administrative costs could have been reduced and resources freed for the humanitarian exemption.

Impact assessments, joint reviews and integrated approaches were absolutely attainable objectives had the UN Security Council conceptualised a sanctions plan for Iraq and shown the political will to implement it. Its absence made the Council vulnerable to misuse by individual member countries or groups of countries within the Council, which resulted in significant political costs to the United Nations, international order and the people of Iraq.

Those who remember that the purpose of a UN sanctions structure in Iraq was to deal with an irresponsible dictator and the threat he posed to his people, are correct. During the early years of sanctions more transparent and honest Iraqi Government cooperation with the United Nations could have made a difference to the direction in which the Iraqi crisis moved. Would this have been an additional hurdle for a Bush administration which, from January 2001, was determined to change the Iraqi regime by force? Former British Foreign Secretary Robin Cook told me in October 2004 that he did not think so. This is also my view. The fact that Saddam Hussein chose to pursue a different political path makes him accountable for the high price his people had to pay under his leadership. This, however, cannot possibly serve as a justification for maintaining a thirteen-year UN sanctions structure which largely bypassed the perpetrators and increasingly punished the wrong party. Acceptance of this fact constitutes a precondition for further analysis of the approach used by individual organisations of the UN sanctions system in carrying out their mandates.

UNSCOM and Iraq played an eternal cat and mouse game during the course of which the cat became more daring and the mouse more frightened and paranoid. By the time UNMOVIC arrived in 2002, as the new 'cat', the Iraqi Government was thoroughly suspicious of the United Nations and its agenda.

The Bush administration vocalised unveiled intentions to remove the Government of Saddam Hussein. Unequivocal pronouncements were made by members of the Clinton and Bush administrations that sanctions would not be removed as long as Saddam Hussein was in power. The existence of the 1998 Iraq Liberation Act passed by the US Congress formalised a US policy of regime change. All of the above confirmed to the Iraqi Government that there was nothing they could do to achieve a removal of the embargo.

The misuse of UNSCOM by the United States and the United Kingdom for their national intelligence interests accentuated the Iraq Government's reluctance to cooperate with the United Nations. It also influenced relations between Government and other UN entities such as UNOHCI and complicated the implementation of the Oil-for-Food Programme.

Based on the UNSCOM experience, Iraqi Government suspicion of UN intentions made UN data collection in health, education, household food consumption and other areas much more difficult and often impossible to obtain. The fact that incremental progress in the disarmament of Iraq did not prompt incremental reduction in the severity of economic sanctions further complicated overall UN-Iraq relations.

The very fact that not only disarmament and a military embargo, but also disarmament and economic sanctions had been linked should have resulted in a close involvement between UNSCOM and the UNOIP. Other humanitarian organisations under the leadership of the UN Security Council and the UNCC should also have been involved.

The UN Compensation Commission, similar to other 'tenants' in the UN Sanctions House, operated in splendid isolation. UNCC was remotefed by substantial funds taken out of the Oil-for-Food Programme. By mid-2004 these amounted to over $18 billion. It cannot be disputed that such an amount would have made a substantial difference to the Iraqi people. Surprisingly, during the entire lifespan of the Oil for Programme there was not a single occasion when the UN Office of the Iraq Programme in New York, the UN Office of the Humanitarian Coordinator in Baghdad and the UN Office of the Compensation Commission in Geneva arranged to meet in order to brief each other on the situation in Iraq. Neither the UN Security Council nor the UN Secretariat had such an idea. We in Baghdad did not have the imagination to press for such an important joint assessment: the UNCC and the UNOIP/UNOHCI were not only physically far apart, but a mental wall separated us. The latter could have easily been removed by enlightened leadership in New York. Had we all understood this, we could have put together a compelling document for the UN Security Council outlining the humanitarian picture of the victims of Iraq's invasion into Kuwait and the humanitarian situation within Iraq.

It would not have been difficult to identify those UNCC claimants who would truly have suffered without compensation. These were primarily workers from South and South-East Asia and the Middle East. No one would have objected to the payment of indemnities for this group. However, UNOIP/UNOHCI had the data to convincingly portray the intolerable socio economic conditions in Iraq, thus making the case for other less urgent claims be put on 'hold' until conditions in Iraq had returned to acceptable standards of living. Had there been an overall sanctions plan for Iraq and leadership in following such a plan, a more equitable strategy for the compensation of invasion victims and humanitarian assistance for victims of economic sanctions could have been developed. Instead, fragmented approaches within the UN Sanctions House and ad hoc interventions in response to critical developments in Iraq's social sectors prevailed. The total separation of the operation of these two sanctions bodies is a particularly grave default of UN Security Council responsibility.

The reports of the UN Human Rights Commission on Iraq were not only available to the Commission and the UN Secretariat, but also to the UN Economic and Social Council and the UN General Assembly. In other words, each one of the 191 member governments of the United Nations had access to these reports.

When Iraq human rights reporting began in 1991, the world was appalled by Iraq's invasion of Kuwait and by what transpired during the dictatorship of Saddam Hussein. The impact of imposed economic sanctions on the country was at this point only beginning to be felt by the Iraqi people. Moreover, only a few Iraq specialists[2] anticipated the collapse of Iraqi society because of the totally inadequate preparations made by the UN Security Council and the UN Secretariat for handling the humanitarian emergency. This may explain why the mandate of the UN Human Rights Rapporteurs for Iraq was limited to an assessment of human rights violations committed by Saddam Hussein's Government; it does not explain why this mandate was not changed when the impact of UN sanctions policy on the lives of the Iraqi people became known. The mandate should have been broadened at that time to include factors other than those of a dictatorship which impinged on conditions in Iraq. It was a grave bias of the UN Security Council to assess human rights violations by the Iraqi Government only but not those for which the UN Security Council and individual members within the Council were responsible.

Rights enshrined in international covenants disallow freezing national assets when funds are needed for survival. Refusing to release funds in personal accounts and blocking billions of US dollars-worth of needed humanitarian supplies is an abuse of such rights, as is limiting the sale of oil and the rehabilitation of the oil industry. Introducing a procurement bureaucracy leading to significant delays in the arrival of humanitarian goods and the slow pace of repairing the water, sanitation and electricity structures also compose abuses, as do the gradual collapse of the education and health systems. This disregard for international covenants and its impact on human rights should have been included in a human rights rapporteur's agenda to properly analyse the causes for the human conditions in Iraq. The Commission on Human Rights in 2000 had access to a comprehensive report on 'the adverse consequences of economic sanctions on the enjoyment of human rights'[3] which should have, but did not, lead to an immediate mandate revision for human rights reporting. To leave the 'sanctions factor' out of human rights reporting has become a heavy UN liability.

Like UNSCOM, UNCC and UNOIP/UNOHCI, the Human Rights Rapporteur had his own agenda during the period 1991 to 1999. There was no institutionalised contact between the Rapporteur in Geneva and

2. These included Professor Richard Garfield of Colombia University in New York and Professor Ulrich Gottstein of IPPNW, the International Physicians for the Prevention of Nuclear War, in Frankfurt.
3. Reference is made here to UN Economic and Social Council document E/CN.4/sub.2/2000/33, 21 June 2000, in which Professor Bossuyt outlines succinctly how sanctions could be evaluated to help prevent the wrong parties from being punished, as had been the case in Iraq.

UN staff in Iraq. Had there been, it could have enabled the Rapporteur to better understand the constraints sanctions had put on an adequate food supply, medical attention and water and sanitation services, as well as the damage that resulted from other international sanctions policies.

Those in the UN Sanctions House had no influence over the implementation of the two no-fly zones in the early 1990s, nor could they have halted the provocation of foreign air forces in Iraqi airspace. None of the UN sanctions organisations vocalised this violation of international law. The Security Council itself had been unable to prevent the establishment of these zones: it did not even discuss their illegality. Interventions by individual member countries to protest the existence of the no-fly zones and their damage to civilian life and property were few: there was some 'barking' but there was no 'biting'. The pressure of hidden agendas prevented the Security Council from standing united to object to bilateral exceptionalism. Human costs made little difference.

UNOIP and UNOHCI maintained close links with UN specialised agencies and programmes concerned with humanitarian issues in Iraq. They avoided interaction with other operational UN sanctions organisations such as the UNCC, the UN Human Rights Commission and the disarmament agencies. The 1995 de-linking of the UN Iraq Humanitarian Programme from the UN Department of Humanitarian Affairs signalled a UN preference for converting the Iraq programme into a self-contained UN entity. This was a serious mistake, with consequences for the quality and impact of the UN humanitarian exemption. It was a convenient way of controlling and limiting the extent of humanitarian assistance in Iraq for those in the UN Security Council with a particular interest in uncompromising, tough sanctions operations. During its seven years of existence UNOIP/UNOHCI was always aware of the fundamental inadequacy of the Oil-for-Food Programme and argued for improvements. Some support was received from the Security Council, but ultimately the key objectives of a UN humanitarian programme were not achieved. These should have been to ensure that the United Nations would in no way be party to the suffering of ordinary Iraqis, and succeed in significantly raising the level of well-being of the population. Integrated approaches to Iraq by all relevant political, social, economic and humanitarian units within the UN Secretariat could have made a difference in the quality and impact of the Oil-for-Food Programme.

There was no such initiative, either within the UN Secretariat itself or from the UN Security Council. There was an absence of coordination between UNOIP/UNOHCI and other (non humanitarian) UN sanctions organisations, and an unjustifiable independence in decision-making by UNOIP. These were compounded in their negative impact by the absence of an overall Iraq sanctions plan vetted by the UN Security Council, including the built-in monitoring of the state of human conditions in Iraq.

It is a hard but unavoidable conclusion that the UN humanitarian programme in Iraq was carried out with neither vision nor courage, and never graduated from its supply and distribution mentality. It cannot be argued that a critical review of thirteen years of comprehensive economic sanctions and the concurrent humanitarian exemption constitute wisdom after the fact. The Government of Saddam Hussein, the UN Security Council and the UN Secretariat all had options; protagonists were aware of these but chose to neglect them. Had they not done so, the Iraqi people would have been treated more humanely.

There was no shortage of warning from the international community, professional organisations, governments, the UN Secretary-General, UN civil servants, church leaders and people with healthy consciences that humanitarian law and human rights were ignored year after year. A nation was destroyed by dictatorship and sanctions.

The profound seriousness of the Iraqi tragedy is that it was not accidental nor the result of ignorance. The impact of sanctions and the inadequacy of the humanitarian exemption were known and documented. Some governments, academic institutions and citizen groups saw an urgent need to go beyond protest in response to the conditions created by sanctions policy in Iraq. The result was an increasingly refined catalogue of measures which were meant to protect innocent civilians while retaining sanctions as a legitimate and peaceful international response to threats by individual governments or groups against peace and security.

There were early voices in the US Congress, the UK House of Commons, the European Union, the International Committee of the Red Cross, the United Nations, churches and civil society at large, who argued against the comprehensive nature of the UN Iraq sanctions regime which was unique in the history of sanctions. Awareness, however, did not translate into political commitment to alter the course of Iraq sanctions, as the outline in Table 6.2 makes clear.

Sanctions impact awareness based on sanctions experience and sectoral analyses in such key areas as food and nutrition, health, water and sanitation and education has been translated into valuable documentation that will in the future make it difficult to justify an international policy of the kind which prevailed for Iraq during the thirteen-year period.

Furthermore, available documentation can put an end to sanctions and humanitarian exemption experimentation as was practised by the United Nations Security Council in Iraq, if future political will exists to do so. The Iraq experience has unequivocally shown that comprehensive economic sanctions should be eliminated as a coercive tool in international relations.

Thanks to the commitment of the Governments of Switzerland, Sweden, Germany and Canada, in cooperation with the University of Uppsala,

Table 6.2 Impact of Sanctions and Humanitarian Exemption on Civil Society in the Case of Iraq

A. The UN's Institutional awareness*	B. The UN's Institutional reaction**
I. Preparations for sanctions and humanitarian exemption	
UN Security Council resolutions require *interpretable* measurable objectives *for managing economic sanction and humanitarian exemption.*	*UN Security Council Iraq sanctions resolutions were vague and with no detailed sanctions and humanitarian exemption objectives.*
Pre-sanctions assessment of *Iraq's socio-economic conditions.*	*No pre-sanctions assessment for Iraq*
II. Implementation of sanctions and humanitarian exemption	
Sanctions strategy; *definitions of purposes, targets and roles; action plan for all UN sanctions units.*	*Sanctions strategy for Iraq limited to linkage between disarmament and comprehensive economic sanctions. There were definitions of purposes, targets and roles, yet no integrated UN action plan.*
Sanctions time-frame *and provisions for termination or renewal.*	*The sanctions time-frame for Iraq was open-ended as were provisions for termination, suspension or renewal.*
Security Council oversight *mandate (ongoing monitoring) of sanctions and humanitarian exemption.*	*No continuous and comprehensive Security Council Iraq oversight.*
Consultative mechanisms *between Security Council and UN sanctions units; between sanctions units and with NGOs.*	*Ad hoc consultations only between Security Council and UN sanctions units; no consultations between sanctions units and only sporadic consultations between Security Council and non-UN entities.*
UN sanctions coordinator.	*No sanctions coordinator for Iraq.*
UN sanctions ombudsperson.	*No sanctions ombudsperson for Iraq.*
Standardised terms of reference *for Security Council Sanctions Committees.*	*Iraq Sanctions Committee had evolving terms of reference.*
Regular reviews *between Security Council and targeted party.*	*Intermittent contact only between Security Council and Government of Iraq.*
Standard reporting *for Security Council and Secretariat.*	*No standard format for reviews of humanitarian situation in Iraq; standard format on Oil-for-Food Programme only.*
Regular (continuous) Security Council assessments *of impact of sanctions on targeted country.*	*No regular sanctions impact assessments for Iraq.*
Special humanitarian exemption measures for vulnerable *groups.*	*Special measures for targeted nutrition only.*
Provision of special funding *for servicing and supporting humanitarian exemptions.*	*No special funding; humanitarian exemption and overheads financed entirely by Iraq.*

continued

Table 6.2 *continued*

Training *and* institution building *for the management of targeted sanctions and humanitarian exemptions.*	*Limited training and UN institution-building for implementation of comprehensive economic sanctions and humanitarian exemption.*
Public communications *on substantive issues of sanctions and humanitarian exemptions.*	*Ad hoc interaction with media only.*

III. Post-sanctions and post-humanitarian exemption

Final assessment *of sanctions and humanitarian exemption programmes.*	*No final assessments for Iraq available.*
Feedback *of lessons learnt from sanctions and humanitarian exemptions methodologies.*	*No lessons learnt for Iraq identified yet.*
International support for national rehabilitation and nation-building.	*Security conditions in 2006 in Iraq do not yet permit international support for national rehabilitation and nation-building.*

*Institutional awareness refers to 'known requirements'.
**Institutional reaction refers to 'what was actually done'.

Brown University, the Bonn International Centre for Conversion and the UN Office for the Coordination of Humanitarian Affairs in New York, methodologies for targeted sanctions have been identified which reflect sanctions experience over many years.[4] They will allow, if followed, well thought-out approaches to ensure that the negative effects of sanctions on innocent civilian populations are kept to a defensible minimum and stay within the boundaries of international humanitarian law.

Those in power must be reminded that sanctions as an international tool, blunt as this tool may be, do not have to cause the harm they did in Iraq. The sanctions process must begin with an in-depth pre-sanctions assessment to understand the socio-economic conditions in which the population of the country to be sanctioned lives. Without such knowledge,

4. See: (1) The Swiss Confederation in cooperation with the United Nations Secretariat and the Watson Institute for International Studies at Brown University, *Targeted Financial Sanctions: A Manual for Design and Implementation*, 2001. (2) Bonn International Centre for Conversion in cooperation with the German Foreign Office and the United Nations Secretariat, *Design and Implementation of Arms Embargos and Travel and Aviation-Related Sanctions*, 2001. (3) Uppsala University and the Swedish Ministry of Foreign Affairs, *Making Targeted Sanctions Effective: Guidelines for the Implementation of UN Policy Options*, 2003. (4) The United Nations Interagency Standing Committee, *Sanctions Assessment Handbook*, 2004.

the monitoring of sanctions to understand how international policies impact on the lives of people will not be possible. In Iraq such an assessment was not carried out and therefore evaluations of the Security Council's handling of the evolving Iraq situation would have been difficult.

Iraq resolutions were passed in the Security Council without any quantifiable objectives. This made political misuse easy since the resolutions could be interpreted at will. Iraq must have 'completed all actions'[5] and 'cooperated in all respects' is the wording of two key Iraq resolutions.[6] This is not the wording required to measure 'compliance'; the international call for quantifiable objectives is, therefore, fully justified.

No country should be subjected to economic sanctions without the Security Council identifying a sanctions strategy. Such a strategy should translate into an action plan, including definitions of purpose, target and roles of the parties implementing sanctions.

The single sanctions strategy for Iraq was to link comprehensive economic sanctions to a military embargo and disarmament. This linkage held the civilian population accountable for the acts of armament of their Government and therefore became a tool for the punishment of innocent people for something they had not done. An overall strategy, action plan, targets and roles were never identified for Iraq; instead, a free-for-all without coordinating leadership constituted the preferred alternative.

The UN Security Council has as one of its fundamental tasks the responsibility of oversight in order to be aware of international political developments in general and to know, at any given time, the impact of its own policies. It would be wrong to maintain that the Security Council was not following Iraq developments in some detail. Yet, it is correct to point out that the Council did so in an ad hoc manner: there was no continuous oversight and no regular consultation between the Council and those within the UN charged with the implementation of sanctions and the humanitarian exemption. In contravention of the spirit of the United Nations as a conflict-prevention and conflict-resolving institution, there were only infrequent opportunities for dialogue between the Council and Iraq, the targeted party. The Security Council's Iraq Sanctions Committee had the opportunity to oversee and monitor the implementation of Council policy. Instead, the emphasis of the Sanctions Committee's preoccupation was to function as a micro-manager of bureaucratic detail and as a licensing office for humanitarian supplies.

Security Council oversight should have included regular in-depth assessments of conditions within a targeted country. With the exception of

5. UN S/RES/687 (1991), para. 22.
6. UN S/RES/1284 (1999), para. 33.

one such Iraq assessment in 1999,[7] the Security Council defaulted in this most important review responsibility.

A particularly serious omission on the part of Council and Secretariat relates to the type of reporting on the humanitarian situation in Iraq. The so-called 90- and 180-day reports were simplistic and, for policymakers in the Security Council, often unintelligible supply and distribution reports: they were not reports that transparently related the achievements of the Oil-for-Food Programme to the needs and conditions of Iraqi society. Comprehensive reporting on human conditions in targeted countries and the international humanitarian response, as well as support from non UN sources, will have to become standard features of future sanctions structures.

There should have been regular contact with non-UN parties involved with Iraq beyond the sporadic and rare exchanges between the Council and organisations such as the ICRC. Demands for Security Council oversight, consultative mechanisms and sanctions coordination have been made repeatedly from within the UN system and from outside. These are well reflected in the documentation coming out of the Interlaken, Bonn/Berlin, Stockholm processes and the important work of the UN Office of Humanitarian Affairs.

Responsibilities of the UN Office of Humanitarian Affairs must include reminding decision-makers that the Security Council should discharge its duties 'in accordance with the purposes and principles of the United Nations'.[8] The temptation by those in power to use international structures such as the Security Council for their own political self-interest was ever-present in the Iraq debate and, as we have seen, carried a high price for the people of Iraq. To protect against such misuse in the future a personality of recognised integrity could function as a sanctions ombudsperson charged with the task to observe, as an independent authority, the sanctions process and the actions of the parties involved.

In 1990 the UN Security Council decided to freeze Iraqi assets abroad as part of sanctions measures. For several years, until the Oil-for-Food Programme had been negotiated in 1995, there was disagreement between Iraq and the Council over an acceptable humanitarian exemption programme. During this period, and throughout the years of the Oil-for-Food Programme, Iraq had no authority over its financial resources. This authority rested with the UN Security Council, the UN Treasury and the Banque Nationale de Paris as the holder of the Iraqi oil account.

---

7. The 'Amorim Panel' on Humanitarian Issues – see UN S/1999/56. Two other assessments carried out of the implementation of the Oil-for-Food Programme – not the human condition in Iraq – had been initiated by the UN Secretariat, not the UN Security Council.
8. UN Charter, chap. v, article 24.2.

Until 1996, the humanitarian programme for Iraq was financed entirely by voluntary contributions. These were far below minimum needs. The UN Security Council established the rules on financing permissible under Iraq sanctions and therefore became responsible for ensuring adequate support for these humanitarian programmes. The Security Council, neither at that time nor after 1996, when similar inadequacies arose during the Oil-for-Food Programme period, felt compelled to recognise this responsibility.

Future sanctions programmes based on careful pre-sanctions assessments and continuous evaluations during sanctions must be equipped with adequate finance for servicing and supporting humanitarian exemptions for the protection of innocent groups. Similarly, the Council has to recognise the special needs of vulnerable groups in such areas as health, food and nutrition and education. The Council did introduce special Iraq-financed targeted nutrition programmes for infants and lactating mothers. Important as this was, the Council did not go beyond this individual special measure and did not ensure adequate financing. Iraq sanctions were initially perceived as short term and requiring humanitarian programmes of an emergency nature. This approach did not change even when it became clear that sanctions had become long term.

The Security Council's oversight mandate should have recognised that short term had become medium and then long term and, on that basis, adjusted the content of the humanitarian exemption. This did not happen, even though signals were given for the need of reorientation. Already in the mid-1990s the development dimension of training and institution building should have become a priority concern. Instead, the engrained perception remained that the humanitarian exemption was to be only a feeding and survival programme.

Lastly, the UN Security Council had a public communication responsibility which it persistently neglected. Informing the public was more than announcing new sanctions measures for Iraq. The UN Security Council and the UN Secretariat faced the daily challenge of the politicisation of the Iraq situation by the Government of Iraq and key members of the UN Security Council. The Council should have responded with transparent presentations to the media on substantive issues such as the management of sanctions, the financing of humanitarian programmes, and what the UN Inter-Agency Standing Committee in New York has termed 'core' human security issues. These include health, food and nutrition, water and sanitation, education and 'systemic' issues such as governance, the economic situation, the physical environment and demographic circumstances. This would have made it much more difficult for the protagonists to manipulate information, fight propaganda battles and misuse the multilateral network.

Over the years, the UN perfected diplomatic language. More often than not, concern within the Department of Public Information was not to cause offence even when clear and serious misrepresentation of facts had occurred or when the department was aware of injustices that had been committed in the name of the United Nations. Examples are how members of the Security Council were handling the no-fly zones in Iraq and the US and UK carried out Operation Desert Fox, and the accusation that Oil-for-Food Programme commodities were sold in large quantities in the Iraqi open market or abroad. Bilateral intelligence gathering within the UN disarmament programme and the irresponsible compensation payments using Iraqi money are further examples. The United Nations Secretariat proved to be too timid in setting the record straight.

Much has been learnt from the many years of Iraq sanctions and the concurrent humanitarian programmes. Knowledge exists in ample measure to prevent a recurrence of the international failure in Iraq.[9] However, knowledge alone, as we have seen, is not enough. The international machinery and, in particular, the United Nations, the Security Council and Secretariat alike, must be normatively and structurally refitted with strong international armour. They must regain independence in order to pursue a global agenda and withstand the powers of narrow self-interests.

9. The high-level plenary meeting of the UN General Assembly recognised in the summer of 2005 that it is necessary '... to ensure that sanctions are carefully targeted in support of clear objectives ... and are implemented and monitored effectively with clear benchmarks and accountability, to comply with sanctions established by the security council, and to ensure that sanctions are implemented in ways that mitigate the adverse consequences, including socio-economic and humanitarian'. See A/59/HLPM/CRP./REV.2, p. 24, para. 88. The Iraqi people would have been spared from much hardship and death had this position been maintained by the UN security council for sanctions against Iraq during 1990–2003.

Postscript

A week after my arrival in Baghdad in November 1998 an Iraqi journalist greeted me with the words: 'Welcome to Iraq, why don't you resign like your predecessor did?' I smiled, since I really did not have a good answer.

The UN Secretary-General's offer to me to be the Humanitarian Coordinator for Iraq was tempting. I knew of the humanitarian crisis that had befallen the Iraqi people and I knew that the Oil-for-Food programme was meant to reduce their suffering. I thought that my thirty years of UN service had equipped me to handle the assignment in Baghdad. This is why I accepted the appointment.

I assumed my functions in Iraq at a time when the confrontation between Baghdad, Washington and London was escalating and UN disarmament personnel were leaving the country. I was under no illusion concerning the implications this would have for the work of the United Nations in Iraq. Under such circumstances, it would be of paramount importance to avoid vacillating across the positions of the different parties. Under no circumstances did I want to play games for the sake of good relations with everyone involved in the conflict. My positions would be determined solely by the issues relating to the effectiveness of the humanitarian intervention.

I came to Iraq neither as an administrator of sanctions nor as an ally of a repressive regime. Instead, I wanted to pursue a two-pronged approach: to enhance the efficiency of the humanitarian programme and to troubleshoot where the Oil-for-Food programme faced obstacles. This did not go down well with those governments which had steadfastly pursued a single-minded Iraq containment policy. Facts such as the shortage of permitted funds and the blocking of needed supplies were realities that Washington and London did not wish to discuss, nor did they want to receive information from the UN in Baghdad relating to the human condition in Iraq resulting from UN Security Council policies. Politics clearly had precedent over people.

In the spring of 1999 hearings on the humanitarian situation in Iraq had taken place. Ambassador Amorim had presented his courageous report to the UN Security Council showing the failure of the international Iraq policy. I regained hope that in the light of such evidence the Security Council would act speedily and decisively in redressing a situation in Iraq for which no one but the Council itself was responsible. Human rights violations of the Government of Saddam Hussein, appalling as these were, had nothing to do with the rights of a people to receive from abroad what they needed to survive.

When I realised that the Security Council acted neither 'speedily' nor 'decisively', I began to seriously question my role in the UN's Iraq operation. The State Department in Washington and the Foreign Office in London did the same, albeit for different reasons. They questioned my competence to implement 'their' policies. Right they were. Angered by my outspokenness and critical observations on the mechanics and content of UN Iraq policies, they wanted to see an end of my tenure.

This did not trouble me since I knew that I had the confidence of Secretary-General Kofi Annan. It was my conscience that troubled me. How could I, in good faith, implement a policy that the majority of the members of the Security Council had, year after year, themselves criticised as a failure? How could I look into the eyes of Iraqis when I was party to their plight?

In late 1999 I knew that I had to make a choice between what I stood for as a UN civil servant and what the policymakers in the UN Security Council wanted to achieve with my help.

On 10 February 2000, I wrote to Secretary-General Kofi Annan asking him to release me from my position, thanking him for his confidence and expressing my deep concern 'over the continuation of a sanction regime in Iraq despite overwhelming evidence that the fabric of Iraqi society is swiftly eroding and an international awareness that the approach chosen so clearly punishes the wrong party'.

H.C. von Sponeck

Appendix A

Technical Discussion of Data on the Oil-for-Food Programme

This Appendix presents some data on the Oil-for-Food Programme (OFF, or 'the Programme'), with details on data sources and documentation on how aggregate data has been constructed from constituent parts. Some example charts are given towards the end of the document.

Data and phases of reporting

The data included here derive from the so-called 180-day reports of the UN Secretary-General. In using this data, it must be remembered that the time period covered by these reports deviated to some extent from the programme phases given in UN Security Council Resolutions, see e.g. Phases VI and X; for details see Table A.1.

Table A.1   Dates of Official Oil-for-Food Programme Phases

Phase	Start date	End date	No. days in phase
I	10/12/96	7/06/97	179
II	8/06/97	4/12/97	179
III	5/12/97	29/05/98	175
IV	30/05/98	25/11/98	179
V	26/11/98	24/05/99	179
VI	25/05/99	11/12/99	200
VII	12/12/99	8/06/00	179
VIII	9/06/00	5/12/00	179
IX	6/12/00	3/06/01	179
X	4/07/01	30/11/01	149
XI	1/12/01	29/05/02	179
XII	30/05/02	4/12/02	188
XIII	5/12/02	3/06/03	180

This can be compared to the periodisation implied by the reporting periods of the Secretary-General's 180-days reports detailed in Table A.2.

Table A.2 Dates for Secretary-General's Reporting on the Oil-for-Food Programme

Phase	Cut-off date for data	No. of days
I	28/05/97	169*
II	15/11/97	171
III	15/05/98	181
IV	31/10/98	169
V	31/03/99	151
VI	31/10/99	214
VII	30/04/00	182
VIII	31/10/00	184
IX	30/04/01	181
X	31/10/01	184
XI	30/04/02	181
XII	31/10/02	184
XIII	30/04/03	181

* Starting from 10 December 1996, the date for the inception of the programme.

As this shows, the dates given are not identical to the termination dates for the official phases. Given this discrepancy, there is no way of exactly reconstituting data on the official phases. When referring to data in a particular phase, it is therefore data up to the cut-off date for the SG 180-day report that is the relevant figure. Naturally, this makes no difference to cumulative figures, but as the periodisation is different the in-figures phase may be different from retrospective statistics (e.g., OIP data on oil exports in a particular phase). In addition, Distribution Plan (DP) data were envisaged for a 180-day period. Comparing, say, the amount of goods arrived with the amount envisaged in the corresponding DP would be potentially inaccurate if the differences in reporting periods were not taken into account.

There is a particular difficulty in presenting data for phases V and VI. The OIP chose to report S/1999/573 with a cut-off date of 31 March 1999. This causes the reporting period for Phase V data to be only 151 days, or five months, while Phase VI is 214 days, or seven months. Put differently, compared to other phases, Phase VI figures contains some of the data that should be in Phase V (this is true even allowing for the fact that Phase VI was extended by twenty days with Security Council Resolutions 1275 and 1280). Using the data straight off therefore understates programme delivery during phase V and overstates it somewhat for Phase VI.

The problem may be addressed in various ways. One method would be to assume that all the months of Phase VI are similar, and simply transfer one-sixth of goods' delivery, revenue, etc. to phase V. This would have the advantage of keeping the cumulative total untouched. However, the underlying assumption is rather questionable, i.e., that all months in Phase VI are identical. In fact, oil revenue generation accelerated enormously during this phase (from a cumulative of $6.8bn in March to $11.5bn in October) and it is unlikely that the first month (April) was of a similar scope to the later phases.

The preferred method is instead to adjust figures for Phase V by pro-rating them for a period of 180 days, i.e., to scale any number derived from SG reports by a factor 1.19 (or 180/151). This method is justifiable for Phase V if we can assume that programme delivery during April 1999 was not too dissimilar from that of the months Nov 1998 to March 1999. This is likely to be a reasonable assumption and has been used throughout when comparing Phase V data with those of the corresponding DP.

Revenue data

Table A.3 overleaf provides a summary of revenue data in Phases I–XIII.

Construction and definitions of categories of data

The data provided in the reports and used to construct Table A.3 are the following categories:

a) total revenue paid into the United Nations Iraq Account from the inception of the Oil-for-Food Programme;
b) funds allocated for the purchase of humanitarian goods by the Government of Iraq, as specified in paragraph 8 (a) of Security Council Resolution 986 (1995);
c) funds allocated for the purchase of humanitarian goods to be distributed in the three northern governorates by the United Nations Inter-Agency Humanitarian Programme, as specified in paragraph 8 (b) of Resolution 986 (1995);
d) funds transferred directly into the United Nations Compensation Fund, as specified in paragraph 8 (c) of Resolution 98 (1995); and
e) other expenses, including: operational and administrative expenses of the United Nations; operating expenses of the United Nations Special Commission and its successor, the United Nations Monitoring, Verification and Inspection Commission; transportation costs of petroleum and petroleum products originating in Iraq exported via the Kirkuk-Yumurtalik pipeline; reimbursement described in paragraph 6 of Security Council Resolution 778 (1992).

Table A.3 Summary of Revenue Data, Phases X–XIII, Oil-for-Food Programme

Phase	Cumulative total revenue (million $US)	Total revenue in phase (million $US)	Cumulative humanitarian revenue (million $US)	Humanitarian revenue in phase (million $US)	Proportion humanitarian revenue (percent of cum. total)	Proportion humanitarian revenue (percent in phase)
I	1,747	1,747	1,094	1,094	62.6	62.6
II	3,283	1,536	2,013	919	61.3	59.9
III	5,573	2,290	3,452	1,439	61.9	62.8
IV	8,399	2,827	5,223	1,771	62.2	62.7
V	10,993	2,594	6,858	1,636	62.4	63.0
VI	18,142	7,148	11,490	4,632	63.3	64.8
VII	25,342	7,200	16,139	4,650	63.7	64.6
VIII	35,157	9,815	22,595	6,456	64.3	65.8
IX	41,421	6,264	27,047	4,452	65.3	71.1
X	47,833	6,413	31,584	4,537	66.0	70.8
XI	53,675	5,842	35,656	4,072	66.4	69.7
XII	57,794	4,119	38,449	2,793	66.5	67.8
XIII	64,665	6,871	43,143	4,694	66.7	68.3

Referring to Table A.3:

- the cumulative data in column 2 is directly obtained from the data in category (a);
- the per-phase data in column 3 is calculated for each phase as the difference between the cumulative revenue at the end of that phase and the cumulative revenue at the end of the immediately preceding phase.;
- the cumulative humanitarian revenue of column 4 is calculated as the sum of categories (b) and (c);
- the per-phase humanitarian revenue of column 5 is calculated for each phase as the difference between the cumulative humanitarian revenue at the end of that phase and the cumulative humanitarian revenue at the end of the immediately preceding phase.;
- the proportion in column 6 is the percentage represented by the revenue in column 4 of the revenue in column 2; and
- the proportion in column 7 is the percentage represented by the revenue in column 5 of the revenue in column 3.

Exchange rates

From Phase IX, category (b) revenue is reported in euros. Conversion into a consistent series of revenue denominated in US dollars requires a definition of the dollar-euro exchange rate. The one used is that implicit in OIP figures when stating euro and dollar equivalents of per-phase oil revenue. Figures were available on the UN/OIP website.[1]

An alternative approach would have been to use the exchange rate implied by the fact that compensation payments are 30 percent of total revenue for Phases I to IX, and 25 percent in Phases X to XIII. As the compensation payments are given in US dollars but revenue in euros, the implied exchange rate is that of the time of transaction. The discrepancies between this approach and the one above are small for most phases, but for Phase XII the difference in the approaches is 8.4 percent. This indicates a potential inconsistency in the OIP's figures and may merit further investigation.

1. http://www.un.org/depts/oip/background/basicfigures.html

'Holds'

Holds data is available for phases VI–XII, as seen in Table A.4.

Table A.4   Data on 'Holds' on Contracts, Phases VI–XII, Oil-for-Food Programme

Phase	Date	Total value of holds (million $US)	Number of applications on hold
VI	31/10/99	808	621
VII	31/03/00	1,957	1,203
VIII	31/10/00	2,600	1,293
IX	14/05/01	4,152	2,244
X	31/10/01	4,034	1,544
XI	17/05/02	5,170	N/A
XII	31/10/02	5,511	1,566

Remarks on data on 'holds'

The data in Phase XII are complicated by the fact that the procedures for approval of goods were changed with the adoption of SCR 1409 (2002). The figure of $5,503 million is the sum of $2,283 million worth of applications declared non-compliant/inactive at the stage of OIP processing; and $3,220 million-worth of applications declared GRL non-compliant/GRL inactive by UNMOVIC/IAEA. The inclusion of the first category is potentially non-conservative, as it includes applications that are simply incomplete rather than containing any goods that would not have been banned from entry to Iraq had more information been available. Excluded from the figure are 543 contracts worth $1,513 million, which were under UNMOVIC/IAEA review. This potentially understates the amounts of 'holds', as many of these will later have been found to be 'GRL non-compliant' and thus put on hold. From the point of view of Iraqi end-users, it matters little if it is UN explicit regulation or UN bureaucracy that holds up the arrival of the good.

The same problem arises for Phase XII, for which less detailed information is available. The figure stated is the sum of the categories 'GRL non-compliant/inactive', 'GRL notice/GRL processing', and 'Returned hold'.

Goods arrived

Table A.5 Value of Goods Arrived under the Oil-for-Food Programme

Phase	Date	Cumulative value of goods arrived ($US million)	Value of goods arrived in phase ($US million)
III	15/05/98	2,016	N/A
IV	10/31/98	3,532	1,516
V	31/03/99	4,744	1,213
VI	31/10/99	6,628	1,884
VII	01/06/00	8,071	1,443
VIII	31/10/00	8,834	763
IX	18/05/01	11,100	2,266
X	19/11/01	15,890	4,790
XI	17/05/02	22,000	6,110
XII	12/11/02	25,000	3,000
XIII	12/05/03	28,120	3,120

Remarks on data on goods arrived

The data for phases III and VII–XIII are stated directly in the respective 180-day reports, as detailed in Table A.5. For phases IV–VI, however, no aggregate sum is given, but data for each sector is available, as detailed in column 4. Judging by the corresponding distribution plans, these sectors should be exhaustive and therefore give an accurate total when summed. No data are available for Phases I and II. Where figures for goods arrived for these phases are stated they are extrapolated from the implied average arrival rate until the end of the reporting period for Phase III, i.e., $672 million in each of the first three phases.

The per-phase data in column 3 were calculated as the difference of the value of goods arrived at the end of the phase and that which had arrived at the immediately preceding phase.

Distribution plans

Summary distribution plan data is given in Table A.6, while Table A.7 contains a detailed breakdown by sector and phase.

Table A.6 Distribution Plan Budgets

Phase	Total distribution plan budget (million $US)	Source
I	N/A	N/A
II	1,321	S/1997/606
III	1,321	S/1998/4
IV	3,100	S/1998/446
V	2,746	S/1998/1158
VI	3,116	S/1999/671
VII	3,527	S/2000/18
VIII	7,131	S/2000/733
IX	5,556	S/2001/134
X	5,505	S/2001/758
XI	4,432	S/2002/19
XII	5,083	S/2002/666
XIII	4,327	S/2003/6

Remarks on distribution plan data

The names and remits of different sectors change over time and to simplify representation, sectors have been mapped into broader categories. In particular:

- Agriculture includes 'agriculture' and 'irrigation'.
- 'KAR specific' refers to categories relevant only to the Kurdish Autonomous Region, including 'mines related activities', 'capacity building', and others.
- 'Infrastructure' includes 'construction and materials', 'transport and communication/rehabilitation of railway network'
- 'Medicines and health' includes 'health rehabilitation'
- 'Other' includes 'Board of Youth and Sports', 'Central Bank', 'culture', 'finance', 'labour and social affairs', 'religious affairs', 'special allocation'.

Table A.7 Distribution Plan Data by Sector and Phase

1996–2003 Sector	I	II	III	IV	V	VI	VII	VIII	IX	X	XI	XII	XIII
Agriculture		50	50	250	180	274	292	805	522	703	474	442	444
Education		27	27	100	100	127	119	389	283	287	188	236	192
Electricity		55	62	411	409	440	321	752	583	487	294	311	273
Food and nutrition		817	815	1,125	1,072	933	1,057	1,282	1,294	1,282	1,291	1,287	1,296
Food handling and support		99	101	180	120	207	230	518	209	305	195	200	282
Housing and settlements		6	11	55	40	166	260	959	424	338	293	207	239
Infrastructure		0	0	0	0	0	0	489	440	407	231	425	343
KAR specific		2	1	11	9	9	12	37	10	17	14	19	25
Medicines and health		220	210	308	240	250	363	696	401	352	222	198	143
Other		0	0	151	126	130	75	0	387	384	309	701	731
Water and sanitation		44	44	210	150	280	198	604	402	343	323	458	360
Sub-total	1,321	1,321	1,321	2,800	2,446	2,816	2,927	6,531	4,956	4,905	3,832	4,483	4,327
Oil	0	0	0	300	300	300	600	600	600	600	600	600	0
Grand total	1,321	1,321	1,321	3,100	2,746	3,116	3,527	7,131	5,556	5,505	4,432	5,083	4,327

Source: Distribution plan budgets for phases II–XIII.
Notes: The distribution plan for Phase I is not available; the totals have been extrapolated from the maximum allowable oil sales.

Table A.8 Compensation Payments

Phase	Cumulative compensation payments (million $US)	Proportion of total revenue paid in compensation (percent)
I	$497	28.5
II	$915	27.9
III	$1,672	30.0
IV	$2,492	29.7
V	$3,269	29.7
VI	$5,397	29.8
VII	$7,533	29.7
VIII	$10,473	29.8
IX	$12,344	29.8
X	$13,960	29.2
XI	$15,330	28.6
XII	$16,276	28.2
XIII	$17,960	27.8

Appendix B

Statistical Tables

Table A.9   Distribution Plan Budgets and Humanitarian Revenue

Phase	Distribution plan budget for phase (planned revenue)	Humanitarian revenue in phase (actual revenue)	Value of goods arrived in phase
I*	1,321	1,094	672
II*	1,321	919	672
III*	1,321	1,439	672
IV	3,100	1,771	1,516
V	2,746	1,636	1,213
VI	3,116	4,632	1,884
VII	3,527	4,650	1,443
VIII	7,131	6,456	763
IX	5,556	4,452	2,266
X	5,505	4,537	4,790
XI	4,432	4,072	6,110
XII	5,083	2,793	3,000
XIII	4,327	4,694	3,120

Source: *UN Secretary-General's 180-day reports on the Oil-for-Food Programme, Phases I–XIII.*
Notes: *Figures for the value of goods arrived in Phases I–III are not available. The figure stated is the average over Phases I–III, based on the cumulative value of goods arrived at the end of Phase III.*

Table A.10 Contracts Approved and Humanitarian Revenue Per Phase

Phase	Contracts approved in phase	Humanitarian revenue in phase	Proportion humanitarian revenue / contracts approved (percent)
VIII	17,550	6,456	272
IX	6,043	4,452	136
X	5,084	4,537	112
XI	5,298	4,072	130
XII	4,183	2,793	150
XIII	6,813	4,694	145

Source: *UN Secretary–General's 180-day reports on the Oil-for-Food Programme, Phases VII–XIII.*
Notes: *No data are available on the value of contracts approved before Phase VII.*

Table A.11 Comparative Data for Phase V Period

Category	Actual Data	Pro-rated Data
Total revenue	2,594	3,092
Distribution plan budget	2,746	2,746
Hum. revenue	1,636	1,950
Goods arrived	1,213	1,446
Value of holds	212	212
Comp. payments	777	926

Source: *Secretary-General's 180-day reports on the Oil-for-Food Programme, Phases V–VI.*
Notes: *Holds data for Phase V refers to contracts from Phases IV and V only and might therefore understate the total number of holds. Data have been pro-rated for a 180-day period. The reporting period for Phase V stretches from 31 October 1998 to 31 March 1999, a period of 151 days. The distribution plan is for the whole 180 days of Phase V, from 26 November 1998 to 27 May 1999. In order to render data comparable, the figures for revenue, goods arrived, and compensation payments have been scaled up by a factor 180/151, i.e., pro-rated for a 180-day period.*

Table A.12 Phase v Budget and Value of Goods Arrived Per Person

Sector	Budget per person ($US)	Value of goods arrived per person ($US)
Total	122.0	53.9
Food	47.6	36.7
Electricity	18.2	2.5
Oil	13.3	0.0
Health	10.7	5.8
Agriculture	8.0	4.1
Water and sanitation	6.7	1.6
Other	5.6	0.0
Food handling	5.3	0.0
Education	4.4	1.0
Housing and settlement	1.8	1.7
KAR specific	0.4	0.4

Source: *Distribution Plan for Phase v and UN Secretary-General's 180-day reports on the Oil-for-Food Programme, phases IV and V.*
Notes: *Food includes nutrition; health includes medicines; KAR Specific includes various activities relevant only to the Kurdish Autonomous Region.*

Table A.13 Oil Revenues and Oil Prices

Phase	Price ($US/barrel)	Oil revenues ($US millions)
I	17.9	2,150
II	16.7	2,125
III	11.5	2,085
IV	9.8	3,027
V	10.9	3,947
VI	19.0	7,402
VII	24.2	8,302
VIII	25.5	9,564
IX	19.2	5,638
X	17.8	5,350
XI	20.3	4,589
XII	24.2	5,639
XIII	26.0	4,413

Source: *UN Office of the Iraq Programme 'Basic Figures' on the Oil-for-Food Programme (http://www.un.org/Depts/oip/background/basicfigures.html).*
Notes: *The oil prices calculated are the phase averages, using volume and revenue information from the Office of the Iraq Programme.*

Table A.14 Balance of Holds in Phases v–xiii

Phase	Value of goods on hold ($US millions)
V	212
VI	808
VII	1,957
VIII	2,600
IX	4,152
X	4,034
XI	5,170
XII	5,511
XIII	3,257

Source: *UN Secretary-General's 180-day reports on the Oil-for-Food Programme, Phases IV–XIII.*
Notes: *No data are available on holds before Phase v. Data for Phase v refers to contracts from Phases IV and v only and might therefore understate the total number of holds. Also, the definition of holds is different in Phase XIII, owing to the introduction of new procedures for the approval of contracts.*

Table A.15 Oil Exports and Oil Revenues

Phase	Export volume total (barrels)	Oil revenues ($US millions)
I	120	2,150
II	127	2,125
III	182	2,085
IV	308	3,027
V	361	3,947
VI	390	7,402
VII	343	8,302
VIII	376	9,564
IX	293	5,638
X	300	5,350
XI	226	4,589
XII	233	5,639
XIII	170	4,413

Source: *UN Office of the Iraq Programme 'Basic Figures' on the Oil-for-Food Programme (http://www.un.org/Depts/oip/background/basicfigures.html).*

Table A.16 Holds and Goods Arrived

Phase	Balance of value of applications on hold	Cumulative value of goods arrived	Holds / goods arrived (percent)
V	212	4,744	4
VI	808	6,628	12
VII	1,957	8,071	24
VIII	2,600	8,834	29
IX	4,152	11,100	37
X	4,034	15,890	25
XI	5,170	22,000	24
XII	5,511	25,000	22
XIII	3,257	28,120	12

Source: *UN Secretary-General's 180-day reports on the Oil-for-Food Programme, phases IV–XIII.*
Notes: *No data are available on holds before Phase V. Data for Phase V refers to contracts from Phases IV and V only and might therefore understate the total number of holds. Also, the definition of holds is different in Phase XIII, owing to the introduction of new procedures for the approval of contracts.*

Table A.17 Compensation Payments to UNCC and Goods Arrived (Cumulative)

Phase	Compensation payments to UNCC	Value of goods arrived
IV	$1,672	$2,016
V	$2,492	$3,532
VI	$3,269	$4,744
VII	$5,397	$6,628
VIII	$7,533	$8,071
IX	$10,473	$8,834
X	$12,344	$11,100
XI	$13,960	$15,890
XII	$15,330	$22,000
XIII	$16,276	$25,000

Source: *UN Secretary-General's 180-day reports on the Oil-for-Food Programme, Phases III–XIII.*
Notes: *No data are available for the amount of goods arrived per phase before Phase III.*

Appendix C

Three Examples of Presidential Decrees

Decree No. 96

Date of Decree: 19 Safar 1451 A.H./28 July 1994

In accordance with the provisions of article 42, paragraph (a), of the Constitution, the Revolution Command Council has decreed as follows.

I. Offences punishable by the penalty of amputation of the hand or the foot shall be deemed to constitute felonies.

II. If a criminal court sentences a convicted person to amputation of the hand or the foot, it must send the case file to the headquarters of the Department of Public Prosecutions within 10 days from the date on which the sentence was passed. The Department of Public Prosecutions must examine the file and submit its contents and petitions in that connection to the Court of Cassation, for consideration, within 15 days.

III. The person sentenced to the penalty of amputation shall be placed in the custody of the Adult Reform Department until the procedures required for enforcement of the sentence have been completed.

IV. The penalty of amputation shall be carried out at a public hospital designated by the Ministry of Health at Baghdad or in any governorate and shall be witnessed by the Enforcement Board consisting of a judge, a member of the Department of Public Prosecutions and a representative of the Ministry of the Interior and of the Ministry of Labour and Social Affairs.

V.   The public hospital at which the penalty of amputation is carried out shall make available the technical medical requisites needed to facilitate the enforcement of this penalty.

VI. In the case of a pregnant woman, enforcement of the penalty of amputation shall be deferred until four months after her delivery.

VII. This Decree shall enter into force from date of its publication in the Official Gazette until further notice.

Saddam HUSSEIN
Chairman of the Revolution Command Council

Decree No. 109

Date of Decree: 11 Rabi I. A.H. 1415/18 August 1994

Pursuant to the provisions of article 42, paragraph 1, of the Constitution, the Revolution Command Council has decreed as follows:

1.   Every person legally punished by amputation of the hand for a crime punishable by amputation of the hand shall be tattooed with a cross between the eyebrows. Each intersecting line of the cross shall be 1 centimetre in length and 1 millimetre thick.

2.   The tattoo shall be carried out in the same public hospital in which the amputation was performed.

3.   The public hospital shall prepare the technical and medical requirements to facilitate the performance of the tattooing procedure.

4.   The Decree shall enter into force from the date of its publication in the Official Gazette until further notice, and shall apply retroactively to every person who has already been punished by amputation of the hand.

Saddam HUSSEIN
Chairman of the Revolution Command Council

Decree No. 115

Date of Decree: 18 Rabi I. A.H. 1415/25 August 1994

Pursuant to the provisions of article 42, paragraph 1, of the Constitution, the Revolution Command Council has decreed as follows:

1. The auricle of one ear shall be cut off any person committing the following crimes:

    a) Evading to perform military service;
    b) Deserting from military service;
    c) Sheltering or protecting anyone who has evaded or deserted from military service.

2. The auricle of the other ear shall be cut off in the case of a second offence involving any of the crimes specified in paragraph 1 of this Decree.

3. A horizontal line 1 millimetre thick and no less than 3 centimetres and no more than 5 centimetres shall be tattooed on the forehead of every person whose ear has been cut off.

4. The cutting off of the auricle of the ear, and the tattooing, shall be performed in accordance with the directives to be issued by the Office of the President in this respect.

5. Death by firing squad shall be the penalty for anyone who:

    a) Has deserted from military service three times;
    b) Has evaded military service and subsequently deserted twice;
    c) Has three times protected or sheltered any deserter from or evader of military service.

6. For the purposes of the application of the provisions of this Decree, a deserter shall be considered to be any person who has been absent from his unit without authorized leave for more than 15 days.

7. a) These legal processes shall not apply to any evader of or deserter from military service who surrenders within seven days of the date of the promulgation of this Decree to authorities to be specified by the Office of the President.
    b) The period specified in paragraph (a) of this article shall be 30 days for anyone outside Iraq.

8. The provisions of this Decree shall apply to those who evaded or deserted from military service prior to the promulgation of this Decree, should they fail to surrender themselves within the period specified in article 7 of this Decree.

9. The authorities competent to implement the provisions of this Decree shall be specified by the Office of the President.

10. a) This Decree shall enter into force from the date of its promulgation until further notice.
    b) Any text which conflicts with the provisions of this Decree shall be null and void.

Saddam HUSSEIN
Chairman of the Revolution Command Council

Appendix D

A Letter from the Permanent Representatives to the President of the UN Security Council (1995)

**UNITED
NATIONS**

S

Security Council

Distr.
GENERAL

S/1995/300
13 April 1995

ORIGINAL: ENGLISH

LETTER DATED 13 APRIL 1995 FROM THE PERMANENT REPRESENTATIVES
OF CHINA, FRANCE, THE RUSSIAN FEDERATION, THE UNITED KINGDOM
OF GREAT BRITAIN AND NORTHERN IRELAND AND THE UNITED STATES
OF AMERICA TO THE UNITED NATIONS ADDRESSED TO THE PRESIDENT
OF THE SECURITY COUNCIL

We have the honour to transmit to you the non-paper on the humanitarian impact of sanctions which has been agreed upon after consultations by China, France, the Russian Federation, the United Kingdom of Great Britain and Northern Ireland and the United States of America.

We would be grateful if you would have the present letter and its annex circulated as a document of the Security Council for the information of its members and other States Members of the United Nations.

(Signed) LI Zhaoxing
  Permanent Representative of
  China to the United Nations

(Signed) Jean-Bernard MERIMEE
  Permanent Representative of
  France to the United Nations

(Signed) Sergey V. LAVROV
  Permanent Representative of
  the Russian Federation to
  the United Nations

(Signed) David HANNAY
  Permanent Representative of
  the United Kingdom of Great
  Britain and Northern Ireland
  to the United Nations

(Signed) Madeleine Korbel ALBRIGHT
  Permanent Representative of
  the United States of America
  to the United Nations

/...

S/1995/300
English
Page 2

<u>Annex</u>

<u>Humanitarian impact of sanctions</u>

The five permanent members emphasize the importance of the peaceful settlement of international disputes in accordance with the Charter of the United Nations. While recognizing the need to maintain the effectiveness of sanctions imposed in accordance with the Charter, further collective actions in the Security Council within the context of any future sanctions regime should be directed to minimize unintended adverse side-effects of sanctions on the most vulnerable segments of targeted countries. The structure and implementation of future sanctions regimes may vary according to the resource base of the targeted country. The relevant considerations include:

-   To assess objectively the short- and long-term humanitarian consequences of sanctions in the context of the overall sanctions regime. The more information the Security Council and sanctions committees have on the humanitarian situation at any stage in existing or potential target countries, the better. In this respect, a coordinating role for the Department of Humanitarian Affairs would be welcomed. The Department should draw on the expertise and assistance of States, agencies, appropriate international bodies and non-governmental organizations, and report to sanctions committees. The committees could draw on those reports in making operational decisions and when necessary refer matters beyond their competence to the Security Council for decision (for example, recommendations which would require changes to Security Council resolutions).

-   In case of emergencies or <u>force majeure</u> situations, the Security Council and/or the sanctions committees may review the application of sanctions and take appropriate actions.

-   In reviewing sanctions in the Security Council, to give due regard to the humanitarian situation.

-   To envisage in the sanctions regimes provision for all States, including targeted States, to allow unimpeded access to humanitarian aid. To elaborate measures aimed at discouraging the targeted States from impeding humanitarian aid and encouraging them to render their assistance in this respect.

-   To ensure that procedures for consideration of humanitarian applications by sanctions committees are as expeditious as possible. The simplest possible authorization procedure should be developed in the case of essential humanitarian supplies - vital to the civilian population - with arrangements for monitoring by United Nations humanitarian agencies when it is necessary. Clearly defined categories of medical supplies and foodstuffs should be allowed to be supplied even without notification of relevant sanctions committees.

/...

S/1995/300
English
Page 3

- To facilitate the expeditious process in the sanctions committees of applications from United Nations humanitarian agencies and the International Committee of the Red Cross.

- To pay particular attention to the improvement of the effectiveness of the sanctions committees by drawing on the experience and the work of different sanctions committees.

Appendix E

The United Nations Compensation Commission

Compensation for Permanent Members of the UN Security Council (as at mid-2004)*

Country	Category	Claims awarded amount	Awarded amount	Actually payment made
China	A	10184	40,761,500	40,769,000
	B	2	5,000	5,000
	C	46	396,999	396,999
	E	24	72,799,466	72,799,466
	Total	**10256**	**113,962,965**	**113,970,465**
France	A	329	1,427,000	1,425,000
	B	47	117,500	117,500
	C	334	10,561,913	10,564,413
	D	26	1,225,177	1,225,177
	E	29	52,331,353	47,331,353
	F	3	2,833,382	2,833,382
	Total	**768**	**68,496,325**	**63,496,825**
Russian Federation	A	6363	28,096,000	28,121,000
	B	1	2,500	2,500
	C	3	100,341	100,341
	E	4	89,887,591	72,926,541
	F	2	1,916,352	1,916,352
	Total	**6373**	**120,002,785**	**103,066,734**
United Kingdom	A	1,124	4,029,500	4,022,000
	B	148	402,500	402,500
	C	2,650	77,192,846	77,172,309
	D	272	17,543,630	17,543,630
	E	212	286,816,455	175,082,785
	F	4	5,103,899	5,103,899
	Total	**4410**	**391,088,830**	**279,327,123**
United States of America	A	655	2,996,000	2,967,500
	B	50	135,000	135,000
	C	2,053	57,388,258	57,216,614
	D	219	25,023,178	23,023,178
	E	72	607,083,258	166,495,807
	F	12	12,782,581	12,782,581
	Total	**3,061**	**705,408,275**	**262,620,680**

*UNCC press releases of payments and panel of commissioners' reports

Bibliography

Aburish, S.K. 2000. *Saddam Hussein: The Politics of Revenge*. New York: Bloomsbury.

Ali, T. 2003. *Bush in Babylon: The Recolonisation of Iraq*. London and New York: Verso.

Anderson, L. and G. Stansfield. 2004. *The Future of Iraq: Dictatorship, Democracy, or Division?* New York: Palgrave, Macmillan.

Benjamin, J.-M. 1999. *Iraq, l'apocalypse*. Lausanne: Editions Favre.

Bessler, M., R. Garfield and G. McHugh. 2004a. *Sanctions Assessment Handbook: Assessing the Humanitarian Implications of Sanctions*. New York: United Nations Office for the Coordination of Humanitarian Affairs (OCHA) in collaboration with member agencies of the Inter-Agency Standing Committee (IASC).

————. 2004b. *Field Guidelines for Assessing the Humanitarian Implications of Sanctions*. New York: United Nations Office for the Coordination of Humanitarian Affairs (OCHA) in collaboration with member agencies of the Inter-Agency Standing Committee (IASC).

Blix, H. 2004. *Disarming Iraq*. New York: Pantheon Books.

Bonn International Center for Conversion in cooperation with the German Foreign Office and the United Nations Secretariat, 2001. *Design and Implementation of Arms Embargoes and Travel and Aviation Related Sanctions: Results of the 'Bonn-Berlin Process'*. Bonn: Michael Brzoska, BICC.

Butler, R. 2000. *Saddam Defiant: The Threat of Weapons of Mass Destruction and the Crisis of Global Security*. London: Weidenfeld and Nicolson.

Campaign Against Sanctions on Iraq. 2000. *Sanctions on Iraq: Background, Consequences, Strategies*. Proceedings of the Conference hosted by Campaign Against Sanctions on Iraq, 13–14 November 1999. Cambridge: Cambridge University Press.

Chaliand, G. 1994. *The Kurdish Tragedy*. London and New Jersey: Zed Books Ltd.

Chomsky, N. 2003. *Towards a New Gold War: U.S. Foreign Policy from Vietnam to Reagan*. London and New York: The New Press.

Cockburn, A. and B. Cockburn. 1999. *Out of the Ashes: The Resurrection of Saddam Hussein*. New York: HarperCollins Publishers.

Conlon, P. 2000. *United Nations Sanctions Management: A Case Study of the Iraq Sanctions Committee, 1990–1994*. Ardsley, New York: Transnational Publishers Inc.

Cook, R. 2003. *The Point of Departure*. London: Simon and Schuster UK Ltd.

Cordesman, A.H. and A.S. Hashim. 1997. *Iraq: Sanctions and Beyond*. Oxford: Westview Press.

Cortright, D., A. Millar and G.A. Lopez. 2001. *Smart Sanctions: Restructuring UN Policy in Iraq*. Washington DC: Fourth Freedom Forum and the Joan B. Kroc Institute for International Peace Studies.

Cortright, D. and G.A. Lopez. 2000. *The Sanctions Decade: Assessing United Nations Strategies in the 1990s*. Boulder CO: Lynne Rienner Publishers Inc.

———. 1995. *Economic Sanctions: Panacea or Peacebuilding in a Post-Cold War World?* Boulder CO and Oxford: Westview Press Inc.

Curtis, M. 1998. *The Great Deception: Anglo-American Power and World Order*. London and Sterling VA: Pluto Press.

Europaïsche Hochschulschriften. 2003. *Die Vereinbarkeit der vom Sicherheitsrats nach Kapitel VII der UNO Charta Verhängt Wirtschaftssanktionen mit den Menschenrechten und dem humanitären Völkerecht*, Reihe II, Rechtswissenschaft, Bd./Vol. 3689. Frankfurt: Peter Lang, Europaïsche Hochschulschriften.

European Law Journal. 2002. *The Impact on International Law of a Decade of Measures Against Iraq* 13(1). Oxford: Oxford University Press.

Fabian, K.P. 2003. *The Commonsense on the War on Iraq*. Mumbai and New Delhi: Somaiya Publications PVT Ltd.

Foreign Affairs. 2004. *Rethinking Iraq*. New York: Council on Foreign Relations.

Graham-Brown, S. 1999. *Sanctioning Saddam: The Politics of Intervention in Iraq*. London: I.B. Tauris Publishers.

Haass, R. 1998. *Economic Sanctions and American Diplomacy*. New York: Council on Foreign Relations.

Hafez, K. and B. Schäbler. 2003. *Der Iraq: Land Zwischen Krieg und Frieden*. Heidelberg: Palmyra Verlag.

Hiro, D. 2003. *Iraq: A Report from the Inside*. London: Granta Books.

———. *Neighbours, not Friends: Iraq and Iran after the Gulf Wars*. London; Routledge.

International Development Community. 2000. *The Future of Sanctions*. House of Commons, London, 27 January.

International Institute of Strategic Studies. 2002. *Iraq's Weapons of Mass Destruction: A Net Assessment*. London, 9 September.

Ismael, T.Y. and J.S. Ismael. 2004. *The Iraqi Predicament: People in the Quagmire of Power Politics*. London: Pluto Press.

Johnstone, I. 1994. *Aftermath of the Gulf War: An Assessment of UN Action*. Boulder CO and London: Lynne Reinner Publishers Inc.

Mackey, S. 2003. *The Reckoning: Iraq and the Legacy of Saddam Hussein*. New York: W.W. Norton and Company.

Makiya, K. *Republic of Fear: The Politics of Modern Iraq*. Berkeley, CA and London: University of California Press.

Pilger, J. 2004. *Tell Me No Lies: Investigation Journalism and Its Triumphs*. London: Jonathan Cape.

Pollack, K. 2002. *The Threatening Storm: The Case for Invading Iraq*. New York: Random House.

Rampton, S. and J. Stauber. 2003. *Weapons of Mass Destruction: The Uses of Propaganda in Bush's War on Iraq*. New York: Jeremy P. Tarcher/Penguin.

Randal, J.C. 1999. *After Such Knowledge, What Forgiveness? My Encounters with Kurdistan*. Oxford: Westview Press.

Ritter, S. 1999. *End Game: Solving the Iraq Problem Once and For All*. New York; Simon and Schuster.

Simons, G. 1999. *Imposing Economics Sanctions: Legal Remedy or Genocidal Tool*. London: Pluto Press.

————. 1998. *The Scourging of Iraq: Sanctions, Law and Natural Justice*. New York: St Martin's Press.

Sluglett, P. 1970. *Britain in Iraq, 1914–1932*. London: Ithaca Press.

Thesiger, W. 1967. *The Marsh Arash*. London: Penguin.

The Swiss Confederation in cooperation with the United Nations Secretariat and the Watson Institute for International Studies Brown University 2001. *Targeted Financial Sanctions: A Manual For Design and Implementation*. Providence, RI: The Thomas J. Watson Jr. Institute for International Studies, Brown University.

The UN Blue Books Series. 1995. *The United Nations and Human Rights, 1945–1995*, vol. VII. New York: Department of Public Information, United Nations.

————. *The United Nations and Iraq-Kuwait Conflict 1990–1996*, vol. IX. New York: Department of Public Information, United Nations.

Trevan, T. 1999. *Saddam's Secrets: The Hunt for Iraq's Hidden Weapons*. New York: HarperCollins Publishers.

Tripp, C. 2000. *A History of Iraq*. Cambridge: Cambridge University Press.

UNICEF. 2002. *The Situation of Children in Iraq, 2002: An Assessment Based on the UN Conventions of the Rights of the Child*. Baghdad.

United Nations Office of Legal Affairs, Codification Division. 1992. *Handbook on the Peaceful Settlement of Disputes Between States*. New York: UN Publications.

von Braunmühl, C. and M. Kulessa. 1996. *The Impact of United Nations Sanctions on Humanitarian Activities*. Berlin: Gesselschaft für Communications Management, Intervention Training.

Wallensteen, P., C. Staibana and M. Eriksson. 2003. *Making Targeted Sanctions Effective: Guidelines for the Implementation of UN Policy Options*. Stockholm: Uppsala University.

Young, G. 1989. *Return to the Marshes*. London: Penguin Books.

Subject Index

Index of Names